Analyzing *Adventure Time*

CRITICAL EXPLORATIONS IN SCIENCE FICTION AND FANTASY
A series edited by Donald E. Palumbo and C.W. Sullivan III
Earlier Works: www.mcfarlandpub.com

61 *The Fabulous Journeys of Alice and Pinocchio: Exploring Their Parallel Worlds* (Laura Tosi with Peter Hunt, 2018)

62 *A Dune Companion: Characters, Places and Terms in Frank Herbert's Original Six Novels* (Donald E. Palumbo, 2018)

63 *Fantasy Literature and Christianity: A Study of the Mistborn, Coldfire, Fionavar Tapestry and Chronicles of Thomas Covenant Series* (Weronika Łaszkiewicz, 2018)

64 *The British Comic Invasion: Alan Moore, Warren Ellis, Grant Morrison and the Evolution of the American Style* (Jochen Ecke, 2019)

65 *The Archive Incarnate: The Embodiment and Transmission of Knowledge in Science Fiction* (Joseph Hurtgen, 2018)

66 *Women's Space: Essays on Female Characters in the 21st Century Science Fiction Western* (ed. Melanie A. Marotta, 2019)

67 *"Hailing frequencies open": Communication in* Star Trek: The Next Generation (Thomas D. Parham III, 2019)

68 *The Global Vampire: Essays on the Undead in Popular Culture Around the World* (ed. Cait Coker, 2019)

69 *Philip K. Dick: Essays of the Here and Now* (ed. David Sandner, 2019)

70 *Michael Bishop and the Persistence of Wonder: A Critical Study of the Writings* (Joe Sanders, 2020)

71 *Caitlín R. Kiernan: A Critical Study of Her Dark Fiction* (James Goho, 2020)

72 *In* Frankenstein's *Wake: Mary Shelley, Morality and Science Fiction* (Alison Bedford, 2020)

73 *The Fortean Influence on Science Fiction: Charles Fort and the Evolution of the Genre* (Tanner F. Boyle, 2020)

74 *Arab and Muslim Science Fiction* (eds. Hosam A. Ibrahim Elzembely and Emad El-Din Aysha, 2020)

75 *The Mythopoeic Code of Tolkien: A Christian Platonic Reading of the Legendarium* (Jyrki Korpua, 2021)

76 *The Truth of Monsters: Coming of Age with Fantastic Media* (Ildikó Limpár, 2021)

77 *Speculative Modernism: How Science Fiction, Fantasy and Horror Conceived the Twentieth Century* (William Gillard, James Reitter *and* Robert Stauffer, 2021)

78 *English Magic and Imperial Madness: The Anti-Colonial Politics of* Susanna Clarke's Jonathan Strange & Mr. Norrell (Peter D. Mathews, 2021)

79 *The Self and Community in* Star Trek: Voyager (Susan M. Bernardo, 2022)

80 *Magic Words, Magic Worlds: Form and Style in Epic Fantasy* (Matthew Oliver, 2022)

81 *Discovering* Dune: *Essays on Frank Herbert's Epic Saga* (eds. Dominic J. Nardi and N. Trevor Brierly, 2022)

82 *Nnedi Okorafor: Magic, Myth, Morality and the Future* (Sandra J. Lindow, 2023)

83 *Science, Technology and Magic in* The Witcher: *A Medievalist Spin on Modern Monsters* (Kristine Larsen, 2023)

84 *Analyzing* Adventure Time: *Critical Essays on Cartoon Network's World of Ooo* (ed. Paul A. Thomas, 2023)

85 *Schools of Magic: Learning in Children's and Young Adult Fantasy Fiction* (Megan H. Suttie, 2023)

Analyzing *Adventure Time*
Critical Essays on Cartoon Network's World of Ooo

Edited by Paul A. Thomas

CRITICAL EXPLORATIONS
IN SCIENCE FICTION AND FANTASY, 84
Series Editors Donald E. Palumbo *and* C.W. Sullivan III

McFarland & Company, Inc., Publishers
Jefferson, North Carolina

This book has undergone peer review.

ALSO BY PAUL A. THOMAS
AND FROM MCFARLAND

I Wanna Wrock! The World of Harry Potter–Inspired "Wizard Rock" and Its Fandom (2019)

ISBN (print) 978-1-4766-7858-0
ISBN (ebook) 978-1-4766-4909-2

LIBRARY OF CONGRESS AND BRITISH LIBRARY
CATALOGUING DATA ARE AVAILABLE

Library of Congress Control Number 2023013505

© 2023 Paul A. Thomas. All rights reserved

No part of this book may be reproduced or transmitted in any form or by any means, electronic or mechanical, including photocopying or recording, or by any information storage and retrieval system, without permission in writing from the publisher.

Front cover images (c) 2022 Shutterstock/
Dana.S, Shutterstock/YUCALORA

Printed in the United States of America

McFarland & Company, Inc., Publishers
Box 611, Jefferson, North Carolina 28640
www.mcfarlandpub.com

To all the *Adventure Time* fans who have spent hours analyzing the show—this one is for you.

Acknowledgments

First, I wish to offer a special thanks to Pendleton Ward, Adam Muto, Patrick McHale and all the wonderful artists who brought *Adventure Time* to life.

Second, on behalf of this book's contributors, I wish to thank all the friends, colleagues, and family members who helped make the essays in this work as solid as they are.

Third, I would like to extend my gratitude toward the fine folks at McFarland, especially the editor for this project, Layla Milholen. When this book was proposed in late 2018, I intended for it to be a single-authored monograph; an unfortunate roadblock in 2020, however, forced me to reapproach the book as an edited volume. During all this time, Layla worked patiently with me, ensuring that the finished product was well-written, accessible, and scholarly.

Finally, as this work's editor, I wish to thank everyone who contributed essays to this volume. I had high hopes for the finished product, but I really am quite blown away at what you all have produced. (Simon Petrikov would be so proud!)

Table of Contents

Acknowledgments	vi
Introduction	
Paul A. Thomas	1
Prelude: The Three Levels of Adventure Time	
Paul A. Thomas	17

"One isn't purely defined by their sex or gender": Gender, Sexuality, and Representation in *Adventure Time*

Be More Than the Binary: Experiencing Queer Subjectivity with BMO	
Olivia M. Vogt	29
From Censorship to "Obsidian": A Critical and Historical Look at "Bubbline"	
Mage Hadley	43
Rainbows and Unicorns: The Influence of Bubbline on Apocalyptic Film and Animation	
Steven Holmes	55
"Get your hero on, dude!" Charting Jake's Growth as a Positive Masculine Role Model	
Bridget M. Blodgett *and* Anastasia Salter	71
Yellow Voices and Rainbow Bodies: Accent, Multilingualism, and the Politics of Representation in *Adventure Time*	
Camille Chane	84

"Behind this curtain of patterns…": The Philosophy of Ooo

Mikhail Bakhtin in the Land of Ooo: The Carnivalesque, Heteroglossia, and the Fun That Never Ends
    Aaron Kerner *and* Birdy Wei-Ting Hung   105

"And we will happen again and again": *Adventure Time* and the Sisyphean Struggle
    Sequoia Stone   122

What Time Is It? Postmodernity! Postmodern Praxis in *Adventure Time*
    Jenine Oosthuizen   137

Making a New Meaning for Man in The Land of OOO: Object-Oriented Ontology, the NonHuman, and Difference in Distant Lands
    Al Valentín   158

"Mind Games": Mental and Emotional Toiling

Too Close for Comfort: On Finn the Human and Princess Bubblegum's Relationship
    Zhi Hwee Goh   179

Of Lacan and Lemons: A Psychoanalytic Reading of Season Six's "The Mountain"
    Paul A. Thomas   192

Trauma and the Body in *Adventure Time*
    Steven Kielich   207

"Is that where creativity comes from?" *Adventure Time* and the Artistic Medium

The Japanese Spirit and Aesthetic in Western Animation: The Influence of Anime on *Adventure Time*
    Kendra N. Sheehan   225

"Bad Jubies": Giving Value to the Intangible in Artistic Professions
    Catalina Millán Scheiding   243

About the Contributors   259

Index   261

Introduction

PAUL A. THOMAS

In 2010, Cartoon Network debuted the animated series *Adventure Time* that follows two brothers, Finn the Human and Jake the Dog, as they travel across the magical fantasy land Ooo, going on adventures and saving the day from all sorts of evil-doers. Created by Pendleton Ward (a CalArts alumnus and former storyboard artist on the CN series *The Marvelous Misadventures of Flapjack*) and produced by Frederator (the production studio behind the Nickelodeon series *The Fairly OddParents* and *ChalkZone*), *Adventure Time* was unique at the time of its creation for being a "board-driven" show; this meant that storyboard artists worked in pairs to hammer out episode plots, dialogue, and scene blocking. This gave each episode its own distinct flair, as the idiosyncrasies of the show's storyboard artists were able to shine through in the finished product. Between April 5, 2010, and September 3, 2018, the show aired 283 episodes, and was followed by two limited run spin-off series, *Distant Lands* (2020–21) and *Fionna and Cake* (forthcoming).[1]

A *Dungeons and Dragons* pastiche with a penchant for non sequiturs and absurd jokes, *Adventure Time* struck many upon its debut as just another "random" gross-out comedy appealing only to the most immature of children. But even in its first season, when the series was arguably at its "wackiest," there were hints that *Adventure Time* was more than what its technicolor designs and sugar-sweet setting otherwise suggested. And as the seasons began to unfold, the storylines grew darker, and soon enough, Finn and Jake were beating up monsters while also tackling decidedly more mature topics, like love, loss, sacrifice, puberty, and death. This storytelling turn caught the eye of viewers, and soon a show that was initially written for kids began attracting a teen and young adult audience. By the time the show's fifth season debuted in late 2012, *Adventure Time* had grown from just a fun cartoon into a pop culture behemoth that boasted a healthy—and diverse—fan following.

Around this time, *Adventure Time* also became something of a darling among media critics, and during the second half of the series' run (when the series was largely under the direction of Ward's right-hand man, Adam Muto), *Adventure Time* was routinely lauded by media journalists as one of the great television works of the 2010s. In one notable *New Yorker* article from 2014, television critic Emily Nussbaum praised *Adventure Time* for being "childlike, nonlinear, poetic" and "one of the most philosophically risky and, often, emotionally affecting shows on TV."[2] A year later, the jurors responsible for selecting the recipients of the George Foster Peabody Award applauded the series for "subtly teach[ing] lessons about growing up, accepting responsibility, and becoming who you're meant to be."[3] In 2018, following the series' finale, "Come Along with Me," Darren Franich of *Entertainment Weekly* named the series one of the "greatest TV shows ever,"[4] and James Poniewozik of the *New York Times* dubbed the program a "surreal masterpiece." This is all quite the praise for a silly little cartoon ostensibly about a boy and his dog!

However, despite the critical admiration and the legions of cosplaying fans, not many works of scholarship have seriously engaged with *Adventure Time* or considered the series through an academic lens. For a show that regularly engaged with profound topics and engendered a strong following in the process, this is quite the oversight. The collection that you are now reading was at least, in part, organized to begin filling this hole in the literature by providing the series with the scholarly attention it deserves.

What Is "Ooo"? And Why Should We Study It?

When first introduced to *Adventure Time*, it is not uncommon for people to dismiss the show as the mad scribblings of a kindergartener who has eaten one too many cookies. But when given a fair chance, *Adventure Time* often wins over critics with its unapologetically vibrant aesthetic, silly humor, and surprising emotional depth. Set in the fantasy land of Ooo, *Adventure Time* follows the eponymous adventures of Finn the Human (voiced by Jeremy Shada) and Jake the Dog (John DiMaggio, perhaps best known as the voice of Bender from *Futurama*). While Jake has magical powers that allow him to shape-shift and change the relative size of his body, Finn is a normal, 12-year-old boy. But what he lacks in magic, Finn makes up for in spirit, and when the series begins, he has already established himself as one of Ooo's champion warriors.

Throughout the show's run, Finn's defining trait—aside from his sometimes-naïve bravery—is his steadfast commitment to Good, and many an episode is focused on Finn attempting to navigate a tricky or complex moral dilemma to save the day. Interestingly, Finn breaks from longstanding cartoon precedent by aging, and over the course of the show's 283 episodes, we as the audience bear witness to Finn as he develops an increasingly sophisticated understanding of morality and what "doing good" actually means. Because of this emphasis on Finn's personal growth, *Adventure Time* can thus be understood in many ways as a sort of surreal *Bildungsroman* (albeit one with a plethora of fart jokes).

Adventure Time ostensibly stars Finn and Jake, but the show has an enormous cast of supporting characters upon whom the spotlight often shines. One of these characters, Princess Bubblegum (voiced by Hynden Walch, of *Teen Titans* fame), is Finn and Jake's liege and the leader of a city-state known as the Candy Kingdom. An 800+-year-old manifestation of the candy elemental, Bubblegum is an immensely ancient being made from chewing gum; she is also a scientific genius who has created an entire kingdom of candy citizens from scratch. In the earliest seasons of the show, Bubblegum is portrayed as your standard fantasy princess who often requires Finn and Jake to save the day, but as the show progresses, it becomes increasingly apparent that there is more to Bubblegum than just tiaras and tea parties. In time it becomes clear that the princess, while well-meaning, is an autocratic dictator who rules a surveillance state. The show does not just play this revelation for laughs—it very clearly codes Bubblegum's actions as morally wrong—but it also provides her with an opportunity to move away from her unique brand of "benevolent fascism."[5] By series' end, thanks in large part to the support of her friends, Bubblegum matures into a truly good ruler.

Another pal of Finn and Jake's is the mysterious Marceline the Vampire Queen (voiced by Olivia Olson). A one-thousand-year-old half-human, half-demon vampire, Marceline enjoys putting on a façade of villainy to pull pranks on others. At first, she clashes with Finn and Jake, but the trio quickly form a bond when Marceline recognizes our heroes' chutzpah. Marceline shares a more complex relationship with Princess Bubblegum; at one point prior to the series' main timeline, the two were in a romantic relationship that unfortunately went south. Consequently, the two leading ladies spend much of the series avoiding or making snide comments about one another (luckily, the two manage to reconcile, reaffirm their feelings for one another, and reunite as a couple by the end of the show). Marceline is also a gifted musician, whose preferred instrument is an old battle axe that she converted into a bass guitar. As a centuries-old being, Marceline has experienced her fair share of tragedies, and she likes to use music to express her lifetimes of trauma.

During the show's first few seasons, the principal antagonist is the Ice King (played by Tom Kenny, perhaps best known as the voice of the eponymous character in Nickelodeon's *SpongeBob Squarepants*), a deranged wizard who lives in the heart of the ever-frozen Ice Kingdom. Ice King is, at the start of the show, really nothing more than your standard cartoon villain, whose maniacal scheming is outdone only by his general incompetence. However, by around season three, the show's writers began to shift Ice King's characterization, playing him less as a "bad guy" and more as an awkward weirdo whose villainy is an unfortunate side effect of extreme loneliness. In time, Ice King's nefariousness is practically forgotten, and in the show's final seasons, he often interacts peacefully—albeit awkwardly—with the show's main characters. A major reason for this shift in Ice King's characterization was the season-three reveal that Ice King was once a human named Simon Petrikov, who fell victim to an ancient curse contained within the ice crown. And while this curse kept Simon alive for centuries, it destroyed his mental faculties in the process. This narrative curveball instantly made Ice King a sympathetic character who, by series' end, was best read as allegory for those suffering from mental illnesses like Alzheimer's or dementia.

Contra the more pitiful Ice King, the real villain of the show is revealed during season two to be the Lich (voiced by Ron Perlman), a primeval being from before the beginning of time who personifies death, destruction, and the inevitable corrosiveness of entropy. The Lich's only goal is to annihilate all of existence, and he will stop at nothing to accomplish this task. Naturally, Finn and Jake are having none of this, and the three routinely clash throughout the series. While the Lich is a being of immense power, he constantly finds himself bested by a child and dog: a testament both to the righteous prowess of Finn and Jake, as well as the optimism that shines at the show's heart.

The final character to consider is the Land of Ooo itself, and while it is not active and "alive" in the same ways as the show's other characters, it nevertheless plays a major role in the development of the show. Recalling a bizarro sort of Medieval Europe-meets-Candyland, Ooo is a large continent divided into a variety of principalities, all of which are ruled by an eclectic range of princesses (e.g., Slime Princess, Embryo Princess). For many viewers, this setting, with its pastel beasties and magical atmosphere, is likely to come across as your standard fantasy land, but sprinkled in the background of episodes are clues—e.g., a wrecked car here, a derelict building back there, an unexploded bomb in that corner—suggesting there is something rotten at the heart of Ooo. In time, the audience comes to learn the ominous truth: Ooo is actually the crumbling remnants of our very own Earth, one thousand years in the future. That is right: *Adventure Time* is post-apocalyptic, taking place centuries after a global conflict known as the "Mushroom War" wiped out modern human society while also reawakening magic. This war is a specter that looms in the background of every episode, infusing a generous helping of melancholy into an otherwise bright and saccharine show.

This is all well and good, a cynic might say, but why does this show deserve critical study? After all, we live in an era with no shortage of cartoons, fantasy shows, and post-apocalyptic adventure serials. For one thing, *Adventure Time* was unique among children's programming at the time in that it often dealt quite plainly with profound topics like death (e.g., "The New Frontier," "Together Again"), sexuality (e.g., "Frost & Fire," "Breezy"), depression (e.g., "Incendium," "The Music Hole"), love (e.g., "What Was Missing?," "Obsidian"), forgiveness (e.g., "The Comet," "Varmints"), and abandonment (e.g., "Escape from the Citadel," "Obsidian"). In this way, the series offered viewers—both young and old—a safe place to explore many of life's more challenging moral, philosophical, and existential questions, often in a fun, silly way. Another reason it is important to study *Adventure Time* is simply because the series was popular. Put another way, there was something about the series that resonated with its audience and enabled it to grow into a pop culture behemoth. By analyzing the show, we can better understand the reasons why it reeled in an audience, and by exploring those reasons, we can better understand the wants, desires, interests, and beliefs of the society that created and consumed it. The study of *Adventure Time*, in other words, allows scholars and theorists of twenty-first-century media and culture to better understand the complexities of the world in the 2010s.

The Library of the Undead: A Brief Recap of "Adventure Time *Studies*"

As the first edited collection about *Adventure Time* aimed squarely at academics, it seems fitting to kick things off by reviewing the foundational literature of the nascent field one might call "*Adventure Time* studies." This domain of study can be traced back to 2015, when the media and gender scholar Emma A. Jane published her article "'Gunter's a Woman?!'— Doing and Undoing Gender in Cartoon Network's *Adventure Time*." In this essay, Jane explored the unique, creative, and often subversive ways that *Adventure Time* performed and played around with gender. In doing so, Jane argued that the series "unsettles gender binaries, namely, through non-stereotyped, and trans- and multi-gendered characters, as well as via cross-dressing, role play, and exaggerated displays of masculinity and femininity as performance."[6]

Aspects of Jane's arguments were later picked up by the communication scholars Christopher J. Olson and CarrieLynn D. Reinhard in their 2017 book chapter "A Computer Boy or a Computer Girl? *Adventure Time*, BMO, and Gender Fluidity." This work, as its title likely makes clear, focuses on the robot character BMO and the character's gender fluidity. Olson and Reinhard see the character as one who both consciously performs gender, while at other times, performatively cites gendered behavior unconsciously. BMO can thus be seen as a synthesis of Erving Goffman and Judith Butler's ideas about gender.[7] The gender and media studies scholar Al Valentín would later make a similar case in their chapter "Using the Animator's Tools to Dismantle the Master's House? Gender, Race, Sexuality and Disability in Cartoon Network's *Adventure Time* and *Steven Universe*," (2019) which also builds off Jane's observations about the subversive portrayal of gender in the show. Perhaps the strongest and most novel portion of Valentín's chapter is the close analysis of the season four episode "Princess Cookie," which the author convincingly reads as a trans allegory.[8]

In 2019, the media scholars Bridget M. Blodgett and Anastasia Salter shifted the conversation toward the show's portrayal of sexuality with their book chapter "What Was Missing: Children's Queerbaiting and Homoromantic Exclusion in *Adventure Time* and *Steven Universe*." This essay focuses on instances of "homoromantic exclusion"[9] and "queerbaiting" (that is, the act of repeatedly suggesting but never canonizing the queerness of a character or couple). The authors take particular interest in the *Adventure Time* miniseries *Stakes*, which they argue is important for the way it "hint[s] at romantic tensions"[10] between Marceline and Bubblegum long before their relationship was "officially" confirmed in the series finale. In 2020, the independent vampire and horror scholar Simon Bacon would follow-up on Blodgett and Salter's ideas about "Bubbline" in his chapter "'A Dream Within a Dream': Children's 'Horror' Television and Lesbianism in the World of Marceline the Vampire Queen" (2020). Bacon also focuses on *Stakes* but reads it as a liminal and liberatory space that allows "Marceline to move beyond the purposefully normative structure of the fantasy world [of Ooo into] a dream-world within which she can express her normally repressed transgressive lesbian sexuality."[11]

So far, the research I have discussed has focused on the way *Adventure Time* creatively explores queerness, gender, and sexuality. But there are also those publications that look at *Adventure Time* more broadly by exploring the show's underlying philosophies. This more abstract, theory-oriented variant of "*Adventure Time* studies" was inaugurated by Nicolas Michaud's *Adventure Time and Philosophy: The Handbook for Heroes* (2015), an edited collection published by Open Court as an entry in their celebrated "Popular Culture and Philosophy" series.[12] Intended for lay audiences, this book is not as rigorous as the research that preceded or followed it, but it nevertheless serves as an accessible entrée for those interested in exploring many basic philosophical questions vis-à-vis *Adventure Time*.

A few years after Michaud's edited collection, the English and American studies scholar Grzegorz Czemiel published an article entitled "Speculative Cuteness: Adventures of Ideas in *Adventure Time*" (2017). Czemiel applied critical theory to explain the *je ne sais quoi* of the show's appeal, taking the philosophical study of *Adventure Time* to a new level. Czemiel's central argument invokes the theories of cultural and feminist scholar Sianne Ngai by arguing that "cuteness is the key aesthetic category deployed in *Adventure Time*."[13] The show, Czemiel, argues, is constantly vacillating between cute and mature set pieces. In doing so, the program "utilize[e] [cuteness's] ability to subvert the accepted norm of 'maturity.'"[14]

The year 2017 also saw the publication of Elijah Siegler's book chapter "*Adventure Time* and Sacred History: Myth and Reality in Children's Animated Cartoons," in which the author makes the argument that as a show with a rich and vibrant mythology concerned heavily with the topic of time, *Adventure Time* should be understood as mythic and thus analyzed through the lens of comparative religion.[15] The connection between *Adventure Time* and religion would be made once more in 2019, when Emma A. Jane published her book chapter "It's Not the End of the World: Postapocalyptic Flourishing in Cartoon Network's *Adventure Time*." This work explores *Adventure Time* through the ideas of René Girard. Detailing the show's depiction of mimetic desire, sacrifice, and scapegoating, Jane examines the ethics of Ooo and the way its "inhabitants routinely face and defuse various personal and planetary catastrophes."[16] In doing so, Jane proposes an alternative to Girard's conclusion that only literal mass conversion to Christianity can stave off the destruction of the human world.[17]

Around the time that Jane's Girardian analysis was published, the cinema scholars Aaron Kerner and Julian Hoxter released their book *Theorizing Stupid Media: De-Naturalizing Story Structures in the Cinematic, Televisual, and Videogames* (2019). Of particular interest to this project is this book's fourth chapter, "The Stupid as Narrative Dissonance," wherein Kerner and Hoxter detail the ways in which *Adventure Time* is "joyously stupid."[18] By describing the show as such, they do not mean that the show is bad, but rather that it is unconventional, "throw[ing] off the shackles of contemporary storytelling conventions," while also "celebrat[ing] the topsy-turvy world of the carnivalesque."[19] Kerner and Hoxter see *Adventure Time* as a show whose narrative takes place in what literary theorist Mikhail Bakhtin (coincidentally?) dubbed "adventure time," i.e., a narrative temporality in which "nothing changes: the world remains as it was, the biographical life of the heroes does not change, their feelings do not change, people do not even age."[20] *Adventure Time*'s predication on "adventure time," (at least in its earliest seasons), Kerner and Hoxter reason, means that the show is better understood as one that "follows a videogame logic where narratives rely on spatialized storytelling, rather than standard cause and effect progression."[21]

As of the writing of this introduction, the most recent work in *Adventure Time* studies is a project of my own: *Exploring the Land of Ooo: An Unofficial Overview and Production History of Cartoon Network's Adventure Time*. This book covers the production history of the series and the development of its characters over the course of the show's run. Select chapters also discuss the guest animators who directed certain episodes, the music of the series, the way *Adventure Time* told its stories, and the show's expansive fandom. The entire book was based in part on interviews with many of the show's writers and designers, and I intended for it to fill a hole in the literature by focusing on the show's cultural history while also illuminating the often mysterious "behind-the-scenes" happenings that influenced the way certain episodes turned out. The work was originally published by the University of Kansas Libraries in 2020, and a greatly expanded version is slated for release in 2023 by the University Press of Mississippi.[22]

Outline of This Book

After this Introduction, the book features a "prelude" followed by four sections, each of which has been organized around a general theme. The prelude is entitled "The Three Levels of *Adventure Time*." In this work, I—following the lead of the critical theorist Douglas Kellner—set the stage for the book by arguing that *Adventure Time* is not just a simple, straightforward kid story, but instead a knotty work that functions on three increasingly complex levels of meaning. The first level, the realistic, enables us to empathize with the characters. The second level, the mythological, has a ludic element that draws viewers in and encourages them to "connect the dots" and piece together the show's overarching story. The final layer, the allegorical, allows *Adventure Time* to talk about "serious" topics that might otherwise feel inappropriate for a children's show.

The prelude is followed by the book's first section, "'One isn't purely defined by their sex or gender': Gender, Sexuality, and Representation in *Adventure Time*." In this part of the book, I have grouped essays that (as the section's title might suggest) interrogate the question of identity vis-à-vis *Adventure Time*. The inaugural essay is Olivia M. Vogt's "Be More Than the Binary," in which the author performs a queer discourse analysis aimed at better understanding the queer subjectivity of BMO. Vogt reads BMO as a representation of nonnormative gender experience, and a character who not only validates but also encourages queer resistance, queer identity, and queer subjectivity. Vogt notes that because BMO is a character in a children's television show, the robot can inspire viewers to question the binarist understandings of gender and sexuality in which they find themselves embedded. BMO is a revolutionary character, Vogt argues, and this aspect should be celebrated.

In the second essay, "From Censorship to 'Obsidian,'" Mage Hadley provides a critical and historical overview of Princess Bubblegum and Marceline the Vampire Queen's romantic relationship (known in the fandom as "Bubbline"—a portmanteau of "Bubblegum" and "Marceline"). Hadley's essay traces this relationship back to the production and debut of the third-season episode "What Was Missing?"; in particular, the essay explores how the Frederator web series *Mathematical!* caused controversy when it suggested that Marceline and Bubblegum had romantic feelings for one another. Following this drama, the Bubbline pairing was then sidelined for several seasons—a move that Hadley reads as network censorship—before being gradually reintroduced into the show and officially canonized in the finale. The explicit celebration of queer romance in both the show's finale and the *Distant Lands* special "Obsidian" is worthy of praise, Hadley argues, but that praise should not erase the homophobic censorship that prevented Bubbline from being openly celebrated seasons prior.

In his essay "Rainbows and Unicorns: The Influence of Bubbline on Apocalyptic Film and Animation," Steven Holmes continues the look at Bubbline by providing an overview of the way LGBT+ themes have developed in film and animation. Holmes places particular emphasis on the queer romance between Princess Bubblegum and Marceline, arguing that the canonization of this pairing was a watershed moment that has had a noticeable impact on subsequent animated works, including *She-Ra and the Princesses of Power* and *Harley Quinn*. Holmes also considers the way *Adventure Time* and Bubbline impacted media depictions of the "post-apocalyptic," supplanting the once popular "grimdark" aesthetic for one that emanates a bright sort of "rainbow fantasy." In discussing *Adventure Time* and its impact, Holmes's essay argues that the pervasiveness of queer representation in apocalyptic animation coincides with an emphasis on rejecting commonplace assumptions about human nature, forcing viewers to re-evaluate the relationship of humankind to natural environments, and encouraging audiences to re-evaluate their relationships to the media they consume.

In Bridget M. Blodgett and Anastasia Salter's essay, "'Get your hero on, dude!,'" the authors zero in on and interrogate the nature of Jake's masculinity. The two argue that at the onset of the series, Jake is characterized by a "passive toxic masculinity" that clashes with the show's otherwise "genderfluid, progressive, and queer fantasy elements." Over the show's run, however, Jake experiences several life-changing events (e.g., he becomes a father), each of which impact him deeply. Blodgett and Salter argue that these events change Jake, moving his characterization vis-à-vis masculinity far beyond toxic passivity. By the time *Adventure Time* ends, Jake has become a truly a multifaceted character, who demonstrates a far more complex understanding of gender. This, the authors contend, makes Jake an unexpected "icon," who models to viewers a positive, "alternative," and ever-changing understanding of masculinity in a mediascape saturated with characters who conform to the hegemonic gender binary.

In "Yellow Voices and Rainbow Bodies: Accent, Multilingualism, and the Politics of Representation in *Adventure Time*," Camille Chane focuses on whether the decision to cast Korean animator Niki Yang as the voice of BMO (an adorable genderfluid robot), is innovative or regressive, considering the racist history of cartoons misrepresenting Asian voices and bodies. Chane briefly surveys this history of racialized accents in animation before considering the case of BMO, as well as Lady Rainicorn (another character voiced by Yang, who speaks only in Korean). Chane argues that the multilingualism and accent diversity in *Adventure Time* is a complex topic and that the show uses accents and multilingualism to not only generate humor, sell characterization, and contribute to the series' worldbuilding, but to also index a sort of ethnic "otherness."

The book's second part, "'Behind this curtain of patterns....': The Philosophy of Ooo," concerns itself, broadly speaking, with the philosophical currents that run throughout the series. Aaron Kerner and Birdy Wei-Ting Hung begin this section with their essay, "Mikhail Bakhtin in the Land of Ooo: The Carnivalesque, Heteroglossia, and the Fun That Never Ends." In this essay, the authors contend that *Adventure Time* is colored heavily by the ideas of Russian literary critic Mikhail Bakhtin. To make this point, Kerner and Hung first explore the many ways the series, with its emphasis on body humor, embraces the carnivalesque and the spirit of "grotesque realism." The authors then shift to a discussion of Bakhtin's (coincidentally-named) conception of "adventure time"—a sort of cartoon-like narrative common in the Greek romance tradition wherein individual events have little impact on the overall narrative. Kerner and Hung conclude their essay with a Bakhtinian exploration of language, arguing that, in particular, the slang of Ooo illustrates Bakhtin's idea of "heteroglossia," or multi-voicedness.

In the essay entitled "'And we will happen again and again': *Adventure Time* and the Sisyphean Struggle," Sequoia Stone tackles the dual topics of existentialism and joy, arguing that *Adventure Time* manages to synthesize both in a meaningful way. Although the show time and time again suggests that people cannot control the larger whims of fate, Stone argues that *Adventure Time* never embraces vulgar nihilism. Instead, the series emphatically states that joy can still be found by embracing the moment and enjoying it for what it is. Stone explores this seeming contradiction by invoking Albert Camus's *The Myth of Sisyphus*. By recognizing that his situation is absurd, Camus's Sisyphus exercises what freedom he has by finding happiness in his task, *Adventure Time* urges its viewers to accept the unchangeable and instead find happiness in the spaces where our agency remains. This central message leads Stone to categorize *Adventure Time* as an "optimistically existential" piece of media.

In "What Time Is It? Postmodernity! Postmodern Praxis in *Adventure Time*," Jenine Oosthuizen takes a close look at what might best be described as the series weirdness, arguing that this peculiarity is best read as a manifestation of the postmodern. Oosthuizen first sets up a theoretical framework with which to better identify and articulate postmodern tendencies within the series. The author then focuses on two key issues: narrative structure (fragmentation) and narration (meta-fiction). In the first part of the essay, Oosthuizen unpacks *Adventure Time*'s postmodern use of "fragmentation," discussing it in connection with the narrative structure of the series itself. In the essay's second part, the author considers the series' treatment of "meta-fiction." This discussion includes a close analysis of Ice King's fan-fiction, Cuber's narrative style and guest-animated episodes. These constituents are put in dialogue with the postmodernist's preoccupation with form and self-reflexivity.

Al Valentín's essay, "Making a New Meaning for Man in The Land of OOO," closes out the philosophy section of this book. In their essay, Valentín discusses the *Distant Lands* specials with regard to "object-oriented ontology" (abbreviated, quite coincidentally, as OOO), an approach to metaphysics that seeks to not privilege the human at the expense of everything else. Instead, object-oriented ontology recognizes that humans exist on the same ontological level as fire, bacon pancakes, and video game consoles. Valentín illustrates the many ways that *Adventure Time* embraces the core tenets of a decidedly feminist object-oriented ontology that places emphasis on nonhuman subjects and their importance. Valentín proposes that the *Distant Lands* specials can function something like a guide, demonstrating how we can create a future that celebrates the interconnections of everything—human and nonhuman, alive or inanimate.

12 Introduction

The third part of this book, "'Mind Games': Mental and Emotional Toiling," contains essays exploring the emotional and psychological depths of the show's characters. The opening work is Zhi Hwee Goh's "Too Close for Comfort," which reads the complex relationships between Finn and Princess Bubblegum. Goh notes that this relationship has long been debated within fandom spaces, and many have opted to read their interactions through the lens of (unrequited) romance. With this essay, Goh rejects romantic readings; instead, he argues that the two are united by *storge*: a familial sort of love that, at times, recalls the fraternity of brothers, and at other times, recalls the bond between a mother and her child. Creatively, Goh uses the philosopher Karl Popper's realistic situational logic to link dramatic and literary interpretations of Finn and Bubblegum's onscreen interactions and dialogue to make his overall argument.

The conversation then turns from love to desire in my own essay, "Of Lacan and Lemons," wherein I consider the sixth-season episode "The Mountain" through the lens of psychoanalytic—and, in particular, Lacanian—theory. My essay puts forth the thesis that "The Mountain" is best read as a psychoanalytic "self-analysis," focusing on Lemongrab's longing to merge with the great being known as Matthew. This act, Lemongrab believes, will enable him to find that "missing piece" of his soul (or, as Lacan put it, his *objet petit a*), which he hopes will provide him with pure *jouissance* in the totality of the impossible Real. The episode concludes, however, with Lemongrab "traversing his fantasy," resulting in him recognizing that the happiness Matthew offers is impossible and that the Real is forever out of reach. It is worth noting that by explicating "The Mountain" using Lacanian psychoanalysis, I aim to not only explore the episode's "unconscious" meaning, but also illustrate many of Lacan's trickier ideas.

Steven Kielich likewise uses Lacanian psychoanalysis in his essay, "Trauma and the Body in *Adventure Time*," to discuss the role that trauma plays in the series. In particular, Kielich sees the show as a "trauma fiction," or a story wherein the characters find themselves in the aftermath of a catastrophic event (e.g., the Mushroom War). *Adventure Time*, Kielich argues, is unique in that it places particular emphasis on the ways that trauma inscribes itself on the body. By displaying trauma visually on the body rather than through textual or oral means, the series demonstrates the difficulty of translating traumatic experiences into an easily digestible narrative. In considering the materiality of trauma, Kielich's essay also pays particular attention to the Land of Ooo itself (a land almost entirely defined by the trauma of a nuclear war), and the Ice King (whose body serves as a visual example of that trauma's impact).

The book's concluding section, "'Is that where creativity comes from?' *Adventure Time* and the Artistic Medium," considers the artistic and aesthetic elements of *Adventure Time*, regarding both its inspiration and its impact. The section's first essay—Kendra N. Sheehan's "The Japanese Spirit and Aesthetic in Western Animation: The Influence of Anime on *Adventure Time*"—explores the relationship between *Adventure Time* and Japanese animation (better known as "anime"). After first considering the cultural allure of "cool Japan," Sheehan delves into the history and defining elements of anime itself. The author then shifts into a discussion of *Adventure Time*, pointing out the various ways in which the series seems imbued with a distinctly Japanese approach to animation and storytelling. Sheehan concludes her essay with a close analysis of *Stakes*, detailing the various ways in which the miniseries reflects elements of anime, with regard to its characterization work, its philosophical considerations, and its visuals. By exploring *Adventure Time* in this way, Sheehan argues that we can better understand how different cultures inform and influence one another through their art forms.

The book comes to a close with Catalina Millán Scheiding's essay, "'Bad Jubies': Giving Value to the Intangible in Artistic Professions." In this essay, the author uses the seventh-season episode "Bad Jubies" to explore the complexity of pursuing music as a career. Scheiding notes that for many, employability is a key factor when it comes time to pick a career, but this proves a challenge for those interested in art—a field whose outcomes are generally intangible. To further probe this problem, Scheiding brings "Bad Jubies" into the discussion, arguing that it succinctly demonstrates the importance of art by showing its worth in times of crisis. Scheiding concludes her essay by discussing the use of "Bad Jubies" in the Berklee College of Music's "Professional Development Seminar." After analyzing the results of a quantitative survey administered to 25 students, Scheiding argues that "Bad Jubies" encourages artistic career assessment by exploring the creative process, the nature of "productivity," and the "support systems" needed to allow an artistic career to flourish.

The scholars who contributed essays to this book are from a range of disciplines, and as such, each approaches the series in their own distinct ways. However, they are all united by not only a love for the Land of Ooo but also their belief that *Adventure Time* is more than just "that weird show with the boy and his talking dog." These essays thus function as a collective argument that *Adventure Time* is a work of pop art worthy of increased critical attention.

Notes

1. For a full production history of the series, see my work, Paul Thomas, *Exploring the Land of Ooo*.
2. Emily Nussbaum, "Castles in the Air."

14 Introduction

 3. Brian Steinberg, "*Cosmos, Adventure Time, Doc McStuffins* Among Peabody Winners."
 4. James Poniewozik, "*Adventure Time*, TV's Surreal Masterpiece, Comes to an End."
 5. To borrow a turn of phrase that Hynden Walch often uses to describe the character.
 6. Emma A. Jane, "'Gunter's a Woman?!,'" 243.
 7. Christopher J. Olson and CarrieLynn D. Reinhard, "A Computer Boy or a Computer Girl?," 177–193.
 8. Al Valentín, "Using the Animator's Tools to Dismantle the Master's House?," 175–215.
 9. Joseph Brennan, *Queerbaiting and Fandom*, 20.
 10. Bridget Blodgett and Anastasia Salter, "What Was Missing," 148.
 11. Simon Bacon, "'A Dream Within a Dream,'" 105.
 12. Nicolas Michaud, *Adventure Time and Philosophy*.
 13. Grzegorz Czemiel, "Speculative Cuteness: Adventures of Ideas in *Adventure Time*," 4.
 14. Czemiel, 24.
 15. Elijah Siegler, "*Adventure Time* and Sacred History," 71–84.
 16. Emma A. Jane, "It's Not the End of the World," 178.
 17. Jane, 177–203.
 18. Aaron Kerner and Julian Hoxter, *Theorizing Stupid Media*, 111.
 19. Kerner and Hoxter, 111.
 20. Mikhail Bakhtin apud Kerner and Hoxter, 122.
 21. Kerner and Hoxter, 21.
 22. Thomas, *Exploring the Land of Ooo*.

References

Bacon, Simon. "'A Dream within a Dream': Children's 'Horror' Television and Lesbianism in the World of Marceline the Vampire Queen." In *New Queer Horror Film and Tv*, edited by Darren Elliot-Smith and John Edgar Browning, 105–19. Cardiff, UK: University of Wales Press, 2020.

Blodgett, Bridget, and Anastasia Salter. "What Was Missing: Children's Queerbaiting and Homoromantic Exclusion in Adventure Time and Steven Universe." In *Queerbaiting and Fandom: Teasing Fans through Homoerotic Possibilities*, edited by J. Brennan, 142–55. Iowa City: University of Iowa Press, 2019.

Brennan, Joseph, ed. *Queerbaiting and Fandom: Teasing Fans through Homoerotic Possibilities*. Iowa City: University of Iowa Press, 2019.

Czemiel, Grzegorz. "Speculative Cuteness: Adventures of Ideas in *Adventure Time*." *View. Theories and Practices of Visual Culture*, no. 19 (2017). http://pismowidok.org/index.php/one/article/view/509/1074.

Franich, Darren. "*Adventure Time* Finale Review: One of the Greatest TV Shows Ever Had a Soulful, Mind-Expanding Conclusion." *Entertainment Weekly*, 2018. https://ew.com/tv/2018/09/04/adventure-time-finale-review/.

Jane, Emma A. "'Gunter's a Woman?!'—Doing and Undoing Gender in Cartoon Network's Adventure Time." *Journal of Children and Media* 9, no. 2 (2015): 231–47. https://doi.org/10.1080/17482798.2015.1024002.

———. "It's Not the End of the World. Postapocalyptic Flourishing in Cartoon Network's Adventure Time." In *Mimetic Theory and Film*, edited by Paolo Diego Bubbio and Chris Fleming. Violence, Desire, and the Sacred, 177–203. New York: Bloomsbury Academic, 2019.

Kerner, Aaron, and Julian Hoxter. *Theorizing Stupid Media: De-Naturalizing Story Structures in the Cinematic, Televisual, and Videogames*. Cham, Switzerland: Palgrave Macmillan, 2019.

Michaud, Nicolas, ed. *Adventure Time and Philosophy: The Handbook for Heroes*, Popular Culture and Philosophy. Chicago: Open Court, 2015.

Nussbaum, Emily. "Castles in the Air: The Gorgeous Existential Funk of *Adventure Time*." *New Yorker*, 2014. https://www.newyorker.com/magazine/2014/04/21/castles-in-the-air.

Olson, Christopher J., and CarrieLynn D. Reinhard. "A Computer Boy or a Computer Girl? *Adventure Time*, Bmo, and Gender Fluidity." In *Heroes, Heroines, and Everything in Between: Challenging Gender and Sexuality Stereotypes in Children's Entertainment Media*, 177–93. Lanham, MD: Lexington Books, 2017.

Poniewozik, James. "*Adventure Time*, TV's Surreal Masterpiece, Comes to an End." *New York Times*, 2018. https://www.nytimes.com/2018/09/02/arts/television/adventure-time-appraisal-series-finale.html.

Siegler, Elijah. "*Adventure Time* and Sacred History: Myth and Reality in Children's Animated Cartoons." In *Religion and Popular Culture in America*, edited by Bruce David Forbes and Jeffrey H. Mahan, 71–84. Berkeley: University of California Press, 2017.

Steinberg, Brian. "*Cosmos, Adventure Time, Doc McStuffins* Among Peabody Winners." *Variety*, 2015. https://variety.com/2015/tv/news/peabody-awards-cosmos-adventure-time-doc-mcstuffins-1201478277/.

Thomas, Paul A. *Exploring the Land of Ooo: An Unofficial Overview and Production History of Cartoon Network's* Adventure Time. Lawrence, KS: University of Kansas Libraries, 2020.

Valentín, Al. "Using the Animator's Tools to Dismantle the Master's House? Gender, Race, Sexuality and Disability in Cartoon Network's *Adventure Time* and *Steven Universe*." In *Buffy to Batgirl: Essays on Female Power, Evolving Femininity and Gender Roles in Science Fiction and Fantasy*, edited by J.M. Still and Z.T. Wilkinson, 175–215. Jefferson, NC: McFarland, 2019.

Prelude

The Three Levels of Adventure Time

Paul A. Thomas

In his essay "Teens and Vampires: From *Buffy the Vampire Slayer* to *Twilight*'s Vampire Lovers," the critical theorist Douglas Kellner argues that the cult television series *Buffy the Vampire Slayer* (which aired on The WB/UPN from 1997 to 2003 and followed the adventures of the titular heroine as she faced vampires, the forces of darkness, and the perils of being a teenager) can be read on three distinct levels, the first being the realistic, the second being the mythological, and third being the allegorical. The realistic level, as the name suggests, is the layer focused on realist depictions of our everyday reality. The mythological level, conversely, is the level of the show's overarching story. The final level, that of the allegorical, is built on symbolism and metaphor that lets the show express "deeper" ideas through visual and storytelling poetics. While these layers each serve their own purpose, they also intersect and overlap, resulting in "a complex structure [with] polysemic depth of meaning ... that demands levels of interpretation."[1]

Kellner's layered dissection of *Buffy the Vampire Slayer* is revealing, proving that a television show can appear straightforward on the surface while actually containing several levels of meaning. But I believe that *Buffy* (as much as it revolutionized television) is far from the only show that can be constructively analyzed in this way. What follows is thus a consideration of *Adventure Time* vis-à-vis Kellner's three levels. The purpose of this endeavor is to support the essays contained in this volume by pre-emptively demonstrating that *Adventure Time* is a multivalent piece of media that functions—and can thus be analyzed—at various levels of narrative depth.

A Slice of Life: The Realist Layer

For someone who knows of *Adventure Time* only from its pop culture shadow, the claim that the show has a "realistic" layer might appear, at best, suspect and, at worst, totally preposterous. After all, is not *Adventure Time* just a silly cartoon with nonsensical dialog, goofy characters, and "random" comedy? (When writing this book, I encountered this question, often expressed with amplified exacerbation, far more times than I would like to admit.) The short answer is no; over its ten-season run, *Adventure Time* proved itself more than capable of blending its surreal brand of adventure stories with a relatable sense of normality, often resulting in episodes that many fans both on- and offline have taken to calling "slice of life" narratives.

According to Robert Barton and Annie McGregor, "slice of life" as a descriptive term was introduced by the French playwright Émile Zola in the 19th century to label "naturalistic drama."[2] By the 20th century, it had developed into a theatrical subgenre that attempted "to depict natural everyday life … [by] follow[ing] a character's life for the duration of the realistic time the actual play lasts."[3] By the 1980s and '90s, the term had come to anchor an anime subgenre of the same name, featuring episodes that "focus on school … or on interpersonal relationships, either within family or a romance."[4] Now compare this last definition of "slice of life" narratives to Kellner, who in writing about "realistic shows," contends that they present "down-to-earth and revealing relations between teenagers, and between young people and parents, teachers and mentors, and a diverse range of authority figures."[5] These definitions are strikingly similar and can thus be logically connected to one another.

Most of *Adventure Time*'s "slice of life" episodes focus on the truly mundane: the Emmy-award winning episode "Jake the Brick," for instance, opens with a minute-long sequence showing Finn wandering lackadaisically through the hills and forests of Ooo, stopping only to consult a map and eat an apple. The rest of the episode revolves around the inhabitants of Ooo tuning into and becoming absorbed with Jake's radio broadcast, which details the story of a (non-magical) rabbit whose home is threatened by a (non-magical) summer rain storm. Another excellent example is the ninth-season episode "Cloudy," in which Finn and Jake spend 11 minutes talking about their feelings while pretending to give one another haircuts.

It is important to note that not every episode of *Adventure Time* is a "slice of life" narrative—far from it!—but even in the most fantastical of episodes, there is often one or two realistic vignettes that see Finn, Jake, and their many friends: go to the library, take naps, cook real-world dishes (e.g., sandwiches, spaghetti, bibimbap), pay taxes, play video games, and casually surf the Internet, among many other things; these are all simple, "down-to-earth" occurrences that happen in our regular, quotidian reality.[6]

Adventure Time's interest in realism, however, is not limited only to the small happenings of the everyday; in fact, several episodes see the characters deal with many of those "painful and heavy problems" that define the human condition.[7] For instance, the sixth-season episode "Breezy," which sees Finn go on a kissing spree to cope with the loss of his father and his arm, is a rather frank depiction of depression that episode co-writer Jesse Moynihan claimed was based on his own lived experiences.[8] Likewise, the climax of the seventh-season episode "Varmints" is a quiet scene wherein Princess Bubblegum tearfully apologizes to Marceline and reaffirms their friendship. Finally, while the eighth-season miniseries *Islands* is replete with talking sea dragons and futuristic technology, the core of its story is authentic: It is the simple tale of Finn's brave attempt to find his biological mother. Loss, forgiveness, and personal reconnection—these are all things that "real" humans deal with, and the show often handles them in ways that are surprisingly relatable.

Adventure Time's realist level likely serves a number of purposes, but in terms of simple narrative and storytelling techniques, the show's depiction of normal happenings in an otherwise strange world allows audience members to see themselves in the characters: We recognize their situations, their struggles, and their choices as ones that we routinely face. By connecting the viewer to the show's characters, *Adventure Time* manages to produce a sort of "narrative empathy" that encourages us to intimately care about the show's many fantastical characters. This investment leads us to continue our viewership of the program (and, in the case of fans, speculate about characters' behaviors, intentions, hopes, and future actions).

The Lore of Ooo: The Mythological Layer

The second layer of *Adventure Time* is its mythological level. A reader will be forgiven if the word "mythology" initially conjures up mental images of Hercules fighting the Hydra or Theseus slaying the Minotaur. These are figures from *classical* mythology, and this is not what is meant when the word "mythology" is invoked by media and fandom scholars. In these fields, the term refers to a "serialized narrative plus backstory plus world building," according to the religious studies scholar Elijah Siegler.[9] Kellner provides a slightly more technical definition, writing that "mythology" denotes "the particular mythical universe and narrative of

[a] series."[10] Regardless of which definition is preferred, the point here is that when people nowadays talk about a show's "mythology," they are usually referring to that program's overarching storyline, its often supernatural elements, and the backstories of its many characters.

This unique use of the term "mythology" (which is often referred to by both fans and scholars alike as a show's "mythos" or its "mytharc"),[11] was popularized by the screenwriter Chris Carter in reference to the overarching story of his hugely popular sci-fi television series *The X-Files*. This program first aired on the Fox network from 1993 to 2002 and followed the adventures of FBI agents Fox Mulder (played by David Duchovny) and Dana Scully (Gillian Anderson) as they investigated paranormal phenomena across the United States. Episodes that focused exclusively on random mutants or cryptids were called "Monster-of-the-week" episodes, while those that focused on a broader plot about a planned alien invasion were dubbed the "mythology" episodes.[12] In time, this use of the term "mythology" was appropriated by audiences to refer to the narrative arcs of other media franchises, such as the aforementioned *Buffy the Vampire Slayer*, the ABC series *Lost* (2004–10), the Fox series *Fringe* (2008–13) and the WB/CW series *Supernatural* (2005–20).

When *Adventure Time* debuted, it was largely devoid of any mythological pretensions, as the show's producers assumed that Ooo was just a generic fantasy land. This all changed by accident when the writers were hammering out the plot for the first-season episode "Business Time," in which Finn and Jake find a group of businessmen frozen in an iceberg. When reviewing the storyline, Pendleton Ward recognized that the appearance of businessmen as frozen relics implied that not only was the world of *Adventure Time* the same as our own, but also that the series took place at a point in the distant future following some apocalyptic event.[13] Ward readily embraced the idea, and at the 2012 Toronto Comic Arts Festival, he told the crowd: "I love post-apocalyptic movies.... I was so glad when [the show became post-apocalyptic]. I thought, 'Oh great, now I can explore that!'"[14]

Ward first attempted to purposefully introduce this element into the series when he storyboarded the first pass of the show's intro, which would have concluded with a gigantic nuclear blast. According to former creative director Patrick McHale:

> If I remember correctly, Pen kept [the idea that Ooo was post-apocalyptic] close to the vest early on. He didn't really even talk to me about it until he storyboarded an intro sequence that ended with a huge explosion. And when I asked him about it, he said he was thinking that the show was actually post-apocalyptic and the explosion was a reference to how the world (as we know it) ended. I think he had that idea for a while. He always wanted a lot of junk littered around in the backgrounds for that reason.[15]

This take on the intro was vetoed by the executives at Cartoon Network, who were likely concerned that it was too violent for a children's program. But while a "tamer" version was eventually approved, even this intro contains references to nuclear war: Eagle-eyed fans who pause the intro as soon as it begins will notice that the ground is strewn with unexploded atom bombs and scattered detritus from a by-gone era!

Ward finally got a chance to make the post-apocalyptic aspect of the show fully apparent when production began on the second-season episodes, "Mortal Folly"/"Mortal Recoil." This two-parter introduced the series' principal antagonist, the Lich, and as soon as this new character entered into the Land of Ooo, the writers realized that he needed a compelling backstory. Ward and the writers thus made the decision to connect the character's origins to the mysterious extinction event that had rendered Ooo post-apocalyptic in the first place—and thus the gruesome mythology of the "Great Mushroom War" was born.

Direct allusions to this war are few and far between, and most are subtle, appearing as blink-and-you-will-miss-them easter eggs in the backdrop of episodes. (Numerous background pieces, for instance, contain unexploded bombs, wrecked military equipment overgrown with plant life, or the crumbling ruins of shell-ravaged buildings; other episodes depict the Earth with a huge chunk of the crust missing.) Occurring sometime around the turn of the 21st century, the war was carried out presumably with atomic weapons, whose distinctive mushroom clouds gave the conflict its name. Who the combatants were remains a mystery, but thanks to the fifth-season episodes "Finn the Human"/"Jake the Dog," we do know that the war ended with the dropping of a doomsday weapon known as the mutagenic "Mushroom Bomb," which—in addition to unleashing a burst of irradiated doom—also gave corporeal form to the Lich.

When the dust finally settled, the destruction wrought by the Mushroom War was incomparable: it had vaporized whole cities, rearranged entire landmasses, and polluted large swaths of the land with radioactive sludge. While a handful of the privileged elite took to the stars to escape Armageddon, most humans were not so lucky; it is implied that the Mushroom War cost the lives of millions—if not billions—of humans, and when the bombs stopped falling, only a fraction of terrestrial humanity remained. This remnant eventually fled on ships to a string of remote islands, where they spent centuries rebuilding their society, far away from what would one day become the Land of Ooo.[16]

As episodes of *Adventure Time* were written, the story of the Mushroom War soon became entwined with the backstory of several other major characters, most notably Ice King and Marceline the Vampire Queen (both of whom were revealed to be direct survivors of the war), and the Lich (whose existence was heavily tied to the Mushroom War's explosive finale). Season after season, these mythological connections continued to develop, and in no time, they had become an integral part of the show's spirit.

It is interesting to note that despite starting out merely as thematic window dressing, the mythological aspects are compelling for many fans. (This can be attested by searching "*Adventure Time* mythology" on Google, YouTube, or Reddit, which will turn up page after page of fans trying to explicate the show's complicated lore or make esoteric connections between episodes.) But why is this? What purpose does the mythology serve and why have fans latched onto it? In terms of purpose, I believe that as with the realist level, the mythology serves the larger narrative: It provides the series with an internal consistency and a sense of structure by providing the world with a mappable history. While this does not confer "believability" in the way that the realist layer does, it nevertheless establishes an in-universe logic that allows for consistent, long-form storytelling over the course of several episodes (if not seasons).

But this still does not answer why the mythological level in particular has intoxicated so many viewers. Based on my own experiences as a viewer who avidly kept track of the mysterious world of Ooo, I believe the mythology of the show is appealing because it functions like a mental puzzle: By creating (often subtle) details that hint to previous happenings within the Oooniverse, the show actively challenges viewers to "connect the dots" and "unlock" the mysteries of the world's and its characters' origin. Focusing on the mythological clues also allows viewers to speculate about alternate developments, or to come up with theories about what "might have happened" if events in the series' universe were handled differently. The mythological level of *Adventure Time* thus has a ludic quality to it, and the viewers who zero in on this facet of the series become players who "dabble with [the] content and adopt a playful disposition of imagination and make-believe. They are players ... because they engage with the content through their fantasy and playfully recreate it" in their discussions or simply in their mind.[17] Put most simply, people love a good mythology because there is a certain pleasure in piecing it all together; it is akin to a game, and a fun one to boot!

Going Deeper: The Allegorical Layer

Adventure Time also has a final layer: that of the allegorical. The *Columbia Electronic Encyclopedia* defines "allegory" as a "story that serves as a disguised representation for meanings other than those indicated on the surface,"[18] with the "hidden message" often being a moral, philosophical, or religious one.[19] A storytelling tool that has been used for millennia, allegory is so powerful, Kellner reasons, because it allows humans to explore the unpleasant truths inherent in "reality" in a way that is safer and perhaps more socially acceptable.[20]

Adventure Time's use of allegory functions the same way. Consider, for instance, the looming specter of death. It is an unpleasant fact of human existence that all of us will die one day, and the stark realization of this mortality is one that has impacted almost everyone the world over. But by watching episodes in which Finn, Jake, and their friend symbolically deal with loss, abandonment, and even death, a viewer might be able to contemplate and process their own mortality in a way that is not only thought-provoking, but also funny. While discussing in an interview the episode "The New Frontier" (in which Jake frankly discusses his eventual demise), *Adventure Time*'s head writer Kent Osborne touched on this same idea when he said: "Hearing Jake talk about his perception of death and dying, I remember when that was pitched, it made me feel better about my own mortality…. It prepared me for death better."[21]

Arguably, *Adventure Time*'s allegorical masterminds were Tom Herpich and Jesse Moynihan, and most of their episodes are full of material that can be mined for additional meaning. Herpich has been especially upfront about his interest in taking grand life lessons and molding them into 11 minute cartoons, noting in an interview that many of his episodes—including "Puhoy," "Dungeon Train," and "The Hall of Egress"—are best understood as "allegorical escape stor[ies]."[22] "The Hall of Egress" is perhaps the best example. In the episode, Finn finds himself trapped in the titular dungeon, and the only way he can seemingly escape is by closing his eyes and running blindly through its labyrinthine passages. The problem is, once he returns to the outside world, he finds that he cannot open his eyes, lest he be teleported right back to the dungeon where he was previously trapped. After dozens and dozens of attempts to escape (all of which end with Finn somehow opening his eyes), Finn realizes that the only way to escape is to keep his eyes shut and wander until he somehow finds the *real* exit. He is unable to trust anyone (he is unable to trust even his own sense of sight!)—he can only trust his lonely consciousness. Eventually, after blindly wandering across Ooo for what appears to be a few seasons, he bumbles his way into another Hall of Egress, and when he passes through this dungeon, he finds that he is finally able to open his eyes and emerge out the other side.

In the episode, Finn remembers that "egress" is a fancy word that means "exit." Usually, it is invoked as a noun, but it can also function as a verb; this means that it not only describes an exit hatch, but also the *action* of exiting. It is the latter meaning of the word that the episode seems focused on, as almost all the action is placed not on the dungeon's exit hatch but rather the process by which Finn attempts to break out of his bizarre prison, which he is only able to do by closing his eyes, isolating himself from his friends, and trusting his instincts. When taken into account, the allegorical message is made all the more clear: Life is not about who we should or could be, or what we should or could do: it is about becoming who we *are* in the moment and listening only to what our heart tells us is correct. To properly "know thyself" is as simple as being, just as leaving the dungeon is as simple as egressing. "The Hall of Egress" can thus be seen as a giant allegory for the tricky process of self-discovery, all wrapped up in a deceptively simple story about dungeon-crawling.

Contra Herpich (whose episodes often centered on humanistic meditations about life), Moynihan was more interested in playing around with explicitly spiritual or mystical themes. According to Kellner, "complex … allegor[ies] [usually have] theological and religious dimension[s] that cop[e] with life and death; sin, guilt, and redemption; the choice between good and evil; and how to understand and deal with life and an afterlife."[23] It should be no surprise as to why Moynihan is being discussed in this section. During his years-long tenure as an *Adventure Time* storyboard artist, he wrote a plethora of episodes that fit neatly into the dimensions that Kellner discusses, including episodes that deal with the nature of gods, such as Glob, Prismo, and Abraham Lincoln ("Sons of Mars," "Is That You?"); redemption and atonement ("You Forgot Your Floaties," "Normal Man"), the meaning of life ("Astral Plane"), and the existence and nature of the afterlife ("Death in Bloom," "Ghost Princess").

Among the fandom, Moynihan was one of the show's more popular storyboard artists, and almost certainly some of this admiration was due to the way he tackled heady spiritual issues in a way that was not only fun, but also readily digestible. Take, for example, the sixth-season episode "Astral Plane," wherein the four-headed quasi-deity Glob Grod Grob Gob willingly sacrifices themselves to protect Mars from an errant comet. There is something powerful and touching about a celestial being willing to risk death for a lesser creation that the being loves so dearly. Indeed, this idea is so powerful that it has inspired a whole litany of religious beliefs about a "dying god," with perhaps the most well-known example in the modern world being the Christian conviction that Jesus of Nazareth willingly died at the hands of the Romans to save the world that he loved from sin. By storyboarding his portion of the episode in this way, Moynihan draws an allegorical parallel between Glob Grod Grob Gob and Jesus (or the many Jesus-like figures appearing in folklore the world over), illustrating the paradoxical idea that death can be the greatest act of life; what is more, he does this all within 11 minutes.

The beauty of *Adventure Time*'s allegorical level, as was mentioned at the start of this section, is that it allows the show to consider those topics that are otherwise "out of bounds" in everyday conversations—let alone children's media!—but which nevertheless play a major role in the human experience. Topics like this (such as death, depression, dementia, and sexuality) are often seen as "too distressing and traumatizing for [...] realist aesthetic depiction,"[24] and as a result, realist children's programs rarely address them, outside of an occasional "very special episode." But ignoring these "traumatizing" problems does not make them go away—instead, it causes them to linger in the dark cellars of the mind. And if repressed long enough, these problems can explode into wild phobias or anxiety. The producers of *Adventure Time* seemed to have been aware of this, and so they used allegory as a way to explore otherwise "traumatizing" problems in a controlled, less visceral way. Allegory in *Adventure Time* thus functions like an escape valve, providing the viewers with an opportunity to ponder often troubling question in a serious but funny way.

Notes

1. Douglas Kellner, "Teens and Vampires," 56.
2. Robert Barton and Annie McGregor, *Theatre in Your Life*, 312.
3. Barton and McGregor, 464.
4. Robin Brenner, *Understanding Manga and Anime*, 112.
5. Kellner, "Teens and Vampires," 57.
6. Kellner.
7. Kellner, 58.
8. Jesse Moynihan, "Breezy was a deeply personal episode…" Twitter, 2014, archived at https://archive.is/gdwZg.
9. Elijah Siegler, "*Adventure Time* and Sacred History," 74.
10. Kellner, "Teens and Vampires," 59.
11. A.J. Black, *Myth-Building in Modern Media*.
12. Siegler, "*Adventure Time* and Sacred History," 74.
13. Smith, "Adventure Time Creator Talks '80s."
14. Ward et al., "*Adventure Time* Panel" (TCAF, May 5).
15. Patrick McHale, interview with author, July 2, 2021.
16. For a complete rundown, see Jagm's excellent resource: https://atchronology.com.
17. Nicolle Lamerichs, *Productive Fandom*, 237.
18. Columbia Electronic Encyclopedia, 6th ed. (New York City, NY: Columbia University Press, 2019), s.v. "Allegory."
19. Kellner, "Teens and Vampires," 62–66.
20. Kellner, 63.
21. Bustillos, "How Adventure Time Came to Be."
22. Thomas, "Tom Herpich Interview."
23. Kellner, "Teens and Vampires," 62.
24. Kellner, 63.

References

Barton, Robert, and Annie McGregor. *Theatre in Your Life*. 2nd ed. Boston, MA: Cengage Learning, 2011.

Brenner, Robin. "Teen Literature and Fan Culture." Article. *Young Adult Library Services* 11, no. 4 (2013): 33–36.
Bustillos, Maria. "How *Adventure Time* Came to Be." The Awl, 2014, accessed https://popula.com/2018/09/03/the-literature-of-the-universe/, http://theholenearthecenterofthe world.com/.
Kellner, Douglas. "Teens and Vampires: From *Buffy the Vampire Slayer* to *Twilight*'s Vampire Lovers." In *Kinderculture*, edited by Shirley Steinberg, 55–72. Boulder: Westview Press, 2011.
Lamerichs, Nicolle. *Productive Fandom: Intermediality and Affective Reception in Fan Cultures*. Amsterdam, Netherlands: Amsterdam University Press, 2018.
Siegler, Elijah. "*Adventure Time* and Sacred History: Myth and Reality in Children's Animated Cartoons." In *Religion and Popular Culture in America*, edited by Bruce David Forbes and Jeffrey H. Mahan. Berkeley: University of California Press, 2017.
Smith, Zack. "*Adventure Time* Creator Talks '80s." *USA Today*, 2012. http://www.usatoday.com/story/popcandy/2012/11/01/adventure-time-creator-talks-80s/1672583/.

"One isn't purely defined by their sex or gender"
Gender, Sexuality, and Representation in Adventure Time

Be More Than the Binary
Experiencing Queer Subjectivity with BMO

Olivia M. Vogt

Our cultures are engrained with deeply held beliefs, values, and norms which permeate all facets of society. Because of this, creative products such as art, literature, and film always reflect the culture in which they were created.[1] The information we glean from media, in turn, impacts our understanding of the world and has some level of influence on what we believe. Without exception, television programs of every kind fit into this model. From the nightly news to the latest Netflix series, we are always learning from media. The value in televised cartoons, in particular, lies in the fact that, as aforementioned, both their messages and images are produced by human beings who participate in a shared cultural reality.[2] In this way, cartoons are a fiction derived of meanings from the real world, with real-world ideas and values. This often results in cartoons which uphold cultural norms, or which echo the beliefs of dominant cultural groups.[3] Cartoons thus fill a dual role of entertainment and socio-cultural education. Young viewers learn, episode by episode, what behaviors and identities are acceptable.[4] Likewise, the quality and quantity of human representations on screen impact how children understand their peers. Seeing many similar characters can lead a viewer to be more accepting of certain demographics, as the meanings of race, gender, and age are depicted onscreen.

Gender stereotypes abound in cartoons, teaching children how to act according to their gender, so that they may avoid ostracism by their peers.[5] Like most human beings, children will seek to fit into their peer group rather than find themselves singled out as "weird." The gender stereotypes from television become scripts for children to act out in the real world.[6] Young boys absorb the expectation that they should be strong and brave, while young girls learn their place as mothers or arm candy. Any child outside of the gender binary (transgender, nonbinary, genderqueer, or otherwise) learns that they are ignorable, disposable, or unwanted, as they rarely see themselves represented. It is the latter statement which drives the present discussion. As someone who was once a child categorized by gender otherness, I now find myself in the unique position to analyze and celebrate instances of revolutionary pieces of media. My early formative years are in the past, but the present essay allows me to explore a new world in which children (and adults) who do not fit in are given the opportunity to see themselves represented in media. Through an analysis of the *Adventure Time* character BMO, and a consideration of queer identity,[7] I hope to document and illustrate the importance of gender nonconforming characters.

Adventure Time *and Gender*

Previous analyses of *Adventure Time* found that the series subverts and reimagines gender stereotypes in a way that does not simply reverse the script but reimagines it. Emma Jane[8] focuses on the ability of the series to present normalized examples of gender role subversion and the subversion of strict gender binaries. The main characters Finn and Jake, for example, frequently have heartfelt conversations about love, fear, and loss—something other programs shy away from with male characters. Additionally, Jane claims, the overall gender symbolism of the series encourages all viewers to question the ways they have learned to perform gender in their own lives, and to wonder at the potential of other gender expressions. This potential is salient especially to children, who will learn from characters that break the traditional media mold. She highlights Gunter, the assumed male penguin who lays an egg, and BMO, the very character who is the driving force of the current discussion. These characters and their experiences, she argues, provide a space for queer and transgender experience and presentation to thrive.

In an analysis of both *Adventure Time* and another Cartoon Network animated program, *Steven Universe*, Al Valentín argues that both series provide spaces of potential resistance for anyone who is not white, straight, cisgender, or able-bodied. Worth noting, as seen in this analysis, is that *Adventure Time* storyboard artist Rebecca Sugar played a major role in pushing for queer inclusion, first on *Adventure Time*, and later as the showrunner of *Steven Universe*[9] (a point of discussion I explore further in my own work, as well).[10] Valentín explains that BMO's gender identity seems to fluctuate and "makes possible a read of the character as bigender, placing BMO on the transgender spectrum."[11] Valentín further argues that all characters—not just BMO—repeatedly exhibit nonnormative gender and sex roles: Princess Cookie embodies a transgender symbolism, Jake takes on stereotypically feminine traits, and there is a queer romance between Princess Bubblegum and Marceline the Vampire Queen.

Likewise, Christopher Olson & CarrieLynn Reinhard argue BMO has proven to be a powerful symbol of nonnormative gender performance.[12] Through textual analysis, the authors concluded that BMO's actions and interactions situate them as a genderfluid being whose gender expression and identity exist in a state of flux. "BMO self-presents and interacts via a fluid gender identity,"[13] they explain, highlighting how BMO's social network verifies this reading in the narrative. The interchangeable use of gender role performance and pronouns give way to a character who teaches audiences that "anyone can be a hero and take part in adventures."[14] The current essay expounds on the idea that anyone is worthy of feeling proud of their place in the universe. To present it from another angle, I explore BMO specifically as an exploratory space for queer subjectivity and identity, seen through the lens of my own subjectivity.

As discussed previously, children too often learn that heroes must meet a set of criteria to be "real" heroes—they must exist at a particular intersection of dominant social identities, such as whiteness, heterosexuality, and a binary gender expression. Children also learn that everyone, hero or otherwise, must also meet certain criteria of social acceptance or risk ostracism by their peers. Those with the desired mix of traits are more likely to succeed in society, both socially and economically.[15] As a critical researcher, I realize that a culture which unproportionally benefits people for their race, gender, sexuality, and other demographic traits is a culture with immoral systematic foundations. My work here is driven by the possibility for a generation which does not vilify people for their differences. The simple fact that BMO exists as a character beyond the gender binary can serve to validate queer children who otherwise feel lost between the extremes of maleness and femaleness. As a queer person raised in a culture which valued gender polarity of girls and boys, I feel the need to look back and imagine what would be different if *Adventure Time* was airing in my own formative years. Likewise, I wish to consider the lessons which television is teaching younger generations.

The position of this analysis thus comes from a place of queer subjectivity, which I embody through a queer identity of my own. This present analysis reinforces and expands on the findings of Valentín, Jane, and Olson and Reinhard, to a place suggested by queer scholars as a place of resistance.[16] Beyond the cultural and societal implications of a nonnormatively gendered character (which, indeed, are impressive implications already), the existence of BMO in the *Adventure Time* narrative opens a site for identity exploration through which queer identities are normalized and celebrated. BMO represents the possibility and validity of queer resistance to a gender binary, with *Adventure Time* operating as a space wherein queer viewers of any age can see themselves positively portrayed.

A Queer Discourse Analysis

The current essay takes the form of a queer discourse analysis. "Discourse analysis" itself is a research method primarily concerned with the power relationships and meaning making in a text.[17] This approach is especially helpful when considering television programs, as they are rife with symbolism that can be fruitfully analyzed. Furthermore, the use of queer theory in this discourse analysis allows us to analyze not only power but the binaries and norms which constitute it.[18] When a researcher views a sample through the lens of queer theory, gender and sexuality become particularly salient in the message of a text. We can see the gendered implications behind seemingly genderless meanings, including the assumptions and messages that an audience may receive through gendered readings.[19] With queer theory, we can understand the nonbinary nature of gender, the fluidity of sexuality, and the possibility to challenge creators to reach for these realities.

Finally, the authorial position of queer subjectivity becomes relevant as we consider the importance of queer perspectives in cultural and academic work.[20] In the discussion of queer rights and society, no voices are as important as those living the queer experience. When gendered media is analyzed through queer experiences, the messages become increasingly nuanced and valuable to research.[21] Although it is amicable to welcome research on queerness from straight and cisgender researchers, queer researchers provide an indispensable glance at the truth of existing in a space outside the norm. In a society which too often privileges sameness and familiarity for the sake of profit, it is increasingly important to give platforms to those who have been historically othered. Thus, the perspective of diverse viewers is more important than ever in the goal of reaching an equitable society. Specifically, I read BMO as genderqueer from my lived of experiences as a genderqueer nonbinary researcher. In the following sections, I argue that BMO provides a space for viewers' queer embodiment and resistance to heterosexism and homophobia. I support these claims with discussion and examples taken directly from *Adventure Time*.

BMO as Queer Embodiment and Resistance

Viewers of *Adventure Time* will recognize that "BMO" is the name of a small blue robot character whose appearance is reminiscent of a Game

Boy handheld gaming console. BMO's face is displayed on the screen of the device, with two blue arms extending from the sides, and two blue legs holding up the device. They are voiced by South Korean actress Niki Yang, who also provides the voice of Lady Rainicorn. BMO is shown to have multiple technical capabilities: they can allow others to play video games on their screen, take photos, capture video, print documents, play music, power other electronics, and display documents, data, photos, and video. BMO is primarily referred to with he/him pronouns,[22] often simply referring to himself in third person in statements like "BMO is so pretty and smart!"[23] Between BMO's appearance, pronouns, and voice, it would be easy to conclude that BMO is a robot manifestation of a male child whose feminine voice reflects his age. However, as we will explore, BMO's gender is a much more interesting space than what the surface suggests.

The story of BMO's life begins when they were created, rather than born, in a factory by an inventor named Moe; this positions BMO immediately as something outside of our norms of human reproduction. Unlike human babies, BMO was not born into the world with the declaration "It's a boy!" or "It's a girl!" Instead, BMO was created to "be more" than a simple robot,[24] and as we will discuss, he also became more than binary gender limitations would have allowed. This call to "be more" complicates and foresees readings which would criticize the association of the nonhuman robot with the queer. Too often, human fear of the queer unknown manifests in nonhuman characters like aliens, monsters, and robots. To position queer people as inherently different is one way to remove them from human society and empathy.[25] In cases where most characters are human, this argument makes more sense. Especially in children's media, it can be particularly harmful to code queer people as freaks or outcasts, or conversely, to hold them to superhuman standards.[26] However, in *Adventure Time*, very few characters are human. In fact, creatures like candy-people, magic animals, and other supernatural entities are far more commonplace. As such, BMO's inhuman nature suddenly becomes a lot less insidious, and much more comfortable to relate to as a queer person. It positions BMO firmly within the category of "normal" for the world, where having a unique appearance or being imbued with techno-magic is not something to be feared, but something to be celebrated.

Normalization of queer people outside of heteronormativity poses a possibility for a world where hetero- and cis- are not the presumed default categories.[27] This acceptance integrates nicely with the fact that fantasy genres are places where queerness and difference thrive. Magical beings are not hunted because of their magic. BMO, like other characters, is valued for their uniqueness. Interactions in the *Adventure Time* narrative show BMO as an accepted character. Similarly, I feel most accepted as a queer person when my difference is seen as something unique or magical rather than something monstrous.[28] True allies and friends to queer people value and accept the differences of their loved ones. Like how BMO's creativity and personality are beloved by his friends, queer people can experience a similar love from those who celebrate their differences as normal and valuable. All things considered, BMO's character is valued for more than just his perceived gender or technological capabilities.

As previewed above, BMO's voice and appearance are sensory signifiers of queer gender. He primarily uses he/him pronouns and refers to himself as a boy on several occasions. When speaking to his reflection, who he has named "Football," he identifies himself as "a little living boy."[29] In other children's animated media, nonhuman characters tend to default to male, unless otherwise specified.[30] However, in the Land of Ooo, it is normal for all characters to behave outside of the Western conceptions of gender roles. We see this when BMO's reflection, Football, claims that they are "a real baby girl." On one separate occasion, Finn is even shown referring to BMO as "milady,"[31] and on another, BMO refers to himself with the oft-femininely gendered adjective "pretty."[32] Likewise, BMO is sometimes referred to as "it" by other characters, *The Adventure Time Encyclopedia* contends that "the machine [i.e., BMO] is obviously genderless,"[33] and the Cartoon Network website notes that BMO "is neither male nor female."[34] In one episode, the characters attend a murder mystery party where they are given pseudonyms, such as "Lady Quietbottom" and "Prince Hotbod." BMO, however, is given the ungendered honorific "Professor Pants."[35] From the gendered language employed by BMO and the characters around them, we can infer that BMO is not restrained to any single binary gender identification—something that firmly places them on the genderqueer spectrum (as likewise claimed by other authors).[36] In fact, BMO's interchangeable use of pronouns and identities shows a transcendence of the gender binary altogether. Genderqueer people may find comfort in this fact, due to BMO presenting the possibility to live outside of societal restrictions.

The fluidity and ease with which BMO's friends use respectful gendered language is refreshing and utopian. In daily life, this is often not the case. Real people living in a queer gender identity are sure to recognize the uncomfortable interactions with non-queer people who feel entitled to personal information about them. A glance at any headline containing the phrase "transgender" is telling of the current political turmoil queer people are experiencing, as people may feel threatened or offended when their perceptions of the world are challenged. Issues of human rights suddenly come into question when the majority becomes unsure of our gender and/or genitalia. Likewise, media audiences unsure about the gender of a character may try to justify a character's gender by observing displays of sex, romance, and attraction.[37] This often doubles back on the assumption that all people are cisgender by default (they identify with the gender and sex they were assigned at birth based on perceived physical appearance) and that all people are heterosexual (attracted to the "opposite" gender or sex). Necessarily, by this logic, males must be attracted to females, and vice versa. Alternatively, a person may be read as strictly homosexual if they display attraction to the perceived same sex. BMO complicates both assumptions as he enacts relationships with friends, family, and romantic partners. His queer ways of living, acting, and relating to other characters present a point of resistance against societal expectations of the self, love, and family.

Like other *Adventure Time* characters, BMO lives in a world of creativity and imagination. He does not have a 9-to-5 job, a nuclear family, or bills to pay. He exists in a place outside of our Western understanding of what it means to be a normal person. BMO's interactions with a wide variety of characters show that he is not a "normative" person, nor is he a robot who sits at home all day as some lonely pet. While he sometimes chooses to stay at home to solve mysteries (like the case of Finn's missing sock),[38] or to talk with Football, we see him in a multitude of settings. Sometimes, he accompanies Finn and Jake on adventures to places around the Candy Kingdom,[39] and sometimes, he goes on adventures alone.[40] BMO is shown to have a sense of agency, creativity, and freewill—things that could easily be omitted from robot characters. He displays emotions of curiosity, joy, fear, sadness, and anger. The fact that he shows support and emotion to his friends, and that his friends reciprocate, places him relationally[41] in a found family that comprises his close friends. This gender-transgressive familial practice rings true to my own queer experience, wherein queer people tend to emotionally gravitate towards one another. We understand the "weirdness" and "difference" inherent to other queer people, and so, we seek comfort in our found families of those who love and accept us (and often times, this is done out of emotional, mental, or physical necessity). Consequently, BMO's discovery of a family outside of his place of creation makes sense as part of a queer narrative; he was created, did not fit into the world of the factory he was raised in, and journeyed out to find his own identity and family outside of normative constraints.

Through his travels, BMO finds a stable home alongside Finn and Jake, who serve as his friends and caretakers. In one episode, Jake states that BMO is "like a baby, almost,"[42] a characterization that Marceline the Vampire Queen affirms when coaxing BMO towards her by stating softly, "come here, baby."[43] On another occasion, Finn proudly declares of BMO: "He's our son!"[44] These statements by other characters, alongside displays of naivety and emotional vulnerability, make BMO seem like a young, childlike character. This aging down of the character can seem problematic when the audience remembers that he is voiced by an Asian woman—someone who already has an increased likelihood of being infantilized or fetishized because of her identity. However, BMO also refutes this oversimplified reading of his age by queering our normative understanding of "straight time."[45]

As detailed by Muñoz, "straight time" is the ideal and normative timeline that Western capitalism expects us all to follow if we want to be accepted as a productive member of society. This timeline starts with the nuclear family, follows a person through marriage and heterosexual reproduction, and ends with the patriarch of the family passing on his wealth and property to his children. As stated above, BMO already challenges this path by his very creation, which seems to take place years before the main storyline. From there, he goes out into the world on his own, demonstrating childlike curiosity alongside an advanced understanding of technology and a robust understanding of survival. The fact that he exists as an object further queers his existence, as he resists the expectation of being a tool for human use. Instead, he maintains his technological abilities while creating his own identity using the very human traits of empathy, curiosity, and optimism.

BMO's mastery of technology brings him to outer space in his eponymous *Distant Lands* special,[46] and through this special, his potential for imagination and invention are repeatedly lauded. Instead of the normative movement away from parents at a certain age for the purposes of reproduction or capital production, BMO sails through the stars, meets new characters, and sufficiently finds his way home to Earth. In "Imaginary Resources," he demonstrates his nonsexual ability to (re)produce technology and data in an artificial reality world, eschewing heteronormative marriage and childbirth.[47] In the digital world of "Imaginary Resources"—cheekily called "Better Reality"—BMO takes the form of a massive, muscular man. The color of his blue skin and the lack of genitalia denote a mystical god more so than a hypermasculine human man, thereby queering BMO's appearance in the virtual, too. The campy nature of a "big, beautiful man"[48] walking around wearing nothing but his blue skin and three weirdly placed eye patches also invites queer readings of pride in different bodies and the celebration of beauty.

BMO's incredible mastery of technology, alongside his lack of knowledge or interest about sexuality, create a complex and multilayered character who escapes the straight and binary categories of age, sexuality, biological sex, and even death. After all, the finale reveals that, hundreds of years after Finn and Jake's demise, BMO is still "alive," living on top of a secluded mountain as the (new) "King of Ooo." BMO ultimately embodies an alternative queer reality[49] that exists outside of straight time, where life and death are not standard measurements, and individuals can simultaneously live in multiple time-spaces, echoing what BMO sang to Jake in the show's finale: "You and I will always be back then."[50]

Finally, BMO showcases a boundless understanding of love that goes well beyond the limits imposed by straight time. In many cases, this love is platonic; for example, he clearly loves and admires Finn and Jake. In other instance, this love is more parental. Consider, for instance, the episode "BMO Lost," which begins with BMO carrying an egg in a plastic cup taped to his chest.[51] "Who is the mother? Who is the father?" he sings. Although BMO's song and dance are silly and charming, they invoke a sense of foster parenthood or birth through means other than simple intercourse and conception, as he carries an egg from an unknown mother and father. Later in the episode, BMO attempts to adopt a lost baby he finds in the forest, whom he names Ricky. Accompanied by the talking, genderless Bubble (voiced by Levar Burton), BMO carries Ricky around and attempts to care for him. By episode's end, BMO and Bubble finally locate Ricky's true mother (who angrily informs them that "his name is Sparkle!"), and BMO begrudgingly returns the baby. I related to these scenes as a queer person who desires children but understands that my relationship makes this more than a matter of simply having sex.

The show also discloses that BMO's love has a romantic side. In "BMO Lost," for instance, the audience learns that BMO was once in a relationship with the treehouse chicken, Lorraine.[52] "She is red-hot like pizza supper!" BMO exclaims before revealing that the two shared a "secret grown-up kissing spot" somewhere in the house. Likewise, at the end of "BMO Lost," BMO and Bubble confess their love for one another—a feeling that mutually developed during their time spent in the forest. The two agree to get married before Jake accidentally pops Bubble, revealing that he was actually Air, who had merely been trapped in the bubble. As Air disperses invisibly around BMO, the romance around the two transcends gender, sex, and physicality. They achieve the ultimate queer fantasy of finding love outside of boundaries, inhabiting a space where neither of them will be harmed for being (un)seen together.

Come Along with Me, Beyond the Binary

The way that BMO acts, adventures, and learns evokes an essentially queer exploration of self-identity and the constraints of the world around us. When BMO speaks to Football in his reflection, I recognize the pure curiosity that accompanies queer gender exploration. When BMO puts on a cowboy hat,[53] or bandeau bra,[54] or flower headband,[55] he escapes normative gendered bodies in a way that I only wish I could; his friends never mock his appearance or question his attire. Though the appearance of his videogame console may denote masculine gender (with its blue coloring, rectangular shape, and boxy appearance), he is completely unconstrained by societal expectations of sex or gender performance. He comfortably enacts "powerful moments in animation that confound the binary through proud appropriation of the feminine,"[56] and in some cases, the masculine. As queer people, we often wish to experiment with our own identities in a way that may be frowned upon by the public. We constantly face the specters of harassment, rejection, and violence from those around us. A well-intentioned peer may misgender us, an unknowing acquaintance may address us incorrectly as "ma'am" or "sir," and a stranger may feel entitled to know our gender or "biological" sex identity.

BMO may just be a tiny robot, but he enacts profoundly large human behaviors and emotions, all while freely avoiding any sort of gender role or stereotype. He explores what it means to be alive, what it means to be a person, and what it means to love. The fact that this character exists in such a hugely popular television program provides a space for queer resistance in a normatively gendered media landscape. While children have long learned about societal norms through television, they now have the unique opportunity to learn about gender fluidity and queer joy from a seemingly insignificant cartoon character. Thankfully, streaming services allow us to revisit this space in *Adventure Time* whenever and wherever we want. In an artistic medium that directly resists capitalism's demand for productivity, in a show that actively resists sex and gender simplicity, BMO provides a site for the queer viewer to be affirmed, validated, and celebrated. He is not purely a robot, but not quite human, either. He exists as an intermediary between worlds of life and nonsentience, time and timelessness, magic and science, a borderland of a character that, ironically, defies binary coding.[57]

This leaves us questioning the importance and next steps in this discussion. How can an analysis of a cartoon impact the real world?[58] Ultimately, I hope that this exploration of BMO provides a queer reading that others can use in their own research and exploration. Like BMO, I am constantly seeking new ways to express ideas of gender, identity, and knowledge. This curiosity and want for something better are what make us human. This feeling of hope for a better tomorrow comes right alongside the experience of queerness[59]; we acknowledge the problems we face now as a society and hope to face them to find solutions. Through *Adventure Time* and BMO, we comparatively see our world as a place that could use more of the morals exhibited by Finn, Jake, and BMO. Perhaps, we hope, the ability to love and thrive would advance humanity past our current grapples of systematic inequality and threats to our livelihoods. We could all be better people for going on emotional adventures.

While this might seem like a heavy demand for a cartoon, it is but one piece of the overall puzzle that is a societal advancement towards empathy and openness. Through the creation of queer spaces and the celebration of minorities, the media around us can mediate change for the better. Queer or not, young or old, *Adventure Time* viewers can emulate BMO's genuine love of life, loyalty to friends, and commitment to kindness. Audiences and creators alike can bring these ideals to their own lives and can encourage discussions of gender. For queer people specifically, spaces like this provide us with the possibility of community, comradery, and comfort. BMO shows a wonderful example of a queer character whose personality is not solely based on queerness, or on the creator's criticism of queerness. He simply is. His existence opens a space and a time where we can step outside our narrow cultural teachings of gender and sex identity. I hope that by noticing and celebrating BMO as a space of queerness, we can encourage and support people, shows, and ideas that go beyond the binary.

Notes

1. Gillian Rose, *Visual Methodologies*.
2. Stuart Hall, *Encoding and Decoding in the Television Discourse*.
3. Theodor Adorno, *The Culture Industry*.
4. Tony Kelso, "Still Trapped in the U.S. Media's Closet," 1058–1097.
5. I use the term "gender" rather than sex throughout this essay as an acknowledgment that children's television, as dictated by ratings and appropriateness, does not highlight the "biological sex" of characters. While other media may use these socially accepted categories through revelations of anatomy, it is rare to see children's imagery which features (non-comical) nudity. Additionally, the fact that children's shows do not demand any "biological proof" of gender or sex should be seen as another opportunity for the exploration and encouragement of queer identities which are not dictated by traditional boundaries of reproductive heterosexuality.
6. Edward Schiappa et al., "Can One TV Show Make a Difference?," 15–37.
7. Because this essay relies on my own experiences for discussion, it is necessarily Western-oriented in perspective. As such, my views are informed by an upbringing in a capitalist and colonial society. It is with this knowledge that I argue the essay is all the more compelling, as I seek to explore possibilities outside of Western sex and gender norms.
8. Emma Jane, "Gunter's a Woman?!," 231–247.
9. Nick Romano, "From Steven Universe to Voltron."
10. Olivia M. Vogt, "(De)Constructed Gender and Romance in Steven Universe."
11. Al Valentín, "Using the Animator's Tools to Dismantle the Master's House?," 197.
12. Christopher Olson and CarrieLynn D. Reinhard. "A Computer Boy or a Computer Girl?," 177–193.
13. Olson and Reinhard, 190.
14. Olson and Reinhard, 191.
15. Imani Perry, *Vexy Thing*.

40 "One isn't purely defined by their sex or gender"

16. Frederik Dhaenens, "The Fantastic Queer," 102–116.
17. Rose, *Visual Methodologies*.
18. Guillermo Avila-Saavedra, "Nothing Queer About Queer Television," 5–21.
19. Judith Butler, *Gender Trouble*.
20. Rob Cover, "Material/Queer Theory," 293–310.
21. Cris Mayo, "Queer and Trans Youth, Relational Subjectivity, and Uncertain Possibilities," 530–538.
22. Note that I interchangeably address BMO using he/him and they/them pronouns as a demonstration and affirmation of people whose pronouns are not static signifiers of identity
23. "We Fixed a Truck" (season 5, episode 39).
24. "Be More" (season 5, episode 28).
25. Tom Sandercock, "Transing the Small Screen," 436–452.
26. Lucy Nicholas, and Sal Clark, "Leave Those Kids Alone," 36–55.
27. Dan Michael Fielding, "Queernormativity," 1135–1154.
28. Perry, *Vexy Thing*
29. "Five Short Graybles" (season 4, episode 2).
30. Jessica Birthisel, "Body, Heterosexuality and Patriarchal Entanglements," 336–352.
31. "Conquest of Cuteness" (season 3, episode 1).
32. "We Fixed a Truck" (season 5, episode 39).
33. Martin Olson, *The Adventure Time Encyclopaedia*, 69.
34. Cartoon Network, "Character Facts of the Week."
35. "The Creeps" (season 3, episode).
36. Olson and Reinhard, "A Computer Boy or a Computer Girl?"; Valentín, "Using the Animator's Tools."
37. Frederik Dhaenens, "Teenage Queerness," 304–317.
38. "BMO Noire" (season 4, episode 17).
39. "What Was Missing" (season 3, episode 10).
40. "The Creeps" (season 3, episode 12).
41. Olson and Reinhard, "A Computer Boy or a Computer Girl?"
42. "The More You Moe, The More You Know" (season 7, episodes 14–15)
43. "What Was Missing" (season 3, episode 10).
44. "Imaginary Resources" (season 8, episode 23).
45. José Esteban Muñoz, *Cruising Utopia*.
46. "BMO" (*Distant Lands*, episode 1).
47. This likewise demonstrates a use and acceptance of asexuality, an orientation which remains misunderstood by many.
48. "Imaginary Resources" (season 8, episode 23).
49. Jack Halberstam, *The Queer Art of Failure*.
50. "Come Along With Me" (season 10, episodes 13–16).
51. "James Baxter the Horse" (season 5, episode 19).
52. "BMO Noire" (season 4, episode 17).
53. "Angel Face" (season 7, episode 17).
54. "The Invitation" (season 8, episode 20).
55. "Apple Wedding" (season 5, episode 44).
56. Valentín, "Using the Animator's Tools," 191.
57. Glorida Anzaldúa, *Borderlands/La Frontera*.
58. Jane, "Gunter's a Woman?!"
59. Muñoz, *Cruising Utopia*.

References

Adorno, Theodor W. *The Culture Industry*. London: Routledge, 1991.
Anzaldúa, Gloria. *Borderlands/La Frontera: The New Mestiza*. San Francisco: Aunt Lute Books, 1987.

Aultman, B. Lee. "Nonbinary Trans Identities." In *Oxford Research Encyclopedia of Politics*, edited by Thompson, William R. Oxford, UK: Oxford University Press, 2019.

Avila-Saavedra, Guillermo. "Nothing Queer About Queer Television: Televised Construction of Gay Masculinites." *Media, Culture, & Society* 31, no. 1 (2009): 5–21.

Barbee, Harry, and Douglas Schrock. "Un/gendering Social Selves: How Nonbinary People Navigate and Experience a Binarily-Gendered World." *Sociological Forum* 34, no. 3 (2019): 572–593.

Birthisel, Jessica. "How Body, Heterosexuality and Patriarchal Entanglements Mark Non-Human Characters as Male in CGI-Animated Children's Films." *Journal of Children and Media* 8, no. 4 (2014): 336–352.

Butler, Judith. *Gender Trouble: Feminism and the Subversion of Identity*. New York: Routledge, 1990.

Capuzza, Jamie C., and Leland G. Spencer. "Regressing, Progressing, or Transgressing on the Small Screen? Transgender Characters on US Scripted Television Series." *Communication Quarterly* 65, no. 2 (2017): 214–230.

Cartoon Network. "Character Facts of the Week: BMO from *Adventure Time*." Cartoon Network, 2012. https://web.archive.org/web/20130729204359/http://www.cartoonnetwork.co.uk/blogs/character-facts-of-the-week-bmo-from-adventure-time.

Clark, Joseph. "Virtually Queer: Subjectivity Across Gender Boundaries in Second Life" in *MG 2009 Proceedings*, 19–21. Atlanta: Association for Information Systems, 2009.

Compton, Bradley J. Bond, and Benjamin L. "Gay On-Screen: The Relationship Between Exposure to Gay Characters on Television and Heterosexual Audiences' Endorsement of Gay Equality." *Journal of Broadcasting & Electronic Media* 59, no. 4 (2015): 717–732.

Cover, Rob. "Material/Queer Theory: Performativity, Subjectivity, and Affinity-Based Struggles in the Culture of Late Capitalism." *Rethinking Marxism* 16, no. 3 (2004): 293–310.

Darwin, Helana. "Doing Gender Beyond the Binary: A Virtual Ethnography." *Symbolic Interaction* 40, no. 3 (2017): 317–334.

Dennis, Jeffery P. "The Boy Who Would Be Queen: Hints and Closets on Children's Television." *Journal of Homosexuality* 56, no. 6 (2009): 738–756.

Dhaenens, Frederik. "The Fantastic Queer: Reading Gay Representations in *Torchwood* and *True Blood* as Articulations of Queer Resistance." *Critical Studies in Media Communication* 30, no. 2 (2013): 102–116.

Dhaenens, Frederik. "Teenage Queerness: Negotiating Heteronormativity in the Representation of Gay Teenagers in *Glee*." *Journal of Youth Studies* 16, no. 3 (2013): 304–317.

Dines, Gail. "Toward a Critical Sociological Analysis of Cartoons." *Humor: International Journal of Humor Research* (1995): 237–255.

Fielding, Dan Michael. "Queernormativity: Norms, Values, and Practices in Social Justice Fandom." *Sexualities* 23, no. 7 (2020): 1135–1154.

Foucault, Michel. *The History of Sexuality*. New York: Vintage Books, 1978.

Hall, Stuart. *Encoding and Decoding in the Television Discourse*. Birmingham: University of Birmingham, 1973.

Halberstam, Jack. *The Queer Art of Failure*. Durham: Duke University Press, 2011.

Jane, Emma A. "'Gunter's a Woman?!'—Doing and Undoing Gender in Cartoon Network's *Adventure Time*." *Journal of Children and Media* 9, no. 2 (2015): 231–247.

Joyrich, Lynne. "Queer Television Studies: Currents, Flows, and (Main)streams." *Cinema Journal* 53, no. 2 (2014): 133–139.

Keegan, Cáel M. "Getting Disciplined: What's Trans* About Queer Studies Now?" *Journal of Homosexuality* 67, no. 3 (2020): 384–397.

Kelso, Tony. "Still Trapped in the U.S. Media's Closet: Representations of Gender-Variant, Pre-Adolescent Children." *Journal of Homosexuality* 62, no. 8 (2015): 1058–1097.

Leslie, Carolyn. "*Adventure time* and Gender Stereotypes." *Screen Education* 78 (2015): 44–47.

Manganello, Jennifer, Amy Franzini, and Amy Jordan. "Sampling Television Programs for Content Analysis of Sex on TV: How Many Episodes Are Enough?" *Journal of Sex Research* 45, no. 1 (2008): 9–16.

Mayo, Cris. "Queer And Trans Youth, Relational Subjectivity, and Uncertain Possibilities: Challenging Research in Complicated Contexts." *Educational Researcher* 46, no. 9 (2017): 530–538.

Muñoz, José Esteban. *Cruising Utopia: The Then and There of Queer Futurity*. New York: New York University Press, 2009.

Netzley, Sara Baker. "Visibility that Demystifies: Gays, Gender, and Sex on Television." *Journal of Homosexuality* 57, no. 8 (2010): 968–986.

Nicholas, Lucy, and Sal Clark. "Leave those kids alone: On the uses and abuses and feminist queer potential of non-binary and genderqueer." *Journal of the International Network for Sexual Ethics and Politics* 8, INSEP Special Issue (2020): 7–8.

Olson, Christopher, and CarrieLynn D. Reinhard. "A Computer Boy or a Computer Girl? Adventure Time, BMO, and Gender Fluidity." In *Heroes, Heroines, and Everything In Between: Challenging Gender and Sexuality Stereotypes in Children's Entertainment Media*, edited by Christopher Olson and CarrieLynn D. Reinhard, 177–193. Lanham, MD: Lexington, 2017.

Olson, Martin. *The Adventure Time Encyclopaedia*. New York: Harry N. Abrams, 2013.

Pearce, Ruth. "Inadvertent Praxis: What Can 'Genderfork' Tell Us about Trans Feminism?" *MP: An Online Feminist Journal* 3, no. 4 (2012): 87–129.

Perry, Imani. *Vexy Thing: On Gender and Liberation*. London: Duke University Press, 2018.

Robards, Brady, Brendan Churchill, Son Vivienne, Benjamin Hanckel, and Paul Byron. "Twenty Years of 'Cyberqueer.'" In *Youth, Sexuality, & Sexual Citizenship*, edited by Peter Aggleton, Rob Cover, Deana Leahy, Daniel Marshall and Mary Lou Rasmussen, 151–167. London: Routledge, 2021.

Romano, Nick. "From *Steven Universe* to *Voltron*: The Fight to Bring LGBTQ Characters to Kids' Shows." *Entertainment Weekly*, 2018. https://ew.com/tv/2018/08/22/steven-universe-voltron-kids-cartoons-lgbtq-characters/.

Rose, Gillian. *Visual Methodologies: An Introduction to Researching with Visual Materials*. Thousand Oaks: Sage Publications, 2016.

Rosenbaum, Richard. "What Time Is It? Gender Time! An Exhaustive Analysis of the Gender-Swapping Episode of the Cartoon Network Show *Adventure Time*." Overthinking It, 2013. https://www.overthinkingit.com/2013/01/18/adventure-time-gender/.

Salamon, Gayle. *Assuming a Body: Transgender and Rhetorics of Materiality*. New York: Columbia University Press, 2010.

Sandercock, Tom. "Transing the Small Screen: Loving and Hating Transgender Youth in *Glee* and *Degrassi*." *Journal of Gender Studies* 24, no. 4 (2015): 436–452.

Schiappa, Edward, Peter B. Gregg, and Dean E. Hewes. "Can One TV Show Make a Difference? *Will & Grace* and the Parasocial Contact Hypothesis." *Journal of Homosexuality* 51, no. 4 (2006): 15–37.

Shull, Dee Daniel. "Communicative Acts of Identity: Non-binary Individuals, Identity, and the Internet." Master's thesis, Hayward: California State University.

Valentín, Al. "Using the Animator's Tools to Dismantle the Master's House? Gender, Race, Sexuality and Disability in Cartoon Network's *Adventure Time* and *Steven Universe*." In *Buffy to Batgirl: Essays on Female Power, Evolving Femininity and Gender Roles in Science Fiction and Fantasy*, edited by J.M. Still and Z.T. Wilkinson, 175–215. Jefferson, NC: McFarland, 2019.

Vogt, Olivia M. "(De)constructed Gender and Romance in *Steven Universe*: A Queer Analysis." Master's thesis, North Dakota State University, 2019.

Xie, Jasmine. "Deconstructing and Developing Gender: The Nonbinary Search for Identity." Bachelor's honor thesis, Carnegie Mellon University, 2015.

From Censorship to "Obsidian"
A Critical and Historical Look at "Bubbline"

Mage Hadley

After airing its finale in 2018, Cartoon Network's animated hit *Adventure Time* returned to the small screen in 2020 with the release of the first two *Distant Lands* specials on the streaming service HBO Max. While the first of these specials was a prequel that followed the character BMO, the second episode, titled "Obsidian," was a post-finale adventure starring Marceline the Vampire Queen and Princess Bubblegum. This episode ostensibly centers on Marceline and Bubblegum attempting to slay a magma-dragon that has been terrorizing a neighboring kingdom, but the real heart of the episode is the romantic relationship between the two leading ladies, which the special explores both in the past and the present.

"Obsidian" was a well-woven look at trauma and love, and the episode was generally well received by most viewers, with William Hughes of *The A.V. Club* calling it "fan service at its finest."[1] It is not hard to see why: A look at the relationship between Marceline and Bubblegum was one that many fans and critics had long yearned for, and "Obsidian"—being an explicitly queer meditation on the relationship between a sentient piece of candy and an ageless vampire demon—delivered on this yearning in a way the show previously had not. Indeed, "Obsidian" reads as the long-awaited reckoning fans had anticipated for years after the queer relationship was finally canonized in the finale, affording it the same level of recognition as heterosexual pairings within the show. For this reason, it is easy to see why "Obsidian" received praise for its portrayal of two queer characters, but the episode also comes almost ten years after the pairing was first hinted at—and ten years after the queer content in *Adventure Time* was initially censored. In this essay, I take an historical look at the Marceline/Princess Bubblegum pairing (known to fans as "Bubbline," a portmanteau of "Bubblegum" and "Marceline"), exploring how the producers of *Adventure*

Time created, censored, and eventually canonized the queer pairing over the course of the show's run.

The Origin of "Bubbline"

Adventure Time began its story with a focus on main characters Finn and Jake, but during the first two seasons, it also introduced us to Marceline and Bubblegum. The two present first as side characters in Finn's narrative before sharing a scene in the second-season episode "Go with Me." In this episode, Marceline and Princess Bubblegum interact on screen for the first time, and all indications within the episode imply that they have met before and are not on the best of terms: Princess Bubblegum greets Marceline with a level of disdain and Marceline responds by invoking the Princess's full name in a sarcastic sort of way. In "Go with Me," neither Marceline nor Princess Bubblegum ask who the other is at any point, and given that they are both older than Finn, the idea that the characters have interacted before exists as a viable scenario.

The next entry in which we see Marceline and Princess Bubblegum interacting is the tenth episode of season three, "What Was Missing," which is infamous among fans. In this episode, an evil door lord steals prized possessions from our cast of main characters and locks himself behind a magical door, necessitating that the leads team up to defeat the enemy and reclaim their stolen items. Throughout the episode, tensions are high between Bubblegum and Marceline; both of the characters seem annoyed at each other's presence, and the two constantly argue with one another about how to unlock the magical door. The answer to this question is accidentally revealed to be truthful music when Marceline directs at Bubblegum an emotional song entitled "I'm Just Your Problem," with lyrics that suggest she is both angry at and hoping to reconcile with Bubblegum for some unknown slight. However, Marceline's song ends abruptly when she is distracted by Bubblegum's presence, and this leads to another argument. After Bubblegum and Marceline angrily storm away, Finn sings his own song about truth and friendship, which opens the door and allows the characters to be reunited with their stolen items. Marceline, it is revealed, had lost nothing and simply stuck around to hang out with her friends; meanwhile Bubblegum's prized possession is revealed to be a t-shirt that Marceline had given to her at some point in the past.

Before I discuss the Bubbline pairing and its censorship, it is important to look at how the relationship between these two characters came to be, and to do this, I will need to first talk about one Rebecca Sugar. A gifted cartoonist, Sugar is well-known in the animation scene for creating another Cartoon Network show, *Steven Universe* (which may arguably be queerer than *Adventure Time* on some levels), but before she helmed her own production, she worked as a storyboard artist on a number of early *Adventure Time* episodes. One of these episodes was "What Was Missing," which she co-storyboarded with fellow *Adventure Time* writer Adam Muto. In addition to writing out dialogue and blocking out action, Sugar also wrote the episode's songs, including the infamous "I'm Just Your Problem," and because of this Sugar is the person most people credit with creating the Bubbline relationship.[2] But was this Sugar's intention? The answer, to be frank, is yes. In *Exploring the Land of Ooo*, author Paul Thomas cites an interview with Rebecca Sugar, revealing that:

> ...after receiving the outline for "What Was Missing," [Sugar] pitched to Adam Muto ... the idea that Marceline and Bubblegum had been in a romantic relationship that had gone south, thereby explaining the characters' prickly demeanor toward one another. Muto and the *Adventure Time* crew were receptive to this idea, but due to the prejudices of the time, Sugar and Muto had to be strategic in how they worked this romantic angle into their storyboard. The two eventually decided to make the characters' relationship a bit more subtextual than it perhaps would have been had they been given free rein by the network.[3]

What this means is that the queerness in "What Was Missing" was intentional, and Bubbline was meant to be canon.

Controversy and Censorship

Upon its debut, "What Was Missing" stirred up quite the reaction from fans, many of whom read the interactions between Marceline and Bubblegum as romantic and therefore queer; soon the fan forums lit up with discourse about this new "ship," with some calling the pairing "Sugarless Gum" and others referring to it as "Bubbline" (the latter of which eventually stuck, no pun intended). In 2011, this kind of potential, queer representation in a cartoon watched by children on Cartoon Network was truly groundbreaking in western media. When this episode aired, there was nothing comparable to Bubbline, and, as Steven Holmes discusses in the following essay, this moment paved the way for additional queer media, like *She-Ra* and *The Owl House*. Bubbline also helped spark a fandom of queer people, mostly young teens, who were looking for queer content in animation and actually finding it for the first time. However, after "What Was Missing" aired, the excitement of many fans was muted by the almost immediate controversy generated by a web series called *Mathematical!*

46   "One isn't purely defined by their sex or gender"

Mathematical! was a companion web series produced by Dan Rickmers on behalf of Frederator (the studio that produced *Adventure Time*). Webisodes of this series, which were posted to YouTube after the debut of a new *Adventure Time* episode, largely discussed what had happened in the most-recently aired episodes, and they also speculated as to what might happen in the future (previous webisodes had, for instance, discussed ideas about the heterosexual Princess Bubblegum/Finn pairing). In the episode recap for "What Was Missing"—following a joke about Finn having "special time" with a lock of Princess Bubblegum's hair—mention is made of the Bubblegum/Marceline relationship. The webisode then asked fans to comment on whether or not they thought Marceline and Bubblegum should date.[4] It might seem innocuous to us now, but this recap ended up causing one of the most pronounced *Adventure Time* controversies ever—one that has left an enduring stain on the Bubbline relationship.

Mathematical! was produced not by the *Adventure Time* writing team but by Frederator, and therefore the things said in these videos were not canon, which many fans recognized; these web episodes were just recaps that tried to express the mood of the fandom. Nevertheless, *Mathematical!*'s open discussion of a queer relationship seemed to rock the boat at Cartoon Network, and a few days after the recap video dropped, Fred Seibert, CEO of Frederator, took to his company's Tumblr account and posted:

> Well, I completely screwed up.
> There's been chatter on the internet recently about our latest *Adventure Time* "Mathematical!" video recap that we created, posted, and removed here at Federator. I figure it's time to clear up the matter.
> In trying to get the show's audience involved we got wrapped up by both fan conjecture and spicy fanart and went a little too far. Neither Cartoon Network nor the *Adventure Time* crew had anything to do with putting up or taking down our latest re-cap. The episode "What was Missing" remains a terrific short and will be shown again and again just like any other *Adventure Time* episode.
> I let us goof in a staggering way and I'm deeply sorry it's become such a distraction for so many people.[5]

While showrunner Pendleton Ward remained silent through the ensuing drama,[6] Rebecca Sugar's storyboarding partner Adam Muto also implied that *Mathematical!* had crossed a line between fanon and canon, posting on the question-and-answer site Formspring:

> If it was just a fan video there would be no problem at all. The problem was that it was made by a production company actively involved with the show. The video took something that was a possible subtext and declared it, in effect, text and made it seem like the production was actively seeking out input on plot development.[7]

After Seibert and Muto's posts, Rickmers tried to smooth things over on his blog, writing:

> Let's talk about this whole Bubbleine [sic] thing. I direct the *Adventure Time* fan videos and episode recaps at *Mathematical*, and there's some stuff going on about Cartoon Network and censorship. I think fanfics and shipping and LGBT relationships are AWESOME. Seriously. Personally, I also think Bubbleine is adorable and definitely my OTP [i.e., "one true pairing"] for the series so far. *Mathematical* can at most be considered a reaction to you guys, the fans. It's a place for us to talk about what we like, and geek out about *Adventure Time*, and the production staff has nothing to do with it. So yeah, I think we all were thinking about Marceline and Bubblegum possibly crushing on each other after that episode, so I wanted us all to talk about it, but getting upset at anyone isn't going to solve anything. If you still want to talk about it, I think it would be a really cool development in the show, and between you and me, I'd be excited to see an american cartoon that is able to casually discuss LGBT relationships. I'm open, *Mathematical* is open, and we're still going to put up a fan video tomorrow about … something. And if anyone else isn't open, then that's too bad for them, because I still love ALL OF YOU. I also just wanted to say sorry to Adam Muto (Because it seems like I offended him, I guess?) and Rebecca Sugar for possibly distracting anyone from the excellent episode they wrote with two of the BEST songs in the series! Nothing but love for you two.[8]

Nevertheless, Rickmers was subsequently fired from Frederator Studios and the *Mathematical!* series was cancelled. For many queer fans of *Adventure Time*, Rickmers' firing and the dismissive comments made about Bubbline by some of the show's producers were distressing, and it was hard for these individuals to sense that queer content—and not fan conjecture—was the real issue. In time many of these fans came to see this "controversy" and its fallout as nothing short of blatant censorship of queer content.

The Slow Transition to Canonicity

In the episodes following "What Was Missing," Bubblegum and Marceline were essentially separated from one another, and for several full seasons, the two hardly interact. But whilst Bubbline was sidelined within the show itself, the relationship was gaining more and more traction in online spaces. This included members of the *Adventure Time* crew, like storyboard revisionist and character designer Natasha Allegri, who posted less than subtextual fan art of the two characters on her personal blog.[9]

In 2013, Marceline and Bubblegum were finally reunited on screen in the fifth-season "Sky Witch." This episode follows Marceline and Bubblegum as they fight Maja, a witch with terrible powers. (Maja has stolen

Marceline's teddy bear, Hambo, because the toy's "body is all juice-logged with sentimental affection," which Maja can use in her magic spells.) At the start of this episode, we see Bubblegum wearing the t-shirt from "What Was Missing" as pajamas, and by episode's end, Bubblegum trades the shirt with Maja for the return of Hambo, noting that "the psychic resonance on Hambo is nothing compared to" the shirt; Maja then demonstrates the power of the shirt by tossing a piece into a bubbling cauldron, which erupts violently. Needless to say, this episode, like "What Was Missing," "whipped the fandom into a frenzy,"[10] and all the talk of the t-shirt being full of emotional power was widely read by fans and reviewers as queer. But still, those who worked on the show denied this queerness. For instance, one of the episode's storyboard artists, Jesse Moynihan, implied that it was more of a "buddy film" story and that it had been inspired by an "intense" heterosexual friendship he had in the past.[11]

The following year, Marceline's voice actress Olivia Olson would renew discussion of Bubbline's ambiguous canonicity, when at a book signing, she mentioned that, according to Pendleton Ward himself, Marceline and Bubblegum had previously been in a relationship:

> I was at the recording studio [the other day] and Pen was actually there because he was recording for Lumpy Space Princess. And I ... wanted to pick Pen's brain a little bit [about Marceline and Bubblegum's relationship]. And he said, "Oh, you know they dated, right?" ... I said, "Are they going to [date] on the show at all? Or can we say anything about it in the [*The Enchiridion & Marcy's Super Secret Scrapbook*]?" And he's like, "I don't know about the book, but in some countries where the show airs [queer relationships are] illegal." So that's why they're not putting it in the show.[12]

Unfortunately for the shippers, after the signing Olson tweeted that she "like[s] to make things up at panels."[13] With this one-two act, it was like a queer relationship had been offered to fans and then immediately retreated on. For many, Bubbline started to shift from a canon ship that had been censored into a frustrating exercise in queerbaiting.

Luckily, season seven of *Adventure Time* marked a real turning point for Bubbline. This change is notable almost immediately in the season's second episode, "Varmints," which is centered firmly around Bubblegum's relationship with Marceline. At the start of the episode, we learn that Bubblegum is embarrassed about her dethroning, and has not yet told Marceline that she has been living in exile. When Marceline finds out, she calls Bubblegum out before realizing that Bubblegum doesn't need a lecture: she needs a friend. As such, Marceline and Bonnie go on an adventure, talk rather openly about their (still ambiguous) past relationship, and fight a monster that symbolizes Bubblegum's trauma. Marceline and Bubblegum are seen conversing in "Varmints" with a maturity that they had lacked previously, and given that it explicitly foregrounds their past relationship and their continuing reconciliation, many fans read the episode, like "Sky Witch" before it, as queer.

It is also worth noting that "Varmints" aired at an interesting time. Rebecca Sugar, who had helped establish the relationship between Bubblegum and Marceline, had long ago resigned from her role as a storyboard artist on *Adventure Time* to create and run the show *Steven Universe*. Sugar's show was explicitly queer from the beginning, and Adam Muto, who at this point was showrunning *Adventure Time*, later admitted in interviews that he felt more comfortable writing Bubblegum and Marceline as queer (or, at least, queer-coded) knowing that Cartoon Network had not yet censored Sugar's show.[14] "Varmints" aired in 2015, right in the middle of *Steven Universe*'s run, and its influence on *Adventure Time* seems undeniable: Bubblegum and Marceline grew closer and the writers became less resistant to the pairing. But whilst *Adventure Time* grew queerer, there was still a lack of solid confirmation from the people at the top that Bubbline was canon.

A few episodes after "Varmints," the show debuted a Marceline-centered miniseries called *Stakes* that follows Marceline's quest to rid herself of her vampirism and face down vampiric foes from her past; appropriately, Bubblegum is heavily involved in the story, serving as Marceline's closest ally. And even if the phrase "Marceline and Bubblegum are queer" is never said aloud in *Stakes*, it is not hard to read the miniseries as queer.[15] This is because *Stakes* routinely goes beyond subtext by allowing Marceline and Bubblegum to intimately express their friendship in a way that we had never before seen. For instance, near the beginning of the miniseries, there is a scene wherein Marceline thinks Bubblegum is about to reveal to her something emotionally important. When Bubblegum does not deliver, Marceline is visually saddened. Later, in the miniseries episode "Take Her Back," Marceline dreams about her and Bubblegum growing old together, and in this dream, Bubblegum even kisses Marceline on the forehead. Finally, at the end of the miniseries, after Marceline has reverted back to being a vampire, Bubblegum invites Marceline to live with her, and Marceline happily declares that, because she is once again immortal, she and Bubblegum "get to hang out forever." Of them all, this last example is one of the easiest to read through a queer lens, given that it is centered around the idea of Marceline and Bubblegum living together as a couple for eternity.

But while *Stakes*—through animation choices and subtle dialogue—arguably offered fans a form of queer content, that queerness still seemed to exist within the show's liminal space. Whilst Finn and Jake were explicitly allowed to have girlfriends in the show, Bubblegum and Marceline were not allowed to explicitly be "girlfriends," regardless of how "coupley" they acted. The show's refusal to explicitly confirm the characters' romantic relationship despite mounting evidence to the contrary is perhaps most noticeable in the season eight episode "Broke His Crown." In this "meet the parents" episode, Marceline brings together Bubblegum and her adoptive Ice King dad for dinner. In addition to the episode's set-up—which is reminiscent of the many television episodes or movies that see characters introducing their romantic partner to their parent(s)—there are several moments in the episode that suggest Bubblegum and Marceline are closer than "just friends": For instance, the two are seen holding hands, Bubblegum calls Marceline her "girlfriend" (although this is done in a jovial tone), and when Simon asks Marceline if she has a boyfriend, Marceline says "No!" and laughs whilst looking at Bubblegum. The queerness of these moments is not exactly subtle, but considering that the writers were still not explicitly confirming the canonicity of Bubbline, it was not exactly overt representation either. As such, many fans saw the episode as another exercise in queerbaiting.

In the final season of *Adventure Time*, Marceline and Bubblegum do not get much screen time together—a strange decision on the part of the writers, considering that the season ends with the two being explicitly portrayed as a couple. And while the two act somewhat like a couple at Finn's birthday in "Seventeen" (for instance, Marceline is incredibly protective of Bubblegum when she is threatened, and the two hold hands in one scene at the very end), it is really only in the episode "Hunson & Marcy" that the "Bubbline question" is revisited. In this episode, Hunson Abadeer (Marceline's neglectful and comically useless demon dad) returns to Ooo and causes all sorts of problems for Marceline while trying to rekindle a relationship with his daughter. Interspersed amongst all the shenanigans are several "hints" suggesting that Marceline and Bubblegum are in a relationship: In one scene, for instance, Hunson asks Finn if Marceline is dating anyone, and Finn implies that she *might* be. In another, Marceline is shown wearing one of Bubblegum's sweaters—a sweater that Bubblegum prominently wears in *Stakes*. And like "Broke His Crown" from season seven, "Marcy & Hunson" also features a "dinner with a parent" (although this time, it is a different dinner and a different dad). But perhaps the most obvious hint comes when Marceline sings a song called "Slow Dance with You," which details a woman's desire to dance with another woman; the scene even features a ghost voiced by Hynden Walch (Bubblegum's voice actress) on backup vocals! Many Bubbline fans were exhilarated by these hints, but upon reflection, it all seems rather strange. A confirmation of Marceline and Bubblegum's relationship *almost* feels as if it comes in this episode but it never quite does. Because of this, there are definitely arguments to be made that this episode, like several of the ones that preceded it, was queerbaiting its audience.

Even the big kiss in the series' finale "Come Along with Me"—a scene which CinemaBlend called an "iconic moment"[16] and which *them.* magazine called "the ending [queer fans] deserved"[17]—is more problematic than it might initially seem. According to showrunner Adam Muto, the reveal in the finale that Bubblegum and Marceline are romantically interested in one another was never originally scripted by the writers; the outline given to the storyboard artists merely noted that the two were to "have a moment" after Bubblegum is nearly killed. Hanna K. Nyström, the artist responsible for storyboarding the scene, however, drew the characters kissing and added the note "come on!" in the storyboard's margin. In an interview with TV Line, Muto admitted that he and the producers "[could not] argue with that."[18]

The way that many of the (male) *Adventure Time* writers and producers have (not) spoken about the Bubblegum and Marceline relationship over the years is, arguably, indicative of the problematic treatment of Bubbline. Adam Muto, for instance, was reticent to explicitly confirm that the characters were an official couple after the finale aired, even after their very prominent on-screen kiss.[19] (Remember, this is the writer who was most vocal about the *Mathematical!* situation, which led to a man losing his job.) Meanwhile, writer Jesse Moynihan encouraged fan "shipping" of Bubblegum and Marceline before telling fans that he saw them mostly as friends.[20] And finally, Pendleton Ward, the creator of the show, decided to never comment on, or defend the existence of, queer characters in his own show.[21] Whilst these creators were never maliciously homophobic, they were hardly supportive of the queer content that they had created. As such, there is a real sense of creator-audience gaslighting here—or what we could more lightheartedly call "Schrödinger's Bubbline": For years, the producers and writers claimed that a relationship was not definite, only to then confirm in the series' finale that Bubbline had been there all along. This behavior, and all the online drama, caused some fans (many of them young and queer themselves) real distress at the time.

An Ambivalent Victory

"Obsidian" received positive reviews and—judging by the fan discourse on sites like Twitter and Reddit—was adored by fans, but for many of these fans, the episode comes with a pang of sorrow, too. The story of Bubblegum and Marceline was one that was initially censored, and while *Adventure Time* is now being applauded for its queer representation, the shadow of that censorship still hangs over the program. To make matters more complicated, Cartoon Network has not simply let Marceline and Bubblegum be a couple within the show and left it at that—now the network is actively promoting their queer relationship. On the Cartoon Network and HBO Max Youtube and Instagram pages, the studio has made posts confirming that scenes once described only "friendly'" by the writers are now seen as definitely queer. There is even a studio-sanctioned "Ultimate Bubbline Playlist" of *Adventure Time* songs available on most music streaming services. Now that *Adventure Time* technically airs on a streaming service, instead of an "children's channel," it seems that those at Cartoon Network have no issue celebrating the couple, and now that American media (and culture) as a whole has become more accepting of queer representation, the creators of *Adventure Time* seem to have grown prouder of their once-shunned creation. But for many fans, it is hard to forget the moments of queer suppression that occurred in a show they adore.

The love between Bubblegum and Marceline in "Obsidian" is powerful, but it makes one think about what could have been if the pairing had not been initially censored. And in this "lost future" where Bubbline was allowed to shine, what would the impact have been on other shows? If Bubblegum and Marceline's romantic relationship had been explored explicitly after "What Was Missing," would the writers of Nickelodeon's *Legend of Korra* have felt the need to censor their own queer ending in 2014? And if *Legend of Korra* had not waited until the last moment to canonize its queer couple, would Dreamwork's *She-Ra* still have done the same in 2020? Is the fight for queer relationships in children's animation easier now, or is it simply more lucrative? Is it unfair to even expect the writers to have fought for queer representation in 2010, or is it hard to argue allyship ever occurred when so much muting of that representation had happened? "Obsidian" was a wonderful love letter to Bubbline and in many ways an apology to fans, yet to some it is still a solemn thing that such a gesture needed to be made in the first place.

Notes

1. William Hughes, "*Adventure Time: Distant Lands*—Obsidian is Fan Service at its Finest."
2. Allegra Frank, "*Adventure Time* Showrunner Doesn't See the Finale as a Happy Ending."
3. Paul Thomas, *Exploring the Land of Ooo*, 38–39.
4. Dan Rickmers, "Mathematical—What Was Missing Recap."
5. Fred Seibert, "Well, I screwed up..."
6. Zack Smith, "*Adventure Time* Creator Pen Ward Talks Before Season Finale."
7. Adam Muto, "Could you explain..."
8. Dan Rickmers, "Let's talk about this whole Bubbleine [sic] thing..."

9. Natasha Allegri, untitled Bubbline picture.
10. hawnjf's comment on Jesse Moynihan, "Sky Witch."
11. Moynihan.
12. Olivia Olson in Thomas, *Exploring the Land of Ooo*, 41
13. Olson in Thomas.
14. Frank, "*Adventure Time* Showrunner."
15. See, for instance, Simon Bacon, "A Dream within a Dream."
16. Mick Joest, "*Adventure Time*'s Producer Explains That Finale Kiss."
17. Mey Rude, "Bubbline Is Canon."
18. Swift, "Bubblegum and Marceline's Series Finale Moment."
19. Swift. See also Charles Pulliam-Moore, "*Adventure Time*'s Producer Was Concerned."
20. Jesse Moynihan, "Sky Witch."
21. Smith, "Pen Ward Talks

References

Allegri, Natasha. Untitled Bubbline picture, Tumblr, 2011. https://natazilla.tumblr.com/post/5680916215.

Bacon, Simon. "'A Dream within a Dream': Children's 'Horror 'Television and Lesbianism in the World of Marceline the Vampire Queen." In New Queer Horror Film and TV, edited by Darren Elliot-Smith and John Edgar Browning, 105–19. Cardiff, UK: University of Wales Press, 2020.

black and white thinking. "The History of *Adventure Time*'s Bubblegum + Marceline." YouTube, 2020. https://www.youtube.com/watch?v=rn7BLqzaetI.

Blodgett, Bridget, and Anastasia Salter. "What Was Missing: Children's Queerbaiting and Homoromantic Exclusion in *Adventure Time* and *Steven Universe*." In *Queerbaiting and Fandom: Teasing Fans through Homoerotic Possibilities*, edited by J. Brennan, 142–155. Iowa City: University of Iowa Press, 2019.

Bollis, Lexi. "Romance Between *Adventure Time*'s Princess Bubblegum and Marceline Confirmed." Geek Insider, 2014. https://geekinsider.com/romance-adventure-times-princess-bubblegum-marceline-confirmed/.

Frank, Allegra. "*Adventure Time* Showrunner Doesn't See the Finale as a Happy Ending." Polygon, 2018. https://www.polygon.com/tv/2018/9/3/17806570/adventure-time-finale-finn-bubblegum-marceline-adam-muto-interview.

Hughes, William. "*Adventure Time: Distant Lands*—Obsidian Is Fan Service at its Finest." The A.V. Club, 2020. https://tv.avclub.com/adventure-time-distant-lands-obsidian-is-fan-service-a-1845677393.

Joest, Mick. "*Adventure Time*'s Producer Explains That Finale Kiss." Cinema Blend, 2018. https://www.cinemablend.com/television/2456944/adventure-times-producer-explains-that-finale-kiss.

Kylie. "*Adventure Time*, Bubbline, and when subtext stops cutting it." The Fandomentals, 2016. https://thefandomentals.com/adventure-time-bubbline-subtext-stops-cutting/.

Moen, Matt. "In Conversation: Rebecca Sugar and Noelle Stevenson." *Paper*, 2020. https://www.papermag.com/rebecca-sugar-noelle-stevenson-2646446747.html.

Moynihan, Jesse. "Sky Witch." JesseMoynihan.com, archived on October 13, 2013. https://web.archive.org/web/20131013142608/http://jessemoynihan.com/?p=2042.

Muto, Adam. "Could you explain…" Formspring, archived on January 7, 2012. https://web.archive.org/web/20120107112009/http://www.formspring.me/MrMuto/q/243840879511470446.

Outlaw, Kofi. "*My Hero Academia* Reveals Izuku's New Black Whip Form." ComicBook.com, December 8, 2020. https://comicbook.com/anime/news/my-hero-academia-manga-293-spoilers-izuku-black-whip-froppy-style-tongue/.

Polo, Susana. "Is *Adventure Time* Confirming More-Than-Friends Subtext Between Two

Female Characters?" *The Mary Sue*, September 28, 2011. https://www.themarysue.com/adventure-time-lesbian-characters/.

Pulliam-Moore, Charles. *"Adventure Time*'s Producer Was Concerned Queer Representation Might Draw 'Too Much Attention.'" io9, September 4, 2018. https://io9.gizmodo.com/adventure-times-producer-was-concerned-queer-representa-1828807397.

Rickmers, Dan. "Let's talk about this whole Bubbleine [sic] thing…" Tumblr, 2011. https://danrickmers.tumblr.com/post/10783950746/lets-talk-about-this-whole-bubbleine-thing-i.

Rickmers, Dan. "Mathematical—What Was Missing Recap." YouTube, 2011. Archived at https://www.youtube.com/watch?v=4G55ZV9ITY8.

Rude, Mey. "Bubbline Is *Canon*: 7 Gayest Moments From *Adventure Time*'s Cutest Relationship." *them*. magazine, September 5, 2018. https://www.them.us/story/bubbline-is-canon-adventure-time.

Sedghi, Sarra. "Adam Muto on Why an *Adventure Time* Reboot Is Inevitable." *Dot & Line*, August 30, 2018. https://dotandline.net/adam-muto-adventure-time-interview/.

Seibert, Fred. "Well, I Screwed Up." Frederator, 2011, https://web.archive.org/web/20111004154306/http://adventuretimeart.frederator.com/post/10825331450/well-i-completely-screwed-up-theres.

Smith, Tyler. "Olivia Olson Spills the Beans on PB & Marceline." YouTube. August 7, 2014. https://www.youtube.com/watch?v=_EleCNWfwTY&feature=emb_title.

Smith, Zack. "Adventure Time Creator Pen Ward Talks Before Season Finale." Newsarama, 2012. Archived on May 27, 2013. https://web.archive.org/web/20130527140217/http://www.newsarama.com/9077-adventure-time-creator-pen-ward-talks-before-season-finale.html.

Sugar, Rebecca. "What was missing, Monday at 8!" Tumblr, September 22, 2011. https://rebeccasugar.tumblr.com/post/10542659493/what-was-missing-monday-at-8-this-one-took.

Swift, Andy. "*Adventure Time* EP Talks Bubblegum and Marceline's Series Finale Moment: 'There's Enough to Draw a Conclusion.'" TV Line, September 3 2018. https://tvline.com/2018/09/03/adventure-time-series-finale-bubblegum-marceline-kiss-bubbline-confirmed/.

Thomas, Paul. *Exploring the Land of Ooo: An Unofficial Overview and Production History of Cartoon Network's* Adventure Time. Lawrence: University of Kansas Libraries, 2020.

Rainbows and Unicorns

The Influence of Bubbline on Apocalyptic Film and Animation

Steven Holmes

In understanding the history of queer themes in western animation, one text serves as a watershed: *Adventure Time*. The relationship between Princess Bubblegum and Marceline defined new trends and broke ground in representing queer themes in western animation, particularly children's animation. In particular, it showcased how queer themes could successfully be integrated into this type of animation. But because this relationship was never fully confirmed until the series finale, "Come Along with Me," and the post-finale special, "Obsidian," *Adventure Time* also established a pattern in children's animation where the confirmation of queer relationships is deferred until near the ending of a narrative series. This pattern is visible in productions including *She-Ra and the Princesses of Power* (2018–20), as well as the adult animation show *Harley Quinn* (2019–present).

Although the practice of deferring the confirmation of LGBT+ relationships in the narrative may seem conservative—especially when compared to some shows, like *Steven Universe* (2013–19)—this essay argues that given its place in time, *Adventure Time* helped push the boundaries of LGBT+ representation in children's animation. This essay will also show how *Adventure Time* changed trends not only in animation, but also in the larger discourse surrounding the topics of the "apocalypse" and the "post-apocalypse," which have been an increasingly common narrative subject matter since the early parts of the 20th century. In that discourse, as a rejection of grimdark aesthetic, *Adventure Time* helped usher in a new wave of rainbow fantasy.

First, let me briefly clarify one key concept, that of "apocalypse." Although the word has Greek origins, contemporary usage generally uses it to refer to any major catastrophic event or disaster. This means that "apocalypse" and "post-apocalypse" can sometimes seem to be loose organizing principles; a show where the world is threatened to end, but is still saved, might still be considered "apocalyptic" because the narrative action was driven by the threat of world-ending events. Even so, some people might hear the word and think of specific well-known post-apocalyptic narratives, such as *Mad Max*. I do not think a belabored debate about whether each of these shows is a perfect example of either apocalyptic or post-apocalyptic television is very interesting. Instead, I am using the terms in relation to what Michel Foucault in *The Archaeology of Knowledge* would call a "discursive formation." Something is a part of discourse if people think of it or talk about it in relation to that topic. "Discursive formation" is a very expansive way of conceptualizing terms. So, for *Adventure Time*, we might say it is post-apocalyptic because in the intro to each episode, there are dilapidated nuclear weapons, which imply the world exists after nuclear holocaust. This does not preclude *Adventure Time* from belonging to other genres or categories as well; as a discursive formation, it is no problem whatsoever to describe *Adventure Time* as being both a fantasy and a post-apocalyptic narrative (in addition to many other descriptors). *Adventure Time* has unicorns, magic, vampires, and other elements commonly associated with fantasy, and *Adventure Time* has world-threatening events, flashbacks to what we think of as contemporary human civilization, and references to "The Great Mushroom War." When it comes to discursive formations, it's both/and, not either/or.

"What Was Missing" in Adventure Time

Running from 2010 to 2018 on Cartoon Network, *Adventure Time* focused primarily on the adventures of a boy, Finn the Human, and his brother/friend Jake the Dog. During its duration *Adventure Time* won multiple awards, including Annie Awards for Best Animated Production for Children, and consequently we can understand one of its primary commercial demographics being boys between ages 6–11.[1] In the early seasons, Finn pines after Princess Bubblegum, the princess of the Candy Kingdom, and many of his quests are done on her behalf. As the series progresses it introduces other major characters, including Marceline the Vampire Queen. Throughout season one, Princess Bubblegum is primarily presented in heterosexual terms, with increasing frustration on Finn's part in season two as his relationship with Princess Bubblegum does not begin to develop further.

Despite occasional playfulness with gender representation, in the early seasons the show is mostly framed around the heterosexual desires and frustrations of Finn the Human and Jake the Dog. The show seems like it will play with a heteronormative love triangle in moments like the second-season episode "Go with Me," in which Finn wants to ask Princess Bubblegum to the movies, a prospect he finds challenging because Jake tells him that going to the movies on "couples night" has "romance initiation" requirements. Finn spends much of the episode seeking the advice of Marceline, who seems to deliberately give him bad advice. Is Marceline sabotaging Finn's relationship with Bubblegum because Marceline is secretly enamored with *Finn*? Does this mean the show will develop a love triangle, with Finn pining after Bubblegum and Marceline pining after Finn? No and no. The show plays this off all as a misunderstanding and has Finn and Marceline go to the movies as friends; in doing this, the show avoids a Finn-Bubblegum-Marceline love imbroglio.

I draw attention to "Go with Me" to highlight the extent to which the early seasons did seem to be playing with the idea of love triangles with Finn, Marceline, and Bubblegum without ever fully developing them; yet the ambiguity of this failed love triangle set the stage for the more developed romantic prospects as the series progressed. Paul Thomas, in *Exploring the Land of Ooo,* observes that in the initial pitches for the characters, Bubblegum and Marceline were originally planned to be romantic rivals for Finn in the vein of Betty Cooper and Veronica Lodge from *Archie Comics*.[2] Transforming the relationship between Bubblegum and Marceline was the work of storyboard artist Rebecca Sugar, who later went on to create *Steven Universe,* which featured one of the first queer weddings on Cartoon Network. Although in print comics, Northstar in the *X-Men* franchise had been revealed as gay by 1992 and was married in print comics in 2012,[3] the transition to those relationships being depicted in animation has lagged behind. But this essay is focusing here specifically on American animation, and as Yomi Adegoke observed in a discussion of Rebecca Sugar's work, American television networks have long censored queer representation that otherwise would have been imported from Japan, as in the case of *Sailor Moon*.[4]

Sugar's intervention into the show's sexual dynamic begins in season 3, episode 10, "What Was Missing." In this episode, a "Door Lord" steals various important objects from each of the primary characters, including Finn, Princess Bubblegum, and seemingly Marceline. The structure of the episode focuses on the revelation that Bubblegum and Marceline have an estranged relationship that was potentially romantic in the past. The Door Lord stole a T-shirt that had been given to Bubblegum by Marceline, a T-shirt that clearly has sentimental value for Bubblegum given she prefers to sleep in it. Coupled with a song earlier in the episode, "What Was Missing" introduces one of the most notable queer relationships in animated television, the eventually confirmed romantic relationship between Princess Bubblegum and Marceline, "Bubbline." A fuller discussion of the historical trajectory of *Adventure Time's* depiction of the relationship between Princess Bubblegum and Marceline is discussed in the preceding essay, entitled "From Censorship to 'Obsidian': A Critical and Historical Look at 'Bubbline.'"

Even in 2011 when "What was Missing" was airing, Cartoon Network was still very reticent about an explicit queer relationship, and for that reason Sugar's pitch kept the relationship subtextual rather than explicit. Thomas speculates that the fan controversy, particularly the push to have the relationship explicitly confirmed by users on the internet, made the creators more reticent to depict the relationship. After the controversy, the show's depiction of Marceline shifted more to her daughter/father relationship with the Ice King. Hadley's essay in this volume suggests that rather than backlash to fan culture, the pullback on the depiction of Bubbline is better understood as censorship. In either explanation, Cartoon Network, as a company attempting to have a broad reach to an international market, had created enough normative opposition to openly queer relationships that the showrunners felt very cautious about being too direct in their approach or foregrounding that element. In the long term, the show does end with a kiss between Marceline and Princess Bubblegum, after ten seasons and two hundred and eighteen total episodes.

While Bubbline's kiss does serve as a narrative climax for the series, it is also worth considering that the long delay in the development of the characters is likely more linked to the trepidations of Cartoon Network in representing confirmed queer relationships up through the 2010s. The idea that children must be protected from queer representation is one of the most insidious and widespread forms of homophobia currently existent in cultural discourse, as Lee Edelman observes in *No Future*, which he characterizes as "Reproductive Futurism." For Edelman, the image of the heteronormative family has definitional political power because the child acts as the guarantee of a social future, and so heteronormativity is interwoven with almost all deliberative politics. Thus according to Edelman, "Reproductive Futurism" is:

> an ideological limit on political discourse as such, preserving in the process of absolute privilege of heteronormativity by rendering unthinkable, by casting outside the political domain, the possibility of queer resistance to this organizing principle of communal relations.[5]

Children's programming is precisely where queer representation is most important insofar as which representations people will accept being depicted to their children showcases their social and discursive norms.

Both Princess Bubblegum and Marceline are survivors, having emerged out of the post-apocalyptic landscape following the destruction of humanity in the "Mushroom War," an overt implication of nuclear holocaust. Princess Bubblegum and Marceline both break away from heteronormativity in their being; Princess Bubblegum emerged out of the radioactive wasteland as a mutant of pink slime, reshaping the world as she saw fit, creating the denizens of the candy kingdom, as well as the next in line for the throne, Lemongrab. At no point is there an indication that Princess Bubblegum needs a heteronormative relationship to maintain her line, nor is there an indication there is a line to maintain; she seems functionally immortal, and is in control of her reproductive life through cloning. Marceline, meanwhile, as a vampire, is also immortal (or at least undead), and also rejects any sort of biological mandate for reproduction. It is important to emphasize that the "queerness" of *Adventure Time*'s depiction of Bubbline goes beyond simply having two characters that present as female in a relationship with one another; structurally, the universe of the show impressively rejects many of the core tenets of "reproductive futurism."

Despite Cartoon Network's hesitation, *Adventure Time* did serve as a breakthrough work, setting the stage for shows like *Steven Universe* that would more openly depict LGBT+ themes. To perhaps play a cynical game of devil's advocate, I do also wonder whether structuring the confirmation of a queer relationship until the series finale does allow some minor benefits, namely that the show is not at risk of killing off the queer characters in the midst of their relationship—in this way, the show did manage to avoid the #BuryYourGays trope, which I will discuss further later. Moreover, the overall transformative impact of *Adventure Time* is even more powerful when understood in terms of its intervention into apocalyptic and post-apocalyptic television.

Adventure Time *Through the Lens of the Post-Apocalyptic*

Natalie Kouri-Trowe observed in 2013 that "mainstream depictions of postapocalyptic survival largely centre on the archetypical figure of the male saviour or hero, and advance a familiar patriarchal instrumentalization of women's bodies as vessels for the survival of the human species."[6] While that was still largely true in 2013, although there had been some strides made in the preceding decades, there has been an explosion of queer representation in certain media forms and genres. Western young adult and adult animation has seen a dramatic rise in both the frequency of queer relationships as well as noticeable qualitative changes in the style of queer relationships.

To be clear, the *qualitative* change in the depiction of queer relationships may be more significant than the *quantitative* change, although this may seem counter-intuitive. As Guillermo Avila-Saavedra argues in "Nothing Queer about Queer Television: Televized Constructions of Gay Masculinities," although there have been quantitative changes in the representation of queer identities on television, particularly since 2003,[7] the queerness of queer characters is not usually the driving force of a show, and in this sense the "perceived progressiveness" of the depiction of queer characters on television does little to "translate into social tolerance or recognition"[8] because "the fictional media narratives tend to emphasize the interpersonal issues of homosexuality and avoid the political ones."[9] So, for example, while the existence of Benson in *Kipo and the Age of Wonderbeasts* is notable insofar as highlighting how far LGBT+ representation in children's animation has come in the last decade, he is more notable in the context of this essay for the banality of his gay identity; him being gay is not obviously important for the plot or structure of the show. (That said, Petrana Radulovic argues that the coming-out moment there is "beautifully understated," and it is also important to have some queer characters in children's animation whose queerness is banal and normal to the narrative world.)

To this extent, simple quantitative changes in the demographics of the characters in apocalyptic narratives may seem underwhelming. It may seem "progressive" to see a show like *The Walking Dead* move past mere queer subtexts, such as the explicitly homosocial but subtextually homosexual relationship between Michonne and Andrea in early seasons, to the depiction of explicitly queer characters such as Aaron, Tara, and Jesus. Yet, as Avila-Saavedra would observe, while the characters are depicted as queer, their queerness is never a driving force in the narrative, and the narrative arcs continue to revolve around largely heterosexual matrices. Still, moving from subtext to overt representation is noticeable progress.

The transformation in the depiction of sexual identity in the last twenty years should not be hand-waved as irrelevant or as merely a token effort. In 2004, characters like R.D. Reid's "Glen" were still typical in films like Zack Snyder's remake of *Dawn of the Dead*. In that film, Glen antagonizes Michael Kelly's CJ with his coming out story while CJ is imprisoned in the mall, and there are later shots of him trying on women's shoes in a montage. Still, Glen's queerness is primarily played for comic relief. The film also foregrounds a cameo by Ken Foree, who as a recurring actor from the original film seems to reflect some level of thematic concern when he acts as a televangelist arguing that the zombie apocalypse is caused because, as the director's cut states: "Hell is overpopulated and Satan sends his dead to us on earth. Why? Because you have illegitimate sexual intercourse. Because you kill unborn children. Because men fornicate with men. Because you contract same-gender marriages." In Snyder's film, at least, the apocalyptic rationale is couched in American political progressive and reactionary terms, where the white heterosexual antagonist is taunted with the queerness of side characters while accepting homosexuality in America as the cause of the end of civilization.

Likewise, science fiction prose, since moving into the "New Wave" and leaving the pulp era and golden age, has had some notable queer characters, certainly, with breakthrough authors like Octavia Butler having bi-sexual main characters or non-binary aliens in her many fictional worlds through the 1980s and 1990s. Still, although there have been breakthrough, against-the-grain authors and characters, it is worth emphasizing that "men saving women" in a heterosexual context was one of the defining features of post-apocalyptic narratives throughout the 20th century. In this regard, *Adventure Time* can be seen as an intervention into the norms of post-apocalyptic narrative generally, not only children's media. In Jack London's 1912 "The Scarlet Plague," much of the narrative's conflict revolves around a lower-class individual named Chauffeur abducting and marrying Vesta Van Warden against her will. Chauffeur getting to decide which man is paired with which woman is one of the defining features of the apparent depravity of London's post-apocalyptic world. In Harlan Ellison's "A Boy and his Dog," the young boy Vic actively plans to assault and rape a woman after tracking her using his faithful companion. In David Brin's *The Postman*, one of the first heroic acts of Gordon Krantz is saving a woman from rape from bandits; protecting women from rape is one of the key moments that pushes Krantz to not just continue to use a postman's uniform as a disguise to move around the post-apocalyptic world, but pushes him to work to re-create civilization using twentieth-century American ideals as a model. In Cormac McCarthy's *The Road*, the reader learns through flashbacks that the mother of "the man" and "the boy" committed suicide before the full depravity of post-apocalyptic worlds appeared because the threat of rape from unrestrained heterosexual men was so obvious to her. The trend has also continued into the 21st century, including in digital art and computer games. The game *This War of Mine* creates a similar conflict to that posted in Brin's *The Postman*, where the player has to decide whether they can save a woman from rape or not, depending on their resources in the game. Finally, the entire premise of the *Mad Max* franchise is that Max is "mad" precisely because gangs and post-apocalyptically depraved heterosexual men murdered his wife, themes that reiterate themselves in *Mad Max: Fury Road* where Max strives to protect "wives" from Immortan Joe. While much of that film also revolves around Charlize Theron's Imperator Furiosa, it remains the case that throughout the 20th century, and continuing on into the 21st century, "men saving women" has been one of the defining narrative and structural elements of post-apocalyptic narratives. Scenes of heteronormative sexual conflict are very often the defining moments of character motivation for novels, films, and short stories. *Adventure Time* challenges this formula.

Queer characters are becoming more central to the structure of narrative in animation. There has certainly been a rise in queer characters in post-apocalyptic media generally, as noted above, and not only in animation. A representative example here is the character of Lexa (Alycia Debnam-Carey) from *The 100*. Lexa's queerness was both prominent and also central to the plot—since, as "Commander," Lexa organized the 12 tribes of "grounders" into a coalition to wage a war against the "mountain men." Lexa's relationship with the series lead Clarke (Eliza Taylor) caused conflict with her "flame-keeper," and as a result she was assassinated. This caused a fair amount of backlash from the fan community, since Lexa's death, occurring shortly after she consummated her relationship with Clarke, seemed to play into the "Bury Your Gays" trope wherein television series kill of queer characters after particularly happy moments, or to prop up heterosexual relationships instead. The benefits of queer representation can seem short-lived if it is primarily used as just another vehicle for shocking deaths in a television drama. The "Bury Your Gays" trope is seen as harmful because it seems to link affirming sexual orientation with death; Lexa's death even instigated the website "LGBT Fans Deserve Better" to create a "Lexa pledge" for television creators to stop using queer character deaths purely for shock value.

The appeal of animation in terms of queer representation should be addressed. Regardless of being young adult or adult oriented, animation tends to have fewer major characters killed off in any given season, tends to not veer as heavily into "grimdark," and tends to focus on "save the world" narrative arcs over survival-oriented stories. "Grimdark" is associated with particularly amoral, violent, and dystopian depictions of speculative futures, and was heavily popularized through the game *Warmhammer 40,000*, and the A Song of Ice and Fire series by George R.R. Martin, but it has also been applied to recent popular narrative worlds including *Batman* and *The Walking Dead*. Furthermore, post-apocalyptic animation can more readily include fantastic elements, which can mean queer themes can infuse themselves more readily into the visual style of the world and art as a whole. Whether it is Lady Rainicorn in *Adventure*

Time or a rainbow wave of magical energy in *She-Ra and the Princesses of Power*, animation can visually either play with or convey themes like a flag to the viewer. Additionally, there can be greater emphasis on the overlap between environments and interpersonal human relationships, and this overlap can play into larger thematic distinctions between animated works and live-action dramas.

The prevalence of queer representation in apocalyptic animation coincides with an emphasis on rejecting commonplace assumptions about human nature and re-evaluating the relationship of humankind to natural environments. Katie Hogan argues that deep diving into the interconnections between various systems of oppression reveals contradictory ideas about "women, people of color, nature, and LGBTs as 'against nature'... and the earth as worthless."[10] This, in turn, encourages ecocritics from all disciplines to revisit ecofeminist and eco-queer insights. In the context of *Adventure Time*, we might ask, are Bubblegum and Marceline also "people of color" (pink, grey)? Beyond that, Bubblegum emerges up out of the new natural world of a post-apocalyptic Earth; in the wake of the Great Mushroom War, the bubblegum naturally mutates out of the radioactive wasteland into sentience. In creating the people of the Candy Kingdom, and in presenting an alternative to reproductive futurism, her entire being rejects the idea that the earth, that nature, that women, that queerness is "worthless."

Even then, *Adventure Time* does not present Bubblegum in purely idealistic terms or as a flawless character. There are two plots building up to the kiss between Marceline and Bubblegum. First, there is the "Gum War." Bubblegum is being invaded by an army led by Gumbald, one of her old creations which has come to despise her. Marceline tries to talk her out of total war, but after assassination attempts from Gumbald, Bubblegum declares a full-on war. This conflict is interrupted by the invasion of GOLB. Like other fantasy series, *Adventure Time* presents antagonists who embody the threat of almost total annihilation. In this case, GOLB is a being linked to the idea of chaos, and the threat of its chaos is yet another apocalyptic threat at the end of the series. Although the series protagonists do defeat GOLB in part through harmony and singing songs, no effort or argument outside of GOLB as a distraction prevents the "Gum War" between Bubblegum and Gumbald. Although the series ends with the world being saved from GOLB, the series also ends on the bittersweet sense that Princess Bubblegum and "Bubbline" was not on its own capable of preventing the cycles of violence that seemed to have led into the Great Mushroom War.

In broad strokes (hinting at a relationship, and then delaying the realization of that relationship until the narrative's ending), *Adventure Time* emulates many of the points that we may typically expect in heteronormative cultural depictions. Whether it be *Spider-Man 2* or *How to Train Your Dragon*, audiences are well familiar with the idea that the hero will often "get the girl" in the end of the show. If anything, this is slightly less true in apocalyptic media, where more often than not heteronormative relationships have broken down due to violence, particularly the death of one member of a romantic pairing, as in *The Road*, *Mad Max*, or *Children of Men*. Nonetheless, in save-the-world narratives that drift toward apocalyptic frameworks, this remains a common framework, whether it be Neo and Trinity in *The Matrix*, Thor and Jane in *Thor*, or The Postman and Abby in *The Postman*. This structure persists in media directed at children, including Pixar's *Wall-E*, where the relationship between Wall-E and Eve is a major focal point of the film's narrative structure. *Wall-E* can loosely fit as a descriptive model for the typical romantic subplot in young-adult animated narratives, wherein one character typically pines for a female participant who eventually responds at the climax of the film.

In some ways then, *Adventure Time* simply remaps conventional action-adventure tropes into a queer framework. Through adventure, two characters are forced to work together in a variety of situations, until a world-threatening event causes them to re-evaluate where they are going in their lives and their foundational values, at which point at the narrative conclusion they decide to connect with each other and express love that they previously kept on a back-burner. Certainly *Adventure Time* could have stayed even more closely to this model had it maintained the Archie Comics structure of Betty Cooper and Veronica Lodge it had played with in "Go with Me." Even if we accept *Adventure Time* as remapping action-adventure tropes to a queer framework, and very cautiously deferring clear representation of lesbian love until the final episode, it nonetheless also helped usher in a new wave of animation.

From Harley Quinn *to* She-Ra: *The New Wave in Animation*

This new wave is characterized by a trend to reject grimdark narrative archetypes, and to move LGBT+ themes away from the periphery and toward the center of fantasy narrative structure. Works like *Steven Universe*, *She-Ra and the Princesses of Power*, and *Harley Quinn* imbue their worlds with LGBT+ characters, yes, but they do so to an extent that destabilizes heteronormative assumptions in narrative progression. The subtext of queer desire gives shape to the narrative structure and arcs, and eventually becomes directly represented. The new normal these shows seem to be grappling with, then, is the paradigm established by *Adventure Time* of deferring the confirmation of queer identities until late in the series. In *Steven Universe* these themes enter the narrative earlier and give shape to more of the narrative overall. These narratives tend to avoid the pitfalls of LGBT+ themes in the otherwise popular grimdark, including the frequent use of killing off LGBT+ characters as a pretext for character drama and conflict. This wave may have begun with children's animation, but importantly, we can still see the structural model *Adventure Time* established for the depiction of queer relationships in newer animated productions aimed at older audiences. Chris Kanther characterizes *She-Ra and the Princesses of Power* as "rainbow fantasy." Although Kanther does not theorize his formulation, "rainbow fantasy" could aptly describe many of the works of this new wave of animation.

Consider, for instance, *Harley Quinn*, which was originally designed to be part of a new subscription television service, DC Universe, that was meant to compete with the likes of Disney+ and Netflix. This service did not last long, however, and most of the contents of that service were transferred to HBO Max where it persists now. In addition to being content that is primarily tailored for an on-demand online service, rather than a general cable channel, *Harley Quinn* is tailored for a very different demographic than *Adventure Time*, and has been shown on *SyFy* as well; it has R-rated language and graphic bloody animated violence, but is still part of the DC Comics Universe, making it adult oriented animation veering toward young-adults as a core audience.

Of course, Harley Quinn is fast becoming one of the DC Universe's most visible characters. Created for the 1992–1995 *Batman: The Animated Series* television production, Harley Quinn was first introduced as girlfriend of the Joker, Batman's most iconic antagonist and villain. Joker's sadistic and domineering relationship with Harley is one of the main focal points that different iterations of the character respond to in varying ways, a point that both the directors and fan community are aware of: Kate Roddy observes how the fan community is aware that "Harley Quinn, being a character entwined within an abusive relationship, is often the subject of discourse around the use of misogynistic tropes in comics: her relationship with the Joker is seen as something she must escape from, lest DC [Comics] be sending 'bad messages' to 'female comic book readers'—often described as 'young,' to boot."[11] She has gained much more visibility with Margot Robbie's portrayal of the character in David Ayer's *Suicide Squad* (2016), Cathy Yan's *Birds of Prey* (2020) and James Gunn's *The Suicide Squad* (2021). The visibility of the character combined with the oftentimes violent or abusive relationship she has with the Joker already made Harley Quinn a controversial character; as Kate Roddy argues in

"Masochist or Machiavel?" fan responses to Harley Quinn as a character can depend on attitudes toward sexual submissiveness and sexual masochism, concepts that often do not gel very easily with some strands of contemporary feminism which tend to focus on empowerment and liberation.

The animated series *Harley Quinn* focuses on Harley Quinn living with her friend Poison Ivy after having a falling out with the Joker. For most of the first season, their relationship is presented as homosocial and friendly. Nonetheless, Harley and Ivy's relationship changes in Season 2, Episode 7, when Harley and Ivy escape an underground jail and, celebrating their triumph, romantically kiss. After this, though, Ivy is not prepared to advance their relationship and she rejects Harley as a romantic partner, leading Harley to go on a spontaneous and successful attempt to rally an army and take over the city entirely. The most apocalyptic elements of the show go hand in hand with Harley's frustrated sexual desires. Harley consistently emphasizes that her desire to use a demonic army to take over the city is purely because she's spontaneous and not due to her kiss with Ivy; in actuality, however, it highlights the extent to which Harley is repressing her romantic feelings for Ivy: Her invasion of the city is a spillover of her closeted, repressed desire.

This formula, of rewriting large-scale conflict as a means of understanding the repression of queer identity, also ends up being the central conflict of the Netflix series *She-Ra and the Princesses of Power*. Like *Adventure Time*, *She-Ra and the Princesses of Power* is a family, kid-oriented show, although unlike *Adventure Time*, it is developed by Dreamworks and distributed by Netflix, which is not as beholden to commercial sponsors and as a result perhaps has slightly more autonomy in its depiction of relationships. It also is distinct from the 1980s television serial *She-Ra: Princess of Power* which was developed by Filmation in conjunction with Mattel to sell Mattel's line of toys. The 2018–2020 show did not feel particularly reluctant to depict queer relationships as the show progresses, with one supporting character, Bow, occasionally spending time with his two dads, and the fifth season in part revolving around a conflict between Netossa and her wife Spinerella. Nonetheless, these relationships, although a stark contrast from the wholescale reluctance for any confirmed queer relationships on Cartoon Network during the 2010s and a huge departure from filmic depictions through the early 2000s, are not as impactful to the show's larger narrative as is the relationship between Catra and Adora.

She-Ra and the Princesses of Power primarily revolves around the conflict between the Princess Alliance, led by Princess Glimmer and Adora, otherwise known as She-Ra, against the forces of Hordak and his top general, Catra. In the beginning of the show, it's established that Adora and Catra have an almost sisterly relationship, arguably competitors but tightly connected. This changes when Adora defects from Hordak's army and joins the Princess Alliance after coming into contact with a mysterious sword. In the final season of the show, an even more powerful version of Hordak, Horde Prime, invades the planet, creating circumstances wherein the entire planet might fall to his army once and for all. To stop Horde Prime, Adora opts to sacrifice herself for the greater good. Faced with her friend's imminent death to save the world, Catra chooses to reach out to Adora, and through the power of love they manage to survive. In celebration of this reversal of fortunes, Catra and Adora share a kiss.

Adventure Time defined the trope of ending a series on a romantic lesbian kiss; *The Legend of Korra* also ends on similar terms. What is distinctive about *She-Ra and the Princesses of Power* though is the way in which the lesbian relationship reframes the narrative trajectory of the series. Although Hordak and then later Horde Prime remain the arch-villains that serve as the pretext for the struggle, most of the show's confrontations take place between Catra and Adora. While the show always makes clear that much of Catra's motivation in hating the princess alliance is her sense of abandonment by Adora, it reframes that sense of abandonment away from a homosocial sense of sisterly love and repositions it as thwarted homoerotic love; in a sense most of the struggle of the show could have perhaps been avoided if Catra had simply been willing to be more upfront about her emotions with Adora, and if Adora was more self-aware on her sense of identity. Of course, much of the show is about Adora discovering her sense of identity overall, but nonetheless the overarching plot structure still hinges on conflict writ large revolving around the frustrations of closeted or refuted love.

Returning to Avila-Saavedra's discussion of the *qualitative* change in LGBT+ representation, recent productions are foregrounding the thematic and structural centrality of LGBT+ themes in animation, which may be more significant than mere increasing frequency, which is nonetheless also significant. The stylistic overtones of LGBT+ representation have also become more pronounced in these more recent shows. This is particularly the case in *She-Ra and the Princesses of Power* episode "The Battle of Brightmoon," when the heroes defeat the forces of Hordack through the use of a massive rainbow tidal wave. While the structural shift from broadcast cable to streaming platforms has certainly had a big impact on this explosion of LGBT+ themes in children's animation, it also cannot be denied that Bubbline, in breaking that barrier for broadcast animation, had a big impact on enabling shows like *She-Ra and the Princesses of Power* and *Steven Universe* to represent their themes without as forceful a backlash.

Bubbline has also had a successful post-series life, with an after-the-finale spinoff series of television specials named *Adventure Time: Distant Lands* featuring Bubbline in its second special, "Obsidian" (2020). In "Obsidian," the glass kingdom (a kingdom composed of glass people) is threatened by the dragon Molto Larvo, and they ask Marceline for aid, since she previously had defeated the dragon. In the course of journeying to the glass kingdom to help, Princess Bubblegum and Marceline relive and reflect on the conflict that caused them to break up previously, since it was during that earlier confrontation with Molto Larvo that their relationship had initially ended. Through flashbacks, the episode dwells on Marceline's survival in the immediate aftermath of the Mushroom War, the different approaches Marceline and Bubblegum take to solving problems, and Marceline's loss of her mother. In the "television special" format, hosted on HBO Max instead of being broadcast on Cartoon Network directly, and freed from the serialized constraints of the main run of the series, "Obsidian" offers a deeper view of the romantic relationship of Bubbline and the emotional complexities of Marceline as a survivor. "Obsidian" does an excellent job highlighting how, as the relationship between two women who care for each other but approach problems very differently, "Bubbline" continues to offer narrative conflict and compelling drama.

With "Obsidian," Cartoon Network has shown that in the online format of HBO Max, they are willing to more deeply explore the afterlife of Bubbline, even without the continued input of Rebecca Sugar (who had since moved on to *Steven Universe*); of course, this also risks showcasing the extent to which the Bubbline relationship could have been further developed during the televised broadcast of the series. Nevertheless, the willingness of Cartoon Network to now openly return to Bubbline and depict it directly further highlights how much has changed since the show originally aired and the transformative power Bubbline has had on LGBT+ representation in animation. In works ranging from *Steven Universe*, to *Harley Quinn*, to *She-Ra and the Princesses of Power*, we see the major plot elements becoming more directly tied to the personal sexuality of the characters. We are not just seeing narrative structures where there is greater LGBT+ representation, we are seeing post-apocalyptic narratives where the apocalypse itself mirrors the confrontation with individual sexuality and then the rebirth and hope of rekindled love in a reborn world.

Notes

1. ASIFA-Hollywood, "Best TV/Media—Children."
2. Paul Thomas, *Exploring the Land of Ooo*, 38.

3. Matthew Perpetua, "Marvel Comics Hosts First Gay Wedding."
4. Yomi Adegoke, "Move Over, Disney! Meet the Woman Leading the LGBT Cartoon Revolution."
5. Lee Edelman, *No Future*.
6. Natalie Kouri-Trowe, "Queer Apocalypse."
7. Guillermo Avila-Saavedra, "Nothing Queer about Queer Television: Televized Constructions of Gay Masculinities," 10–11
8. Avila-Saavedra, 5–6
9. Avila-Saavedra, 6.
10. Katie Hogan, "Queer Ecofeminist Apocalypse."
11. Kate Roddy, "Masochist or Machiavel?"

References

Adegoki, Yomi. "Move Over, Disney! Meet the Woman Leading the LGBT Cartoon Revolution." *The Guardian*, 2019. https://www.theguardian.com/tv-and-radio/2019/oct/01/move-over-disney-meet-rebecca-sugar-the-woman-leading-the-lgbt-cartoon-revolution-steven-universe-adventure-time.
ASIFA-Hollywood. "Best TV/Media—Children." 48th Annual Annie Awards. Accessed March 13, 2021. https://annieawards.org/rules-and-categories/production-categories/best-tv-media-children.
Avila-Saavedra, Guillermo. "Nothing Queer about Queer Television: Televized Constructions of Gay Masculinities." *Media Culture & Society* 31, no. 1 (2009): 5–21.
Branagh, Kenneth, dir. *Thor*. Hollywood: Paramount Pictures, 2011.
Brin, David. *The Postman*. New York: Bantam Books, 1985.
Cuarón, Alfonso, dir. *Children of Men*. Universal City: Universal Pictures, 2006.
"Dawn of the Dead: Comparison." Movie-censorship.com. Accessed March 13, 2021. https://www.movie-censorship.com/report.php?ID=1988.
DiMartino, Michael and Bryan Konietzko, creators. *The Legend of Korra*. Studio City, LA: Nickelodeon Animation Studio, 2012–2014.
Drozdowski, Michał, and Przemysław Marszał, dir. *This War of Mine*. 11 bit studios, 2014.
Edelman, Lee. *No Future: Queer Theory and the Death Drive*. Durham: Duke University Press, 2004.
Ellison, Harlan. "A Boy and his Dog." Open Road Media, 2016.
Foucault, Michel. *The Archaeology of Knowledge: And the Discourse on Language*. New York: Vintage, 1982.
Gunn, James, dir. *The Suicide Squad*. Burbank: DC Films, 2021.
Hogan, Katie. "Queer Ecofeminist Apocalypse: Tony Kushner's *Angels in America*." *International Perspectives in Feminist Ecocriticism*, edited by Simon Estok, Greta Gaard, and Serpil Oppermann, 235–253. London: Routledge, 2013.
Kanther, Chris. "The Rainbow Fantasy of She-Ra and the Princesses of Power." Medium.com, 2020. https://medium.com/@chriskanther/the-rainbow-fantasy-of-she-ra-and-the-princesses-of-power-3b23e9f4b4bf.
Kirkman, Robert, creator. *The Walking Dead*. New York: AMC Studios, 2010.
Kouri-Trowe, Natalie. "Queer Apocalypse." *Fuse Magazine* 36, no. 3 (2013): 4.
"The Lexa Pledge: Misunderstandings and a Fan Perspective." *LGBT Fans Deserve Better*, 2016. https://lgbtfansdeservebetter.com/lexa-pledge-misunderstandings-fan-perspective/.
London, Jack. "The Scarlet Plague." Project Gutenberg, 1912. https://www.gutenberg.org/files/21970/21970-h/21970-h.htm.
Martin, George R. R. *Game of Thrones*. New York City, NY: Bantam Spectra, 1996.
McCarthy, Cormac. *The Road*. New York City, NY: Alfred A. Knopf, 2006.
Miller, George, dir. *Mad Max*. Sydney, Australia: Kennedy Miller Productions, 1979.

———. *Mad Max: Fury Road*. Sydney, Australia: Roadshow Entertainment, 2015.
Perpetua, Matthew. "Marvel Comics Hosts First Gay Wedding in *Astonishing X-Men*." Rolling Stone, 2012. https://www.rollingstone.com/culture/culture-news/marvel-comics-hosts-first-gay-wedding-in-astonishing-x-men-235209/.
Raimi, Sam, dir. *Spider-Man 2*. Los Angeles: Columbia Pictures, 2004.
Roddy, Kate. "Masochist or Machiavel? Reading Harley Quinn in Canon and Fanon." *Transformative Works and Cultures* 8, special Issue 2 (2011). https://doi.org/10.3983/twc.2011.0259.
Rothenberg, Jason, creator. *The 100*. New York: Alloy Entertainment: The CW, 2014–2020.
Rudolovic, Petrana. "2020 was animation's biggest, gayest year so far." Polygon, 2020. https://www.polygon.com/animation-cartoons/2020/12/15/22174955/2020-animated-shows-lgbtq-representation.
Sanders, Chris, Dean DeBois, dir. *How to Train your Dragon*. Glendale, CA: DreamWorks Animation, 2010.
Sechrist, Radford, creator. *Kipo and the Age of Wonderbeasts*. Glendale, CA: DreamWorks Animation Television, 2020.
Snyder, Zack, dir. *Dawn of the Dead*. Los Angeles: Strike Entertainment, 2004.
Stanton, Andrew, dir. *Wall-E*. Burbank: Walt Disney Studios, 2008.
Stevenson, ND, creator. *She-Ra and the Princesses of Power*. Glendale, CA: DreamWorks Animation Television, 2018–2020.
Sugar, Rebecca, creator. *Steven Universe*. Burbank: Cartoon Network Studios, 2013–2019.
Thomas, Paul. *Exploring the Land of Ooo: An Unofficial Overview and Production History of Cartoon Network's* Adventure Time. Lawrence: University of Kansas Libraries, 2020.
Timm, Bruce, and Paul Dini, creators. *Harley Quinn*. Beverly Hills: Yes, Norman Productions, 2019-.
Timm, Bruce, Paul Dini, and Mitch Brian, creators. *Batman: The Animated Series*. Burbank: DC Entertainment, 1992–1995.
Wachowski, Lana, and Lilly Wachowski, dirs. *The Matrix*. Burbank: Warner Bros, 1999.
Yan, Cathy, dir. *Birds of Prey*. Burbank: Warner Bros. Pictures, 2020.

"Get your hero on, dude!"
Charting Jake's Growth as a Positive Masculine Role Model

BRIDGET M. BLODGETT *and* ANASTASIA SALTER

Hegemonic, often toxic, representations of masculinity are common not only in geek-targeted media properties,[1] but also in children's media, even those productions that star nonhuman characters.[2] Consider, for instance, Pendleton Ward's *Adventure Time*. One of the show's main characters, Jake the Dog, is an archetypal animal sidekick and anthropomorphized best friend who has a complex relationship with masculinity. In the show's early seasons, he voices a type of passive toxic masculinity. This is often positioned in contrast to the Men's Rights Activist villainy of the Ice King (villainy that is driven, at least in part, by the Ice King's adherence to the principles outlined in the book *Mind Games* by Jay T. Doggzone, which the show heavily implies was written by Jake under a pseudonym). Initially, Jake's affable toxicity coexisted uncomfortably with the gender-fluid, progressive, and queer fantasy elements the show has been noted for.[3] But after several mid-series events (namely, his experience with parenthood and his grappling with the evolving friendship he shares with his brother, Finn), Jake demonstrates a growing self-awareness and reflexivity in the face of mutable models of gender and identity. By examining key moments of Jake's character evolution, this essay reveals Jake's significance as a role model for positive masculine representation in a media landscape of underdeveloped, persistently hegemonic, children's heroes.

Cartoon Characters as Moral Markers

In the world of children's cartoons, the lines between villains and heroes were traditionally drawn clearly and broadly. Cartoons of the 1970s,

72   "One isn't purely defined by their sex or gender"

'80s, and '90s did not leave many areas for a gray or ambiguous morality to find a home. Skeletor, Magneto, Shredder, Aku, and the Joker were all clearly coded to viewers as evil. Cartoons were designed to both entertain children and sell toys—a task made easier when kids have a clear understanding of who the "good" and "bad" guys are. Cartoons were in essence the morality plays of the era. Unfortunately, these cartoons often treated children as simplistic thinkers who required clear moral guidance as to the correct actions. Children viewers, it was believed, were unable to distinguish between villain and hero if there was any degree of moral ambiguity at play. This consequently led to reductive characters whose growth reset after each episode.

In the mid–2000s there was a shift away from the "traditional approach" to cartoon character development, to one that encouraged a more nuanced understanding of character development and moral complexity. On Cartoon Network, this shift ultimately culminated in *Adventure Time*, which drew on patterns from comic books and similar changes to the television sitcom that enable more meaningful character growth and learning. Although the earliest episodes reflect the traditional approach of having clear "good guys" (i.e., Finn and Jake the Dog) and "bad guys" (i.e., Ice King and Marceline the Vampire Queen), by the end of the first season, these distinctions already begin to break down: The episode "Henchman," for instance, shows that Marceline enjoys putting on a show of evil more so than actually *being* evil, and in the episode "What Have You Done?," Finn and Jake consider the larger moral implications of their actions after they imprison the Ice King despite his having done nothing wrong. From here, the show begins to further break down the clear-cut nature of heroes and villains.

Throughout the entire show there is only one clear-cut villain: The Lich, a character whom IGN's Matt Fowler has described as "basically, a real, grotesque villain inserted into the *merely semi-dark* world of *Adventure Time*. No quirks. No hangups. The Lich just wants to destroy all life."[4] By comparing the Lich (a character who clearly embodies what one could call "genuine evil") against its other, more morally ambiguous antagonists, *Adventure Time* highlights the relative rarity of true evil within the world. Pendleton Ward described the intentional decision to explore a range of character representations rather than fall into familiar cartoon tropes in an interview: "It's candyland on the surface and dark underneath, and that's why it's compelling, I think, if at all. Those are my favorite kind of emotions—the ones that conflict with each other, and they feel weird inside of you."[5]

Ward's desire to make the audience feel conflicting emotions—for instance, rooting against the Ice King's schemes while still liking and understanding his background—resulted in a more nuanced approach to how the show's characters are understood by the audience, and it invited complex connection-making and self-recognition on the part of the viewer. This also resulted in the show having a cross-age demographic appeal. While the main adventures of Finn and Jake (which, when taken together, constituted a *Bildungsroman* coming-of-age narrative) drew in younger viewers, the show's dystopian world and its interest in the complexity of morality resonated deeply with an adult audience, as well. The developmental arcs of Princess Bubblegum, Marceline, Ice King, and Jake, in particular, resonated with young adult viewers who had to deal with the more grown-up struggles of becoming parents, dealing with stressful family members, or helping loved ones who struggle with degenerative mental illnesses.

Part of *Adventure Time*'s appeal also lay in its demonstration that, just as there are rarely clear-cut heroes and villains, people rarely fall into traditional gendered roles. Journalists have noted that *Adventure Time*'s creative team imbued the show "with a progressive ethos that few shows— children- or adult-oriented, animated or live-action—have matched."[6] A shift towards a "progressive ethos" is often associated with more agency on the part of represented women: however, studies of such representation have noted that while "programming sends the message that girls should aspire to stereotypically masculine behaviors in roles ... the reverse does not hold true."[7] *Adventure Time* importantly offers characters room to explore gendered roles, and demonstrate character growth through connections with characters and mentors across the gender spectrum, offering room both for queer representation and non-normative parental relationships. As a modern morality play, the show offers its audience a cartoonish version of the real struggles they may encounter. In doing so, the show emphasizes that overcoming these struggles requires growth, which can be an uncomfortable process marked by moments of both progress and backsliding. And of the show's many characters, the one who perhaps best illustrates this growth—in particular, a growth toward a more positive form of masculinity—is Jake the Dog, Finn's brother, side-kick, and comedic foil.

Jake the Delinquent

Jake's origins are not in positive masculinity: importantly, the character transcends origins in regressive, and even toxic, masculinity to become a mentor to others. Several episodes and b-plots revolve around Jake's troubled past of petty crime and thievery, offering an opportunity for contrast and the demonstration of his personal growth. Three big themes are considered during these episodes: traditional presentations of masculinity, history following the character, and form following function. Jake acts out the role of a petty criminal gang leader in these arcs, pulling off or otherwise reminiscing about the crimes he committed in his youth. These mentions illustrate a way of living that Jake has long since moved away from. Generally, he only references these periods when forced to by other outside forces or when placed in a setting that naturally evokes a reminiscence.

As seen in the fifth-season episode "One Last Job," when Jake engages in criminal activity, he changes both his attitude and appearance. While normal Jake is laid back—the prototypical slacker mixed with party animal—Jake the thief is a man in charge. He is firm, aggressive, distrustful, and cunning; he covers all eventualities with his planning and execution. Physically, he also develops a more stated brow bone, which shadows his eyes, making him appear suspect. Jake's Neanderthal-like brow also visually conveys the rough, aggressive masculinity of his thief persona. Jake's physical form and altered personality reflect the more traditional rough-and-tumble hypermasculinity often featured in heist and noir films. Men in these works are expected to be logical, cunning, and aggressive. They should take chances, alter plans on the fly, lead those around them, and reject any authority. They should, in other words, embrace the ideals of toxic, hegemonic masculinity.

When this version of Jake is shown or mentioned, it is done so with the emotional overtone of regret. In the third season episode "Apple Thief," for instance, Jake admits that he only stole because he did not know his actions were wrong:

> JAKE: Oh, the candy tavern, man. I used to hang out there back when I used to snatch old ladies' purses.
> [Finn looks shocked]
> JAKE: Don't worry. I stopped doing that a long time ago. I didn't know it was wrong.[8]

In later episodes, Jake makes it clear that he does not wish to return to his life as a thief and that he has since moved on. But in the episode "One Last Job," after someone threatens his daughter, Jake is forced to return to his life of crime. When Tiffany, one of Jake's old gang members, questions his ability as a thief, given the "soft" life he is currently living, Jake responds by pounding the table and snapping back: " I'm the same Jake, I just stopped stealing mostly! ... When you get older you're supposed to get into other stuff, like graphic design, or pottery. It's called 'growing up'!"[9] Notably, the "other stuff" Jake references includes behaviors frequently gendered as feminine, which suggests that, for Jake, "growing up" is associated with a broad range of personal expressions not restricted by hegemonic masculinity. While the episode demonstrates Jake's challenges and his regression, his awareness of that "growth" reaffirms his commitment to moving forward.

For Jake, the performance of toxic masculinity is tied to the physical presentation of his body. To change between them—that is, to shapeshift from "normal Jake" to "criminal Jake"—is to become a different person from how he presents himself in the day-to-day of the show. His different personalities and attitudes are literally embodied in his physical representation, best showing off his current mentality. It is only at the end of the episode, when Jake dons a different masculine role—that of the caregiving father—that Jake relinquishes the rough-and-tumble noir version of masculinity featured throughout much of the episode. In this way, the episode proves a point made by Emma Jane, who, in an examination of the show's nontraditional representational choices, argued that "the textured nature of Jake's character cannot easily be mapped onto the masculine stereotypes usually found in children's media entertainment."[10]

Jake the Brother

Throughout the show, Jake acts as the big brother to Finn, both literally and figuratively. Implied to be in his late twenties or thirties to Finn's early teens, Jake has a wider array of experiences he likes to draw upon, and by offering advice to Finn, he often plays a role that would have originally been filled by Finn and Jake's deceased parents. However, because many of Finn's questions center on the nature of puberty and romantic relationships, Jake's advice tends to straddle the line between the wink-and-nudge of an older brother and the firm denial-oriented approach of a parent. In a memorable exchange from the fourth-season episode "Burning Low," Jake tries to give Finn the "talk" but struggles with what and how much information he should provide, given his brother's age and species. An example of Jake's wording is as follows:

> Let me explain some junk about dating. Right now, you're at Tier 1, which is hugging, but pretty soon, you'll be at Tier 2, which is smooching. [After that], you'll make it to Tier 5, where she'll let you discover all fifteen feet of her long, beautiful stomach. Then ... you'll make it to Tier 8, where you touch her horn for the very first time. Very special.[11]

The surrogate parent figure (and the displacement of adults as central to the parenting role) is typical in this type of animation: the early death of parents in Disney films, for instance, has attracted commentary and has even obtained trope status. Finn's isolation is taken as a given in the narrative, without major contextual development in the early framing of the show, but so too is his reliance on Jake as a mentor and support. Despite taking care of his physical needs just fine on his own, Finn still needs the guidance that an older, non-romantic adult can provide.

But at times, Jake himself clearly struggles to fulfill this role. When Jake discusses the 15 tiers, for instance, his tone initially suggests amorous hidden secrets that he wants to urge his brother to enjoy, but he rapidly alters to a forceful and parental yell when Finn asks about tier 15. While Jake wants his brother to enjoy his physical romantic journey, when it comes to a discussion of sex, he switches to the stance taken by many parents when they first address the topic with their children: "You're not ready. Don't do it." Of course, it is obvious from this exchange that Jake actually does know about these experiences but is struggling to guide Finn in a way that is appropriate to his age, development, and the unusual relationship they share.

Jake also struggles with how to present a form of strong masculinity to Finn that differs from that embraced by Joshua, Finn and Jake's deceased canine father. Joshua is emphatically a "man's man" kind of dog, embodying in many ways the ideal masculinity of 1940s pop culture: Joshua loves his woman, hits hard, and takes no guff. When the audience is finally introduced to Jake's father, it is easy to see how Jake initially became a delinquent youth. In the season-three episode "Dad's Dungeon," in which a recording of Joshua guides Jake and Finn through an adventure, Jake is repeatedly told by Joshua's recording to let Finn take on risks, and Jake is even encouraged to insult his brother; this is done because Joshua fears that Finn is too soft:

> JOSHUA: [*On tape*] All right. Hey, Jake, I wanna remind you what this dungeon's for. [*Holds up baby Finn who is crying*] In order for Finn to stop whining, he needs to be put through a trial that forces him to take charge of a situation.
> JAKE: But Dad, Finn's already figured that out. He's a good kid with a kind heart.[12]

Near the end of the episode, Jake finally reveals the goal of the recording to Finn, and in doing so stands up to his dad—and thus his brand of masculinity. Jake then helps build back Finn's broken confidence by remixing Joshua's recording, turning them into an inspiring message about how Finn is both loved and makes his adopted father proud. While it is easy to say that Jake is just repeating Joshua's words, it is clear that the sample dialogue Jake uses in his remix indexes his own pride and love of Finn.

The overall message that Jake always tries to support, advise, and cheer on Finn as he goes through the emotional rollercoaster of human teen years is repeated throughout the series. In this way, Jake takes on multiple roles in his relationship to Finn, functioning as a brother, best friend, confidant, parent, advisor, and sidekick. He even functions as an emotional counselor, ensuring that Finn grows up with a strong understanding of how to treat other people correctly. Finn and Jake's complicated relationship illustrates the different ways that people often relate to one another, and parents to their children specifically, during a person's life. Jake tries his best to relate to his brother as Finn grows older. In doing so, he both models that there is not one right way to interact with others while also breaking dramatically from how Joshua treated his own sons, both natural and adopted.

Jake the Dad

When it comes to his own kids, Jake is cast as both a caring father and a deadbeat dad: his own struggles to handle his regressive tendencies and learn parenting are sincere, if unusual. In the fifth-season episode "Jake the Dad," Jake attempts to learn how to be a father and care for his new pups while Lady Rainicorn recovers from their birth. In doing this, he follows a book written by Margaret, his mother, that mixes both sensible and terrible advice, mirroring many baby raising guidebooks in our world. This episode makes it clear that many of the commonsense behaviors of a parent are missing in Jake's case, as he literally sleep deprives himself to the point of endangering his children by leaving them vulnerable in the woods while a hungry fox is around. His naivety is played for humor, but ultimately serves as a reminder to the viewers that nurturing behaviors need not be inherent to be sincere. His emphasis on learning from experts, including his partner and children, is in tension with the narrative's frequent need for his absence, due to their own sensibilities and the rapid aging of rainicorns.

After the initial demonstrations of parental interest, Jake is very disconnected from his children's lives, an issue raised several times in the series. In the sixth season episode "Ocarina," Jake's children have an open discussion about their father's flaws—one that may very well be heard in some real households:

> JAKE JR.: Seriously, Mom, Dad's already three hours late with the food!
> VIOLA: You hush, Junior. You know Dad's a wonderful cook.
> JAKE JR.: Viola, when's the last time you even heard from Dad?....
> T.V.: Yeah, I love Dad and everything, but he's only ever met me twice.[13]

We see this further disconnect between Jake and his children in the fifth season episode "Another Five More Short Graybles," wherein Jake tries to bond with his daughter through a game of make believe—something wildly inappropriate for her age of "basically thirty."[14]

In "Ocarina," Jake's son Kim Kil Whan, a dry humorless businessman, attempts to parent Jake by buying the deed to the treehouse and forcing Jake and Finn to get real jobs, a move he eventually regrets after realizing that while his father does love him, Jake simply is not capable of living up to Kim Kil Whan's expectations. Upon reflection with his wife, Kim Kil Whan admits: "I think I was wrong about Dad. I think he's good."[15] This reflection shows that Kim Kil Whan finally understands that there are many ways to be an adult and that even though Jake "lives the life of a child," this does not mean that Jake dislikes his son. This episode is thus a firm illustration of two concepts: First, that even within the world of *Adventure Time*, Jake does not match traditional societal expectations of fatherhood and masculinity. Second, that in spite of Jake's inexperience, and naivete, his failings are not necessarily enough to categorize him as a "bad dad."

Near the end of season ten, "Jake the Starchild" introduces Jake's alien "bio-dad," Warren Ampersand. In a plot echoing the storyline of *Guardians of the Galaxy 2*, Warren lures Jake into a trap so that he can steal his son's eternal youth. The episode plays with models of fatherhood, ultimately vindicating Jake's commitment to his own offspring. This episode ties together many of Jake's paternal personas, resulting in a consistent one that proves he is a good father in his own way. In the episode's climactic scene, Jake manages to outsmart Warren Ampersand, using "old-fashioned grifting" taught to him by his adoptive father, Joshua; he then declares that he is "the proud pop of a whole bunch of pups!"[16] This scene (and the episode in general) is important because it provides context for Jake's inexperience: his struggle to transcend a lack of his own parental modeling has much to do with his own dysfunctional upbringing. But unlike his own bio-dad, Jake recognizes the needs of his girlfriend and children, with their unusual backgrounds and aging processes, and he places them before his own needs. Jake and his family find the best balance when his children accept his differences and allow familial feelings to develop outside of the normative expectations of fatherhood. In acting out this form of acceptance Jake and his family strengthen their own connections, while still respecting the individual needs and personhood of those involved.

Jake the Lover

Despite occurring entirely off camera, Jake's romantic relationships play an important role in his development. Jake is only shown in one romantic relationship throughout the series, that with Lady Rainicorn, and while a reading of their relationship could cast them as being an exemplar of the heterosexual pairings often seen in comedy sitcoms, Jake's otherness to his own family prevents this reading from being the dominant framing. Queer readings of Jake's relationship with Lady Rainicorn are a part of *Adventure Time* fandom, as one essay centers: "Jake thinks he's a dog, though he cannot explain his stretchy powers. He later learns that he's part shapeshifting alien, part dog. When Jake prepares to meet Lady Rainicorn's family [in the second season episode "Her Parents"] he's very nervous about how they will feel about a dog and a Rainicorn being together. Their relationship, then, becomes a cipher for how societal norms impact relationships—in this case, a cross-species one."[17] Jake and Lady are a cross-species, unmarried, non-cohabitating couple with multispecies children, whom they are raising with methods that differ from the literal textbook example. The queerness of their relationship is not merely recognizable by this external gaze, but also in their own navigation of romance: the characters live outside a heteronormative convention.

"Her Parents" also breaks down the understanding that even romance advisors know all the rules, as Jake struggles to impress and connect with Lady's parents. Attempts by Jake to perform a normative romance fail, as he foretells at the episode's start following an ill-advised attempt to impersonate the other species: " You know, I thought painting ourselves rainbow-color using condiments and stuff from the fridge so we could pretend to be rainicorns was a good idea when you pitched it to me five minutes ago, but now I'm not so sure, man."

Jake often acts as a source for sage romantic advice to many other characters on the show beyond just Finn, using the lessons and growth from his less conventional relationship to turn a sharp gaze on heteronormative stereotypes. Most notably, he provides feedback to both the Ice King and Prismo through the series' run. When Jake first encounters Prismo, the powerful god-like entity is living alone in a cube in space. Prismo's introduction reads like the set up to many a Hallmark movie wherein the powerful successful businesswoman is too busy with her fulfilling and exciting life to make a relationship work. Like a good wingman, Jake counsel's Prismo on his relationship woes. While Prismo contends that he does not enjoy the work required for a relationship to succeed, his reactions to compliments given by Jake hint that there may be other reasons for his romantic failures. The last line of the episode ends with Jake reflecting: "I gotta get that guy a girlfriend."[18]

While there can be parallels drawn between Jake's love advice to Prismo and his advice to Finn, the role he is filling at the time significantly impacts both that advice's presentation and content. With Finn he struggles to balance the brotherly need to share experiences with the parental desire to protect and safely guide a child. With Prismo, he clearly is upfront and straightforward like one would be with another adult friend. He provides the advice to Prismo but doesn't feel responsible for the choices that the other makes and is willing to be dismissive when he feels his friend has made a misstep; this is something we do not see in his interactions with Finn. His advice to Prismo is like the blunt feedback given at brunch by best friends in a romcom, not the sensitive support of a brother or parent.

This tonal difference is also apparent in romantic advice that he is willing to provide to a general audience. During his "delinquent" past, it is implied that Jake wrote the "dating" book *Mind Games*, attributed to "Jay T. Doggzone." This book, which contains advice similar to that provided by pick up artists in our world, is referenced several times throughout the series by different characters: Ice King, for instance, repeats Doggzone's advice about swinging at every ball[19] and the book's claim that "chicks dig guys with tortured pasts."[20] Broco, a candy citizen, finds the book in his grandfather's tomb and, after reading it, attempts to woo Princess Bubblegum by "peacocking," or wearing ostentatious clothing for attention.[21] Even Finn reads the book, after which he decides to "future farm" possible suitors in case his current relationship with Flame Princess ends.[22] After finding out that Finn has been reading the book Jake tells him:

> JAKE: Oh my gosh! Where is this coming from?!
> FINN: It's called "future farming." I read it in that book you have by Jay T. Doggzone.
> JAKE: Jay T. Dogg—awww, dude! Don't read that book! It's gonna mess up your brain. I keep that book around for laughs. It's all really bad advice.[23]

While Jake obviously believes that some of this advice is not harmful and may even be good, his response suggests that either he no longer stands by what he wrote in the book or that he was deliberately writing a book of bad advice.

Jake's occasional hegemonic masculinity is always disrupted by the presence of the Ice King as the ultimate toxic other: episodes centering on the Ice King will frequently feature MRA tropes (such as the violation of consent and the vilification of women not sexually available to him). Jake's "bro-ness" is always minimized through such a comparison, and Jake's willingness to confront the Ice King on his internalized, ever-present misogyny is a crucial part of his character, setting him on a path in which growth is plausible. As much as Jake is the foil to Finn's naivety, energy, and bravery, the Ice King is a foil to Jake's actual romantic actions and advice. Throughout the series as he interacts with Ice King and other adult male characters, Jake reflects on his own choices for romance and decisions in the past and learns to think about relationships with more nuance and respect. If the Jay T. Doggzone book represents his past views, his advice to Prismo and his non-traditional relationship with Lady Rainicorn show how far his understanding of romance has come.

Jake the Icon

By demonstrating a sentimental, mature yet playful, and continually growing mode of masculinity, Jake offers an enduring model of alternative masculinity for viewers that gently rebukes attempts at binary deconstruction. In a review of the finale, *Entertainment Weekly* author Darren Franich notes that, because of this, it is "more sensible to compare *Adventure Time* to ... [HBO's *The*] *Sopranos*."[24] By placing Jake in conversation with a more complex, adult-oriented look at masculinity, Franich draws attention to how unusually multifaceted Jake's characterization is: in a cast of complex, queer, and nuanced characters, Jake is at first easy to dismiss as a humorous sidekick, but ultimately offers a much-needed critique on the limited models of masculinity typically seen in children's media. Jake's personal character arc across the ten seasons of *Adventure Time* sees him grow as a brother, adventurer, citizen, husband, father, and friend, and while it is not as obvious as Finn's coming of age story, his arc shows that growth and development do not actually stop once you reach adulthood; in fact, Jake's arc emphasizes that healthy development should continue throughout one's life.

Jake's relationships develop alongside him, and with the effort to improve himself and others, he manages to help save both his brother and the world. In the series finale, for instance, Jake is the only character not to fight his doppelganger in a dream world; he instead works to find the key that will help all the others come to understand and accept one another. Jake's insistence on finding a solution helps to bring peace to both his friends and to the kingdom as a whole. In this way, it is a clear indication of his character's growth and his rejection of toxic behaviors that he himself once partook in.

A significant focus of cultural masculinity is on a man's legacy in the world, his ability to ensure that he has both a continuing genetic line and that others outside of his family remember his name and achievements for generations. This focus often leads men in many series to act in their own interests to build fame or acclaim, much like the fabled king Ozymandias. But as the finale of *Adventure Time* makes clear, Jake the Dog leaves a legacy that extends far beyond his own genetic line and instead shows that the values he espouses and the joy he finds in his world continue far into the future. When it comes to masculinity, Jake summarized his own development perfectly, "Dude, sucking at somethin' is the first step towards being sorta good at something."[25]

Notes

1. Anastasia Salter and Bridget Blodgett, *Toxic Geek Masculinity in Media*.
2. Jessica Birthisel, "Body, Heterosexuality and Patriarchal Entanglements."
3. Emma Jane, "Gunter's a Woman?!"
4. Matt Fowler, "*Adventure Time: The Complete Second Season* Blu-ray Review."
5. Yohana Desta, "Adventure Time to End in 2018."
6. Juliet Kleber, "The Progressive, Grown-Up Appeal of *Adventure Time*."
7. Beth Hentges and Kim Case, "Gender Representations."
8. "Apple Thief" (season 3, episode 11).
9. "One Last Job" (season 5, episode 23).
10. Jane, "Gunter's a Woman?!," 238.
11. "Burning Low" (season 4, episode 16).
12. "Dad's Dungeon" (season 3, episode 25).
13. "Ocarina" (season 6, episode 12).
14. "Another Five More Short Graybles" (season 5, episode 24).
15. "Ocarina" (season 6, episode 12).
16. "Jake the Starchild" (season 10, episode 11).
17. S.E. Fleenor, "The Awesome [and Unexpected] Queering of *Adventure Time*."
18. "Jake the Dog" (season 5, episode 2).
19. "Reign of Gunters."
20. "I Remember You" (season 4, episode 25).
21. "The Suitor" (season 5, episode 21).
22. "Reign of Gunters" (season 4 episode 24).
23. "Reign of Gunters" (season 4, episode 24).
24. Darren Franich, "*Adventure Time* Finale Review."
25. "His Hero" (season 1, episode 25).

References

Birthisel, Jessica. "How Body, Heterosexuality and Patriarchal Entanglements Mark Non-Human Characters as Male in CGI-Animated Children's Films." *Journal of Children and Media*, 8, no. 4 (2014): 336–352.

Desta, Yohana. "*Adventure Time* to End in 2018, but Its Legacy Will Live On." *Vanity Fair*, 2016. https://www.vanityfair.com/hollywood/2016/09/adventure-time-2018.

Fleenor, S. E. "The Awesome [and Unexpected] Queering of *Adventure Time*." SyFy Wire, 2019. https://www.syfy.com/syfywire/the-awesome-and-unexpected-queering-of-adventure-time.

Fowler, Matt. "*Adventure Time*: The Complete Second Season Blu-ray Review." IGN, 2013. https://www.ign.com/articles/2013/06/27/adventure-time-the-complete-second-season-blu-ray-review.

Franich. Darren. "*Adventure Time* Finale Review: One of the Greatest TV Shows Ever had a Soulful, Mind-Expanding Conclusion." *Entertainment Weekly*, 2018. https://ew.com/tv/2018/09/04/adventure-time-finale-review/.

Hentges, Beth, and Case, Kim. "Gender Representations on Disney Channel, Cartoon Network, and Nickelodeon Broadcasts in the United States." *Journal of Children and Media* 7, no. 3 (2013): 319–333.

Jane, Emma. "'Gunter's a Woman?!'—Doing and Undoing Gender in Cartoon Network's *Adventure Time.*" *Journal of Children and Media* 9, no. 2 (2015): 231–247.
Kleber, Juliet. "The Progressive, Grown-Up Appeal of *Adventure Time.*" The New Republic, 2017. https://newrepublic.com/article/140225/progressive-grown-up-appeal-adventure-time.
Salter, Anastasia, and Bridget Blodgett. *Toxic Geek Masculinity in Media: Sexism, Trolling, and Identity Policing.* Cham, Switzerland: Palgrave Macmillan, 2017.

Yellow Voices and Rainbow Bodies

Accent, Multilingualism, and the Politics of Representation in Adventure Time

CAMILLE CHANE

A large part of the existing critical work focusing on BMO (Finn and Jake's adorable robotic agender roommate), does so by exploring questions of gender identity and gender expression. This essay, however, sets out to offer new lines of inquiry regarding BMO's perceived ethnic and racial identity, i.e., BMO's presumed Asianness. BMO's voice is provided by animator and voice actress Niki Yang, whose phonology as a first-language Korean speaker (what we would colloquially call "a Korean accent") can be heard in-character. Due to the American cartoon's history of using Pidgin and accents as indicators of race, this results in the incidental coding of BMO as ethnically East Asian.

When playing BMO, Yang performs in English, her second language. She is also heard in the show voicing a second character, Lady Rainicorn, speaking her first language, Korean. In itself, the very presence of Lady Rainicorn, a multilingual character, and the fact that the quasi-entirety of her lines are in a different language than that spoken by the main cast is worth analyzing if we are to discuss representation in *Adventure Time* and racial othering (its continuation and its subversion) in contemporary television cartoons. These two considerations will lead us to broaden the discussion and consider the way world-building and characterization in *Adventure Time* relies on language and accent diversity

BMO Versus Ethnic Stereotyping: Cartoons and Language Discrimination

In 2013, a GameFAQs forum user started a thread entitled "Am I the only one that hates BMO's voice acting on Adventure Time?," in which forum users discussed the voice of BMO, provided by Korean-born storyboard artist Niki Yang.[1]

> ORIGINAL POSTER (OP): I understand that they're trying to make the character sound robotic, but at least use someone that speaks English. So many mispronounced words. —cringe—
> PERSON 2: His voice actress is Asian dude, get over it, in fact she also does Lady Rainicorn.
> PERSON 3: Yeah, his voice actress is South Korean.
> OP: I know she also does Lady Rainicorn, but it's just obnoxious how thick the accent is. It adds nothing.
> PERSON 2: Well BMO is a computer and most computers are made in Asia so ergo he has an Asian accent
> PERSON 4: I don't like it either.
> PERSON 5: I thought I was the only one that thought BMO's VA was pretty bad. Maybe that's the joke though since most video game systems are made in Japan. So that's probably why the voice actress is using a heavy asian accent.
> PERSON 6: I love BMO's Asian accent. It's a reference to how most video game systems are made in Japan.
> I mean, a lot of Asian people sound like that anyway. I should know, since I have Asian family members.
> But then again, I'm mostly black, so when I hear characters who sound really, really stereotypically black, I can get offended.[2]

From a media critical standpoint, there is much to unpack here. The original poster argues that giving a foreign accent to a cartoon character should "add" something to the show, and asserts that either Yang "mispronounces words" when reading BMO's line or that BMO is written to speak broken English (grammatically incorrect English with a markedly foreign accent). If we look at the responses, we may be intrigued by the fact that BMO's accent is unanimously perceived as "Asian" despite there being nothing in the show's text to indicate this. The very concept of a perceived "Asian accent" is interesting and questionable, as Asia is made up of a number of diverse cultures, which are not limited to East Asia (China, Japan and Korea). We can also pause at the fact that a poster mentions Japan in their tentative guess as to why Yang was cast as BMO, despite Yang being Korean. Lastly, and closer to our considerations, is the immediate connection made between accent, ethnicity ("Asian accent") and race ("characters who sound [...] stereotypically black"); What should one make of the very idea that an accent can cause offense, and the question of whether or not this feeling of offense is justified? All these points could stand to be picked apart and unraveled into conversations about accented voices in visual media, and race representation in American animation.

This essay is by no means a response to this decade-old forum thread, and it is very likely that the reactions in this thread are not representative of the general reception of BMO by the show's viewer base and Niki Yang's work as a voice actress. However, the discussion above provides a starting point for our inquiry into the role of language and accent variety in *Adventure Time*'s politics of representation.

This essay is about two distinct topics—accents and multilingualism—and how they relate to the show's representation of characters coded as ethnic and racial minorities.[3] We should clarify that, while multilingualism is relatively simple to identify and define in the context of an animated show (the use of multiple languages by a character), the concept of "accent" in sociolinguistics is a somewhat nebulous concept. In most contexts, when we say 'accent,' we usually mean the phonological features associated with dialect variation. To give a couple of straightforward examples: Tree Trunks the tiny elephant was voiced by Polly Lou Livingston, who had what we can easily identify as a Southern accent if we are familiar enough with American dialects to recognize the monophthongization of sounds such as /aɪ/ ("*Ah*" instead of "*I*"), elongated and diphthongized front vowels ("*weh-uh-dding*" instead of "*weh-dding*"), non-rhoticity, and a slow tempo (a "drawl") as typically Southern. Even though her speech lacks typical grammatical features from Southern American English, Tree Trunks' native dialect is implied to be Southern American English rather than General American English. Extradiegetically, the explanation for this is that her voice actress, Texas-born Polly Lou Livingston, used her natural speaking voice and accent for her character.

Then we have Lumpy Space Princess, whose speech is characterized by what we would commonly call a Valley Girl accent. Unlike Livingston as Tree Trunks, Pendleton Ward affects a mock accent when he plays LSP. The most characteristic feature of Valleyspeak is the use of "*like*" as a filler word, and possibly the frequent use of the phrase "Oh my God" (which is even more comical in *Adventure Time*, in which every instance of "God" is replaced by "Glob" whether as a discourse marker or as a theological concept). In terms of prosody and intonation, Valleyspeak is characterized by uptalk (the use of a rising intonation in a declarative statement), but what is more likely to strike the viewer with regard to LSP is the deep guttural voice Ward affects for this role. The so-called Valley Girl accent, or Valleyspeak, is a social dialect associated with white Anglo-American suburban youths, as depicted in comedy movies such as *Clueless* (1995) or *Mean Girls* (2004). Through intertextual association, the viewer associates LSP's speech with Valley Girl archetypes in popular culture.

Tree Trunks and LSP are written as speakers of a regional or social dialect, from which they exhibit phonological quirks, while mostly sharing the same grammatical features as the rest of the cast.

Before we continue, we should point out that even though most American viewers will probably hear LSP, Tree Trunks and BMO and think "*I hear an accent*" (whereas hearing Finn and Jake will likely make them go "*I hear a teenage boy and John DiMaggio*") the truth is, everyone has an accent. It's simply that we tend to think of General American English as an unaccented, standard, normal way of speaking, especially in movies and national television.[4]

BMO's case is slightly different from that of LSP and Tree Trunks for a number of reasons. We can see from the forum thread cited earlier that BMO's perceived accent is not viewed as an indicator of regional or social origin, but rather of nationality, ethnicity, and race. The surface-level explanation given in this online discussion is quite straightforward: BMO is voiced by a Korean animator and voice actress, Niki Yang. Yang's mother tongue is Korean, and the phonology of her first language carries over to her second language, causing her to "mispronounce" words, to quote the author of the original post.

In her study of Indian American representation on the American screen, Shilpa Davé posits the existence of what she calls "racial accents," since Asian American, Indian American, and South Asian characters in media are made racially identifiable not only by visual factors, but also by the vocal performance of accents.[5] In order to specifically tackle the question of Indian and South Asian representation in television and film, Davé goes on to define "brown voice" as "the act of speaking in accented English associated with Indian nationals and immigrants" which is ultimately instrumental in racializing South Asians. Similarly, considering the fact that BMO and Lady Rainicorn are readily read as "Asian" by fans (as in a racial rather than ethnic or national descriptor), using the term "yellow voice" would be appropriate here to describe the perceived nature of their speech.

All in all, this could be no different from Tree Trunks' regional accent coding her as a sweet Southern old lady, but as noted by the last answer quoted in the forum thread cited above, accents may index racial identity and even cause offense when represented a certain way in media.

How does BMO's voice code him as Asian? How can it impact, positively or negatively, the perception of his character? What about Lady Rainicorn's bilingualism? Such questions can be partly answered by taking a closer look at Niki Yang's delivery of BMO's lines, but only looking at that will not be enough to fully comprehend the question of accents and representation in *Adventure Time*. What we are truly interested in here is language ideology, which is to say: what accents, dialects and languages index in the mind of audiences. This can be understood only if we take into account the history of East Asian representation in American animation, and how language factors into both negative and positive stereotyping.

Yellow Voice and Racial Accents in Historical Perspective

Historically, film and television tended to favor Euro-American (white) performers in yellowface[6] over ethnically East Asian actors and actresses when it came to portraying East Asian and Asian American characters in visual media. In animation as well, casting ethnically East Asian and East Asian American performers as the voice of Asian or Asian-coded characters is a relatively new practice when put in perspective with the history of American cartoons. Much as was the case in live-action cinema, talking East Asian characters in studio-era cartoon would either speak in gibberish meant to approximate a foreign oriental language, or, at other times, they would speak in accented, broken English.

In 1975, the persistence of this linguistic stereotype led the pioneering Asian American studies scholar Elaine H. Kim to publish an essay titled "Yellow English."[7] Kim's text questions the role of language in the discrimination against Asians in the United States. She comments on the fact that even American-born, native English speakers of Asian descent are disproportionately likely to perform poorly in English classes. Kim theorizes that the cause for this is not the students' bilingualism and interference between English and the students' heritage language, but rather, the fact that Asian Americans were constantly made self-conscious about their way of speaking due to the stereotypes that saturate Asian images in American popular culture, which caused them to retreat into silence or stereotypical behavior. Thus, the social reality of the "Asian American college English 'problem,'" as she writes, has less to do with Asian American students' intrinsic command of the English language, and more with the way Asian Americans are reflected in the mirror of American culture.

The term "Yellow English" was coined by Kim to refer to stereotypical images that congealed in popular culture. It was then adapted and reworked by sociolinguists and media scholars alike.[8] The concept of Yellow English does not find any purchase in sociolinguistics and fails to describe any sort of dialect shared by Asians and Asian Americans, but it remains an apt descriptor of the way the speech of racially East Asian characters has consistently been depicted in media.

The most egregious examples of linguistic stereotyping of East Asians in American animation may be found in the Japanese caricatures of World War II cartoons, in which Japanese characters were given a heavy mock Japanese accent, and uttered high-pitched staccato gibberish intended to approximate what non–Japanese speakers hear when they hear spoken Japanese. This, compounded with the use of exaggerated facial features meant to emphasize racial difference, contributed to the racial othering of the wartime enemy.⁹ Despite Hollywood's renewed appreciation of Japan after the war, portrayals of the Japanese (and by extension all East Asian characters in cartoons) rarely lacked the accent and mannerisms with which Japanese enemies were consistently saddled in wartime propaganda cartoons.

The broken English and fortune-cookie prose of the oriental archetypes (the Chinese American detective Charlie Chan, for instance) from earlier decades functioned as signs of cultural maladaptation and racial inferiority. Ultimately, Yellow English contributed to what Eugene Franklin Wong calls "visual media racism," alongside yellowface makeup, typecasting, and so on.¹⁰ If we look at today's television shows, conversely, we find that they can have a multiethnic and multicultural cast and showcase accent diversity while trying to avoid negative stereotyping and caricature. This is true of Asian-coded characters, who are voiced by Asian actors and given a "naturally" accented voice, such as BMO and Lady Rainicorn.

It is worth noting that at some point, *Adventure Time* seems to allude to the history of Yellow English in comedy and animation. In "Her Parents," season 2 episode 12, Finn embarrasses himself by posing as a rainicorn and inviting Lady Rainicorn's parents to do the "traditional rainicorn dance" with him before he starts dancing and chanting nonsense. Since he fails to pass as a rainicorn due to his physical appearance, does not speak Korean, and knows in fact nothing about rainicorn culture, he ends up offending Bob and Ethel (cue Bob, "Please Jake, ask your goblin butler to stop insulting my heritage."). Though Jake fails to keep up with Bob and Ethel's cultural references, he manages to sustain the masquerade longer because, unlike Finn, he knows better than to crudely mimic his rainicorn in-laws' language. This scene can be read as a self-reflexive allusion to how children's media often represent East Asian cultures and languages and as a condemnation of racist linguistic stereotyping.

BMO the White Boy

The concept of "mock language" was first put forward by Jane H. Hill in her work about mock Spanish, and then applied to East Asian stereotypes by Elaine W. Chun in her analysis of stand-up comedian Margaret Cho's parodic impersonation of her Korean-American mother.¹¹

Mock Asian speech can be defined as an impressionistic rendition of English spoken as a second language by immigrants from East Asia, so a non-standard grammar is essential to suggest foreignness (for example, deletion of copula, deletion of articles, simple negation with *no*, plural nouns turned singular). In addition to the Pidgin-like grammatical errors, a mock Asian performance is not quite complete without a racial accent. Salient phonological characteristics found in most varieties of cartoon Yellow English are the undifferentiated use of [l] for [r] and [l] sounds, the addition of a final [ə] schwa sound at the end of checked syllables (epenthesis), simplification of final consonant clusters, and a staccato syllable-timed rhythm.

BMO's speech usually lacks the usual patterns of grammatical errors frequently found in cartoons and comedy skits featuring East Asian caricatures. Only on very rare occasions does he display grammatical features consistent with the broken English spoken by Asian-coded cartoon characters of past decades. For instance, in "The Conquest of Cuteness," when asked to go get a camera by Finn and Jake, who wish to photograph the Cute King, BMO exclaims, "*BMO is camera!*." In this short throwaway line, we can observe the deletion of the article "*the*" before "*camera*" and BMO refers to himself in the third person.

Non-standard, "broken" English is one of the many manifestations of the way the stereotype of the "perpetual foreigner" sticks to members of Asian diasporas. In order to fully invoke this trope, it is necessary that the character be unable to speak idiomatic standard English, which BMO is capable of. "*BMO is camera!*" is an example of diegetic mock language (i.e., in the narrative, BMO, a fluent English-speaker, is using non-standard grammar in order to joke around with Finn and Jake). In short, the show is not making fun of BMO for being unable to speak proper English, possibly on account of him being East Asian.

The intention was probably not to evoke specifically mock Asian speech or the broken English of oriental caricatures in films and television, but the effect is similar: BMO is goofing around and pretending to talk bad. Another interpretation for BMO's exceptional use of mock broken English here could be that he is imitating a sort of mock baby talk, rather than Pidgin. Since he is essentially a little kid, playfulness and childishness are at the heart of BMO's characterization. Either way, this is an instance of *Adventure Time*'s portrayal of BMO coming dangerously close to linguistic stereotypes frequently associated with East Asians, but immediately defusing any potential implications that BMO is comically failing to speak proper English. While this is most probably unintentional, we can read this short line as a subversion of racist linguistic conventions in animation and cinema.

We can assume that the one thing that codes BMO as ethnically Asian in the eyes of some viewers is the phonology of Niki Yang's English. BMO's lines are in fact written in General American English, and it is Niki Yang's accent that makes them sound "Asian," thus infusing them with racial indexicality. Years of typecasting, stereotyping, and linguistic masquerade in cinema and cartoons have conditioned audiences to associate Asian characters with broken grammar and accented speech; and even though *Adventure Time* never addresses nor subverts ethnic stereotypes, BMO's portrayal in the show and its reception by viewers are bound to be influenced by existing representations of East Asians and linguistic stigma that ethnically East Asian non-native English speakers are faced with in real life.

BMO's coding as East Asian is impermanent and conditional. Unlike Lady's bilingualism, BMO's accent, his only marker of Asianness, can be erased in foreign dubs of the show. However, as far as the original version of *Adventure Time* is concerned, BMO is consistently read as East Asian by those who hear him speak with Yang's voice. BMO's assumed Asianness ends up being the source of potential subversion whenever he engages in white boy behavior and in mock Asian humor. BMO engages in mock Asian speech himself, as in the example cited above, or in "Gotcha" (season 4, episode 12) when he makes Jake call him *sensei* and bow to him. BMO exhibits the same attitude to East Asian cultures and languages as Finn and Jake, and he could be read as being white boy-coded if it was not for Yang's voice and the fact that viewers find her Korean accent conspicuous (possibly, again, because of the way popular culture has been portraying East Asians for decades).

It is worth mentioning that series creator Pendleton Ward and the show's first creative director, Pat McHale, are said to have liked Yang as BMO not because of her accent, but rather because of her monotone voice. Yang has recounted at a panel discussion in 2014 that whenever she tried to "act" her lines and sound more like "a little boy," Ward would ask her to stop acting and just stick to her natural, monotonous voice so that it would sound more robotic.[12] The robotic, androgynous, and youthful quality of Yang's voice undoubtedly plays a large part in BMO's development as a character and subsequent popularity with fans, and is something that needs to be separated from her accent and bilingualism.

All of this is complicated even further in foreign dubs of the show in which BMO is given the same ethnically neutral mainstream accent (for lack of better terms) as the other characters. In these versions of *Adventure Time*, BMO's implied and conditional Asianness is completely removed from his characterization. If allusions to a character being something else than straight, cisgender or white-coded can be erased when the show is transposed to another language, network, or medium, then does this part of the character get erased in foreign versions? If the French dub of *Adventure Time* had specifically called for a native Korean-speaking bilingual to be cast as BMO's French voice, it surely would have been a tokenistic gesture. If BMO's French voice actress or actor had chosen to affect a Korean accent in her performance, it would most certainly have come off as offensive, ignorant, and even mean-spirited. The French localization team seems to have deemed that BMO having the same accent as Yang was not textual, or essential to the show.

The question of how translation and dubbing alter the material of a show exceeds the scope of this essay, but it is worth mentioning. Chalking up the disappearance of BMO's accent in the French dub of *Adventure Time* to xenophobia makes little sense, but the fact remains that BMO's Asian-coding in the original version of the show is a noticeable part of his character. This is something that can cause offense or annoy viewers, as pointed out in the forum discussion quoted earlier, but also something that makes BMO's character special, likeable, and even relatable to some other viewers.

To summarize, unlike in typical representations of mock Asian speech seen on television, BMO is not intentionally written as a non–Native speaker of broken English. His accent is not textual, and can be considered to be only incidental to his character. What is interesting about BMO's voice is that there is no in-universe justification for BMO to speak a Korean-accented English. This may be why some viewers may think the "the accent does not add anything." However, unlike BMO's accent, Lady Rainicorn's bilingualism and accented English index foreignness. This makes sense in the diegesis, as Lady comes from a Crystal Dimension, which is geographically and culturally foreign to inhabitants of Ooo.

Multilingualism in Adventure Time

Lady Rainicorn is Yang's other recurring role in the series besides BMO. The Crystal Dimension, as a foreign land in relation to Ooo, is a somewhat metaphorical counterpart for Korea, considering that rainicorn culture is partly based on Korean culture. Furthermore, rainicorns have been intradiegetically stated to speak Korean in the show.[13] In this regard, Lady is heavily coded as Korean. Since Yang uses her own natural talking voice when playing both of her characters (as she has explained herself), it appears that simply switching languages is enough to allow the two characters to sound different—but of course, there is also the fact that BMO and Lady very rarely interact.

The insertion of untranslated Korean dialogue in the show exemplifies two qualities that characterize *Adventure Time* as a series: the unique whimsical humor that made it stand out initially, and the strides in terms of positive representation of minorities (in particular, queer sexualities) the show has been credited for making. Despite never quite willfully pushing back boundaries as it did with LGBT+ representation, *Adventure Time* challenges the status quo in interesting and subtle ways when it comes to portraying characters explicitly coded as foreign and non-white. Lady's status as a multilingual Korean speaker among English speakers factors into her relationship dynamics and her character writing.

The following scene from "My Two Favorite People" (S1E9) is an example of multilingual dialogue in which the language barrier is acknowledged and used as a set up for a gag. In this episode, Jake attempts to bring Finn and Lady Rainicorn closer together. Fan translations are indicated in italics inside brackets.

> JAKE: Anybody have a joke?
> FINN: Oh, I have a joke! [*Laughs.*] Okay [*laughs*] okay. Knock knock.
> LADY RAINICORN: 누구세요 ("*Who's there?*")
> JAKE: She said, "who's there?"
> FINN: Diarrhea!
> JAKE: 쟤가 설사래. ("*He said 'diarrhea.'*")
> LADY RAINICORN: 어, 나도 들었어. 뭐야, 하나도 재미없잖아. ("*Oh, I heard it too. What was that? It hardly qualifies as a joke.*") [*Sips drink*]
> FINN: Did she say diarrhea who?
> JAKE: Uh, no. No, she didn't say, "diarrhea who?" She didn't … say it. Lady, how 'bout you tell a joke?
> LADY RAINICORN: 글쎄.. 뭐가 있었을까? 아! 우리 완전히 다 벗고 상추밭 미친듯이 뛰어다닌 거 기억 나? [*Jake and Lady Rainicorn giggle*] 그 농부 아저씨 완전 맛이 갔었지! ("*Maybe…. What could it have been? Ah! Do you remember when we got completely naked, and frantically ran around in the farmer's cabbage patch?* [*Jake and Lady giggle, both blushing*] *That farmer got crazy mad!*")
> FINN: What's the joke?
> JAKE: Uh…. Well, the joke doesn't translate very well.[14]

While a Korean/English bilingual will understand the scene fully, a monolingual English speaker will rely on subtitles or fan translations, the exact same way Finn relies on Jake as an interpreter.

In most scenes showing Jake and Lady interacting alone, Jake's lines are enough to infer what Lady is saying. This is not the case here: in this discussion, Lady monologues (with subtitles) during a small stretch of the conversation and Jake's replies do not hint at the content of Lady's story. Finn acts as a stand-in for the monolingual viewer and his presence justifies Jake's translations. If the viewer cannot understand Lady's lines, then their perspective is close to Finn's: The monolingual viewer sees a knock-knock joke fall flat (because its recipient fails to follow the conventional script of this kind of joke); and then they hear Lady segue onto an unrelated and unintelligible story. The absence of a punchline to Finn's diegetic (probably mediocre) joke is a twist on comedy conventions, and a surreal punchline in itself. This outcome may arguably be even funnier than hearing the actual joke Finn was intending to tell, whose aborted set up suggests toilet humor.

The non-Korean-speaking viewer may pick up on the insinuation that Lady and Jake, a canon couple, are talking about something dirty because they both blush and laugh as Lady monologues, and Jake refuses to translate what she said when Finn asks him to. Understanding this may allow the viewer to avoid being on the same level of comprehension as Finn, despite being frustrated to miss out on the actual content of Lady's joke. Both Finn and Lady are unable to understand each other's joke: Lady because she either finds Finn's humor unfunny or because she is unfamiliar with the script of knock-knock jokes due to linguistic and cultural difference, and Finn because he does not understand Korean and the joke "does not translate well"—and possibly because Jake may want to shield him from a dirty story or avoid sharing an embarrassing anecdote. The scene has a meta level, hinging on the viewer's assumed inability to understand the language of the joke. Depending on our language skills and cultural background, we can be in the same position as either Finn, Lady, or Jake.

Unintelligible dialogue is a form of a gag in itself. The pilot episode of what would later become *Adventure Time*, made in 2007 for Nicktoon Network, featured an early version of Lady Rainicorn voiced by Dee Bradley Baker. Instead of speaking Korean, she only expressed herself through screams, animal noises resembling a pigeon cooing, and uncontrollable sobs. These iterations of Lady and Finn (then "Pen the Human") end up having an exchange which sounds similar to their conversation in "My Two Favorite People," as Pen attempts to tell the rainicorn a joke to cheer her up as she flies around while crying hysterically. In the pilot, Pen goes "Knock knock" and waits for a response which does not come, as the rainicorn just keeps crying. When Pen then says, "Who's there?," the rainicorn's cries resemble an *ooh~* sound, so he continues with "Oo-woo-wooh who?," which is again responded to with more screaming and sobbing. Ultimately, as the rainicorn continues crying, Pen gives up and concludes "Man.... That wasn't very funny." In the 2007 pilot, Pen and the rainicorn have a one-sided conversation. There is no way of knowing if the rainicorn understands what Pen is saying to her, and whether her screams are responses to Pen's questions. The cartoon frames this exchange as if it were an actual civil and meaningful conversation: not only do the two participants take turns speaking (or screaming in the rainicorn's case), but the camera also cuts between them, following the shot/reverse shot convention. Later on in the pilot, while Pen battles the Ice King in the background, Jake starts chatting up the rainicorn and it is implied Jake can understand her cooing. Their interactions in the second half of the pilot resemble the type of conversations they are seen having in the series later: Only Jake's lines are in English, and monolingual English speakers can deduce what Lady is saying to a certain degree, through Jake's answers ("Are you kidding? I play the viola too!").

The change between Lady's dialogue in the pilot and in the actual series is a significant one. In "My Two Favorite People," the conversation is not one-sided anymore. Jake's presence as a bilingual interpreter makes Finn the butt of the joke, since he is the only monolingual and depends on Jake's translations. The fact that Pendleton Ward went from having Lady talk in gibberish and screams to deciding he wanted her to specifically speak Korean parallels the way *Adventure Time* evolved between the making of the pilot and the beginning of the series, from loud *non sequitur* absurd comedy to multilayered jokes with double meanings, while still holding onto its core aesthetic (for instance, the superposition of overly cute visuals and crude lifelike colloquial dialogue). The change from Dee Bradley Baker's hysterical cooing to Yang's flat voice allowed Lady Rainicorn to break out of her initial animalistic characterization, and become her own character rather than just "Princess Bubblegum's rainicorn" as Pen calls her in the pilot. Whereas the Jake from the pilot could understand her innately, presumably because they are both animals, the Lady from the series needs to be speaking to someone with some proficiency in her native language. The series can still exploit the incongruousness of Korean dialogue for comedy, while using Lady's bilingualism to give extra layers of meaning to her dialogue.

On the other hand, the fact that Ward decided, on Bert Youn's suggestion, to pick exclusive Korean dialogue as a sophisticated replacement for Lady's initial gibberish cooing is very telling in terms of how East Asian languages are perceived by audiences and represented in American cartoons. Could it be that Korean is an adequate substitute for nonsense, with the added benefit of hidden dirty jokes? Could it be linked to the history of mock languages in American animation, where East Asian characters would always speak either in broken English or in gibberish approximations of either Chinese or Japanese? What matters is the end result and the actual impact the show ended up having in terms of representation.

If we now consider the perspective of a multilingual viewer who understands both English and Korean (or the perspective of someone who is able to watch the episode with subtitles), the scene becomes a set up for what may or may not be an adult joke. Lady Rainicorn's joke is multilayered, since we automatically assume that a couple running around naked is a sexual situation, therefore inappropriate to mention in a children's show—but there is also the fact that Lady and Jake do not normally wear clothes, which makes the joke at the same time too dirty to let children hear on national television, and absurdly innocent.

Several episodes show instances of Lady's status as a Korean speaker being used to sneak in borderline adult humor. Most of them take place in early seasons, so it is possible to theorize that the show's gain in popularity allowed viewers to watch the episodes with subtitles (either officially provided closed captioning, or fansubs) and look up translations online, which may have diminished the appeal of using bilingual dialogue as a vehicle for hidden jokes.[15]

Unlike BMO's accent, which is never brought up by himself or other characters, Lady's bilingualism is, if not exactly a plot point, an actual character trait and a set up for gags. Lady's habit of speaking exclusively Korean was probably part of the overall whimsical tone of the first seasons of *Adventure Time*, which introduced a world where an overly sweet aesthetic (rainbows, unicorns, princesses) intermingles with the ghoulish and the uncanny (mad science, zombies, death). Having a character speak a foreign language no doubt contributed to the "random" feel of *Adventure Time*. It is funny because we do not know what Lady says, and it is funny because it is unexpected for a rainbow unicorn to speak Korean, *and* it is funny because if you speak Korean or look up a translation, then you are getting a joke about naked animals offending someone by being naked, or a creepy story about zombies chasing a unicorn.[16]

To go back to Lady Rainicorn's appearances in the first couple of episodes, Lady's risqué lines in response to Finn's childish toilet humor in "My Two Favorite People," told in Korean and left untranslated for both Finn and the monolingual viewer, is a perfect example of how the show addresses both Cartoon Network's target audience, while slipping in some allusions directed at adult viewers—and multilinguals as well.

Adventure Time is far from being the first show to feature untranslated multilingual dialogue,[17] but the case of Lady Rainicorn is still novel in several respects: First, because Lady, while not a main character, appears in a non-negligeable number of episodes and is Jake's love interest. Second, because when *Adventure Time* first started airing, Korean was not a language most American viewers were familiar with. Thus far, East Asian representation in cinema and television, especially in cartoons, had been strongly centered around Chinese and Japanese characters. When *Adventure Time* premiered, the third wave of *hallyu* had yet to begin (Korean culture was not yet as visible to Western youth as it became later in the decade thanks to the growing popularity of Korean popular music) and millennials were all about colorful, whimsical, anime-inspired, random humor—the nyan cat, *Asdfmovies*, Psy's "Gangnam Style," the "Harlem Shake," rage comics going mainstream, bronies…. Pen Ward's show is a product of its time, and also a significant cultural landmark in the media landscape of the early 2010s. However, being a pure product and a cultural pillar of the 2010s does not free *Adventure Time* from the influence of decades of film and cartoon history, and audiences cannot help but to process Lady and BMO's Asian-coding through the lens of ethnic difference as it is traditionally encoded in media.

All of this begs the question of whether the casting of Niki Yang as BMO and Lady Rainicorn in the original dub of the show could have been somehow tokenistic, considering that, to Yang's own admission, she does not really act in these two roles so much as use her natural voice in either Korean or English.[18]

Conclusion: *The Functions of Multilingualism and Accent Diversity in* Adventure Time *Humor*

Recognizing and understanding a dialect in a show when it unexpectedly crops up can cause amusement on its own, and even in some cases, pride—something that puts some viewers on a different level than monolingual viewers. In this regard, the insertion of untranslated foreign language dialogue in English-speaking media is like an inside joke aimed at multilingual and multicultural viewers.

For viewers who can only understand English, there is humor to be found as well in the presence of unintelligible dialogue. Some viewers may appreciate the unfamiliarity of a foreign language and giggle because it sounds strange, and others will find the irruption of gratuitous multilingualism in a children's show amusing, because it disrupts narrative conventions.

The occasional use of a mock language by a character can work as a one-time *non sequitur* gag. For instance, in "Checkmate" (season 7 episode 12) when Jake and Peppermint Butler say, "Yo, pass me the bucket." "どうぞ (*dōzo*)" "*Merci* and *adios*," there is no contextual justification for unprompted mixture of mock Japanese, French and Spanish.

In addition to this, the irruption of multilingual dialogue and mock languages in *Adventure Time* is constantly juxtaposed with the idiolects of the main cast and linguistic oddities that are diegetically endemic to Ooo, from Finn's mathematical swears to "Check please!" becoming both a running gag and an in-universe meme.

Characterization

Accent diversity and implications of multilingualism are tools of characterization. As explained in this essay, LSP's Valleyspeak and Tree Trunks'

Southern drawl allow viewers to associate these characters with character archetypes. Princess Bubblegum being fluent in German is another interesting example of canonical multilingualism in the show. Perhaps the various instances of PB speaking German across the seasons are examples of diegetic mock German, but it seems more likely that PB is indeed fluent in German, as she is seen shouting in German when surprised or emotional in season 1,[19] and in season 7, when she counts in German while exercising with Marceline.[20] When asked about it at a convention panel in 2018, Hynden Walsh clarified that she actually speaks German (having learned the language in school), which initially came as a surprise to the creative team, as PB's bilingualism was written into the show without the knowledge that Walsh's language skills matched that of her character.[21] Incidentally, on the same occasion, Adam Muto interjected to specify that he did not even remember why PB speaks German. Whatever Muto's initial reasoning was, we can observe the effect this character trait has on viewers. Barring the obvious unsavory implications and potential Nazi jokes about PB's dictatorial tendencies, German can be a part of Bubblegum's "mad scientist" persona, an index of her intellect and unethical scientific ambitions.

Worldbuilding

A perfect example of linguistic worldbuilding is the appearance of minor Swedish-speaking character Alva in *The Island* miniseries. When Finn first meets Alva in "Mysterious Island," the language barrier and the age difference between them parallel Finn's disconnection from humanity and human culture (as well as everything that has been lost since the apocalypse, given that Alva's human settler friends have been dying off). In the world of *Adventure Time*, Swedish is implied to be a dead language and Alva the lone speaker of a nearly extinct dialect. Like Finn, the monolingual English-speaking viewer must struggle, or at least, listen and think a little in order to piece out how Alva ended up on her island and what happened to the other humans.

Bicultural and bilingual Swedish/English viewers have access to another level of comprehension and share an insider's knowledge when they recognize Helena Matsson's (Alva's voice actress) authentic Swedish, but no Swedish skills are required to understand the gist of Alva's dialogue and the documentary film she shows Finn. What is important here is that the mutual incomprehension between Finn and Alva is essential to the show's world-building and to the progression of Finn's character arc. The language barrier between Alva and Finn is symbolic of the gap separating Finn from humanity, old human settlements from the new, the land of Ooo from the islands.

Of course, multilingualism as world-building does not function as a perfectly logical system: what would be the in-universe explanation for everyone in Ooo to speak American English? How come Marceline and Simon's dialect has not evolved in a thousand years? Do the Hoomans speak in a mock caveman dialect because of their underground isolation? To be fair, the reason for all of this is that the writing of *Adventure Time* is like a collective painting that is also a jigsaw puzzle and a tabletop role-playing game. All in all, the in-universe internal logic of the linguistics of Ooo is not as important as the effect the show's linguistic landscape ends up having on the viewer.

We are free to speculate as to why rainicorns speak Korean,[22] but in the end what matters is that Korean encodes the foreignness of the Crystal Dimension in relation to the American-coded denizens of Ooo. Rainicorns from the Crystal Dimension are coded as foreign, which is to say: geographically, culturally, and ultimately, *ethnically* different from North American-coded, white-coded, English-speaking Ooo.

Implying and Indexing Ethnic Otherness

This last point brings us to the central question of this essay: the coding of ethnic and racial identity via language and accent. We can come to the conclusion that reading BMO and the rainicorns as East Asian-coded makes a lot of sense, but it is possible to be oblivious to this aspect of their characters, and even outright choose to reject it. A viewer may decide to be colorblind or be unaware of the possible race and ethnicity metaphors, but by doing so, they will miss out on certain interpretations of some storylines, such as Jake's being anxious about meeting Lady's parents because of the Dog-Rainicorn wars, or T.V. learning about his mother's past in the Crystal Dimension, which encourages him to reconnect with his cultural heritage in season 7.[23]

All in all, these are interpretations guided by subtext and allusions. This essay simply sought to put *Adventure Time* in perspective with the history and the state of East Asian representation in media in order to recontextualize these potential readings of BMO and Lady, and get a deeper understanding of the way the show uses dialectal and accent diversity in its aesthetic and narrative.

To be fair, *Adventure Time* itself tends to skirt around the question of ethnic and racial diversity. The Land of Ooo and the surviving human societies are implied to be perfectly post-racial. Racism and racial diversity does not seem to be something the show's writers ever tried tackling; and *Adventure Time* never gives the impression of attempting to capitalize on revolutionary and radically diverse representation.

100 "One isn't purely defined by their sex or gender"

After decades of racist stereotypes being the norm in terms of how racial and ethnic minorities were represented, it is normal for viewers to see cartoon representations of East Asians and wonder if they could carry negative undertones, intentionally or not, maliciously or not. This is a legitimate line of questioning, and not just hairsplitting due to oversensitivity or hyperbolic political correctness. Regarding language diversity, as with many other topics, even though *Adventure Time* is innovative in terms of representation and marked the start of a new era for Western animation, it remains a product of its time and it cannot be completely dissociated from the history of American cartoons.

NOTES

1. Despite BMO being stated to be agender and being referred to with both he/him and she/her pronoun sets in the show (in addition to they/them and neopronouns in supplemental material and fan media), this essay refers to BMO with the pronouns he/him.
2. Cron, "Am I the only one that hates BMO's voice acting on Adventure Time?"
3. The terms "Asian-coded" and "East Asian-coded" occur throughout the essay. "Coding" refers to the way a fictional character is subtextually implied to belong to a certain ethnicity (or a gender identity, etc.) without the text outright stating it. The term "Asian" is sometimes used in quotes, as it refers to the way most people tend to use the term as a racial catch-all for various ethnicities when they in fact mean East Asian people. All derived terms such as 'Asianness' are used in a similarly loose sense. This essay was written while bearing in mind that racial and ethnic identities (often in overlap, though they refer to different things) are social and cultural constructs, and what is generally meant by these terms falls under the scope of perceptions commonly projected onto an individual.
4. For a discussion of the 'standard language myth,' language discrimination, and accents in Disney movies, see Rosina Lippi-Green, *English with an Accent*.
5. Shilpa Davé, "Racial Accents, Hollywood Casting, and Asian American Studies," 142–47.
6. I.e., "Make-up used by a non-East Asian performer playing the role of an East Asian person," *Oxford English Dictionary*, s.v. "Yellowface."
7. Elaine H. Kim, "Yellow English," 44–63.
8. For a sociolinguistic exploration of Asian diasporic communities across North America, see Angela Reyes and Adrienne Lo, *Beyond Yellow English*.
9. Examples and discussions of anti-Japanese propaganda cartoons can be found in Michael S. Shull and David E. Wilt, *Doing Their Bit*.
10. Eugene F. Wong, *On Visual Media Racism*.
11. Elaine Chun, "Ideologies of Legitimate Mockery." For Hill's discussion of mock Spanish and mock languages, see: Jane H. Hill, *The Everyday Language of White Racism*.
12. Thomas Kay Valentine, "Kraken Con 2014."
13. E.g., Finn in "The Pit" (season 5, episode 41): "Yo, my Korean is not that good."
14. "My Two Favorite People" (season 1, episode 9).
15. Lady mentions "merging bodies with Jake all the time" in "The Creeps" (season 3, episode 12), and her wish to be bitten by zombie-Jake in "From Bad to Worse" (season 3, episode 13).
16. "Lady & Peebles" (season 4, episode 19).
17. To give only one example among many others, the original *Teen Titans* series, whose initial run ended four years prior *Adventure Time*'s debut, had recurring minor characters Más and Menos, a pair of Guatemalan twins who appear in a handful of episodes. Both twins were voiced by the same person, Freddy Rodriguez, have a fluent understanding

of spoken English, and consistently spoke Spanish. Similar to Lady Rainicorn, Más and Menos' bilingualism and their use of a foreign language is acknowledged in the show's text and commented on by other characters, and the show offered no English subtitles, letting instead the monolingual viewer infer the meaning of the Spanish lines through contextual cues.

    18. Valentine, "Kraken Con 2014."
    19. "What Have You Done" (season 1, episode 24).
    20. Checkmate" (season 7, episode 12).
    21. Cartoon Network, "Adventure Time."
    22. A YouTube video essay mentions a theory according to which rainicorns were actually the originators of the Korean langage and brought it to Korea: LuLYeah, "¿Por qué Arcoiris habla coreano? (Hora de Aventura)," YouTube, 2019, https://youtu.be/yepgl0SJDgE?t=460.
    23. "Lady Rainicorn of the Crystal Dimension" (season 8, episode 4).

References

Cartoon Network. "Adventure Time | Finale Panel San Diego Comic-Con 2018 | Cartoon Network." YouTube, 2018. https://www.youtube.com/watch?v=2N45801_38g.

Chun, Elaine. "Ideologies of Legitimate Mockery: Margaret Cho's Revoicings of Mock Asian." *Pragmatics* 14, no. 2/3: 263–289.

Cron. "Am I the only one that hates BMO's voice acting on Adventure Time?" GameFAQs, 2013. https://gamefaqs.gamespot.com/boards/203-cartoons-and-animation/65018289.

Davé, Shilpa. "Racial Accents, Hollywood Casting, and Asian American Studies." *Cinema Journal* 56, no. 3 (2017): 142–47. Accessed May 27, 2021. http://www.jstor.org/stable/44867828.

Hill, Jane H. *The Everyday Language of White Racism.* Chichester, U.K.; Malden, MA: Wiley-Blackwell, 2008.

Kim, Elaine H. "Yellow English." *Asian American Review* 2, no. 1 (1975): 44–63.

Lippi-Green, Rosina. *English with an Accent: Language, Ideology and Discrimination in the United States.* 2nd ed. New York: Routledge, 2012.

Reyes, Angela, and Adrienne Lo, eds. *Beyond Yellow English: Toward a Linguistic Anthropology of Asian Pacific America.* New York: Oxford University Press, 2009.

Shull, Michael S., and David E. Wilt. *Doing Their Bit: Wartime American Animated Short Films, 1939–1945.* 2nd ed. Jefferson, NC: McFarland, 2004.

Valentine, Thomas Kay. "Kraken Con 2014: Niki Yang Panel." YouTube, 2014. https://www.youtube.com/watch?v=QMTGTRbnJjQ.

Wong, Eugene F. *On Visual Media Racism: Asians in the American Motion Pictures.* New York: Arno Press, 1978.

"Behind this curtain of patterns…"
The Philosophy of Ooo

Mikhail Bakhtin in the Land of Ooo
The Carnivalesque, Heteroglossia, and the Fun That Never Ends

AARON KERNER *and* BIRDY WEI-TING HUNG

Introduction: It's Got Bakhtin Written All Over It…

Infused throughout Cartoon Network's *Adventure Time* series (2010–2018) are a number of Bakhtinian principles: the carnivalesque and specifically the associated trope of grotesque realism, and not least of which, Mikhail Bakhtin's concept of "adventure time." I (Kerner) have written about this elsewhere.[1] To summarize, whether by design or coincidence, *Adventure Time* is permeated by Bakhtinian principles (as stated above) including his observations about the continental conception of time prior to the Renaissance. In several moments, Bakhtin talks about vertical and horizontal time. With the Enlightenment and the conception of human progress, time is conceived as unfolding on a horizontal axis. The Renaissance transferred time "to one single plane, and the higher and lower stratum became relative. The accent was placed on 'forward' and 'backward.'"[2] However, as Bakhtin points out, the carnivalesque conception of time is vertical—time in effect goes up and down, as symbolized in the somersaulting clown, as in the cycle of life where life is co-present in death and death is pregnant with life. And this cyclical, or vertical conception of time is peppered throughout the Cartoon Network series.

Take, for instance, the episode, "Food Chain" (season 6, episode 7), which celebrates the carnivalesque conception of time. The title, "Food Chain," explicitly references the cycle of life: death is not an end *per se*, but always already pregnant with the potential of re-birth.[3] "Food Chain" starts with children's laughter. We are then introduced to a rambunctious group of Candy Kingdom children, whose bodies are simply different shapes (e.g., triangle, circle, square, oval, cylinder, and so on), running energetically through a playground-like space. At the entrance of a slide (which is effectively a cross section illustration of a bird), a sign reads: "You guys are caterpillars!! Let's try to be eaten!!" We thus follow the Candy Kingdom children's adventure, sliding through a bird's alimentary canal, to underneath the ground, then up to a showroom: "The Catapilla Family: Caterpillars of life." Candy Kingdom children are simply having fun—*their laughter never ends!* More signs invite consumption: "You guys are little birds!!" "Let's try to eat!!" Now, the Candy Kingdom children are not only munching on leaves; they also begin chomping on caterpillars. "Ugh, that's gross, too," Finn pronounces, and adds, "There is no way real caterpillars are delicious." Jake is not so sure, "You think? I bet they taste great if you were a boid." And, of course, later in the episode, this is exactly what Finn and Jake will experience: Magic Man transforms Finn and Jake into a variety of body forms—little birds, bigger birds, a group of bacteria, flowers, then back to caterpillars again. Matter is not fixed *per se*, but rather always in motion, and the human subject is not set apart from this economy, but is caught in this constant state of becoming. *Adventure Time* also invites a rhizomatic worldview. Finn and Jake's transformation cycle is relevant to consumption and excrement. In fact, despite its suggestive title, the "Food Chain" episode is not so much about survival and evolution, but the coexistence of multiple body forms. By the end of the episode, Finn is literally becoming a bird-caterpillar-plant-bacteria hybrid—Finn *embodies* the cycle of life.[4] And the cycle of life does not unfold on a horizontal timeline, but in a spiraling economy of exchange of matter and energy. Thus, Finn's ever-changing bodies hint at this vertical conception of time: birth and death, consumption and excrement, which are in a constant open-ended process.

    The rhizomatic worldview can be understood through Bakhtin's conception of grotesque realism. It is critical to bear in mind that the Bakhtinian "grotesque" has very little to do with the contemporary colloquial understanding of the term (e.g., gross, disgusting, the "ew factor"); instead, Bakhtin draws on its original meaning. Our word, "grotesque," derives from the Italian, "grotto," meaning cave. During the Renaissance, curious explorers discovered in the ruins (read: caves) of the Roman empire, capricious designs decorating the walls of buildings. The designs freely mixed humans, animals, architectural features, foliage, and festoons. Thus, drawn from the word "grotto," these came to be known as "grotesques."[5] These designs were copied and imitated, and even today grotesque-inspired imagery can be found on the backs of playing cards, on flatware, and incorporated into late nineteenth century architecture. In sum, Bakhtin's conception of the grotesque body—related to those capricious Roman designs—is one that is open to the worlds, where all matter—be it organic life, or inanimate—is not an individuated entity set apart from the world, but rather a rhizomatic figure that is inextricably imbricated with the world all around us.[6]

Many Bakhtinian grotesque body tropes can be found in *Adventure Time*. As Bakhtin notes, the comic performers at the market place—the clown, the jugglers, the magicians—have always been a source of the grotesque body.[7] Let us take a look at "Freak City" (season 1, episode 20). Finn and Jake encounter a mysterious man, begging for food, who later reveals himself to be Magic Man. Demonstrating his tricks, Magic Man turns a bird literally inside out (organs are revealed) and he even turns Finn's lower body into a giant foot. As Bakhtin writes, "the grotesque ignores the impenetrable surface that closes and limits the body as a separate and completed phenomenon. The grotesque image displays not only the outward but also the inner features of the body: blood, bowels, heart and other organs."[8] It is Magic Man, as a trickster magician, that effectuates grotesque realism. Along with others in the episode, it is Finn that is made to exemplify the grotesque body, his upper torso literally projects out of the shin of his foot-body. He panics, "I can't be a hero if I'm a big ... foot!" But Jake actually adores Finn's new foot-body: "Here." Jake inflates his hindquarters into an exaggeratedly large ass, "Come on. Kick my butt!" Jake adds imploring, "Let's give your foot-body a shot." Jake then attaches Finn-the-foot, upside-down, onto a catapult. As a two-headed monster comes closer, mumbling, "We are evil, we are evil...." Jake steps on a trigger, launching Finn-the-foot right into the monster's crotch. The monster yells in pain, "Our crotch! Our evil crotch!" Jake gleefully intones, "Let's go set out some more crotch catapults, so we can laugh and be heroes!" Again, the colloquial language (with emphasis on the lower stratums), the mismatch and/or exaggerated displacement of body parts, all fit in Bakhtin's conception of grotesque realism: "The grotesque was the basis of all the abuses, uncrownings, teasing, and impertinent gestures (as pointing at the nose or the buttocks, spitting, and others)."[9] From Magic Man's trickster antics, to Jake's exaggerated ass, to the blow to the crotch, to Finn's uncrowning as the principle hero of Ooo, grotesque realism fuels the humor that we find in *Adventure Time*.

Grotesque realism, as Bakhtin frames it, "never presents an individual body; the image consists of orifices and convexities that present another, newly conceived body. It is a point of transition in a life eternally renewed, the inexhaustible vessel of death and conception."[10] Bakhtin observes two sources of the grotesque body in folklore and literature in the Middle Ages. First, there were folklores of giants, who were "an indispensable part of popular-festive carnival images."[11] Second, there were legends that are related to "Indian Wonders," i.e., the stories of travelers which, "describes India's fantastic wealth and extraordinary natural resources, as well as its purely fictitious phenomena: devils spitting fire, magic herbs, enchanted woods, fountains of youth."[12] Bakhtin brings our attention to the descriptions of the extraordinary, and therefore, exotic human beings in these travelogues: "These creatures have a distinctive grotesque character. Some of them are half human, half animal: the hippopods with hoofs instead of feet, sirens with fishtails, 'sinucephalics' who bark like dogs, satyrs, and onocentaurs."[13] Bakhtin's survey of these travelogues could very well catalog the inhabitants of Ooo, as Bakhtin explains the travelogues offer "an entire gallery of images with bodies of mixed parts. There are also giants, dwarfs, and pygmies." Bakhtin adds that "there are various monsters: the 'scipedes' who have only one leg, 'leumans' without a head and with a face on the chest, Cyclops with one eye on the forehead, others with eyes on their shoulders or on their backs, creatures with six arms, and other who feed through their noses, and so forth. All this," Bakhtin concludes, "constitutes a wild anatomical fantasy, so popular in the Middle Ages."[14] All these imaginative figures, from the dwarves and giants and to the monstrous beings with all their anatomical fancies in medieval folklore and travelogues can be found in *Adventure Time*.

With the Renaissance and the proliferation of Enlightenment ideas, the conception of the human condition underwent a dramatic paradigmatic shift. Whereas the Enlightened subject is conceived as discrete, somehow "above" or "outside" the natural world, the medieval continental conception imagined the subject as open to the world, always in the state of becoming. *Adventure Time* regularly plays with anatomical fancies, analogous to what we find in medieval accounts. Mouths in *Adventure Time*, for example, with some regularity are set on the vertical axis of the body, inviting comparisons with the labia—and it is evident in Hunson Abadeer's monstrous incarnation, as well as other Oooian inhabitants. The labia-mouth motif is yet one more instance where the upper and lower stratums are inverted.

While a modern conception of the body imagines that we are self-contained entities, closed off from the world, the medieval conception of the body was wholly different. "The outward and inward features are often merged into one," Bakhtin observes.[15] Let us look into the second half of the "Freak City" episode. Finn-the-foot fails to be the hero for Rump Town (the inhabitants of which have butts for heads, rump of course yet one more carnivalesque motif) and is thrown under the bridge—a cave-like underworld where he meets Gork, the leader of Freak City. The way in which Gork invites Finn and Jake, "Welcome, travelers!" invites us to draw affinities with Bakhtin's analysis of "Indian Wonders" and the fantastical anatomy found in travelogues. As they all walk into the cave, for example, Gork vomits lava, which turns into a fire. Gork then introduces the inhabitants: Zap the Arm (a pink humanoid arm), Trudy the Waist (a blue lump), Wee Wee and Gorflax (both are tonsils), Kim the leg (a beige leg), and Gork the Head (a Cyclops creature with no legs or arms). Gork explains, "We are the cursed ones, all once normal guys and gals who crossed paths with the Magic Man." Finn then persuades the inhabitants to unite, becoming a Super Freak to defeat Magic Man—while Jake offers to be the pants. Whereas everyone is amazed by their newly formed body, the fanciful anatomy in "Indian Wonders" is embodied in a giant form (Gork exclaims, "We are like a big, normal guy!")—a Super Freak formed by freaks. Magic Man later transforms the inhabitants back to their humanoid forms. Finn and Jake, likewise, assume their normal body-forms. However, while Gork and the rest of the group return to their humanoid form bodies (though still monstrous, Gork, for example is a cyclops), everyone decides to stay together as a Super Freak. Bakhtin reminds us further that the "grotesque imagery constructs what we might call a double body. In the endless chain of bodily life it retains the parts in which one link joins the other, in which the life of one body is born from the death of the preceding, older one."[16] While Super Freak reconstitutes as atomized whole humanoid body forms—Gork is not just a head, Kim is not just a leg and so on—Super Freak lives on as a collection of individuated entities. As individuated entities, Gork and the rest of the misfits are reborn, while retaining an identification with their older Super Freak-self (or was it always plural—selves?).

The title of the program very well might also come from Bakhtin's conception of "adventure time." This stems from Bakhtin's literary concept of the chronotope, which means "time space." Bakhtin develops the conception of the chronotope to account for how time-space is depicted in literature. "Adventure time," though, refers to those interstitial moments in a narrative where the protagonist might face various challenges, trials, or quests, but they have no bearing on the larger narrative. The Greek romance tradition often includes adventure time—a protagonist might go on some long adventure, separated from their beloved, and many things might happen in the intervening time, but this makes no difference to the lover's narrative. In adventure time it makes no difference what the adventures are, the adventures are interchangeable.[17]

Human time means nothing in the literary convention of adventure time. While a conventional narrative typically offers a discrete unit of time in a character's life, with the adventure time, on the other hand, "nothing changes: the world remains as it was, the biographical life of the heroes does not change, their feelings do not change, people do not even age. This empty time leaves no traces anywhere, no indications of its passing."[18] Severed from the conventions of linearity, continuity, and cause and effect determination, adventure time is amorphous. By its very nature, because it is not bound to linearity and driving to a specific conclusion, adventure time is episodic: "It is composed of a series of short segments that correspond to separate adventures," Bakhtin observes. "What is important is to be able to escape, to catch up, to outstrip, to be or not to be in a given place at a given moment, to meet or not to meet and so forth."[19] And this is precisely what happens with the series. While there is an overarching narrative that emerges over the course of the entire series, by and large individual episodes are atomized events (especially at the beginning of the series), and the fact, for instance, that at one point Finn got turned into a foot makes no difference to the overarching narrative.

With *Adventure Time*, the Cartoon Network program that is, time is reversible, and the very concept of space itself is flexible.[20] Thousands of years might be no more than a second by our conventional notion of time, or vice versa. The biographical time of the characters do not always appear to line-up (especially Marceline's timeline), but this is of little consequence in *Adventure Time*, or adventure time.[21] And because human time-space is unbound in the *Adventure Time* story-world, melancholy is built into the series: nothing can ever stay the same, life and the world is always already in a state of becoming. Take, for example, the finale of the program, "Come Along with Me" (season 10, episode 13).[22] The episode is set in the distant future—a thousand years after the Gum War. Beth and Shermy, a pair of good friends (clearly modeled after Finn and Jake), chat at Marceline's house (where Finn and Jake resided). Curious about the past, Beth and Shermy visit BMO, the "King of Ooo," who walks us through, in flashback, the story of the Gum War. Halfway into the episode, Beth and Sherman come to realize that the Gum War was prevented, that the Gum War effectively never happened. Beth exclaims, "Oh! So, you meant, like, the end of the *war*. I thought you meant like the end of the *world*." BMO explains, "No, no, no. That happened next." We then flashback and see GOLB, the mysterious deity who embodies chaos, being summoned to Ooo. Hoping to quell GOLB, BMO sings, "Time Adventure," later joined by Princess Bubblegum, Marceline, and the other Oooian inhabitants, which focuses on eternalistic block time.

The Great Gum War was prevented, the fate of Ooo was eventually saved. But there is nothing to "restore," because there is nothing to "go back to." And yet "people and things have gone through something, something that did not, indeed, change them but that did (in a manner of speaking) affirm what they, and precisely they, were as individuals, something that did verify and establish their identity, their fluid durability and continuity."[23] In fact, while there is an ostensible "happy ending" to *Adventure Time*, there is simultaneously that terrible sublime feeling that change is inevitable, that nothing is permanent—sharing certain affinities with the ephemerality found in Ozu, but dare we say it, far more potent in its sublimity.[24]

In addition to these Bakhtinian principles that I (Kerner) have discussed elsewhere, there is the constant play with language. From colloquial banter, to neologisms and slang, to haranguing insults and to speech that again and again returns to the lower stratums—all of which is the stuff of billingsgate culture, or the "carnivalizing" of language—to various manifestations of what Bakhtin refers to as dialogism. The latter being the local or individual mobilization of language that is inflected with individual and/or socio-cultural context. Language is not stable, or fixed, rather it is subject to recontextualization and any number of idiosyncratic mobilizations. Finn, for example, might exclaim, "mathematical!" meaning that something was done well, executed with precision, or is just simply awesome.[25] This fluid mobilization of language necessitates at once the centripetal force of official discourse (trading in the fiction that meanings are fixed and transcendent), and an individual's own peculiar utterances that tear a signifier away from the gravitational pull of official discourse. Bakhtin refers to this tug between the shared cultural understanding of language, and the language as it is lived in our day-to-day experience, as heteroglossia. "A common unitary language is a system of linguistic norms," Bakhtin observes. "But these norms do not constitute an abstract imperative," Bakhtin adds. Rather linguistic norms "are ... the generative forces of linguistic life, forces that struggle to overcome the heteroglossia of language, forces that unite and centralize verbal-ideological thought, creating within a heteroglot national language the firm, stable linguistic nucleus of an officially recognized literary language, or else defending an already formed language from the pressure of growing heteroglossia."[26] This, and the general play with language in *Adventure Time*, is the subject of the following section.

Yogaballing with Language

FINN: "Whoa. Fudge man, this place is yogaballs huge!"
JAKE: "Ha, ha, yogaballs aren't that really huge, dude."
FINN: "Hey, man, I can't analyze *everything* that comes out of my mouth."[27]

For Bakhtin, heteroglossia materializes in the language of the novel at any number of points: "Authorial speech, the speeches of narrators,

... the speech of characters," and more often than not in the form of dialogue, where the expressions of lived-language are expressed.[28] The language used in *Adventure Time* is at once the realization of a rich fictional diegetic story-world, and at the same time, inextricably bound to our contemporary world. Even in the cited passage above from "The Limit" (season 2, episode 22), "yogaballs," goes from replacing "fuckin'"—as in "this place is fuckin' huge"—to actual yogaballs: "Yogaballs aren't that really huge, dude." The slip between a signifier for actual yogaballs, to its mobilization as an expletive is seamless, and it is this fluidity that is so characteristic of heteroglossia.

While the communicative function of language depends upon "linguistic unification and centralization, an expression of the centripetal forces of language," the individual articulation of language in everyday speech often resists the gravitational pull of official discourse. *Adventure Time* actively resists "the centripetal forces of language," in the constant word-play, the violation of common word-usage, and the violations of syntax, even in intonation and pronunciation. And again, from the cited passage above, "Yogaballs aren't that really huge, dude," there is a violation of syntax—"that really" is awkward. There is thus a constant tug and pull as the official discourse "makes its real presence felt as a force for overcoming this heteroglossia, imposing specific limits to it, guaranteeing a certain maximum of mutual understanding and crystalizing into a real, although still relative, unity—the unity of the reigning conversational (everyday) and literary language, 'correct language.'"[29] There are moments in *Adventure Time* when this is pressed to the absolute limit of intelligibility, where utterances nearly slip into gibberish, or in some cases into complete nonsense.

Part of the brilliance found in *Adventure Time* is the tapestry of contemporary "hipster" language. Each *Adventure Time* character possesses their own "poetic individuality as reflected in his[/her] language and speech," and it is the careful attunement to each character's individual speech patterns and diction that constructs the poetic stylizing of language in *Adventure Time*. And although Bakhtin was writing about the poetic heteroglossia of language in the novel, *Adventure Time* imbues its internal language with "social heteroglossia and the variety of individual voices in it," which is, for Bakhtin, "the prerequisite for authentic novelistic prose."[30] The heteroglossia in *Adventure Time*, its playful use of language, is part of its enduring charm.

Princess Bubblegum, who reigns over the Candy Kingdom (and is in a sense the default ruler of Ooo), comes the closest to anything resembling an authoritative center—and thus her speech, in most instances, serves as the centripetal force that centers and grounds official discourse. In "Food

Chain," for example, Princess Bubblegum appears to scroll through a "Food Chain wheel," lecturing children of the Candy Kingdom, "The caterpillar eats the leaf. Then the bird eats the caterpillar. Then the big bird eats the little bird. The big bird then dies, and its remains decompose into rich, fertile soil. And from that soil a new plant bursts to life. And then the caterpillar eats the plant again. And so the circle of life continues. This is the law of nature we called 'the food chain.' Isn't that fascinating?" In response, a candy child, Terry, askes, "Yo, Princess Bubblegum, do birds play football?" Princess Bubblegum disappointingly responds, "No, Terry. They don't." Disappointed by the discourse of nature, which was demonstrated in Princess Bubblegum's centripetal language, Terry sighs, "That's weak, Ma'am." Now the camera turns to Finn and Jake, who witnessed Princess Bubblegum's lecture. As they walk out from the crowd, Finn appears to agree with the Candy Kingdom children, "No way I am eating a bug's *butt*. Those kids are right. What's the big *deez* about the food chain, anyway?" While Princess Bubblegum's speech emphasizes the consuming cycle and the nutrient value of organic life, Finn and Jake's clowning around via billingsgate language, aligned with children's talk, constantly serves as the centrifugal forces of heteroglossia. Further, Finn's billingsgate language returns to the lower stratum of bodies (i.e., "what's the big deez"), connecting the consuming organ with the defecation organ (i.e., eating a bug's butt). "Everything from consumption to defecation, from fucking to child-birth," as Bakhtin notes, "the lower stratum is the site of condemn, deny (topographically), kill, bury, send down to the underground, abuse, curse; and at the same time they all conceive anew, fertilize, sow, rejuvenate, praise, and glorify. This general downward thrust, which kills and regenerates, unifies such different phenomena as blows, abuses, the underworld, and the act of devouring."[31] In short, via the constant tug and pull—the centripetal and centrifugal forces in heteroglossia—*Adventure Time* celebrates the cycle of life and at the same time "carnivalizes" language.

There are instances, however, when even Princess Bubblegum utters an Oooian expletive, in the face of some calamity, or mishap. Marceline, is interesting in this respect too, because she once reigned over the Land of Ooo as the Vampire Queen. Her timeline is both ambiguous and mysterious: At the start of the series, she is over 1000 years old, but little about her life history is revealed to the audience. Marceline is irreverent, possesses something of a trickster streak, and lives (despite being undead) to create music. Marceline and Princess Bubblegum prior to the diegetic framing of the *Adventure Time* series were a romantic couple, and they reunite at the conclusion of the series. (In addition, there is an episode in the HBO Max series *Adventure Time: Distant Lands*, "Obsidian," that depicts them living as a couple. The HBO series is independent of the Cartoon Network series, featuring narratives that come before and after the *Adventure Time* diegesis properly speaking.) And in their coupling, we have yet another carnivalesque trope: crowning and decrowning, embodied in their respective reigns. Marceline, as a "commoner" and a song-writer and performer, is more inclined to play with language than Princess Bubblegum.

The gravitational pull of the lower stratums also pulls language away from the imagined anchorage of official discourse. In "Hitman" (season 3, episode 4) Ice King hires a hitman, named Scorcher, to hit (as in punch) Finn and Jake. Scorcher the hired assassin is all business—silent and stoic. Ice King is oblivious to the fact that Scorcher intends to kill Finn and Jake. And, of course, things go awry, and when Ice King attempts to distract Scorcher, to make an escape, the crackpot old wizard exclaims, "Look, a supermodel! Look, a hover-board! Look, the apocalypse!" Ice King switches tactics, moving from the spectacle of sex (supermodel), novelty (hover-board), and cataclysm (apocalypse), to the carnivalesque, "Someone got hit in the boing-loins! Hit in the boing-loins! Boing-loins! Boing-loins. Somebody got hit in them." To begin with the image of a strike to the lower stratums is a typical carnivalesque scenario—and it is repeated multiple times no less. As for the play with language though, there appears to be a few things taking place. While the word "loins" anchors the term "boing-loins" in the lower stratums, "boing" on the other hand pulls away from official discourse. It is possible even without the anchoring term, that "boing" might work on its own, but nonetheless this illustrates how heteroglossia still requires some gravitational center to allow the play with language to work. "Boing" is a near onomatopoeia slang for an erection. Recall the titular characters of the MTV program, *Beavis and Butthead*, who, when encountering an attractive woman, might declare, "boing!" Often when Beavis or Butthead utter such a thing, their bodies might go stiff and rigid (echoing the posture of an erect dick) and extend the utterance to mimic the snapping up of a spring: "boooooiiinnnnngggg!" While Ice King does not parrot Beavis and Butthead's enunciation, the (American media cultural) connotations of the word remain. While "loin" grounds the meaning in the official discourse of the nether regions, "boing" at once pulls away and brings us right back through sexual slang. An erect cock. The sudden snapping up of a dick. And, of course, all of this also resonates with other Bakhtinian principles: grotesque realism, the malleable and changing form of the body, procreation, fecundity, sex. The play of language works in the tug and pull between official discourse and the "carnivalizing" of language.

There are many other instances where playful language is employed to refer to the lower stratums—from the genitals, to procreation, to excretion. The series is peppered with creative terms to refer to the genitals (including the ass), and particularly male genitals. In the episode, "Jake Suit," for example, Jake complains to Finn, "You were a little rough with the Jakesuit today, bro. You mashed up my *doggy bag* pretty hard."[32] In addition to the genitals, other body parts are referred to in playful manners. In the episode, "You Forgot Your Floaties" (season 6, episode 38), Finn, having an uneasy feeling, says, "I got a weird feeling in my *fat-basket*."[33] This imaginative phrase—"fat-basket" referring to Finn's belly—could have easily been torn from the pages of François Rabelais's *The Life of Gargantua and Pantagruel*. Prior to the diegetic frame of the *Adventure Time* series, when Finn was found by Jake's parents, he was a baby crying and stewing in his own mess. Recounting his own origin narrative, Finn recalls, "I went boom boom on a leaf—BOOM! BOOM!—and I fell backwards and sat in my own boom boom, and cried for a day."[34] "Boom boom," of course, being shit and another typical carnivalesque motif. What is more, in this case, Finn's shifting of an onomatopoeic phrasing for an explosive action (either the boom of a cannon, or the explosive passing of a turd), is set in a loose chain of associative connotations inviting us to read "boom boom" as shit. And as cited earlier, similar to "boing," it is the associative connection to a bodily transformation and the sounds (if abstractly) that are associated with such transformations that make this all Bakhtinian.

It is instructive to see how *Adventure Time* has been dubbed into other languages, and how the tug and pull of heteroglossia manifests in other cultural contexts. *Adventure Time*, for example, was broadcasted in the Sinophone world and dubbed into Chinese. For one thing, "Chinese" is an umbrella term for multiple languages. In fact, Sinophone speakers likely share a somewhat similar Chinese writing system, yet the pronunciation of the same word could be completely at odds. Despite the fact that Sinophone speakers share a general understanding of written Chinese, the ways in which Sinophone people from different regions speak are not mutually intelligible. A national language *per se* is *never* a coherent entity. From a linguistic perspective, for example, there are multiple languages with major phonetic distinctions: Mandarin, Cantonese (or "Yue"), Hakka, Wu, Min, and the language variants spoken by Mongolians, Manchus, Tibetans, and so on. In fact, as Sinophone Literature scholar Shu-mei Shih reminds us, a good number of ethnic peoples in contemporary China are multilingual: "They are Sinophone to the extent that they speak and write in the standard language of Han, which they willingly acquire or have imposed on them. The historical minorities such as those in the southwestern border areas also are multilingual communities that resist or adapt to Han Chinese assimilation to different degrees."[35] As Shih insists, an uncritical acceptance of the nationalist historiography of modern China as a victim of the Western colonization, along with China's claim of "territorial integrity," is itself an internal colonialist idea propagated by the Chinese state.[36] Bakhtin's heteroglossia, or "other-languagedness" as Linda Park-Fuller frames it, does not only mean the tug and pull between different national languages.[37] Rather, Bakhtin would argue, the inherent ideologies of various languages are at play. The ways in which a speaker chooses how to speak already exemplifies one's social status and cultural identity. A centripetal/centrifugal system was built by the governmental forces, and in so doing, it rendered other languages as "dialects."

Adventure Time embodies Bakhtin's heteroglossia in a playful manner. The Chinese-dubbed version of *Adventure Time* not just suggests lower social status; more importantly, the inherent dialogism of the dub is constantly winking at the Sinophone viewers like me (Hung). Characters often playfully switch between the centripetal language (i.e., Mandarin) and the centrifugal languages (i.e., slang, Taiwanese Hokkien, English, or even Japanese at times). "All rhetorical forms, monologic in their compositional structure," as Bakhtin notes, "are oriented toward the listener and his answer."[38] Moreover, while Finn mostly speaks in Mandarin (i.e., the northern-regional, intellectual, official language), Jake is dubbed with a strong Cantonese accent (i.e., the southern-regional, vulgar, colloquial language).

Lady Rainicorn serves as another example of heteroglossia. In "My Two Favorite People" (season 1, episode 9), Finn cannot understand Lady Rainicorn's utterance without a Universal Translator device that Jake found at the bottom of lake Szelezon.[39] While Lady Rainicorn mostly speaks Korean in the original English version of *Adventure Time*, in the Chinese version she was dubbed in Taiwanese Hokkien (also known as "*Taigi*"). Despite the fact that Taiwanese Hokkien is widely spoken by more than seventy percent of the population in Taiwan, it is rendered a culturally lowbrow, southern "dialect" of Min Chinese.

Something analogous happens with the original American voice-acting, and the appropriation of racially inflected speech differences. Although characters are not outwardly coded as black, Jake's voice and diction, for example, is inflected with African American colloquialisms. Ice King's Finn and Jake fanfiction, *Fionna and Cake*, establishes a very thinly veiled parallel universe of the Land of Ooo—Ice King merely reverses the gender of Ooo's inhabitants, and gives his characters unimaginative names of Ooo's residents. The protagonists of Ice King's fanfiction, Fionna and Cake, closely correspond to their respective Oooian personalities. Fionna is effectively the female version of Finn, while Cake corresponds to Jake. In addition to being coded female, Cake is also a cat. While Jake's inflection and diction is sometimes coded as African American, despite being voiced by John DiMaggio (who is white), Cake, on the other hand, is voiced by Roz Ryan (a black woman), who plays blackness to the hilt, and is snarkily described by the Ice King as "a bottomless dispenser of cheap sassitude."[40]

As discussed on forums and blogs, some *Adventure Time* fans debate the assimilation of black culture as it manifests in the show's speech and music—such as when Finn and Jake break into free-style raps.[41] *Adventure Time* perhaps straddles the line between the assimilation (or the permeation of black culture into other cultural milieus), and appropriation, which might begin to approach something akin to the auditory equivalent of black-face. Without dismissing this problematic possibility, what this illustrates is the significance of black culture in American life. As it has been said numerous times—especially in the wake of the Black Lives Matter campaign—Americans love black culture, but hate black people. There is undoubtedly a fetishistic assimilation of black culture, and *Adventure Time* was not made in a cultural vacuum. The blackness that manifests in *Adventure Time* illustrates how heteroglossic pressure from marginalized communities has a gravitational pull of its own and can exert its own force on speech patterns and diction, which is most discernible in Jake and Cake.

There is something carnivalesque in Ice King's *Fionna and Cake* fanfiction, where certain elements are reversed (namely, as already stated, a character's gender) and the amplification or exaggeration of other characteristics. This is most pronounced in the black-coding of Cake, where blackness manifests in the form of African American Vernacular English (AAVE), which is an "African American linguistic" style that has "its complex histories, structures, uses and politics"; as Angela Reyes argues "AAVE is not 'bad' English; rather, AAVE has its own rule-governed system comprised of phonological, morphological, syntactic and discourse features."[42] And just as billingsgate culture asserts its own gravitational pull-on official discourse (as Bakhtin says of the medieval marketplace), so too does AAVE on the so-called "standard" American English. Cake amplifies the less explicit blackness found in Jake's diction and enunciation.

Adventure Time as an articulation of hipster culture, appropriates elements of blackness as a form of cultural cachet—along with all its other idiosyncratic elements (peculiar narrative rhythms, neologisms, grotesque realism). This lends *Adventure Time* its charming quirkiness and sets it apart from mainstream media that largely peddles in official discourse (and standard accents, etc.). And it is this charming quirkiness that finds affinities with the use of slang, which "is associated with signaling coolness and engagement in youth culture [...] It has also been viewed as signifying resistance to established structures of power."[43] Citing James Sledd, Reyes adds further that "to use slang is to deny allegiance to the existing order."[44] *Adventure Time's* narrative and linguistic quirkiness is in effect its own "slang," which lends it the cultural cachet that it enjoys. And significantly, this quirkiness, again just like slang, does not necessarily "mean" anything as such, but it has a "feeling." Slang does not necessarily mark "a clear lexical territory," as Reyes observes, but rather it "describes a fluid range of words and expressions that locates its users within some social terrain."[45] Just as linguistic shifters (e.g., here, there, I, me) are contingent upon the individual enunciating them, "slang terms also rely partly on surrounding context for their meaningfulness, while making salient particular aspects of context."[46] While particular slang demonstrates an affiliation with a certain social group (e.g., generation, race or ethnic demographic, class), when slang is deployed from an individual outside the specific social milieu it can be painfully awkward, and in fact signal exclusion from the group.[47] *Adventure Time* in its deeply self-aware hipsterism is mildly awkward—when Finn raps, for example, it's a bit "off," but this is also part of *Adventure Time's* charm. Furthermore, in its self-awareness, *Adventure Time* appears to be actively playing with the tug and pull of heteroglossia, and capitalizing on AAVE as part of this playfulness. This use of AAVE is therefore just one more way that *Adventure Time* yogaballs language.

Conclusion: Ooo, Where Bakhtin Lives...

Mikhail Bakhtin lurks everywhere in the Land of Ooo—from the streets of the Candy Kingdom, to the Nightosphere, and everywhere in-between. Bakhtin's notions of the carnivalesque, grotesque realism, adventure time, and heteroglossia make *Adventure Time* the quirky and playful series that it is (and that we love!). The carnivalesque, in all its manifestations—the usurpation of authority, the topsy-turvy world, the clowning around, the celebration of folklife, the turn toward the lower stratums—occur over and over again as common motifs in the series. Perhaps one of the most potent tropes in the carnivalesque, grotesque realism, likewise proliferates throughout the series. *Adventure Time* plays with the human body and with its organs: these displaced, exaggerated, and, in a word, fetishized body parts recall Bakhtin's grotesque realism. And "adventure time," which seems impossibly coincidental, is also an important part of the *Adventure Time* series: from all the myriad quests, all the excursions, all the injuries and deaths (Finn dies at least twice in the series), which hold little or no bearing on the final overarching narrative.

In addition to these carnivalesque and literary tropes, *Adventure Time* regularly yogaballs language. The heteroglot force of hipster culture materializes in the diction, phrasing, syntax, and tone of the various characters that populate the Land of Ooo. Each character serves as a marionette, a device "where centrifugal as well as centripetal forces are brought to bear." The Land of Ooo is the stage upon which "[t]he processes of centralization and decentralization, of unification and disunification, intersect in the utterance; the utterance not only answers the requirements of its own language as an individualized embodiment of a speech act, but it answers the requirements of heteroglossia as well; it is in fact an active participant in such speech diversity."[48] *Adventure Time*, in its 8-year run, actively participated in the tug and pull on official discourse and playfully diversified speech—and this is yet one more place where the fun never ends!

ACKNOWLEDGMENTS

We would like to thank our colleague, Artel Great, for references regarding the appropriation of black culture.

NOTES

1. Aaron Kerner and Julian Hoxter, *Theorizing Stupid Media*, 109–137.
2. Mikhail Bakhtin, *Rabelais and His World*, 363–364.
3. Aaron Kerner, *Abject Pleasures*.
4. "Food Chain" (Season 6, episode 7).
5. Kerner, *Abject Pleasures*.
6. Kerner.
7. "The comic performers of the marketplace were an important source of the grotesque image of the body. They formed a huge and motley world that we can only touch upon here. All these jugglers, acrobats, vendors of panaceas, magicians, clowns, trainers of monkeys, had a sharply expressed grotesque bodily character. Even today this character has been mostly fully preserved in marketplace shows and in the circus." Bakhtin, *Rabelais and His World*, 353.
8. Kerner, *Abject Pleasures*.
9. Bakhtin, *Rabelais and His World*, 341.
10. Bakhtin, 318.
11. Bakhtin, 328.
12. Bakhtin, 344.
13. Bakhtin.
14. Bakhtin, 345.
15. Bakhtin, 318.
16. Bakhtin.
17. Kerner and Hoxter, *Theorizing Stupid Media*, 120–122.
18. Mikhail Bakhtin, *The Dialogic Imagination*, 91.
19. Bakhtin.
20. Kerner and Hoxter, *Theorizing Stupid Media*, 125. The following three paragraphs are adapted from this work.
21. Kerner and Hoxter, 124.

22. "Come Along with Me" (Season 10, episode 13).
23. Mikhail Bakhtin apud Kerner and Hoxter, *Theorizing Stupid Media*, 134.
24. Kerner and Hoxter, 123.
25. See this wiki site for a list of *Adventure Time* slang: https://adventuretime.fandom.com/wiki/List_of_Slang_in_Adventure_Time.
26. Bakhtin, *The Dialogic Imagination*, 270–271.
27. "The Limit" (Season 2, episode 22).
28. Bakhtin, *The Dialogic Imagination*, 263.
29. Bakhtin, 270.
30. Bakhtin, 264.
31. Bakhtin, *Rabelais and His World*, 435.
32. "Jake Suit" (Season 5, episode 27).
33. "You Forgot Your Floaties" (Season 6, episode 38).
34. "Memories of Boom Boom Mountain" (Season 1, episode 10).
35. Shu-mei Shih, "The Concept of the Sinophone," 713.
36. Shih, 711.
37. Linda M. Park-Fuller, "Voices," 1–12.
38. Bakhtin, *The Dialogic Imagination*, 280.
39. "My Two Favorite People" (season 1, episode 9).
40. Martin Olson, *The Adventure Time Encyclopedia*, 104.
41. For example, see Lady Geek Girl and Friends, "Is Being Ambiguously Black a Good Thing or a Bad Thing?"
42. Angela Reyes, "Appropriation of African American Slang by Asian American Youth," 510. Reyes directs us to: John Baugh, *Black Street Speech: Its History, Structure, and Survival* (Austin, Texas: University of Texas Press, 1983); William Labov, *Language in the Inner City: Studies in the Black English Vernacular* (Philadelphia, Pennsylvania: University of Pennsylvania Press, 1972); and Salikoko Mufwene et al. (eds.), *African-American English: Structure, History, and Use* (New York: Routledge. 1998).
43. Reyes, 512.
44. James Sledd, "On Not Teaching English Usage," 699; Reyes, 512-513.
45. Reyes, 513. See Connie Eble, "Slang," in *Language in the USA: Themes for the Twenty-first Century*, Edward Finegan and John R. Rickford eds. (Cambridge, U.K.: Cambridge University Press, 2004), 375-386.
46. Reyes, 514. Reyes references: Emil Benveniste, *Problems in General Linguistics* (Coral Gables, Florida: University of Miami Press, 1971); Charles Peirce, *Collected Papers of Charles Sanders Peirce* (Cambridge, MA: Harvard University Press, 1932); and Michael Silverstein, "Shifters, Linguistic Categories, and Cultural Description," in *Meaning in Anthropology*. Keith Basso and Henry A. Selby eds. (Albuquerque, NM: University of New Mexico Press, 1976), 11–55.
47. Reyes.
48. Bakhtin, *The Dialogic Imagination*: 272.

REFERENCES

Bailey, Benjamin. "Heteroglossia and boundaries." In *Bilingualism: A Social Approach*, pp. 257–274. Palgrave Macmillan, London, 2007.
Bakhtin, Mikhail. *Rabelais and His World*. Translated by Helene Iswolsky. Bloomington: Indiana University Press, 1984.
Bakhtin, Mikhail. *The Dialogic Imagination: Four Essays*. Michale Holquist ed., translation by Caryl Emerson and Michael Holquist. Austin: University of Texas Press, 1981.
Kerner, Aaron. *Abject Pleasures in the Cinematic*. Edinburgh: Edinburgh University Press, 2023.
Kerner, Aaron, and Hoxter, Julian. *Theorizing Stupid Media: De-Naturalizing Story Structures in the Cinematic, Televisual, and Videogames*. Cham: Palgrave Macmillan, 2019.

Lady Geek Girl and Friends. "Is Being Ambiguously Black a Good Thing or a Bad Thing?" *Lady Geek Girl and Friends* blog (August 6, 2014): https://ladygeekgirl.wordpress.com/2014/08/06/is-being-ambiguously-black-a-good-thing-or-a-bad-thing/.

Olson, Martin. *The Adventure Time Encyclopedia: Inhabitants, Lore, Spells, and Ancient Crypt Warnings of the Land of Ooo Circa 19.56 B.G.E. - 501 A.G.E.* New York: Abrams, 2013.

Park-Fuller, Linda M. "Voices: Bakhtin's heteroglossia and polyphony, and the performance of narrative literature." *Text and Performance Quarterly* vol. 7, no. 1 (1986): 1–12.

Rampton, Ben. "From 'multi-ethnic adolescent heteroglossia' to 'contemporary urban vernaculars.'" *Language & Communication* vol. 31, no. 4 (2011): 276–294.

Reyes, Angela. "Appropriation of African American Slang by Asian American Youth 1." *Journal of Sociolinguistics* vol. 9, no. 4 (2005): 509–532.

Shih, Shu-mei. "The Concept of the Sinophone." *PMLA/Publications of the Modern Language Association of America* vol. 126, no. 3 (2011): 709–718.

Sledd, James. "On Not Teaching English Usage." *English Journal* 54 (1965): 698–703.

"And we will happen again and again"
Adventure Time *and the Sisyphean Struggle*

Sequoia Stone

When the miniseries *Stakes* aired in 2015 during the show's seventh season, *Adventure Time* had already begun to shed its seeming silliness and irreverence in order to tackle deeper storylines. By season seven, Finn the Human has lost an arm, confronted his father, accepted his role as a force of good, and effectively "grown from boy to almost-man"[1]; Jake the Dog has become a father and "moved from happy wanderer to something like adulthood"[2]; and Princess Bubblegum has lost her Candy Kingdom and must come to terms with the dawning realization that her reign was anything but perfect. Indeed, as *Vox* writer Emily St. James observes, by the time *Stakes* begins, "everybody on *Adventure Time* is growing up in one way or another."[3]

Maturation arguably distinguishes not just the show's characters, however. The show's increasing complexity—beginning in season four—features it developing its moral and philosophical undertones in earnest. *Stakes* itself is a philosophically weighty narrative, one which prompts St. James to comment "The closest thing *Adventure Time* has to a moral message is this: Change is good. Growth is good. Supporting others' growth is good. And accepting others when they need to change is the best thing you can do. The only thing that's bad is stasis. And nowhere was that more apparent than in *Stakes*, the program's first miniseries" (St. James). While the theme of change appears throughout the series, *Adventure Time*'s engagement with change goes far beyond simply promoting it as "good." This is especially apparent in *Stakes*, as Marceline grapples with her vampiric immortality and gives it up, only to end the miniseries a vampire once again in a seemingly cyclical pattern. In effect, the show suggests that no human effort or labor can control the cycles of fate. While this could yield nihilistic despair, the arc of *Stakes* demonstrates the possibility of joy, connection, and hope in the face of precariousness, absurdity, and existential dread.

In the process, *Adventure Time* becomes a productive space for both existentialism and optimism. Taking place in a world marred by post-nuclear fallout, with the globe literally carved out, *Adventure Time* is set over and against humanity's greatest existential dread. This post-apocalyptic setting also develops *Adventure Time*'s treatment of cyclical patterns, as it does not simply allow the world to rebuild after nuclear war. When the narrative looks towards its imagined future, in episodes such as the finale, it demonstrates a future Ooo that has again succumbed to the "fall" of civilization, potentially suggesting a hopeless and hapless march toward unhappy endings. There are no easy or comforting endings in *Adventure Time*, no ultimate heroic act to change the heart of humanity forever, and no cosmic justice for those who are "bad" or "good." Instead, *Adventure Time* shifts audience's expectation of what an "end" looks like and means in order to illustrate that, while the endless grind of life can feel "pointless and absurd," seemingly "lead[ing] nowhere and add[ing] up to nothing,"[4] there still exists the ability to thrive.

To understand this, the work of Albert Camus is useful, specifically *The Myth of Sisyphus*. In Greek mythology, Sisyphus is a clever mortal man who manages to cheat death. As punishment, the gods sentence him to the eternal torment of endlessly rolling a boulder up a hill in the underworld. The myth has inspired the idea of a "Sisyphean" task or struggle, which "describes a task as seemingly endless and futile—you keep doing it but it never gets done."[5] For Camus, Sisyphus represents a more complex mindset. In Camus' reading, Sisyphus:

> …teaches the higher fidelity that negates the gods and raises rocks. He too concludes that all is well. This universe henceforth without a master seems to him neither sterile nor futile. Each atom of that stone, each mineral flake of that night-filled mountain, in itself forms a world. The struggle itself towards the heights is enough to fill a man's heart. One must imagine Sisyphus happy.[6]

Camus uses the figure of Sisyphus to grapple with the absurd and the seeming purposelessness of modern life, one where mortal life means being caught in an endless grind within which one ultimately achieves nothing. Camus effectively repurposes Sisyphus as a figure still capable of agency, enough to "raise rocks" and "negate gods." In the admittedly endless torment of Sisyphus' labor, Camus believes Sisyphus remains a "master" of his own universe.

Camus' reading of Sisyphus encapsulates the ways in which *Adventure Time* captures both the inescapable patterns of life and the agency that one nonetheless wields within those patterns. In different ways, *Adventure Time* demonstrates that the Sisyphean, circular struggle of life, history, and the future need not be a joyless or despairing grind. While the "struggle itself towards the heights" may seem scary or fruitless at times, *Adventure Time* urges us to stop impossibly hoping that one day we can set down our boulder. Instead, we must find ways to live fulfilling, rich lives within the endless labors of human life. By subverting audience expectations for a "happy ending," *Adventure Time* forces a reckoning with the Sisyphean struggles within which we are all caught. In doing so, the show places emphasis on each individual's ability to thrive within the limitations of ones' own struggles and circumstances.

The Mushroom War and Life After It

Part of what makes *Adventure Time* a productive space for exploring existentialist facts of life is its setting as a post-nuclear-fallout civilization. On the specter of nuclear war, Crosby writes:

> Most of us are citizens of nation states that would become embroiled in a global nuclear conflict, were it to take place. And even if some are not, we must all live on the same earth. So there is no way we can be immune to the threat of unimaginable suffering and devastation posed by these weapons. How can we live secure, meaningful lives in the face of a threat of this magnitude, a threat which can not only wipe out whole cities and millions of lives in a few minutes, but also places in dire jeopardy the structures and resources of human civilization itself? … We seem doomed either actually to suffer the unimaginable carnage of another world war, this time fought with nuclear weapons, or to be consumed by the constant anxiety of our realization that such a war can begin at any moment.[7]

This inescapable fear of "global nuclear conflict" is partly what propelled existential philosophy forward in intellectual spaces as the "constant anxiety" associated with postmodern dangers made previous approaches to understanding life obsolete. *Adventure Time* exists in this place where "human civilization" has violently collapsed, meaning humanity's greatest fear has been actualized. In the beginning of the series, the establishment of this setting is subtle or quick, and never explained. We see, among other things, twisted metal ruins scattered amongst a cartoon forest, an abandoned bombshell in the corner of the screen, and the mysterious crater hollowing out the globe of the earth. However, as the show progresses Ooo emerges as a world built on the bones of human society destroyed by a nuclear holocaust.

One of the ways in which the show illuminates the story and impact of the nuclear war is through Marceline, who is one of the few main characters in the narrative who lived both before and during the war. Different backstory snippets reveal that being half-demon allowed Marceline to survive the apocalypse and eventually grow up under the care of Simon Petrikov. When Simon succumbs to evil magic and becomes the bumbling antagonist Ice King, Marceline once again finds herself alone. In the companion book *Adventure Time: The Enchiridion & Marcy's Super Secret Scrapbook!!!* (2015), the period of Marceline's life immediately after the "Mushroom War" is explored in Simon's journal, titled "Weekly Records in the Wreckage of the World (Or What's Left of It)."[8] Left to fend for herself in "what's left" of the world, Marceline exists in a space that realizes humanity's core existential dread, haunted by the question "How could this once beautiful world turn into a Wasteland?"[9] We also learn from Simon's journal that he and Marceline are totally alone in a world of the dead, with cities populated by "transparent ghosts. Hundreds of ghost pedestrians walking up and down the streets below."[10] Within this "Wasteland" full of ghosts, Marceline—and, thus, *Adventure Time*—is within a space where the worst has come to pass. Marceline's struggle, then, is to understand how one can exist or persist in and through that sort of entropic state. This is highlighted when Simon remarks in *Marcy's Super Secret Scrapbook!!!* that "Marceline and I seem to be the only ones left ... survival comes first."[11] If one can only hope to survive the unknowable, terrible, or inevitable, cursed to push the boulder up the hill, is there any way to thrive?

This tension between surviving and thriving becomes the basis for Marceline's journey in *Stakes*. The first episode of the miniseries begins with Marceline's struggles with her own immortality and her immortal form. Marceline sits in the shade of a tree, trying to extend her hand into the sunlight for her umbrella, only to burn and then instantly heal. As she attempts this again and again, she tells herself: "It'll only hurt for a second. That's nothing in the face of eternity," only to concede that "a second hurts really bad in the face of eternity."[12] In the shade of the tree, Marceline is visually restricted and imprisoned by the confines of her body and the restrictions that being a vampire imposes on her. This brings to a boil Marceline's own existential anxieties as it prompts her to decide to ask Bubblegum to remove her vampiric essence.[13] Explaining to Bubblegum her wish to relinquish both her immortality and vampiric powers, she says, "[When I] became a vampire, I was just a messed-up kid. Now it's 1,000 years later, and I'm still messed up. I don't want to spend eternity like this, with this emptiness. I want to grow up."[14] For Marceline, immortality presents a ceaseless Sisyphean struggle where she is a perpetually "messed up kid" who cannot "grow up." According to Crosby, at the root of much existential dread is the sense that "even if an organism manages to survive the threats and dangers that imperil the course of its life on every side, it cannot escape the finality of its death ... and thus of the aimlessness and futility of the life struggle as a whole."[15] In *Stakes,* however, Marceline views death as her "last adventure"[16] and Bubblegum affirms that her "natural life-span is going to be richer and fuller than you can imagine."[17] If death, then, is not the source of anxiety in *Stakes,* what is Marceline grappling with as she is trapped in the shade of the tree? In short, Marceline's inner battle in *Stakes* reflects the struggle between surviving (or barely surviving) and joyously thriving.

In this manner, we see illustrated Crosby's point that all human "striving is rooted in deficiency and need, and thus in pain. Each organized form of nature, including human beings, everywhere encounters resistance to its strivings and must struggle to wrest from its surroundings whatever satisfaction it can achieve."[18] If "striving" for survival is thus inherently rooted in deficiency, a life based only in survival is one based most acutely in overcoming resistance, obstacles, and barely-met needs. This brings us back to the myth of Sisyphus and the belief "that there is no more dreadful punishment than futile and hopeless labor."[19] This is the life that Marceline had as a child, surviving with Simon post-fallout, and thus what she carries as a frozen "messed up kid" in her immortal life. The desire for something *more* than survival manifests in *Stakes* when, with a group of humans who are rebuilding life after the apocalypse, Marceline sings a theme song from the sitcom *Mr. Belvedere* (1985–90), which notably includes the line: "Life is more than mere survival/And we just might live the good life yet."[20] A desire for a "good life" as opposed to "mere survival" seems to be what haunts Marceline in *Stakes* as she attempts to envision a life that—even if it involves death—feels "fuller" than her immortal existence. What exactly a "good life" entails or looks like remains necessarily ambiguous in *Adventure Time,* but fundamentally the show demonstrates the importance of embracing change, loss, and the unknown in order to fully enjoy and experience ones' own part in the world at large.

While Marceline believes she must relinquish her vampirism to find the "good life," which would imply that in order to be happy or fulfilled Marceline must *not* be a vampire any longer, her journey in *Stakes* ultimately subverts that expectation. After Marceline gives up her vampirism, she has two visions of an imagined future. In the first, she sings, "Time, sweet time/Don't slip away from me/Love/it flows like a garden hose," while dreaming of a slightly older version of herself (complete with grey stripes in her hair) with Simon and his long-lost love Betty in a cozy home.[21] This vision potentially reflects the desire for a stable home and the "love" that "flows" within such a space. In the second vision, Marceline's singing of "It's spring again" lingers in the background as Bubblegum's henchman Peppermint Butler digs a grave. Marceline then continues, "And the yard is full of tiny flowers/You used to call them weeds" while a young Bubblegum kisses a visibly older, gaunt Marceline.[22] Both visions express a fundamental desire to live a life that is "more" than survival. Marceline craves love, safety, and companionship. This newfound ability to articulate what she might need comes across when Marceline muses that she has a "weird feeling in my tums [...] not fear. I know what that feels like. So maybe it's love?"[23] Previously, Marceline could only appreciate "fear" but now she is cautiously able to embrace "love." While these visions involve an aging Marceline, and thus one who is not a vampire, they do not project a future that is only possible if Marceline is not a vampire. They reveal that Marceline truly wants connection and comfort.

Marceline is partly able to evolve into a person who can achieve a "good life" as she confronts her own patterns of survival. Upon facing her past as the "messed up kid" simply surviving, Marceline chooses to do something different. In this choice, Marceline is positioned to "thrive" in and through her own Sisyphean struggles. After spending the whole of *Stakes* battling the vampires from her past, and thus seemingly unable to escape the very things she tried to shed, Marceline feels defeated. In this moment, Simon (as the Ice King) tells her: "You and me—we're survivors, right? Like cockroaches or rats. Sure, you could fight and try to save the day, but what if you lose? Then what? You could die. Better to run and hide like a rat, right, buddy?"[24] This moment captures the opposing forces facing Marceline, who must acknowledge that her pattern of being a "survivor" means running and hiding—from danger as well as difficult feelings. For Marceline, then, resolving existential dread does not mean (simply) facing or accepting death, as might be more traditionally associated with such a journey. Instead, she, like us all, must figure out a way to overcome "survival" in order to thrive.

Breaking the Wheel

With the depiction of Marceline working through these issues, *Adventure Time's* optimistic existential philosophy develops. In particular, the depiction of Sisyphean cycles emphasizes the ways in which it is possible to live in the present and be "happy." One of the "lessons" that Marceline must learn in *Stakes* is that, in order to achieve this happiness, one must be able to relinquish the comfort of the "known" or the familiar in order to give oneself a chance to adapt to new ways of being that are indeed possible within the existential grind of life. This idea first arises when the vampires that Marceline slayed hundreds of years prior return after they are released from Marceline's removed vampiric essence and begin to interact with the modern world with different results. The Empress, a traditionally stylish and aloof female vampire, complains: "Pah! It tastes different here! Where are we? It's like we fell asleep on a raft and woke up in strange seas [...] Where are the comforts of the old hive? The minions ... the blood.... The good blood, with the gold leaf flaked into it."[25] The desire here for the "comforts of the old hive" positions the vampires as creatures of habit, as creatures of the past. Hierophant, a similarly suave vampire, exhorts his fellows to return to tradition in the new world because "surely diverging from the old ways is what made [them] vulnerable the first time" to Marceline's attack.[26] A presumed correlation between vulnerability and progress seems to establish the vampires as representative of a mindset that clings to what is known and so refuses to embrace or adapt to the flux of the present moment, making them antithetical to Marceline's journey to grow in order to find the "good life."

Notably, the necessity of embracing the ever-changing present in order to achieve the "good life" emerges through the Vampire King's rejection of vampiric tradition. Unlike the other humanoid vampires, the Vampire King is a chimera-like being with the head of a lion, lizard hands, and chicken feet. As the most dangerous, and least human, of the vampires, the expectation is for the Vampire King to be the most committed to the vampire's heyday in the past. However, he rejects such an enthrallment, telling the Empress that the "good blood" with the gold leaf was "stupid. It didn't taste like anything."[27] This rejection, while played for humor, demonstrates a frank abandonment of outmoded tradition, which often includes clinging to beliefs or practices that no longer make sense or ever brought joy. Additionally, tradition and its practices can provide a false comfort vis-à-vis continuity and consistency, creating an assurance of permanency that *Adventure Time* argues cannot exist. For the Vampire King, the vampires' rebirth represents a "new era! Old-fashioned ideas have no place here."[28] To demonstrate the peril of bringing "old fashioned" ideas into this "new era," Hierophant is destroyed by his refusal to give up the past. Labeled a "dumb ... sad old relic!" by Peppermint Butler,[29] Hierophant gives up a potential alliance with Marceline because he will not stop drinking blood instead of the color "red" (as does Marceline). The Vampire King, in another demonstration of a true willingness/wish to evolve, tells Marceline: "My thirst for blood is an awesome force. But in these new times, I have a chance to try ... a different course."[30] Because, in contrast, Hierophant cannot change both his ways and the way he interacts with the world around him, he tells the gang: "Because that's what an old-school vampire does!"[31] before entering a (Jake) house uninvited and thus dying. His death—and the death of the other vampires—implies that an old-school vampire who cannot "get with the times" can only perish as they cannot adapt themselves to the ever-changing world around them.[32] This then sets up Marceline's personal growth in *Stakes* as one where she must, in contrast, reject stasis and adapt to the present moment. In rejecting the belief system of the old vampires, Marceline becomes a figure who is not bound to the false "comfort" of familiarity. Instead, she reckons with and understands that in order to "thrive" one must accept both the things that change and, importantly, the things that cannot change.

It is through her relationship with the Vampire King that Marceline learns how to embrace her immortality, and thus realize meaning and purpose within her own Sisyphean struggle, as opposed to fruitlessly attempting to avoid this struggle completely. Because the Vampire King was the vampire who "changed" Marceline in the past, he represents the original loss of Marceline's mortality and thus the impetus for her emotional journey in *Stakes*. Originally, in Marceline's vampire-killing past, the Vampire King saw the changing of Marceline into a vampire not only as "another way ... to save [his] people"[33] after she had driven the vampires to extinction, but also as a way for her to "[pay] a price" for her powers.[34] For the Vampire King, changing Marceline offers to restore a sense of cosmic balance. When the Vampire King bites Marceline, changing her into a vampire, he allows her stake to be pressed into his heart, creating an ouroboros-like transference of death and power,[35] visually indicating the cyclical nature of their relationship and intertwined destiny. When the Vampire King returns, however, he refuses to fight Marceline again, telling her: "This is the old way—Agents of darkness and light in a tug-of-war. But now a creature can step out of that struggle. In this age, why would I want to be the Vampire King anymore?"[36] As the main antagonist urges the protagonist to "step out" of the "struggle" within which they find themselves, *Stakes* becomes fantastically complex.

This complexity is due in part to the ways in which the Vampire King and Marceline are both able to identify but not necessarily break the cyclical patterns within which they are caught. In focusing on these patterns, *Adventure Time* emphasizes the ways in which the Sisyphean struggles of life are unavoidable and often larger than our understanding, but the show does this in order to foreground the potential still within these cycles. When the Vampire King asks Marceline, "What's the one thing you've noticed about the world since you beat me all those hundreds of years ago?" she responds, thoughtfully, that "Everything repeats over and over again. No one learns anything because no one lives long enough to see the pattern, I guess."[37] With her long life, Marceline has the perspective to understand that one *does* have the power of choice even within the relentless circuitry of past precedent. When Marceline expresses that she does not know how to choose a different path as it is like "a black hole—an unknown,"[38] the Vampire King responds,

> I'm not afraid of the unknown! I have the power to change destiny! ... Spill my guts or face the unknown! Either way, I will not bite. For turning you would subjugate me to the wheel of fortune, and I am a King, not a hamster. My path runs straight into the void on a sick, flaming chariot![39]

Importantly, the Vampire King identifies the "wheel of fortune" as something that would "subjugate" him if he chose to follow the same path as before, and that in order to break this cycle one must choose the "void."

However, *Stakes* ultimately does not posit that it is entirely possible for one to change destiny or understand and dismantle cosmic patterns. After all, we are not vampire kings ourselves. Yet as *Stakes* reveals that the "easy" solution of Marceline relinquishing her vampirism is not possible, *Stakes* does demonstrate that it is possible for Marceline to achieve what she wants within the loops of destiny. In essence, Marceline and the audience come to the realization that with "bewilderment and absurdity ... wrenching pain, catastrophic loss, [and] death" (all of which are facts of existence), we can no less try to "live for the present and try to experience as much of life as we can in the present ... with a proud defiance and freedom ... without despair."[40] The first example of this, presented to both Marceline and the audience, is the Vampire King. After the Vampire King removes his vampire energy in an effort to break the wheel and choose a different path, he becomes a nondescript lion. With him now voiceless, it befalls us to imagine whether or not this is the new life he craved. However, the last image that we have of the Vampire King in *Stakes* is of him in his new lion form contentedly laying down on a grassy hill under the stars before he closes his eyes to sleep. After seven episodes' worth of discord and an implied lifetime of violence, this peaceful slumber seems to demonstrate the possibility of finding the "good life" within Sisyphean patterns.

An emphasis on the acceptance of past and future pain and pleasure with accompanying prioritization of living fully in the present emerges through the song "Everything Stays," which becomes the emotional lynchpin of the miniseries. Narrative grounding for this philosophical upshot begins when the Vampire King's vampiric energy, once released, becomes a massive dark cloud. Marceline, after hearing from Simon that they've always been "survivors," chooses a life more than "mere survival" and sucks the soul/essence of the dark cloud in an effort to save her friends. However, confrontation with her past causes the Dark Cloud to "bite" her, thus transforming her once again into an undead entity.[41] Marceline thus ends up a vampire again, once again turned by the Vampire King and repeating the same cycle as before. In highlighting both Marceline and the

Vampire King's desire to change their fate, then indicating how they end up replicating the same pattern, *Adventure Time* underscores the point that avoiding these cycles is impossible. However, that does not mean it is impossible to find the "good life" within them. This is where the philosophy of "Everything Stays" comes into play, providing an emotional and philosophical center to the miniseries and show at large. Poignantly, this song addresses the inevitable cycles of life. All that we have known or will know "will fade.... Ever so slightly, daily and nightly/In little ways." More dangerously, powerful forces such as the ocean are controlled by sublime forces like the "tide," which can "cause you to drown." Both the small changes that all things undergo and the brutal and unknowable forces that threaten human life speak to the existentialist nature of mortal life on earth. While the Vampire King believes they could choose not to be "subjugated" by the wheel of fortune, "Everything Stays" suggests that no individual can fully understand or "break" the unknowable forces of time, destiny, or death. For Marceline, this means ending up—in many ways— right where she started, a vampire again.

Importantly, the fact that "Everything stays right where you left it" offers comfort. To be sure, this idea that "everything stays" still speaks to Sisyphus pushing his boulder up the hill again and again, but *Adventure Time* infuses this reality with optimism. Much of existential dread wraps around the knowledge that all "our longed-for pleasures, attainments, and moments of fulfillment" will "disappear as soon as they have come, and we must learn to live with the fatal realization that nothing can last."[42] While *Stakes*, as demonstrated through "Everything Stays," does not attempt to disprove this fear, it offers a different perspective. As Marceline's mother reassures her in a flashback during *Stakes,* unfamiliar or scary things "might just be something familiar viewed from a different angle. And that's not scary, right?"[43] Yes, all "longed-for pleasures" will come to an end, but this does not have to be a terrifying or dispiriting prospect. Within the cyclical nature of suffering, sadness, toil, and death, there is time and opportunity to make the "good life" that is possible in ones' own lifetime.

After being changed into a vampire once again, Marceline finishes *Stakes* in a new space of acceptance. She does not receive the end we, as the audience, might expect after seeing her begin the miniseries constrained within her own vampiric body. However, even though she is a vampire once more, Marceline no longer suffers under the same mental constraints she began with. Finn asks her, in the final episode of the miniseries, "Are you, uh ... do you feel bad? I don't want to say like, 'I'm sorry about who you are' or anything if you're feeling okay, but I don't know how bad news all of this is...."[44] To this, Marceline responds: "Nah, I'm cool being a vampire again. Being mortal was good. At the same time, it was terrifying. Now I'm a vampire with fresh mortal memories and—I don't know—more empathy or something. More grown-up. Bonnie, thank you for helping me grow up. Now, I guess we get to hang out together forever."[45] Finn's trepidation that Marceline might "feel bad" about what she is speaks to the struggle with which *Stakes* opened, as Marceline had earlier felt she had to give up her vampirism in order to be happy. However, Marceline's narrative arc in *Stakes* endows her with important tools such as "fresh" memories and "empathy" in order for her to feel "grown up." After confronting the patterns of both her life and the world at large, Marceline's ability to be content and accept/appreciate the good amongst the inevitable bad allows her to no longer be that "messed up kid." In her assurance that she and Princess Bubblegum can "hang out" forever, Marceline realizes the visions she had of spending her life with Bubblegum, and she ends *Stakes* ready to embark on that "good life" she once craved.

Will Happen, Happening, Happened

While Marceline's mini coming-of-age ends here in *Stakes,* its philosophy sets up *Adventure Time*'s handling of its own imagined future—one that is cyclical, too. Instead of working only to establish the end of our current civilization, which creates the world of "Ooo" in *Adventure Time,* the series goes on to demonstrate that even "Ooo" will end someday. In the episodes "Lemonhope" and "Graybles 1000+," we are offered glimpses of the future Ooo that demonstrate a Sisyphean cycle of destruction. In both episodes, Finn and Jake's iconic, Peter Pan-esque treehouse home is now a large tree that has grown far out of frame. The surrounding grasslands, once a verdant green and sight of various hijinks, are now brown with the refuse of spaceships and a big, modern city surrounding the Candy Kingdom. This in and of itself might otherwise be a marker of progress and modernization after *Adventure Time*'s narrative ends, but the city, we learn, is also in decay with broken windows and collapsing buildings, with not a citizen to be seen.[46] This, then, implies that the Candy Kingdom has experienced growth, potential prosperity, and, eventually, another fall.[47] Instead of offering an optimistic or utopian vision of its fictional and post-apocalyptic world, *Adventure Time* emphasizes, to borrow from Crosby, the "frequent frustration and perplexity, and the impossibility of arriving at, or ever being able to know that we have arrived at, absolute solutions."[48]

This treatment of the future becomes the basis for the last episode of the series. Just as *Adventure Time* subverts expectations with Marceline's fate in *Stakes,* its finale shifts audience understanding of what a "happy" ending means. Instead of immediately continuing the tense, World War plot that leads up to the finale, "Come Away with Me" begins with a strange—yet familiar—narrative and set of characters. There is a new opening sequence that resembles the original but with new heroes (i.e., "Shermy and Beth" instead of Finn and Jake) situated in a new location (i.e., "far-off future lands"). Without any context for who these characters are, there are still clear visual ties between them and Finn and Jake, with Beth's coloring and design and Shermy's rabbit ears echoing Finn's iconic white hat.[49] The two characters also live in Marceline's home, simultaneously linking them to the familiar while also implying the displacement of beloved characters. The sense of being in a distant future is furthered when Beth and Shermy marvel over Finn's robotic arm and wonder: "It looks so old, Beth. Whose do you think it is, or *was*?"[50]

This sense of discovering or unearthing the past continues when Beth and Shermy find BMO, who now lives in a home full of artifacts from the past.[51] This monument to the past evokes nostalgia for familiar and beloved details of *Adventure Time* while establishing the ephemerality of these things. When presented with Finn's arm, BMO responds that it "belonged to my best friend, Fred [...] No, not Fred. His name was.... Phil."[52] BMO forgetting Finn's name strikes a deeply sad note in this series finale which as a finale is already a heart wrenching exercise in "goodbye." Along with other details, the performance of moving on that occurs with BMO forgetting Finn's name enacts the show's ultimate assertion that "there is no enduring meaning of the past [and] no reliability of the future."[53]

However, within this sense that there is no enduring presence of the past or any certain future remains *Adventure Time's* particular optimism. In the finale, the song "Time Adventure" becomes a kind of mirror to "Everything Stays," similarly expressing a philosophy of embracing the unknowable and living in the present moment as the present moment itself changes. While it is true that "our attempts to restore the past in memory or to embody it in words are bound to fail, partly because little of the vivid detail of past experiences remains with us, and more of it continues to evaporate with the passage of time,"[54] *Adventure Time* offers, in its finale, the image of an eternity that exists even if we cannot experience it. If time truly is an "illusion" then possibly all things, even after their "unforgiving" end, will both "stay" and "happen again and again." Refocusing on little happinesses amongst a more global apocalyptic end, BMO tells Beth and Shermy that Finn and Jake "kept living their lives" after the finale.[55] Even if, as viewers of the finale, we are confronted with the truth that Finn and Jake are dead, and Ooo is once again an apocalyptic place, the assurance that the characters "kept living their lives" provides a premise for embracing the present moment and knowing that it will, in its own way, "stay" and continue to happen. To illustrate this, the show ends with Shermy and Beth positioned just like Finn and Jake in the show's title card, ready to begin their adventure.

With this image, *Adventure Time* summarizes the complexity of its cyclical narrative. There is joy as Shermy and Beth strike a pose, and the promise of many future adventures both wacky and serious. However, just as they have replaced Finn and Jake, there is the implicit knowledge that one day they, too, will be no more. After all, we have seen Marceline become a vampire again, we know that Ooo will fall into ruin eventually, and we know that no good adventurer can outlast death. Just as the cyclical, eternal struggle of Sisyphus is the "unspeakable penalty in which the whole being is exerted toward accomplishing nothing,"[56] *Adventure Time* acknowledges that there is a terror that all life, all effort, all labor "accomplish[es] nothing." This core feature of existential dread can threaten to overwhelm as we must face the "terrible uncertainty that threatens to annihilate us before the fullness of time and bring to ruin much on which we now stake our hopes and focus our energies."[57]

But, just as Camus imagines Sisyphus' descent as an "hour like a breathing-space which returns as surely as his suffering,"[58] so does *Adventure Time* argue that the spaces of time between struggle, between death, and between endings are worth living. Even if the world will end, begin anew, and end again, embracing the present moment allows one to live the "good life." It is possible to thrive, instead of simply survive, if we do not set our sights on a future that we imagine will always be "better" or imagine that in time all suffering will be "fixed." Instead, we must openly accept—in fact, appreciate—the good with the bad, the different boulders that will eternally be pushed up mountains, and the unbreakable wheel of fortune. In doing so, it becomes possible to discover and embrace the possibility of living the "good life." This is where *Adventure Time* ends, with Shermy and Beth ready to embark on their own journey to discover what the "good life" means to them, ready to figure out how they can live it while they have the chance to do so.

Notes

1. Emily St. James, "*Adventure Time* Has Become This Era's Finest Coming-of-Age Story."
2. St. James.
3. St. James.
4. Donald A. Crosby, *The Specter of the Absurd*, 30.
5. Dictionary.com, s.v. "Sisyphean."
6. Albert Camus, *The Myth of Sisyphus*, 123.

7. Crosby, *Specter of the Absurd*, 59.
8. Martin Olson and Olivia Olson, *The Enchiridion & Marcy's Super Secret Scrapbook*, 1.
9. Olson and Olson, 6.
10. Olson and Olson, 19.
11. Olson and Olson, 5.
12. "*Stakes* Part 1: Marceline the Vampire Queen" (season 7, episode 6).
13. "*Stakes* Part 1."
14. "*Stakes* Part 1."
15. Crosby, *Specter of the Absurd*, 29.
16. "*Stakes* Part 1" (season 7, episode 6).
17. "*Stakes* Part 1."
18. Crosby, *Specter of the Absurd*, 28.
19. Camus, *Myth of Sisyphus*, 119
20. "*Stakes* Part 2: Everything Stays" (season 7, episode 7).
21. "*Stakes* Part 6: Take Her Back" (season 7, episode 11).
22. "*Stakes* Part 6."
23. "*Stakes* Part 7: Checkmate" (season 7, episode 12).
24. "*Stakes* Part 8: The Dark Cloud" (season 7, episode 13).
25. "*Stakes* Part 3: Vamps About" (season 7, episode 8).
26. "*Stakes* Part 3."
27. "*Stakes* Part 3."
28. "*Stakes* Part 3."
29. "*Stakes* Part 5: May I Come In?" (season 7, episode 10).
30. "*Stakes* Part 7" (season 7, episode 12).
31. "*Stakes* Part 5" (season 7, episode 10).
32. "*Stakes* Part 5."
33. "*Stakes* Part 3: Vamps About" (season 7, episode 8).
34. "*Stakes* Part 3."
35. "*Stakes* Part 3."
36. "*Stakes* Part 7" (season 7, episode 12).
37. "*Stakes* Part 7."
38. "*Stakes* Part 7."
39. "*Stakes* Part 7."
40. Crosby, *Specter of the Absurd*, 55, 35.
41. "*Stakes* Part 8" (season 7, episode 13).
42. Crosby, *Specter of the Absurd*, 63.
43. "*Stakes* Part 2" (season 7, episode 7).
44. "*Stakes* Part 8" (season 7, episode 13).
45. "*Stakes* Part 8."
46. "Lemonhope" (season 5, episodes 50–51); "Graybles 1000+" (season 6, episode 35).
47. In the finale, "Come Along with Me" (season 10, episodes 13–16), the remaining humans who had previously lived on a series of remote islands return to Ooo, implying that the big city and its eventual destruction could be tied back to humanity.
48. Crosby, *Specter of the Absurd*, 378.
49. "Come Along with Me" (season 10, episodes 13–16).
50. "Come Along with Me."
51. "Come Along with Me."
52. "Come Along with Me."
53. Crosby, *Specter of the Absurd*, 66.
54. Crosby, 64.
55. "Come Along with Me" (season 10, episodes 13–16).
56. Camus, *Myth of Sisyphus*, 120
57. Crosby, *Specter of the Absurd*, 74.
58. Camus, *Myth of Sisyphus*, 121.

References

Camus, Albert. *The Myth of Sisyphus.* Translated by Justin O'Brien. New York: Vintage Books, 2018.

Crosby, Donald A. *The Specter of the Absurd: Sources and Criticism of Modern Nihilism.* Albany: State University of New York Press, 1988.

Olson, Martin, and Olivia Olson. *The Enchiridion & Marcy's Super Secret Scrapbook!!!* New York: Abrams, 2015.

St. James, Emily. "*Adventure Time* Has Become This Era's Finest Coming-of-Age Story." *Vox*, 2013. https://www.vox.com/culture/2015/11/22/9779088/adventure-time-stakes-review.

What Time Is It? Postmodernity!
Postmodern Praxis in Adventure Time

JENINE OOSTHUIZEN

Today *Adventure Time* is known for its eccentric, borderline hallucinogenic character, and it has launched a multitude of online debates on platforms such as Reddit, YouTube, Tumblr, Imgur, Wiki-Fandom, Toonzone Forums, Instagram *Adventure Time* fan pages, as well as various online news outlets. These platforms still provide *Adventure Time* enthusiasts with the opportunity to initiate and engage in discussions that draw on a wide spectrum of intellectual concerns, including but not limited to: symbolism, inter-textuality, psychology, philosophy, morality, generic traits, diversity of themes and narrative techniques. In these debates, one will often find popular "go-to terms" that describe the show in terms of the hallucinatory. The words "kaleidoscopic," "trippy," "inexplicable," "psychedelic," "surreal" are prolific in online discussions/articles surrounding *Adventure Time*, and commonly feature in synoptic reviews that seem to collectively declare some innate quality of the series that is notoriously difficult to define. The under-examined cultural phenomenon that is *Adventure Time* is consequently described through obscure terminology that consigns the series to the indefinite peripheries of that which is simply "weird" or "random." Paul Thomas observes the same issue in his book *Exploring the Land of Ooo* (2020). Thomas writes:

> *Adventure Time* is frequently described as "random," and while this descriptor is usually meant as a way to compliment the show's limitless goofiness, it can also come across a bit dismissive, implying that the show has no "real" or stable narrative. This could not be farther from the truth.[1]

What is this elusive "weirdness" that we so readily designate as the identificatory stamp of *Adventure Time*? What is it about this series that seems to escape definition and instead treads in the unidentifiable shade of that umbrella term "random"?

In this essay, I intend to demonstrate that what *Adventure Time* fans, online journalists, bloggers, critics and the like, have been dubbing as "weird" is its identifiable postmodern tendencies. The aim of my research is to provide a theoretical framework with which to articulate, as well as expand on, the show's dialogue with postmodernity. In the brevity of this essay, I cannot possibly commit *Adventure Time* to the academic consideration it deserves. However, I can make a start by unearthing some of the rich theoretical significance that lie dormant and grossly unexplored in those oversimplifications of what Poniewozick rightly calls, "one of the artistic wonders of the last decade."[2] Most importantly, I seek to replace those circulating labels that evade definition through vague, phantasmagorical descriptors with a more germane vocabulary, namely: the postmodern.

It is perhaps significant to note that these vague descriptions are in fact ambiguous because that which they seek to describe, i.e., postmodern tendencies, evades definition. According to Bennett and Royale, "[postmodernism] resists the totalizing gesture of a metalanguage, the attempt to describe it as a set of coherent explanatory theories."[3] Having said that, postmodernism is commonly understood as either a concept, practice, style or even period that ensued from, and challenges, modernism.[4] For the purpose of this essay, I will draw on the vocabulary of the postmodern instead of providing a fixed definition thereof.

The essay is divided into two parts that largely focus on two salient issues: narrative structure (little-narratives) and narration (meta-fiction). The first part of my analysis includes a brief discussion of *Adventure Time*'s composition and appreciation of little-narratives as well as non-linear narration, the second unpacks *Adventure Time*'s use of meta-fiction through Ice King and Cuber—two characters who both experiment with self-reflexive narration.

Narration and Postmodernism

Before I begin with my consideration of *Adventure Time*'s narration, it is important to understand narration in the context of postmodernism. One crucial feature or effect of postmodern works is almost an intrinsic repudiation of metanarratives. From the perspective of the sociologist Jean-François Lyotard, metanarratives are discourses like religion, politics or science that are structured and controlled by specific ideologies. According to Lyotard, these "grand stories" or metanarratives impose a "false sense of totality and universality on a set of disparate things, actions and events."[5]

Although Lyotard's discussion of metanarratives is philosophic, it can also be discussed with regard to literature. A metanarrative in literature can be understood as the "realist" master-narrative that unfolds naturally in a coherent structure and ends with a sense of finality, i.e., there is no open-ended denouement.[6] This way of storytelling, the master-narrative that, according to "realist" writers, should follow a logical order unto a conclusive end, is rejected by postmodern writers who, as Bran Nicol explains in *The Cambridge Introduction to Postmodern Fiction* (2009), are highly suspicious of any such overarching "Truth":

> Postmodern subjects simply don't believe in metanarratives any more. They instinctively acknowledge instead the rhetorical function of narrative and appreciate that alternative narratives could be fashioned from the same group of events. Postmodernity, Lyotard argues, prefers 'little narratives' (*petit recits*), those which do not attempt to present an overarching 'Truth' but offer a qualified, limited 'truth,' one relative to a particular situation.[7]

Arguably, *Adventure Time* shows the same disdain for master-narratives. Instead, the structure of the series is fragmented into "little narratives" that explore subjective truths. These stories value individual characters who all offer different interpretations instead of a single, cohesive master-narrative.

Adventure Time and Fragmentation

The fragmentary compilation of *Adventure Time* is most significantly marked by: the mini-series that feature in 3 separate seasons, the "Shorts" (2–3 minute episodes), and the series finale. These components demonstrate a clear abandonment of chronological narration by favoring instead a network of highly nuanced and open-ended narratives.

The Mini-Series

It would be difficult to pinpoint a main story that develops chronologically through the series' successive seasons, as the incorporation of the mini-series disrupts any such overarching narrative by fragmenting the structure into three self-contained (8-part) narratives that pertain to specific characters. The mini-series consequently disrupts what the viewer might come to know as the main or "master" narrative of *Adventure Time*. This shift in narrative focus is demonstrated in the new theme songs that are sung by the character who plays a crucial role in each 8-part narrative: Marceline sings the intro to her mini-series *Stakes* (2015); Finn sings the song to his mini-series *Islands* (2017), and lastly Princess Bubblegum sings the intro to *Elements* (2017). This change in the theme songs refocuses the narrative and consequently emphasizes a new voice.

Stakes and *Elements*' theme song displace Finn and Jake as the protagonists, while *Islands* displace other prominent characters featured in the "main" *Adventure Time* theme song. This compilation of mini-series within a series complicates any discussion of a "main" narrative plot as the plot continually breaks down into several stories that are equally significant in themselves. In other words, the mini-series and its altering theme songs are new stories, which do not necessarily develop Finn (except for *Islands*) or Jake's narrative. Instead, they offer us new stories that pertain to characters other than the main protagonists.

I argue that the very inclusion of a "mini-series" points to *Adventure Time*'s proclivity for "little narratives." As the descriptor, "mini-series" itself suggests, we have narratives within narratives. It is thus difficult to distinguish the larger narrative, the meta-narrative, from the smaller, little narratives because they are formed from each other, fashioned, that is, as Nicol explained, "from the same group of events."[8]

The combination of the intermittent mini-series and the unfolding narrative of *Adventure Time* works something like an ever-changing puzzle that, like any postmodern subject, resists an overarching "Truth"[9]: just as the viewer grows comfortable with the characters and thinks that they have finally figured out each character's relative position in the narrative, the mini-series interjects, providing both new information and frustrating uncertainties. As a result, we have no true "main" or rather "master" narrative revealed through an uninterrupted, coherent progression. Instead, what we have are small stories, revealed through fragments that drop off and pick up at varying stages throughout the series. Each story, thus, seems equally important, retaining its own degree of ambiguity, which leaves the viewer to review and piece together whatever information they can glean from these narrative snippets.

The ninth-season episode "Ketchup" seems to deliberately draw attention to narrative fragmentation. The episode starts with BMO showing up at Marceline's place. He is dressed in a red cape, wielding two wooden stakes ready to help Marceline defeat the vampires. Of course, the return of the vampires, which happened in Marceline's mini-series *Stakes*, occurred two seasons ago. From the start of the episode there is a clear confusion surrounding narrative timelines. This confusion only intensifies as the episode continues.

Marceline reminds BMO that the vampire invasion happened long ago and they spend the rest of the day in her house telling each other stories. BMO tells Marceline about their boat trip, a very significant plot for the viewer who recalls Finn's grueling voyage to uncover the mysteries surrounding his birth parents in the mini-series *Islands*. However, BMO's recollection is shockingly divergent. In fact, his entire recollection seems purely fantastical, complete with an island-turned-upside-down cat called

Ted. BMO does not recall any significant event from that trip and finishes by saying: "That's how I remember it."[10] Marceline then decides to share her own story and creates a puppet show for BMO. Her makeshift puppets, crafted from kitchen utensils, closely resemble herself and Princess Bubblegum. From behind her kitchen counter, Marceline continues to tell the story of "Lollipop girl" and "Rockstar girl." Marceline's story recounts a series of events that preceded the mini-series *Elements*. At the end of her story BMO dismisses the ending as "unbelievable" and Marceline reluctantly confesses: "Fine, I sorta copped out. I guess I just got some stuff that's harder to talk about. Maybe 'cuz I've never actually talked about it for real."[11]

BMO admits that he might have "embellished" his story and Marceline is unable to give her story an "honest" ending because the reality of it is too difficult to express. "Ketchup," therefore, ties into a discussion of fragmentation as it emphasizes subjective truth over 'Truth,' i.e., the master-narrative that the viewer accepts as the "real" narrative. The viewer is consequently left feeling uncertain of both Marceline and BMO's stories and their own understanding of what constitutes a "real" narrative. David Perlmutter marks *Adventure Time*'s fragmentation and the affect it has on the viewer in *The Encyclopedia of American Animated Television Shows* (2018):

"[*Adventure Time* is] a series that has little narrative framework to support it as a larger work, save for the setting and characters. Individual segments can sometimes have little to connect them besides these elements. As a result, there is often little continuity in the narratives, nor anything resembling traditional 'stories,' which is as unnerving and frustrating to some viewers as it is enjoyable to others."[12]

The viewer might find "Ketchup" frustrating as it blatantly misrepresents a crucial plotline in *Islands* and fails to uncover the truth behind the events proceeding the *Elements* mini-series. However, this frustration could be tempered if the viewer considers what BMO means when he says his story is "emotionally honest." Truly understanding *Adventure Time*'s use of fragmentation is to understand that the purpose thereof is not to frustrate the viewer's need for a cohesive, reliable, overarching narrative. Instead, fragmentation allows for reinterpretation and individuality in the form of multiplicity as opposed to "Truth" and by extension finality. Instead of understanding *Adventure Time*'s fragmented narratives as simply frustrating, we should come to understand it as poignantly demonstrating a sincere, or to use BMO's words, "emotionally honest," appreciation of little-narratives.

Postmodern works demand their audience to engage with the work itself. *Adventure Time* challenges the viewer to engage with the narrative/narration. The story is no longer just given to the viewer as a product to be consumed without any thought. The narration and the narratives are not to be taken for granted. The viewer is forced to go back, to re-examine what happened, to question their own inferences and to actively engage until they reach their own understanding. This idea of *Adventure Time*'s viewer, i.e., a postmodern viewer, being actively involved is echoed in *Adventure Time* fan Biggerboot's comment (as quoted in Thomas's book):

> Since *Adventure Time* constantly left loose threads as it tied up new ones, and had this whole vast lore that was only in the background, I think it got a lot of people wanting to complete that puzzle in their head.[13]

The Finale

The composition of *Adventure Time*'s finale, "Come Along with Me," continues the tendency of non-linear narration. The finale—which is the length of four 11-minute episodes—opens with a sequence containing a different theme sung by never before seen characters, Beth and Shermy. These two "future" adventurers are told the story of the Great Gum War. The Gum War is the present conflict of the narrative that the viewer has been following throughout season 10. The future re-telling of the Gum War continues the present action of the series, which is paradoxically represented as the past from Beth and Shermy's timeline. It is especially interesting that the series should end by reinforcing the idea of non-linearity. The introduction of Beth and Shermy, however unexpected, is not coincidental. I would argue that these two characters serve as a final reminder of *Adventure Time*'s highly experimental narration, by revealing the crux of the main plot, *significantly* represented as a past plot, through one last momentous deconstruction of chronological narration.

Furthermore, it is interesting to note that Beth and Shermy's world is anything but a utopia. The opening sequence of the series' finale contains images that suggest an even more degraded landscape: mountainous ice peaks that stretch over great distances, sparse landscapes with collapsed sculptures of, what seem to represent Finn and Jake. *Adventure Time* seems to again repudiate a sense of finality that might be evinced by a utopian civilization. I suggest that we consider this dystopian setting in terms of the series' fragmented narrative structure and its alignment with the postmodern. For while a utopian world would lend itself to the realist's coherent, master-narrative that has progressed unto a final end, the dystopian state, irrespective of a totalitarian regime, contains within it a kernel of the postmodern ethos: the continued pessimistic critique of metanarratives and the "false sense of totality" that it suggests.[14] The finale, which should by definition present the finality of *Adventure Time*, reveals at the heart of it a continued state of indeterminacy and the consequent, everlasting adventure. I therefore argue that *Adventure Time*'s preference for maintaining the dystopian setting advocates the postmodern impulse to negate any form of finality or master-narrative.

THE "SHORTS"

The "Shorts" (mini-episodes released at random intervals and grouped together with certain seasons) are non-specific episodes that do not develop any main story-line. These episodes are merely as their title suggests, short stories that explore trivial goings-on in the Land of Ooo. The "Shorts" comprise the following episodes: "The Wand," *Graybels Allsorts* (that consists of 4 parts), and *Frog Seasons* (that consists of 5 parts). Whichever way one interprets these "Shorts," it remains unmistakably clear that they form a subcategory of experimental narration.

For example, *Frog Seasons* (2016) experiments with the idea of progression and by extent the anticipation of finality. The name of each episode is titled after the seasons: spring, summer, autumn, winter and spring (again). The titling clearly underpins the concept of continuity that is also mirrored in the narrative structure itself. Jake and Finn follow a frog carrying a crown throughout all four seasons; however, they never truly uncover what happens once the frog puts on the crown. As a result their curiosity is continually frustrated. In *Frog Seasons: Winter* (2016), Finn decides to give up their seemingly never-ending pursuit of the frog. Almost immediately after they leave, the frog puts on the crown and turns into the two-headed snake, Life (who the viewer might recognize as Death's consort). However, Finn and Jake do not see the transformation. In the final short of the five-part sequence, it seems as though they have forgotten about the frog, but this assumption is short-lived for the crown soon reappears and so too does the frog. Jake mentions that the crown seems familiar although neither of them recalls their tireless journey spent following the frog through several seasons.

The cyclical seasons combined with Finn and Jake's repetitive pursuit of the frog demonstrates continuity without resolve. These short episodes evidently contest the viewer's idea of finality, or more aptly put, a narrative conclusion. Instead, they relate events that follow obscure plot-lines which offer no clear, or even any resolution. By never uncovering the truth and consequently repeating the pursuit of the frog, the narrative avoids a definitive conclusion. Instead of presenting progressive events that lead to an end, we have a narrative structure that is cyclical. In other words, the narrative does not develop progressively towards a final resolution, i.e., an end. Instead, what we're offered is a narrative that repeats itself, like the seasons, avoiding any sense of finality.

Given the obscurity of the shorts it is not surprising that many people find them to be insignificant in relation to the main narrative of *Adventure*

Time. However, their seemingly non-sensical and awkward existence takes on an entirely new dimension in light of postmodern discourse. As with the mini-series and the finale, these 2–3 minute episodes are a clear exemplification of *Adventure Time*'s disinclination to write according to conventional structures of linearity and finality. By simply exploring the compilation of *Adventure Time*, we find a patent tendency toward narrative fragmentation, which is for the postmodernist, "[An] exhilarating, liberating phenomenon, symptomatic of our escape from the claustrophobic embrace of fixed systems...."[15] *Adventure Time*'s defiance of linearity opens the series up to new avenues of narration. The "Shorts," mini-series and the finale successfully erase any conception of one supreme viewpoint, which consequently subverts the more traditional viewer's expectation of coherence and finality. Instead, the series offers the viewer a host of voices, each revealed in their own nuanced narratives. Fragmentation, in *Adventure Time*, becomes an area of narrative experimentation. The show's playful use of the fragment aligns with the postmodern "escape" from any all-encompassing master-narrative.

Ice King, Cuber, and Meta-Fiction

One of the most significant modes of postmodern writing is the literary technique, termed in 1970 by William H. Gass, as meta-fiction.[16] Patricia Waugh, in *Metafiction: The Theory and Practice of Self-Conscious Fiction*, defines meta-fiction as a literary device that exhibits a level of self-conscious writing that deliberately draws attention to the act of representation.[17] For this section, I will be looking at two of *Adventure Time*'s more curious characters who dabble in the art of storytelling: Ice King and Cuber.

Before I discuss these two characters, it is important to first mark the subtle yet paramount distinction between the modernist and postmodernist's use of meta-fiction. The modernist writer focuses on *consciousness* and the ways of representing it, i.e., stream of consciousness, the interior monologue of characters, a near obsession with the idea of self. Conversely, the postmodern writer is more concerned with *fictionality* and the ways in which a story and its mode of narration goes about revealing itself.[18]

Ice King's Fan-Fiction

In *Adventure Time*, Ice King's fan-fiction is a striking example of the postmodernist's use of meta-fiction. *Cambridge Companion to Popular Fiction* defines fan-fiction as, "[The] activity of writing stories that carry on from an origination text—a film, a TV show, or a book."[19] Furthermore, this specific literary genre is relatively modern; its origin dates back to the early 1930s. Per definition fan-fiction is a literary work that exists *separately* from the original fiction that it seeks to continue. Ice King's fan-fiction is based on the original fiction of *Adventure Time*; however, unlike fan-fiction, which exists separately from the original fiction, Ice King's fan-fiction exists paradoxically within the original fiction, i.e., the series *Adventure Time*. Ice King's fan-fiction is therefore mimetic of the narrative in which he himself exists, consequently continuing the original fiction within itself, creating a type of Droste effect.

The introduction of fan-fiction in the original fictional work demonstrates meta-fiction in the form of, what Waugh describes as, "the self-begetting-novel."[20] It is a mode of writing whereby the creative process of narration is undertaken by a character in the work itself. The result is a highly subjective form of narration that is not represented by some detached and all-knowing voice. Thus the "self-begetting-novel" can be understood as a novel that creates itself presumably through itself; it is personal, and therefore subject to distortion. Ice King, a character in the original fictional world of *Adventure Time*, creates his own fan-fiction about Ooo and its inhabitants. He consequently re-creates and disrupts the known universe of *Adventure Time* by self-consciously re-constructing the fictional world of Ooo and its characters through his own immensely unstable perception.

Fionna and Cake make their debut appearance in the third-season episode "Fionna and Cake." We immediately notice that the opening sequence is different: the usual theme song, normally sung by Finn, is now sung by a female voice; Finn has become Fionna and "Jake the dog" has become "Cake the cat." In this alternate reality the characters are all gender-swapped: Ice Queen represents Ice King; Prince Gumball represents Princess Bubblegum; Lord Monochromicorn represents Lady Rainicorn; Lumpy Space Prince represents Lumpy Space Princess; Marshall Lee represents Marceline. This subversion of the characters' genders is indicative of the disruptive effect that the "self-begetting-novel" exerts on the original fiction.

The episode begins with a presumably normal day in the life of Fionna and Cake, whom we recognize as gender swapped versions of Finn and Jake. The viewer, however, remains uncertain whether Fionna and Cake are *real*. Alternate or parallel universes are an actuality in *Adventure Time* and so the viewer cannot be sure whether Fionna and Cake are *real* characters in an alternate reality, or whether they are just a manifestation we have yet to find the cause of. Our suspended indecision is left pending, until the final moments of the episode. In the few remaining minutes we are suddenly, almost jarringly, removed from Fionna and Cake's world upon hearing Ice King's narration:

> "And I can't wait to marry him," said Fionna. Then she turned to Prince Gumball and said: "I hope Ice King will sweep me off my feet and take me to the furthest corner of Ooo where we will do nothing but kiss and eat a whole bunch until we get fat and die." The end.[21]

We return to the original world of Ooo and find that Ice King has imprisoned Finn and Jake. They each have a copy of Ice King's fan-fiction. After having read his work Ice King asks: "So? What did you think of the fan-fiction I wrote about you guys?"[22] Ice King's reading of his own fictional creation (fan-fiction) is an instance of what Waugh describes as the "overt narrational intrusion," that is a typical tendency of meta-fictional writing.[23] The "overt narrational intrusion" occurs when the character interrupts or intrudes the flow of the narration by revealing their part in the literal composition of the narrative. This meta-fictional conceit is further emphasized in Fionna's speech. Throughout the episode, her speech matched the friendly and laid-back style we associate with Finn. However, with this closing sentence Fionna's speech abruptly transforms into something else: an expression nearer to the *real* Ice King's rhythm and word choice. Evidently, Ice King's fan-fiction is a construction of meta-fiction that demonstrates how *fictionality* and the representation thereof becomes an area of postmodern experimentation: in this case a fictional character is given the chance to re-create an already established world, whereby the viewer experiences re-constructed fiction within fiction.

Adventure Time takes this already blurred construction of fiction within fiction one step further, by having Ice King become infatuated with his own creation. In the fifth-season episode "Bad Little Boy," Ice King chases everyone from his castle after listening to Marceline's own rendition of his fan-fiction. He walks down a spiraling staircase, opens a locked door and goes inside a cave-like room that contains a colossal shrine of Fionna and Cake. He kneels at the foot of this statue and says, "I know you're out there somewhere. I just haven't figured out how to get to you but believe me I will."[24] This scene demonstrates the intense involvement of fan-fiction readers who become "unhealthily obsessed by the world of the originating text."[25] However, on a meta-fictional level it cleverly illustrates the complexities of creating fiction within fiction.

One can see how this meta-fictional conceit of fiction within fiction sets a premise of doubt that necessarily becomes the postmodernist's creative sustenance. In *Adventure Time* this doubt, or uncertainty, manifests in Ice King's inability to distinguish the interior from the exterior, between depth and surface. The knowable world (the exterior) suddenly becomes unknowable and therefore confused with a secondary fiction that was paradoxically created by Ice King himself, by his consciousness (his interior), his depth. Ice King's disruption of the original fiction with the co-mingling of a secondary fiction successfully evokes the postmodern concern of the copy and the real. It is worth noting that the animation engenders the same phenomenon by copying the real, i.e., the original fiction, and mirroring it, in terms of representation, in the copy, i.e., Ice King's fan-fiction. The visual interpretation of Ice King's written text might cause the viewer to share Ice King's uncertainty regarding the distinction between the copy and the real as they perceive both narratives (the real and the copy) in the same animated style. As a result, Ice King and the viewer, like readers of fan-fiction, become enthralled in a copy (or copies) of the real.

Ice King's fan-fiction does not remain exclusively his; it soon becomes a creative mode of narration to be taken up by other characters in the Land of Ooo. This turn illustrates what Waugh refers to as "frame breaking."[26] A "frame" is the "essential substructure" of a story.[27] It is a device that guides the viewer through the progression of the plot without revealing the processes, or "frames," required to create that narrative flow. Meta-fiction, however, draws attention to the *act* of representation, the literary technique raises self-reflexivity, and therefore inevitably exposes "framing devices."[28] Marceline essentially uses Ice King's fan-fiction as a "framing device" through which to construct her own story. In "Bad Little Boy," she interrupts Ice King's reading of Fionna and Cake and says, "It's good but maybe it's time to let someone else try. Listen up y'all I've got a story of my own."[29] Marceline's interruption of Ice King's reading exposes the "frame" of his narrative construction. The framing device of narration is consequently exposed and then passed on to a different narrator.

A similar instance (of taking over Ice King's fictional world) occurs in the season six episode "The Prince Who Wanted Everything" (season 6, episode 9). Lumpy Space Princess writes her own Fionna and Cake adventure with the main protagonist being the gender-swapped version of herself, Lumpy Space Prince. Her book is entitled: *The Prince Who Wanted Everything: A Fionna and Cake Adventure*. Lumpy Space Princess asks Ice King to read it. Ice King agrees to read but is quickly interrupted by Lumpy Space Princess. She screams, "No! That's not how I sound! Read in a better voice!"[30] He starts again, and the voice of Lumpy Space Prince is altered.

The viewer becomes self-aware of the narrative process through frame-breaking: Marceline suggests that it might be time for someone else to tell a Fionna and Cake's story and creates a new story through the gender-swapped version of herself, Marshall-Lee. Likewise, the framing is exposed when Lumpy Space Princess demands that Ice King read her character in a better voice. Both episodes explore what meta-fiction intends to foreground: that fiction is not "unprocessed" but that it is a highly *selective* process and therefore a "framed" undertaking.[31] Marceline and Lumpy Space Princess both manipulate the narrative, demonstrated by their continued interruptions and literal re-framing of the narrative. Marceline and Lumpy Space Princess' exposure of the creative process foregrounds the power that resides in controlling a narrative; by breaking or exposing the traditionally concealed process of "framing," the writing becomes self-reflexive.

Ice King's Fan-Fiction and Cuber's Graybles

We jump one thousand years into the future to meet Cuber, in his debut appearance in season four's "Five Short Graybles." Cuber is a peculiar character who acts as a narrator and addresses the viewer directly. He usually presents his audience with five short stories called Graybles. The Graybles, like Ice King's fan-fiction, raise the viewer's awareness of a constructed, framed story. The viewer, who potentially watches each episode passively, i.e., without being actively involved in the narrative process, is suddenly addressed by a narrator, and invited to participate in the ensuing stories.

He encourages audience participation by asking the viewer to identify a theme that patterns across all five stories. Cuber and his Graybles are therefore another instance of meta-fiction. Like Ice King controls his fan-fiction, so too does Cuber select and present specific stories that outline a central theme for the viewer to identify. Of course, Cuber's narration involves another level of meta-fiction: he disturbs the viewer's passivity by breaking the fourth-wall and addressing them directly. This direct address works to change the passive activity of simply watching the episode to actively analyzing it for possible themes.

In the episode "Five Short Tables," which stars Fionna and Cake, there is a comparative play between the narrative styles of Ice King's fan-fiction and Cuber's Graybles. "Five Short Tables" demonstrates a hyper awareness of the act of representation. Throughout the episode Cake tries to capture portraits of events with "narrative flapjacks."[32] Her concern with cooking life-like flapjacks introduces the episode's near obsession with the act of representation. The episode is packed with layers of meta-fictionality.

Mimicry of Narration

In this particular episode Ice King's fan-fiction seems to mirror Cuber's style of narration: 5 short stories that characteristically share an underlying theme. However, there are significant variations in the way both narrators represent their stories: Cuber *watches* his stories on a holo-pyramid viewer whereas Ice King's *reads* his written work; Cuber addresses a viewer while Ice King addresses his penguins; Cuber is a sympathetic character that allows his viewer to take some time before guessing the theme whereas Ice King is much less sensitive in this regard and dismissively says, "No, you're way off."[33]

Similar to Cuber's Graybles the theme in "Five Short Tables" is obscure. However, Cuber is much more precise when he lists all the congruent themes. Ice King, on the other hand, becomes increasingly vague as his list proceeds:

> Fionna and Cake were at the *breakfast table*; Gumball consulted the *periodic table*; Flame Prince set fire to the *table of contents*; the purple thing had a *tablespoon* of syrup; and Ice Queen did a tabley-thing too, probably.[34]

The mimicked narrative is reinforced at the end of the episode when Ice King decides to call his compilation of short stories "Tables," purposefully parallel to that of Cuber's stories, "Graybles." By noticing the differences in the modes of narration our attention is ultimately drawn to the aspect of "framing." The "framing" of Cuber's style of narration is almost "laid bare" in that it draws enough attention to itself to be identified by the viewer as Cuber's style. The viewer thus actively compares Cuber's style with that of Ice King's and the humor lies in the comparison of the two.

The Authentic Author

The issue of the authorial authenticity comes into play at the end of the episode. Just before the episode ends we realize that we have not been the only viewers. We are removed from Ooo when Cuber decides to turn off his screen. He has been at home watching "Five Short Tables" in his living room. He sighs and says, "I'll never look at tables the same way again."[35] Our continual comparison of the two modes of narration is suddenly subverted. Now, we are left asking who the "true" author of the five-themed story structure is.

We have been actively comparing Ice King's narration to Cuber's style and yet we find Cuber watching Ice King's "Five Short Tables." As in most of Cuber's Graybles, we are forced to reconsider our initial interpretation of the whole episode. Upon reflection we come to realize that it was originally, or at least initially, Ice King's narrative style since Cuber lives one thousand years into the future. This contestation of authorship is another consideration of the postmodern. The idea of the *origin* of a voice, a distinct creator, who somehow, as Roland Barthes describes in his essay *The Death of the Author*, "exists before" the work, is evidently being challenged.³⁶ Ice King's version of what we assumed to be an adaptation of Cuber's Graybles, is turned upside down. Cuber, who we initially associated with the five-themed style, now becomes the "author" who borrowed narrative techniques from Ice King. The result is the contestation of originality, a debate of authorial authenticity, a question of Truth. Postmodernism welcomes this avenue of ambiguity as it questions all absolute values.³⁷

To further divulge this issue of authorial authenticity we move beyond the episode and into its very making. Ward and his production team derived the word "Graybles" from the word "fables": short stories that contain moral lessons, much like an identifiable theme.³⁸ The word "table" in Ice King's "Five Short Tables" is another derivative of the production team's play on "fables," showing the style of narration to be significantly linked.

The uncertainty of authorship we find in fables is explicitly tied into the episode "Five Short Tables." Meta-fiction, in this episode, plays with the postmodern concern of "Truth" by shifting between multiple narrators in one episode. The idea of an original author, the one "True" creator of the story, becomes impossibly blurred as there is a continual shift in both the narrative and narrative voice. The episode starts with Ice King creating a "re-mix" of his fan-fiction. When he starts to narrate his edited fan-fiction, a new scene places the viewer in Fiona and Cake's world. Cake's narrative takes over and Ice King's narrative voice disappears.

Cake is in the process of making "narrative flapjacks" but Fionna, unable to tell the difference between them, admits that they look like "formless blobs."³⁹ Cake agrees and decides to base her flapjacks on "real," "non-fictive" characters, namely the gender-swapped characters in Fionna and Cake's world. Of course, the viewer becomes aware of this intensely ironic concept: Fionna and Cake's reality is Ice King's fan-fiction, i.e., a fictive construct based in fiction. Fionna and Cake set out to observe the actions of several characters including: Butterscotch Butler, Prince Bubblegum, Flame Prince, Lumpy Space Prince and Marshall Lee. As the episode comes to a close, Ice Queen's voice takes over the narrative and the viewer is introduced to yet another fictive world occupied by the Ice President, Flynn the human being and Jacques the raccoon. Ice Queen's voice disappears as her fictive character, the Ice President, reads his fiction aloud: "Lynn the person looked at Janet and asked: Am I my feelings? Do I exist because I can't stop feeling? Janet the Fox answered her…."⁴⁰

The viewer's understanding of an original fiction/narrative or true authorial voice is continually challenged as they follow several unfolding narratives and several authorial voices within each other. The result is a seemingly never-ending displacement of narrative and narrator, the primacy of both these concepts evidently contested. With this paradigm of fiction mirroring fiction comes the consequent disintegration of a supreme authorial voice, and what we are left with is an active interrogation of narration, i.e., representation. Through these meta-fictional considerations, the act of representation itself becomes a self-reflexive labyrinth of unexpected turns and infinite narrative possibilities.

Guest-Animated Episodes

Another mode of meta-fiction at work within *Adventure Time* is the few guest-animated episodes in the series: episodes that are animated in radically different styles. The production crew invited guest animators to interpret *Adventure Time* from their perspective and allowed them to re-animate the show. There are five of these specially animated episodes that are considered distinct from the standard animation of *Adventure Time:* "A Glitch is a Glitch" (season 5, episode 15), "Food Chain" (season 6, episode 7), "Water Park Prank" (season 6, episode 37), "Diamonds and Lemons" (aired after season ten as a bonus episode), and "Bad Jubies" (season 7, episode 20).

The first of these "guest animated" episodes feature in season five. "A Glitch is a Glitch" is the first *Adventure Time* episode to be designed and completed entirely in CGI animation. In this episode the usual introduction or opening sequence is re-done in CGI; this 3-D animation, with simple geometric shapes, runs throughout the entire episode, through to the end credits. The episode was written, directed and animated by David OReilly, who was given unreserved artistic control of the making of the episode.[41] OReilly's style of deconstructing 3D graphics is evident in the heavily pixilated episode and the occurrence of glitches resulting in abrupt displacement, funny merges and a disruptive chaos that threatens the integrity of an ordered reality.

On a meta-fictional level, the viewer is placed inside a computer-like world and explicitly keyed into the complicated processes of animation. The difficulties of animation are mentioned at the very start of the episode, establishing the episode's self-reflexive nature, when Finn declares: "Man, I don't have the patience for this animation junk. Whoever does this must have no life whatsoever."[42] As soon as he says this, he inadvertently hits himself and then asks, "Why did I do that?"[43] It is an excellent use of meta-fiction wherein the animator interferes with his own animation by making Finn hit himself after having insulted the vocation of animators, ergo insulting his very creator. On an aesthetic level we are given the opportunity to experience *Adventure Time* through the eyes of a guest animator, and on a meta-fictional level we are reminded of the processes required to create the series, the technicalities that create a fictional reality, and how utterly dependent this reality is on the correct operation of these "codes."

Whereas OReilly focused on the technicalities behind animation, David Ferguson focused on something more visceral. "Water Park Prank" (Season 6, episode 37) is flat and highly stylized. The characters look like cut-out versions of themselves. While previous guest-episodes merely *look* different, "Water Park Prank" looks and *feels* different. This is due to Ferguson's attempt to steer clear of any profound issues; much like his flat animation he focused instead on depthless content that incorporates folly for the sake of folly. The episode allows for no deeper contemplation which is of course unlike *Adventure Time*. Andrew Tran notes that the voice actors "don't even sound like themselves as they perform the lines."[44] This suggests the extent to which Ferguson tried to disrupt the narrative atmosphere of *Adventure Time*. The word "prank," in the title of the episode, comes to demonstrate more than the episode's immediate story. The "prank" can be understood to operate on a meta-fictional level; Ferguson's mischievous act converts *Adventure Time* into something that is its opposite: flat and fixed.

The episode was unfavorably received by most *Adventure Time* fans, but I suspect it to be a perfunctory disdain, the importance of difference unknowingly overlooked. Difference is the marrow of *Adventure Time*—it is why guest animators were invited to re-interpret an already established world. And Ferguson takes this opportunity and turns it into the ultimate postmodern gesture: not only does he alter the animation, but he decentralizes the familiarity of the series' tone of narration through means of deliberately reducing the characters to cut-out versions of their otherwise highly nuanced personalities. *Adventure Time* now contains a re-constructed version of itself that is at once a true representation of itself and a false representation of itself: a meta-fictional play on the construction of fiction.

Seeing *Adventure Time* and its characters represented in different styles makes the viewer self-aware of the series as a constructed product, a creation that has gone through specific processes of storyboards, animation, voice-overs and directing. We are reminded of the mechanics behind the making of an episode; thus the "framing" of the episode is exposed, and we are invited to see *Adventure Time* re-constructed in the hands of a different creator.

Conclusion

Adventure Time has proved to yield an insurmountable quantity of postmodern material, a percentage of which I have attempted to analyze in this essay. The intent of this discussion was two-fold. First, I hoped that my research would serve to raise academic awareness around the interesting literary phenomena in popular culture that is by no means less critically deserving than highbrow literature. Secondly, I proposed to provide the *Adventure Time* community with a theoretical vocabulary that would ultimately replace the tenuous descriptions of "weird" with a truer descriptor: postmodern. My findings not only affirm postmodern praxis within *Adventure Time*, but they begin to reveal the extent to which these tendencies operate.

I think it imperative that I should end this essay with a concluding commentary that reaffirms and, more importantly, exposes the indissoluble link between postmodernity and *Adventure Time*. Keeping my research in mind (*Adventure Time*'s praxis of postmodernism), one should now be able to recognize the reoccurring attempts to describe the series in latent terms that, either knowingly or unknowingly, relate to the postmodern.

In light of these findings, let me now consider *Polygon* journalist Allegra Frank's description of *Adventure Time*. She attributes the show to having launched a new wave of creativity in succeeding cartoons:

> Fans of other cult favorites like *Steven Universe* and *Gravity Falls* have *Adventure Time* to thank for unlocking the potential of imaginative characters who adventure through world not bound to conventional logic; *Adventure Time* gave us the chance to grow alongside Finn the Human and Jake the Dog, our heroes, as they plunged into the depths of their friendly, if tragic, dystopian home.[45]

I can only presume that what Frank, here, refers to as "conventional logic" is in fact formulaic writing: the reliance on stock characters with fixed personalities, predictable and chronological narration and inevitable endings that produce expected and unsurprising conclusions. As I mentioned in my introduction, *Adventure Time*'s disdain for "conventional logic" is what Sorcher initially identified as being unmistakably "new."[46] *Adventure Time*'s rejection of conventionality is a postmodern reaction against coherence, certainty, predictability and totality.

The fragmentary compilation of *Adventure Time* marks the significant abandon of chronological narration. The fracturing plotlines that interrupt the sense of a coherent, narrative flow avoid totality by opting instead for nuanced and open-ended narratives. Furthermore, *Adventure Time*'s use of meta-fiction allows the series to disrupt forms of certainty by exposing and therefore inevitably questioning narration itself. The viewer questions Fionna and Cake's fictionality, characters in the Land of Ooo are reshaped into numerous versions of themselves through Ice King's fan-fiction, and authorial authenticity becomes an area of debate when we discover that Cuber's five-themed structure was initially provided by Ice King in "Five Short Tables."

The postmodern use of fragmentation and meta-fiction works to undermine conventional logic and successfully dislodges *Adventure Time* from a single, fixed interpretation. By using these postmodern devices, the show cultivates "undecidability" that opens the story up to its viewer. "Undecidability" is a postmodern concept explained by Bennett and Royle as the "impossibility of deciding between two or more competing interpretations."[47] Inciting a self-conscious questioning prompts the viewer to resolve the structural ambiguities themselves. The act of watching is no longer passive. The profusion of analysis videos on YouTube, fanfiction and blogs testify to the viewer's active involvement in trying to unravel the ambiguities of the series.

Provided with the theoretical framework of the postmodern, we now come to realize the significance of people's commentary on the series. Frank's quote inevitably arrives at the postmodern. In a similar vein, Oliver Sava, marks that *Adventure Time* ended with a "celebration of what makes it special," namely that "there is no end."[48] Eric Thurm, too, reaches a similar conclusion: "In retrospect, the thought that *Adventure Time* might have had an actual definitive ending feels silly."[49]

People's concluding thoughts unknowingly echo references to postmodern tendencies that operate in the series. I would argue that the connection between postmodernity and *Adventure Time* is so profound that any description of the series will contain some inherent reference to what constitutes the postmodern. Why else would it be "silly" to think that *Adventure Time* should have a "definitive ending?" For the simple reason that postmodernism does not allow for such totality. A thought emphasized in one of the finale's songs called, "Time Adventure Time" (2018), which suggests that "time is an illusion" and that subjects are "always living in the present tense."[50] The postmodern, according to Bennett and Royle, "challenges our thinking about time, challenges us to see the present in the past, the future in the present, the present in a kind of no-time."[51] For this reason, postmodernism and *Adventure Time* are intimately aligned. It is thus exceptionally significant that *Adventure Time* should end with a song that challenges time and by extent the expectation of "finality." If we replace the concept of time with that of linearity, and remove that which it underpins—coherency, totality, certainty—we will find that what remains is the undecided: a fragmentary experience, "a billion tiny frames" as the song itself suggests. Once again, we are reminded in one last momentous deconstruction of the ultimate schematic, i.e., time, that what *Adventure Time* has been celebrating, is celebrating and will be celebrating, is multiplicity over totality, subjectivity over objectivity and difference over convention. It is, therefore, nothing short of a celebration of postmodernity.

Notes

1. Paul Thomas, *Exploring the Land of Ooo*, 209. This section is omitted in the UP Mississippi edition.
2. James Poniewozick, "*Adventure Time*, TV's Surreal Masterpiece, Comes to an End."
3. Andrew Bennett and Nicholas Royle, *An Introduction to Literature, Criticism and Theory*, 248.
4. Hal Foster, *Anti-Aesthetic*, ix.
5. Bran Nicol, *Cambridge Introduction to Postmodern Fiction*, 11.
6. Nicol, 12
7. Nicol.
8. Nicol.
9. Nicol.
10. "Ketchup" (season 9, episode 11).
11. "Ketchup."
12. David Perlmutter, *Encyclopedia of American Animated Television Shows*, 16–17.
13. Thomas, *Exploring the Land of Ooo*, 244.
14. Cf. Nicol, *Cambridge Introduction to Postmodern Fiction*, 11.
15. Barry, *Beginning Theory*, 83.
16. Waugh, *Metafiction*, 2.
17. Waugh.
18. Waugh, 14.
19. Humble, "Reader of Popular Fiction," 96.
20. Waugh, *Metafiction*, 14.
21. "Fionna and Cake" (season 3, episode 9).
22. "Fionna and Cake."
23. Waugh, *Metafiction*, 14.
24. "Bad Little Boy" (season 5, episode 11).
25. Humble, "Reader of Popular Fiction," 96.
26. Waugh, *Metafiction*, 28.
27. Waugh.
28. Waugh.
29. "Bad Little Boy" (season 5, episode 11).
30. "The Prince Who Wanted Everything" (season 6, episode 9)
31. Waugh, *Metafiction*, 30.
32. "Five Short Tables" (season 8, episode 9).
33. "Five Short Tables."
34. "Five Short Tables."
35. "Five Short Tables."
36. Roland Barthes, *Image Music Text*, 145.
37. Bennett and Royle, *Introduction to Literature*, 249.
38. Tom Herpich, "Five Short Graybles" [commentary].
39. "Five Short Tables" (season 8, episode 9).
40. "Five Short Tables."
41. Oliver Sava, "A Glitch Is a Glitch."
42. "A Glitch is a Glitch" (season 5, episode 15)
43. "A Glitch is a Glitch."
44. Andrew Tran, "Experimental Animation."
45. Allegra Frank, "*Adventure Time*' Showrunner Doesn't See the Finale as a Happy Ending."
46. Chris McDonnell, *The Art of Ooo*.
47. Bennett and Royle, *Introduction to Literature*, 249.
48. Oliver Sava, "*Adventure Time* Concludes."
49. Eric Thurm, "*Adventure Time*'s Series Finale Lives Up to the Show's Spirit."
50. "Come Along with Me" (season 10, episodes 13–16).
51. Bennett and Royle, *Introduction to Literature*, 248.

References

Aesop. *Aesop's Fables*. London: HarperCollins, 2011.
Barry, Peter. *Beginning Theory: An Introduction to Literary and Cultural Theory*. 2nd ed. Manchester, UK: Manchester University Press, 2002.
Barthes, Roland. *Image Music Text*. Translated by Stephen Heath. London: Fontana Press, 1977.
Bennett, Andrew, and Royle, Nicholas. *An Introduction to Literature, Criticism and Theory*. 3rd ed. New York: Routledge, 2004.
Cawelti, John G. *Adventure, Mystery and Romance: Formula Stories as Art and Popular Culture*. Chicago: The University of Chicago Press, 1976.
Demott, Rick. "Time for Some Adventure with Pendleton Ward." Animation World Network, 2010. Archived at https://web.archive.org/web/20170329070034/http://www.awn.com/animationworld/time-some-adventure-pendleton-ward.
Foster, Hal. *The Anti-Aesthetic: Essays on Postmodern Culture*. Seattle: Bay Press, 1983.
Frank, Allegra. "*Adventure Time'* Showrunner Doesn't See the Finale as a Happy Ending." Polygon, 2018. https://www.polygon.com/tv/2018/9/3/17806570/adventure-time-finale-finn-bubblegum-marceline-adam-muto-interview.
Herpich, Tom. "Five Short Graybles" [commentary]. *Adventure Time: The Complete Fourth Season*. Blu-ray. Los Angeles: WarnerBrothers, 2014.
Humble, Nicki. "The Reader of Popular Fiction." In *The Cambridge Companion to Popular Fiction*, edited by D. Glover, and S. McCracken, 96–97. Cambridge, UK: Cambridge University Press, 2012.
Jameson, Fredric. *Postmodernism, or, The Cultural Logic of Late Capitalism*. Durham: Duke University Press, 1991.
Jane, Emma A. "'Gunter's a Woman?!'—Doing and Undoing Gender in Cartoon Network's *Adventure Time.*" *Journal of Children and Media* 9, no. 2 (2015): 231–247.
Kohn, Eric. "Does the obsessive *Adventure Time* Fandom Overlook the Depths of Pendleton Ward's Cartoon Network Hit?" IndieWire, 2013. https://www.indiewire.com/2013/10/does-the-obsessive-adventure-time-fandom-overlook-the-depths-of-pendleton-wards-cartoon-network-hit-33862/.
Lyon, Karen. "The Four Humors: Eating in the Renaissance." Shakespeare and Beyond, 2015. https://shakespeareandbeyond.folger.edu/2015/12/04/the-four-humors-eating-in-the-renaissance/.
Lyotard, Jean-François. *The Postmodern Condition: A Report on Knowledge*. Translated by G. Bennington and B. Massumi. Manchester, UK: Manchester University Press, 1983.
Matyszak, Philip. *Greek and Roman Myths*. London: Thames & Hudson, 2010.
McDonnell, Chris. *The Art of Ooo*. New York: Abrams Books, 2014.
Nicol, Bran. *The Cambridge Introduction to Postmodern Fiction*. Cambridge, UK: Cambridge University Press, 2009.
Perlmutter, David. *The Encyclopedia of American Animated Television Shows*. Lanham, MD: Rowman & Littlefield.
Poniewozik, James. "*Adventure Time*, TV's Surreal Masterpiece, Comes to an End." *The New York Times*, 2018. https://www.nytimes.com/2018/09/02/arts/television/adventure-time-appraisal-series-finale.html.
Sava, Oliver. "*Adventure Time* Concludes with a Celebration of What Makes It So Special." *The A.V. Club*, 2018. https://www.avclub.com/adventure-time-concludes-with-a-celebration-of-what-mak-1828785830.
Sava, Oliver. "A Glitch Is a Glitch." *The A.V. Club*, 2013. https://tv.avclub.com/adventure-time-a-glitch-is-a-glitch-1798176447.
Seibert, Fred. "Algebraic!" Frederator, 2007. http://archives.frederatorblogs.com/frederator_studios/2007/11/03/algebraic/.
Thomas, Paul. *Exploring the Land of Ooo: An Unofficial Overview and Production History of Cartoon Network's* Adventure Time. Lawrence: University of Kansas Libraries, 2020.
Thurm, Eric. "*Adventure Time*'s Series Finale Lives Up to the Show's Spirit and Leaves the

Future Open." *Polygon*, 2018. https://www.polygon.com/2018/9/3/17797024/adventure-time-ending-series-finale-come-along-with-me.

Tran, Andrew. "Experimental Animation: The Guest Animators of *Adventure Time*." OverMental, 2015. https://overmental.com/content/experimental-animation-the-guest-animators-of-adventure-time-20957.

Waugh, Patricia. *Metafiction: The Theory and Practice of Self-Conscious Fiction*. London: Routledge, 2001.

Webb, Charles. "It's *Adventure Time* with Series Creator Pendleton Ward." MTV News, 2011. http://www.mtv.com/news/2621472/its-adventure-time-with-series-creator-pendleton-ward/.

Making a New Meaning for Man in The Land of OOO

Object-Oriented Ontology, the NonHuman, and Difference in Distant Lands

Al Valentín

"The greater good," Y5 says shakily, resolving to give up in "BMO."

When reading this sentence, what image is conjured? Who is Y5? What is Y5? Do you imagine a human? Someone else? Something else? Why? What about BMO? What is a BMO? Now if you're given some more details—if you're told that Y5 is a rabbit, a scientist, a girl, and a hero—what changes? Does that change how you perceive Y5? In what ways? Why?

For fans of the popular series *Adventure Time*, the image of Y5, the scientist rabbit, may seem not only normal but obvious, just as the existence of BMO as an assemblage of videogame-machine-robot-sheriff-hero feels natural. In the Land of Ooo, the fictional post-apocalyptic setting for the *Adventure Time* series, the nonhuman reigns supreme. But for those unfamiliar with the series, the sentence that begins this essay likely has less coherence, with names that are outside the frame of reference for today's humans, made even more confusing by the exclusion of gendered pronouns for either party.

This moment of cartoonish reflection is aimed at uncovering what assumptions we have around agency, speech, and conscious thought. It asks us to reconsider what knowledge we believe we gain in the naming of things and our uninterrogated usage of them. Are our assumptions about some innate truth or meaning of people, places, and things shaped by the descriptive, oftentimes identity-based, words we ascribe to them? Furthermore, it begs the question: how does the greater good shift when we seek to embrace radical alterity and radical compassion with a pinch of whimsical absurdity? How can the world change for the better when we consider what it means to be in community and solidarity with all humans, nonhuman animals, and objects, and act with that understanding in mind?

In previous work,[1] I have argued that Cartoon Network's *Adventure Time* teaches children a more expansive and compassionate understanding of human difference as valuable and necessary thereby building healthier interpersonal and social relations amongst children. This essay, in contrast, builds on this work by analyzing the HBO Max miniseries continuing the mainline story, *Distant Lands,* to consider how we can all stand to have a healthier engagement with difference beyond the figure of the human and towards objects. Rather than framing difference as a quality that only has social and political implications for humans, considering how this reverberates to all forms of not just life, but being, gives us a chance to exist beyond traditional hierarchies that lock us within unequal power relations.

By viewing the Land of Ooo as seen in *Distant Lands* through the philosophical lens of Object-Oriented Ontology (abbreviated as OOO and pronounced Triple O), I argue that we can find an ontological framework of being with objects that seeks not to understand them or to know them, but to respect them regardless. By taking OOO's claim of the unknowability of objects seriously, we can embrace the seemingly absurd position of being with objects that is central to the show's charm and that is key in building a world that values all forms of being. An emphasis on being with objects moves away from practices that traditionally seek to dominate difference by imposing truth, names, and purposes onto objects. Instead, we can enter into community and solidarity that asks us to simultaneously take everything seriously but ourselves. *Distant Lands*, in form and content, is a rich source for beginning to understand OOO as well as a model to make use of its framework towards a better life, animate or otherwise.

Introduction to Object-Oriented Ontology

Object-oriented ontology is a branch of philosophy chiefly concerned with metaphysics or ontology, which can be described as the study of being or the study of reality. OOO was formulated by Graham Harman in his dissertation and revised in his first book *Tool-Being: Heidegger and the Metaphysics of Objects.*[2] His 2017 book, *Object-Oriented Ontology: A New Theory of Everything,* is specifically aimed at putting forth a clear, lucid, and accessible explanation of the field.[3]

OOO is a philosophical intervention to philosophy's near-obsession with unraveling the mysteries of the human at the expense of other types of nonhuman life and other forms of being beyond life itself. One of its main tenants is that it rejects the manner through which philosophy (and perhaps society at large) has tended to frame human life as above other forms of life and inert matter. By object, Harman writes, "the only necessary criterion for an object in OOO is that it be irreducible in both directions: an object is more than its pieces and less than its effects."[4] Therefore, objects within OOO are not subject to what Harman would term undermining or overmining. An object is not defined by the smallest parts that make it up, a concept that would undermine the existence of the object as a thing-in-itself. Furthermore, an object is not an ideal that exists somewhere beyond or apart from the object, for this would rob the object of its ability to be in itself, independent of human concepts or inventions. By emphasizing the object alongside the human, Harman, and others in the field, unravel the ways that we have narrowly assumed that being is based on the qualities of able-bodied humans: the capacity for speech, reason, agency, ethics, and thought itself. This is another chiefly important aspect of OOO, as it denies that being has to be bound up with these capacities which would render only humans capable of being and not all other types of objects. Furthermore, these criteria also serve to excise human life without these capacities, emphasizing how the category of the human has ableism built within its structures, a point that will be returned to in-depth later.

But even as Harman encourages us to level the playing field and put forth what he terms a flat ontology, this is not where OOO remains indefinitely. Starting with a flat ontology forces us to have different standards for what counts as being, bringing us to a deeper sense of being as a whole—and not just to humans in particular. That being said, the goal is not to claim that all forms of being are exactly the same. Harman writes:

> If we imagine that after fifty years of philosophizing a OOO thinker were to say nothing more than 'humans, animals, inanimate matter and fictional characters all equally exist,' then not much progress would have been made. In short, we expect a philosophy to tell us about the features that belong to everything, but we also want philosophy to tell us about the differences between various kinds of things.[5]

We must first be able to accept the realness of these different types of objects and afford them a sort of respect before we can attend to the distinctions between them. By emphasizing the manner through which existence can and should be attributed to animals, matter, and fictional characters, we have a fuller understanding of existence. Furthermore, the imperative to consider fictional characters as existing, being real in a deeper sense, enables us to sit with the entities of *Adventure Time* and consider how their existence reveals new ways of being that are just as viable and meaningful.

This push to respect all forms of matter, being, and existence is further built upon by the work of Timothy Morton. Their work considers

OOO in the larger context of ecology and environmentalism. They do this by engaging with the Anthropocene, a marker of geological time acknowledging the negative impact of Capital H Human existence on the planet. The Anthropocene puts into perspective how our lives, choices, and larger policies have reshaped our environment, climate, and other species. In a larger sense, the Anthropocene is an age in which the assumption and near-obsession with human superiority has fundamentally reshaped the planet in ways that threaten all forms of being, both human and non-human.

Morton's *Humankind: Solidarity with Nonhuman People* (2017) posits that our solidarity with nonhuman people is not just a necessity for the survival of all forms of being, but a practice of kindness that can engage our fascination and pleasure, as well as the fascination and pleasure of other forms of life/non-life. Morton writes, "Our capacity for fascination is what fuels solidarity, not some pre-theoretical, pre-fabricated concept of need. Fascination is the aesthetic gravitational pull of entities toward one another, the dynamics of solidarity, within a forcefield-like matrix of sensitivities."[6] Fascination is a force, a feeling, an object that we are pulled in by. Fascination is the heart of what it means to be with objects. You are pulled towards them, not out of a desire to understand them, to lock them in place, or make them concrete and static but because something about them feels good. There is a sensory component to the way that we relate to anything.

But that sensory component is not just a character or quality of human life. Building on this Morton considers how a vegetarian is able to produce more pleasure for animals through their decision to not eat meat. They write, "You become fascinated by enhancing and expanding non-human pleasure modes."[7] And in the decision to not eat meat—or more specifically "piggies" as Morton states—you enable those pigs to be more pig-like. They are more able to fully be what they are through the lack of human intervention. They can have more pleasure in the act of being pigs when their lives are able to "go about their piggy business."[8] Morton points this out as a way of reconceptualizing environmentalism beyond the structural frameworks that maintain little to no value in the pleasure of other forms of being. It is also the construction of an ecological politic that centers pleasure in a democratic way; it is not just about human desire but the pleasure of all parties involved.

If then, we can conceive of the pleasure of pigs and other objects, then we would have to assume that there is some innate sense of being in a meaningful way. Perhaps not exactly a self but a being. This fits in with Harman's theorization of the object and he uses the Spanish philosopher and poet José Ortega y Gasset to continue to build it out. In reading one of his earlier works,[9] Harman shows how Ortega emphasizes the unknowability of any object we can encounter. Harman works with Ortega's point that "there is nothing we can make an object of cognition, nothing that can exist for us unless it becomes an image, a concept, an idea—unless, that is, it stops being what it is in order to become a shadow or an outline of itself."[10] Harman begins to make a distinction between the real object and the sensual object and real qualities and sensual qualities.[11] We have access only to the sensual objects and their sensual qualities and do not have access to the real object and its real qualities. As soon as cognition takes place, what we are experiencing is something distinct from the real object and its real qualities. The real exists beyond our grasp and in Ortega's understanding, this truth constitutes the I-ness of objects. As Ortega writes:

> "I" means, then, not this person as distinct from another, nor, even less, people as distinct from things, but rather all things—men, things, situations, inasmuch as they are occurring, being, executing themselves. Each of us is "I" according to this, not for belonging to a privileged zoological species equipped with a project making apparatus called consciousness, but more simply because he *is* something. The red leather box that I have before me is not an "I" because it is only an image I have, an image is exactly not what is imaged. … There is the same difference between a pain that someone tells me about and a pain that I feel as there is between the red that I see and the being red of this red leather box. *Being red* is for it what hurting is for me. Just as there is an I-John Doe, there is also an I-red, an I-water, and an I-star. Everything from the point of view within itself, is an "I"[12]

Here Ortega reframes what it means to be an I by removing the qualifications of consciousness. To be at all is to always be an I for Ortega and for Harman. Marking the distinction between the I that observes and the I that experiences or feels, we can understand all manner of objects as being the experiencers of particular modes of being. While I may experience the image of the box in front of me, the shadow of its redness, I cannot experience its being red. Thus, for Ortega, the I-ness is ascribed to people, things, places, qualities. The interiority that is emphasized is interesting because it marks us apart from the innate being of one another and yet brings us together in that we are all subject to this truth. If we all have I-ness, then there is even more reason to be concerned with the pleasure of the I's around us.

OOO, in line with Harman's framing, is then most centrally a critique of the possibility and necessity of knowledge itself. Even as philosophy may appear to be a field chiefly tasked with understanding and knowing the world, Harman seems to forge a distinction between the study of an object and our capacity to fully grasp that object at the level of the field. In making this point, Harman writes, "Even Socrates' famous name for his profession, philosophy, means the love of wisdoms rather than the possession of it."[13] This distinction is important firstly because it enables Harman to frame the field of philosophy as one that is more in line with the arts and aesthetics than natural sciences. Furthermore, this framework allows us a way to center Morton's pleasure, fascination, exploration, and play rather than what I argue are colonial and racist practices of capture; after all, this framing of knowledge through possession reflects the colonial and racist practices that have taken people as objects of study in ways that have historically and currently continue to only center domination. Harman's intervention reminds us that there are other ways of being that do not depend on rigid forms of outwardly imposed definitions and a desire to make static objects that are always in motion. OOO then becomes less a form of knowledge production than it is a form of love production. Similar to Morton, Harman frames OOO as a means through which love and respect for the nonhuman, for the non-alive, can be cultivated. This makes *Adventure Time* a perfect bedfellow for OOO because of the means through which this respect is so mentally explored and taught within each of the episodes.

Feminist Politics and OOO

It is with this move away from the domination inherent in knowledge and possession that I see one of the most important connections between OOO and feminist politics. Dehumanization and objectification are two distinct yet interrelated concepts that feminism has traditionally been invested in understanding and pushing back on. Using Morton's terminology, dehumanization and objectification in essence prevent the full pleasure and full being of those who are subject to them. OOO and engagements with posthumanism/transhumanism help us consider what these terms exactly mean, how these processes happen and how to differently relate to animals and objects in ways that can expand that pleasure for all.

Built out of my investment and engagement with Black feminist theory, I define feminism as a project to end oppression on the basis of categories of difference. While feminism is often chiefly framed as a movement built in opposition to sexism, the work of bell hooks[14] and Audre Lorde[15] have both emphasized that oppression has been systemically created and maintained by assigning particular value and worth to categories of difference and identity such as race, gender, sexuality, ability, class, and size. Furthermore, they have both made clear how the oppression of each serves to uphold the oppression of the others. This understanding is the basis of Kimberlé Crenshaw's 1989 intervention into discrimination law where the term "intersectionality" was coined to explain how the interconnectedness of oppression is written into law and has a particular impact on those who exist at the intersection of multiple categories of oppression, particularly black women. And even though this term was coined in 1989, the concept it represents has been central to Black feminist scholars and activists for much longer than that.[16] Human difference (and the meanings and consequences attached to that difference) is a chief concern for feminists.

OOO is implicated with my vision of the project of feminism as it encourages us to consider differences outside the realm of humans alone. By questioning how difference is given meaning in the context of non-human animals and objects, we can think of difference alongside other binaries: alive/dead and animate/inanimate. Building our conception of difference out in this manner enables us to have more meaningful understandings of how interconnected these forms of oppression are and enable us to find new ideas, new collaborators to unravel these systems alongside. A theorist like Sylvia Wynter is of particular use because she emphasizes that the current concept of the Human has been constructed through the shift from religious framings of Man to a scientific understanding of Man as a biological organism.[17] Wynter charts the history of the construction of the Human by showing how colonialism and racism are written into the knowledge project of the scientific understanding of the human and how our conception of what it is to be is shaped by that history. She gives us a history of the colonial and racist capture mentioned before as integral in the sciences. She asks us to consider how the construction of the Human itself has been the problem that must be tended to.

As Zakiyyah Iman Jackson notes, when posthumanism projects or philosophical projects like OOO do not engage specifically with fields like Black feminist thought, they miss powerful ways to understand the larger picture and find different ways of being, different ways of relating.[18] Philosophy is made all the richer through engagement with people asking similar questions in different ways. In fact, in *Becoming Human: Matter and Meaning in an Antiblack World*, Jackson uses racial difference and the sexual difference that it is intertwined with to understand how blackness refigures the Human as well as looks at Black art and cultural production to see how there are different ontological frameworks already on display and in practice.[19] Similarly, the work of Alexis Pauline Gumbs pushes us to find lessons from other forms of life, elucidating the differences and similarities between human life and marine mammal life and showing that humans are not the only arbiters of knowledge and not the only ones with the capacity to change the world in subversive and liberatory ways.[20]

But it is not just nonhuman animal life that has the potential to show us new ways of being. Jane Bennet's *Vibrant Matter* asks us to more deeply consider that objects have the capacity to affect us as much as we affect them, considering things like garbage as having power over us.[21] Mel Chen's *Animacies* builds on Bennet's perspective using linguistics, queer theory, disability studies, and other fields to further argue that the agential or affective capacity of objects and animals also serve to uphold and reshape whose racialized, classed, gendered and sexual lives are worth living and worth protecting by the state.[22] Similarly to Jackson, Chen shows that objects are never neutral and that questions of power hover behind all these messy human animals, nonhuman animals, and object relations. Similarly, Katherine Behar's edited collection *Object-Oriented Feminism* brings together writers to show the generative conversations that can be developed between the two fields.[23] Behar's own essay within looks at Botox to consider what we can learn from death by moving away from the overemphasis on what vibrancy and animacy exists within objects to instead consider what we with animacy and life can learn from death.[24] Instead of seeing death as an abject state to move away from, she considers what we can gain from moving closer to it. While Behar's essay is provocative and thought-provoking, I would still caution that this proximity to death is one that has been and still is regularly experienced by marginalized people. We must be careful to not fetishize this position as people of color, queer people, trans people, disabled people, and others continue to fight for their lives in the face of systematic oppression.

One avenue to walk this tightrope might be through engagement with disability studies. Disability studies allow us to push back on normative understandings of ontology around ableist norms of capacity. Conceiving what it is to be outside of these frameworks are important questions that are implicated in the rights and survival of people with disabilities. Allison Kafer writes, "'Quality of life' is a familiar refrain in the discussions of disability, as the term has often been used as a measure of the worth of disabled people's lives. 'Measure' is perhaps too precise a term, as the meaning or criteria of 'quality' of life are often taken to be common sense."[25] Assumptions around human capacity frame the lives of those with different capacities as not having an appropriative level of "quality" and therefore subject to invasive medical interventions at best and outright extermination at its most extreme. Disabled people who are more aligned with passivity are in a sense marked as already closer to death in ways that frame their lives as not worth living. Through their disability, they are framed as both not having some literal quality of life as well as the more metaphorical sense. The work of Eunjung Kim is particularly provocative in seeing what types of lessons objecthood can provide us and how those lessons can impact disabled humans as well. In considering what passivity can mean in the context of dolls, Kim argues that there are reverberations into the question of disability care and rights. Kim writes, "Instead of defending the fraught definition of 'human' as the basis of a 'moral' and caring world in order to valorize disabled existence, I suggest recognizing the intercorporeal ontology of objects, with the aim not of conferring inherent rights on them but, rather, of undermining efforts to deny a being humanness on the basis of object-like status."[26] Here Kim positions a recognition of the ontology of objects as a means to ease some of the negative associations with passivity that have historically written some being outside the basis of life worth living. By pushing back on how forms of life/nonlife are prevented from having their own I-ness, we can work to see the value in more states of being.

OOO in the Land of Ooo

The *Distant Lands* special "BMO" manages to encapsulate so much of the tenants of OOO in the first few minutes, a testament to the power of art and aesthetics that Harman himself so deeply values. In this episode, videogame-robot-sheriff character BMO narrates visions of existence in space as they fly to Mars with companion potatoes. They ask the viewer:

> Did you know there are more stars in the sky than there are grains of sand in the sky? It's true. This is a rare asteroid made entirely of heavy metal. His name is Lars Darksaber. I don't know any of these guys. Whoa! Look at that big boy go! That's gonna be the biggest comet I ever did I—[*Suddenly a giant moth swallows the comet whole*] What the heck? Let's forget we saw this. Just another ineffable mystery in a universe of mysteries. [*BMO picks up a guitar pick*] I wrote this song for my hat! [*BMO begins to sing*]

The ontological import of this moment is three-fold. First, it shows how the series conceives objects in ways that exist beyond the necessity of speech or conscious thought to be a being. While BMO is an object with what viewers might more easily assume is an obvious consciousness because of their capacity for speech, BMO emphasizes the I-ness of all the objects encountered thereby troubling this anthropocentric hierarchy of being. The asteroid has a name, one that is perhaps imposed by BMO but one that at least makes an attempt at honoring the importance of that asteroid, their agency, and their being. BMO refers to a giant comet as a big boy, marking the comet as a nonhuman person. Second, it emphasizes the fundamental unknowability of the world we experience that is central to OOO. BMO is at first confused about the comet being eaten whole by this galactic moth, but rather than try to understand the why, BMO offers it up to us as "just another ineffable mystery in a universe of mysteries." Space becomes a zone where knowledge and understanding in the typical sense are not framed as the most valuable. Indeed, there is little attachment to that traditional form of knowledge. Lastly, BMO singing a song to their hat emphasizes a politics of pleasure that is central to BMO's characterization throughout the episode, offering us a different way of relating to objects that are politically viable in this world. BMO considers the I-ness, the being of the hat as a nonhuman person deserving pleasure even if it is not alive in the traditional sense. The hat cannot give BMO thanks for the song or show its own pleasure. Still, BMO understands that being kind to it and trying to bring it joy is still a worthy action. BMO sees innate value in all forms of being; one doesn't need to be alive in the traditional sense to deserve respect.

These points are all further expanded upon throughout the episode. When BMO crash lands on The Drift, the home of Y5, they are drawn to making the lives of everybody and everything better. For example, when a farmer laments a sea lard, a floating blob-like creature, is cold and stuck out in space, BMO immediately jumps into action to save them. When BMO returns the sea lard to their owner, BMO is horrified to find that the farmer intends to eat the sea lard. In exchange for saving the sea lard, BMO demands that the farmer take care of the creature and give it the best life possible; BMO then names the sea lard Ricky. As Timothy Morton writes, "Human-kindness goes beyond tolerance, which is based on an emotional economy of need, to appreciation, appreciation for no reason, based on an emotional economy of desire. This entails the possibility not of refraining from pleasure (which is simply displaced pleasure or pleasurable restraint as such) but of allowing other beings to have pleasure."[27] BMO is chiefly concerned with giving other beings access to pleasure, because this giving of pleasure to others gives BMO pleasure. BMO does this regardless of whether an object has the capacity for speech. For BMO then, there is little to no ontological difference between the hat for which they write their song and the sea lard that they believe deserves to have a good life. Thus, BMO is enacting the politics of pleasure for objects that Morton sees as an ecological and political imperative.

In a humorous turn at the end of the episode, the sea lard flies BMO through space back home. When BMO thanks the sea lard for their help, they reply in plain English, "My name is Twinkletoes." The sea lard had a reality outside of the existence of BMO's sense of what and who they were. Even this brief joke embodies OOO's understanding of the limits of our knowledge and the futility of our assumptions around objects. It is the absurdist humor of *Adventure Time* that also embodies the excess that cannot be fully ascertained or explained or described that OOO holds about objects. Harman writes about the ways in which not knowing can be more impactful than when something is made more explicit. It is the mystery and the unspoken that cannot be pulled out of the object that in some ways gives it its power. Using the example of a joke which asks, "How many surrealists does it take to screw in a light bulb?" and answers, "Fish,"[28] Harman writes, "While reasonably amusing in this form, it is utterly ruined as humor if one is forced to explain the literal meaning, as often happens when children are listening in on adult conversation."[29] The form of *Adventure Time* itself rests on the same sense of mystery and excess that BMO sees within space. Part of the humor of the show, and many other children's shows, relies on either taking the mundane and making it magical or taking the magical and making it mundane. This flip works to upend expectations of children and frames the absurdity as part of the pleasure, part of the joy of watching.

This sense of mystery is also on display in the second *Distant Lands* special, "Obsidian." The episode has two intertwined narratives: The first centers on the evolving romantic relationship between fan favorites Marceline the Vampire Queen and Princess Bubblegum from breakup to makeup. The second follows a lizard-like monster named Molto Larvo who has repeatedly threatened The Glass Kingdom, where See-Through Princess rules. Centuries ago, Princess Bubblegum was tasked with saving the kingdom from Molto Larvo with the power of science. Annoyed by Princess Bubblegum being overly focused on her work, and jealous of the way that Princess Bubblegum seems to be valuing the needs of the glass people over Marceline's, Marceline performs a song that embodies her anger at Princess Bubblegum. In the lyrics, she pushes Princess Bubblegum away, asserting that she does not care about her, ultimately breaking up with her after she does so. Marceline is treated as a deity of sorts in the kingdom because she successfully locked Molto Larvo away through the power of music long ago. But after See-Through Princess's best friend, Glassboy, accidentally unleashes Molto Larvo, he goes on a quest to bring Marceline back to defeat the monster again.

Princess Bubblegum and Marceline are thus forced to relive their breakup when Marceline performs the song again, but to Marceline's surprise, it no longer works to stop Molto Larvo. Once this happens, Princess Bubblegum intervenes, aiming to use science to stop the monster from destroying the kingdom. Princess Bubblegum values the traditional forms of knowledge production that mean she can use science to uncover everything about the monster and fix it. Through experimentation, she believes that she can learn "the truth of its weakness." Marceline decides to find a way to write a song even more angry than before believing that this is what will save the kingdom instead. By returning to a previous home, Marceline is able to work through the trauma of feeling abandoned by her mother during the post-apocalypse that created the Land of Ooo, and realize that because of this, she consistently pushes Princess Bubblegum away. By pretending she wants to be alone rather than admit that she feels abandoned, Marceline is given a false sense of power and control.

By the time Marceline returns to the Glass Kingdom, all of Princess Bubblegum's attempts at unlocking true knowledge of the beast have failed. After Princess Bubblegum and Marceline get trapped in the monster's lair and are about to die, Marceline realizes that she must be honest with Bubblegum in their last moments. She thus proceeds to sing the song "Monster." As Molto Larvo listens to this expression of love, connection, vulnerability, and openness, their exterior cracks open to reveal a different form. Molto Larvo was originally a creature who was mocked by others after sustaining a crack in their head; Molto Larvo then emotionally retreated inward and grew into a monster that harmed others. It is only through the song—a piece of art, that has meaning not just for Marceline and Princess Bubblegum but also for Larvo himself—that the "monster" can grow as a being and find a kinder way of relating to the subjects of the Glass Kingdom. There is an excess there that could be unlocked not by the science of Bubblegum, but by art. The song has value to the author and the recipient for which it was penned, but it has value beyond that. While we may be unable to have full knowledge of the object, that does not necessarily impact its value.

This brings us back to the previous episode, "BMO." In one scene, BMO is scanned by Hugo, the leader of The Drift, and judged to be an object both without purpose and thereby without value. BMO cannot be used to fulfill the goal that Hugo has for them: to use their parts to leave the failing space station. That being said, BMO has value, use, capacities that exist beyond the corporeality and physicality of their form. BMO exceeds what their use and value are on the basis of their whole existence of parts as well as in the reducible parts that produce that whole. In fact, Y5 is confounded by BMO at first. She says, "This robot expends energy in ways that yield it no benefit. So weird." This statement reveals that Y5 has no concept of action outside of that which benefits her, a position likely produced by the conditions under which she grew up. BMO's actions are about ensuring the pleasure of as many people as they can, in Morton's terms. And even as BMO's existence and being are not purposefully created to enhance the lives of those around them, it still has that effect. While we cannot impose the meaning and use of an object on how it relates to human existence, we cannot assume that we have nothing to learn from objects. BMO proves that we do.

The third episode of the *Distant Lands* series further troubles the distinction between animate/inanimate as well as alive/dead. "Together

Again" centers on Finn's posthumous travels through the Dead Worlds, the afterlife of the Land of Ooo. Envisioned as a series of 50 levels, with each level representing gradations between torture and paradise, the Dead Worlds are a place of transition from life to death, thereby troubling that binary, but also a transition between different forms of vibrancy and animation within death itself. Those who exist in the "50th Dead World" have moved beyond desire and, in doing so, have been transformed into beings of pure light that transcend their physical form. Jake the Dog has transcended in this way and is at this apex living without a care in a state of pure acceptance. When Finn dies, Finn is put into the 37th Dead World. Whatever merits the 37th Dead World may have, it is missing one key element with which Finn is unable to cope: there is no Jake there.

The episode then centers around Finn in a desperate quest to be reunited with Jake. In his quest, Finn is forced to defy the new ruler of the Dead Worlds, New Death. New Death is the son of the two-headed snake deity Life and the skeleton deity Death. In a moment when, under the influence of the Lich, New Death strikes his father in anger, killing him, Death takes a new form as a tree and New Death is forced to take on his father's role as a guide to and through the Dead Worlds. Now possessed by the Lich and determined to blast the afterlife into oblivion, New Death uses Finn's intense attachment to his brother to draw Jake out of the 50th Dead World. New Death's plan works: Jake is drawn to Finn. But when he appears before his brother, Jake does not recognize Finn. It is only through a piece of gum—Jake's favorite gum—that he begins to be pulled back towards earthly desires. The gum is, in essence, more powerful than Finn at this moment. As he spends more time with Finn, he regains his sense of care and love for Finn as well as his sense of justice that existed before his total acceptance into Nirvana. While this happens, New Death then sneaks into the 50th Dead World and begins trying to eliminate all forms of life and being.

In order to stop this from happening, Finn and Jake appeal to Life, the goddess who oversees reincarnation and the transmigration of souls. They tell her of how New Death, her son, is planning on preventing all forms of being and reincarnation and she decides to aid them. One of the most interesting moments of the episode for the purposes of this essay is the manner through which Life refashions forms of life into something else. In one instance, she sees two spirit essences that "are a package deal," and transforms them into a carrot and a pea. Within the show, then, what we think of as objects have an essence that exceeds their corporeal form. Indeed, the manner through which the new carrot and pea forms are framed as being equivalent to the spirits' previous forms enables a flat ontology. For Life, there is no distinction between the essence, their previous form, and their new form as the carrot and the pea. Here all forms of being can be thought of as alive in that they have inherent value that exists beyond the gaze of the human, as Life herself is not a human but an entity composed of two snake heads.

In Conclusion

This essay began with Y5 talking about "the greater good." In that first episode, "the greater good" exists as a catchphrase of Hugo, the leader of The Drift. What is the greater good? Who is it good for? Hugo, unbeknownst to Y5 and the rest of the space station, has been systematically robbing different pods or sectors of the space station to build what he calls the Unity Pod. Framed as a way to get everybody off of the failing station, Hugo actually intends to save himself at the expense of everybody else. Despite portraying himself as a determined and selfless leader whose goal is to bring everybody with him to survival, to the future, he is actually only concerned with what objects can do for him. As another robot victim of Hugo, named CGO, says to Y5, "Hugo's a great guy … as long as he thinks you're good for something." It is this sense of using, of capturing the object, the animal, the human framed as other that has perpetuated so much of the injustice that exists in the episode and within the world at large.

In some ways, Hugo's position is the opposite of OOO in that he sees everything and everybody as an object to dissect and use, thereby highlighting that the position of the object is not inherently liberatory. However, BMO's path shows us a different way. BMO brings us back to that sense of how we can maximize not just our own pleasure but that of everything else around us. BMO is an object existing among objects, who moves towards a better world for all involved. BMO shows us an OOO framing of the greater good that inspires the citizens of The Drift to work together. It can be seductive and dare I say easy to frame the consumption of objects and the capturing of their potentiality as the only way. But *Adventure Time* pushes past this.

Fittingly in the last episode of *Distant Lands* entitled "Wizard City," we follow series regular Peppermint Butler on his quest to regain his former magical power, having been made younger and weaker by an assassination attempt in the mainline series. Peppermint Butler, having once been banned from Wizard City, is now a small child entering Wizard School. While the ghost of his formerly grown self appears to him and pushes him towards the ill-gotten power he previously had, Peppermint Butler finds a friend in the stage magic-loving wizard student Cadebra.

It is their connection that pushes him to be better, to want to gain power without having to hurt people to get it. Peppermint Butler learns to focus on the power of collaboration that he can have with Cadebra rather than through the forceful taking of power that stands to hurt them both and the world at large. It is not extractive but additive: a beautiful amalgam that enhances the capacities of all involved. It is a hopeful episode that shows we can always choose to be different, to be better, to be more accountable to ourselves and to those we are in community with. That accountability can change the world.

Similarly, in *Hyposubjects*, Timothy Morton and Dominic Boyer come together to consider how hypersubjects (those who have the most power, e.g., white, cis, heterosexual, able-bodied) must find different ways of relating to others if we have any hope of creating a "nonviolent or less violent" world.[30] Hypersubjects connect nicely with Lorde's mythical norm, wherein those in society who fit into the privileged sides of binaries around difference are given the most power.[31] Instead, we must turn to the hyposubjects, those that exist underneath or within the cracks of the larger structures of society. Morton and Boyer write, "Hyposubjects are necessarily feminist, colorful, queer, ecological, transhuman, and intrahuman. They do not recognize the rule of androleukoheteropetromodernity and the apex species behavior it epitomizes and reinforces."[32] Hyposubjects are the beings who focus less on epistemological truths than they do on experimentation. They focus less on hierarchy and domination and more on ways of fostering all types of being. They are obviously not just human and yet, it is central to their position that "…they play; they care; they adapt; they hurt; they laugh."[33] It is the connections between different forms of life in *Distant Lands* that are its strengths. The connections between Y5 and BMO, between Finn and Jake, between Marceline and Princess Bubblegum and Larvo, and between Peppermint Butler and Cadebra, are models of the care, collaboration, play, hurt, and laughter that can still be found even in dire circumstances and that must be centered if we hope to have not just a nonviolent future but any future at all. The Land of OOO, its characters, and stories are visions of solidarity that are sorely needed as we inhabit a world of global warming, pandemic, and systemic inequality and domination.

Distant Lands and Morton and Boyer are both asking us to humble ourselves, to listen to the hyposubjects whether they be cartoon or flesh or plastic, to consider what they need and how we can work to provide for as many of us as possible. We must be aware of how we are implicated in either the suffering or pleasure of others and how we can maximize the latter. Audre Lorde wrote, "Survival is not a theory. In what way do I contribute to the subjugation of any part of those who I define as my people?

Insight must illuminate the particulars of our lives: who labors to make the bread we waste, or the energy it takes to make nuclear poisons which will not biodegrade for one thousand years; or who goes blind assembling the microtransistors in our inexpensive calculators?"[34] The lives of calculators and bread and the planet are implicated in the lives of people. Just as the lives of calculator users are implicated in the lives of calculator makers. Lorde does not need to know the specific person making those calculators to care about how her usage of one may impact them. In the same way, we should not need to know an object to care for it, we should not need to know people to care for them.

The way we define who and what is in community with us shapes the actions that we choose to take. Survival is not a theory but a practice, a way of relating and caring. A more expansive notion of community in an ontological sense is key to reaching that better future. As Morton and Boyer and Lorde and Peppermint Butler all make clear, we must be aware of our implications in the violence of our current world. Morton and Boyer write, "…people like us have a particular responsibility for our present condition. Not to take a savior position but to try to commit ourselves to a program of rebecoming as something less dangerous. To reprogram."[35] While a children's cartoon may seem an odd place to start in the battle for a world of nonhuman solidarity, it is that sense of oddness that belies the point exactly. It is the humor and absurdity of the interconnections of all forms of life that give us a beautiful model of the world that could be. They give us a model of how to reprogram towards something less dangerous. We can be something else. We can be the newly minted Peppermint Butler we want to see in the world.

NOTES

1. Al Valentín, "Using the Animator's Tools to Dismantle the Master's House?"
2. Graham Harman, *Tool-Being.*
3. Graham Harman, *Object-Oriented Ontology.*
4. Harman, 53.
5. Harman, 55.
6. Timothy Morton, *Humankind*, 144.
7. Morton.
8. Morton.
9. José Ortega y Gasset, "An Essay in Esthetics by Way of Preface."
10. José Ortega y Gasset apud Graham Harman, *Object-Oriented Ontology*, 69–70.
11. Harman, 79.
12. José Ortega y Gasset, "An Essay in Esthetics by Way of Preface," 133–134.
13. Graham Harman, *Object-Oriented Ontology*, 5.
14. bell hooks, *Feminism Is For Everybody.*
15. Audre Lorde, *Sister Outsider.*
16. Brittney Cooper, "Intersectionality," *The Oxford Handbook of Feminist Theory.*

17. Sylvia Wynter, "Unsettling the Coloniality of Being/Power/Truth/Freedom: Towards the Human, After Man, Its Overrepresentation—An Argument."
18. Zakiyyah Iman Jackson, "Animal: New Directions in the Theorization of Race and Posthumanism."
19. Zakiyyah Iman Jackson, *Becoming Human*.
20. Alexis Pauline Gumbs, *Undrowned: Black Feminist Lessons From Marine Mammals*.
21. Jane Bennet, *Vibrant Matter: A Political Ecology of Things*.
22. Mel Chen, *Animacies: Biopolitics, Racial Mattering, and Queer Affect*.
23. Katherine Behar, ed., *Object-Oriented Feminism*.
24. Katherine Behar, "Facing Necrophilia, or 'Botox Ethics,'" *Object-Oriented Feminism*.
25. Allison Kafer, *Feminist, Queer, Crip*, 62.
26. Eunjung Kim, "Why Do Dolls Die?"
27. Morton, *Humankind*, 144.
28. Harman, 64.
29. Harman.
30. Timothy Morton and Dominic Boyer, *Hyposubjects*, 85.
31. Audre Lorde, *Sister Outsider*.
32. Timothy Morton and Dominic Boyer. "Hyposubjects."
33. Timothy Morton and Dominic Boyer. "Hyposubjects."
34. Audre Lorde, *Sister Outsider*, 139.
35. Timothy Morton and Dominic Boyer, *Hyposubjects*, 83.

References

Behar, Katherine. "Facing Necrophilia, or 'Botox Ethics.'" Essay. In *Object-Oriented Feminism*, 123–44. Minneapolis: University of Minnesota Press, 2016.
Behar, Katherine, ed. *Object-Oriented Feminism*. Minneapolis: University of Minnesota Press, 2016.
Bennett, Jane. *Vibrant Matter a Political Ecology of Things*. Durham: Duke University Press, 2010.
Chen, Mel Y. *Animacies: Biopolitics, Racial Mattering, and Queer Affect*. Durham: Duke University, 2012.
Cooper, Brittney. "Intersectionality." Essay. In *The Oxford Handbook of Feminist Theory*, edited by Lisa Jane Disch and M. E. Hawkesworth, 385–406. Oxford: Oxford University Press, 2018.
Crenshaw, Kimberle. "Demarginalizing the Intersection of Race and Sex: A Black Feminist Critique of Antidiscrimination Doctrine, Feminist Theory, and Antiracist Politics [1989]." *University of Chicago Legal Forum* 1989, no. 1 (2018): 139–67.
Gumbs, Alexis Pauline. *Undrowned*. Chico, CA: AK Press, 2021.
Harman, Graham. *Object-Oriented Ontology: A New Theory of Everything*. London: Pelican, 2018.
Harman, Graham. *Tool-Being: Heidegger and the Metaphysics of Objects*. Chicago: Open Court, 2002.
hooks, bell. *Feminism Is for Everybody: Passionate Politics*. New York: Routledge, 2015.
Jackson, Zakiyyah Iman. *Becoming Human: Matter and Meaning in an Antiblack World*. New York: New York University Press, 2020.
Jackson, Zakiyyah Iman. "Review: Animal: New Directions in the Theorization of Race and Posthumanism." *Feminist Studies* 39, no. 3 (2013): 669–85.
Kafer, Alison. *Feminist, Queer, Crip*. Bloomington, IN: Indiana University Press, 2013.
Kim, Eunjung. "Why Do Dolls Die? The Power of Passivity and the Embodied Interplay between Disability and Sex Dolls." *Review of Education, Pedagogy, and Cultural Studies* 34, no. 3-4 (2012): 94–106. https://doi.org/10.1080/10714413.2012.686852.
Lorde, Audre. *Sister Outsider Essays and Speeches*. Berkeley: Ten Speed Press, 2007.

Morton, Timothy. *Humankind*. Brooklyn: Verso Books, 2019.
Morton, Timothy, and Dominic Boyer. "Hyposubjects." Society for Cultural Anthropology, January 21, 2016. https://culanth.org/fieldsights/hyposubjects.
Morton, Timothy, and Dominic Boyer. *Hyposubjects: On Becoming Human*. London: Open Humanities Press, 2021.
Ortega y Gasset, Jose. "An Essay in Esthetics by Way of Preface." Essay. In *Phenomenology and Art*, translated by Philip W. Silver, 127–49. New York: Norton, 2013.
Valentín, Al. "Using the Animator's Tools to Dismantle the Master's House? Gender, Race, Sexuality and Disability in Cartoon Network's Adventure Time and Steven Universe." Essay. In *Buffy to Batgirl: Essays on Female Power, Evolving Femininity and Gender Roles in Science Fiction and Fantasy*, edited by Julie Still and Zara T. Wilkinson, 175–215. Jefferson, NC: McFarland, 2019.
Wynter, Sylvia. "Unsettling the Coloniality of Being/Power/Truth/Freedom: Towards the Human, After Man, Its Overrepresentation—An Argument." *CR: The New Centennial Review* 3, no. 3 (2003): 257–337. https://doi.org/10.1353/ncr.2004.0015.

"Mind Games"
Mental and Emotional Toiling

Too Close for Comfort
On Finn the Human and Princess Bubblegum's Relationship

ZHI HWEE GOH

I begin this essay with a personal acknowledgment that this relationship between two main characters in *Adventure Time* which I am about to describe is perhaps the series' most obscure. I argue further that studying it out of deep respect for its form, nuance and strength has been its own reward, having reinforced my beliefs that this is a cartoon replete with philosophical wonder and that it is ultimately the love that its characters derive from the relationships they foster which colors their lives and tides them through the worst of adversity. If among *Adventure Time*'s greatest creative distinctions is the subverting of the cliché that is its hero rescuing and engaging in romantic union with the princess for whom he pines, then it must be acknowledged that its hero then earns and upholds his title not out of an infatuation for her, but out of profound loyalty. Subtle as it is, this dynamic of love and loyalty is steeped in the most trivial of traits Finn and Princess Bubblegum know about each other; for Princess Bubblegum, that he is "terrible at math" ("Slumber Party Panic"), that he can be cheered up with "feel-good waffles" ("The Music Hole"), that he was once a "young lad [who reminded her of] the Marshmallow kids" he once apprehended ("Scamps") and, above all, that she knows that he will be a hero ("The Enchiridion"), in the absence of any logical certainty she would typically demand to affirm a proposition with such reverberating implications for her kingdom, and the show. In abiding by this drive to subvert clichés, I seek to upset the quiescence of this general "affection"[1] which I am certain they share by floating it front-and-center, as I believe that in all that we celebrate about the love which drives *Adventure Time*, a failure to celebrate this bond between two of its main protagonists would be a tremendous loss of its art.

Finn and Princess Bubblegum share a relationship which is peculiar in that while it is one of the show's longest-running dynamics, it is also difficult to characterize closely. While it is a relationship colored by copious amounts of physical affection which includes kissing and cuddling, it is also fundamentally platonic, and therefore reflects a robust intimacy that could only have realistically developed over an extensive period of devoted interaction. Various episodes showcasing the pair inform us of the many roles she plays in Finn's life. She is his ruler, commander, mentor, schoolteacher and, in "The Tower," his advisor and counseller. That he unquestioningly absorbs her confession of deceiving him to teach him a lesson in "The Tower" reflects both his acknowledgment of this, and an utmost trust he places in her authority over him as a monarch, disciplinarian, educator and experienced elder. Therefore, in describing this relationship, we chart Finn's progressive emotional and psychological development throughout *Adventure Time*, which is inextricably tied to the role Princess Bubblegum assumes as a caregiver. More examples which elucidate her thorough influence on him and their closeness will be explored subsequently, but for now, the aforementioned observations collectively form a picture of a relationship premised on, among other qualities: altruism, investment and familiarity. This reading of their dynamic will thus center on this triad of qualities.

In isolating these qualities about them, I distinguish Finn and Princess Bubblegum's relationship from other significant character relationships in the show. Most significantly, I establish that this dynamic is premised on markedly different qualities from that which Princess Bubblegum shares with her canonical love interest, Marceline; for where altruism, investment and familiarity inspire how she relates to Finn, she commiserates with Marceline based on the contrasting premises of mutualism, commitment and the novelty of reconnecting with a long-lost friend from whom she has a lot to learn, and vice versa. Borrowing from ancient Greek parlance about love, I recognize these to be key differences identifying the former relationship as one that runs on *storge* and the latter on *philia*. Denominating Finn and Princess Bubblegum's relationship particularly under this banner of *storge*, a form of platonic affection that stems from a natural compulsion to nurture and protect and is contingent on a kinship which is strengthened through personal investment in the relationship,[2] is crucial for my central thesis: That is, that Princess Bubblegum has consistently adopted a parental outlook towards Finn and ergo, that the relationship they share is a unique permutation of a parent-child dynamic. Validating this relationship as being parental in nature will establish it as one which portrays a conflux of themes in adoptive parenthood, insecure attachment and passionate admiration characteristic of "puppy love" apparent in it in *Adventure Time*'s earlier seasons. It would thus be a rare exhibit even among numerous media examples of individual portrayals of each of these themes which have been widely explored in academia,[3] and one which has the potential to offer deeper insight into all these domains.

I advance this thesis while being cognizant of the fact that the canon of the series has yet to describe their relationship as such and hence, that we would need some ideas to incline ourselves towards it thus far. We might start by noting that the argument proposing the strength of Princess Bubblegum's maternal compulsions stems from her association with the piece of candy known as the "Mother Gum"; specifically, that this association derives from an allegory of postpartum depression illustrated by her creating the Candy Kingdom because she "[missed her] mind and [her] gum [being] in touch with dozens of others," then falling into despair when she is rejected by her created subjects.[4] It also explains her instinctual compassion for young, vulnerable characters like Lemonhope. In this vein, Hynden Walch's statement on Bubblegum's motivations for Finn ("she believes that she's best able to protect Finn while he's still young and vulnerable") aligns with such compulsions. Correspondingly, we recognize the conspicuous absence of a maternal figure in Finn's life following the passing of his adoptive parents, Joshua and Margaret, and that Finn, having grown up alongside his canine companion, Jake, relates to him as an adoptive brother rather than as a parent. Given his tender age at the time, the knowledge that Jake worked in the Candy Kingdom then and that no living parental figures then appeared to exist in Finn's life to fill a maternal role, we can reasonably expect that Finn, who "[reminded Princess Bubblegum of the preadolescent] Marshmallow kids [as] a young lad," would have found that in her. We further consider the history of trauma in Finn's childhood as his experiences with abandonment and bereavement early in life have left psychological scars which continue to haunt him ("I can't stand being abandoned—I'm sensitive to it!"—*Three Buckets*), and thereby reasonably assume that his psychological development, especially that which centers around his attachment to parental figures, has either been stunted or delayed. However, in characterizing Finn and Princess Bubblegum's relationship I hope to give not a psychoanalytical account of this child's development in this unique relationship with his parental figure, but a humanist one, as it is through qualitatively describing this relationship that further ethical and psychoanalytical study about its features can ensue, both for scholars who are interested in exploring thematic portrayals of parental dynamics in animation and scholars of parent-child ethics at large.

Preliminary Assumptions

Motivating this reading entails making reasonable assumptions that ground the perspectives Finn and Princess Bubblegum take on each other, justifying the logic that I propose drives their interactions. The first assumption I make for this purpose is that episodes, scenes and interactions in *Adventure Time* follow the realistic situational logic that we follow as rational, decision-making human agents, insofar as it supports the progression of *Adventure Time*'s plot. We use the original argument for situational logic proposed by Karl Popper[5] as applicable in this diegetic setting, which briefly states that individual wants and needs equally motivate decisions made by plot-influencing agents in diegetic situations as choices under this model are determined in equal weighting by both unless specified otherwise. We know that this logic informs both the chronological order of *Adventure Time*'s episodes as well as the foreshadowing and retroactive continuity which connects them. I quote *Adventure Time* writer and animator Rebecca Sugar, speaking on the gestation of the backstory for Princess Bubblegum and Marceline's romance, for the proof:

> It really goes all the way back to the time I spent on *Adventure Time* and when I got a chance to do some of the earlier episodes with Marceline and Bubblegum … The strategy at the time that I pitched was that because they're both centuries-old, milleniums-old, [they] had a relationship sometime in the past and they're unpacking that in a way that would be apparent. That was the only way to be able to do something with these characters and their relationship on screen.[6]

However, limiting characterization of the dialogue and action which the characters engage in throughout *Adventure Time* to this schema would understate the humanity the show espouses. Finn's iconic tagline, "Let's all be stupid … forever!," perhaps best encompasses the series' attitude to this. Keenly following its interest in celebrating the human condition means that *Adventure Time* celebrates the spontaneity and irrationality which characterizes us as much as our capacity for reason does. In the context of our discussion, we may recognize that our desires to form romantic relationships would never be determined by as simple a means as a cost-benefit analysis, nor would they be purely explicable by the whims and fancies of our emotions and afflictions. Additionally, our outlooks on "romance" are not pre-programmed within us. Thus, insofar as Princess Bubblegum becomes romantically involved with Marceline and not with Finn, both she and Finn do not engage in such a union for reasons which can be either rational or irrational and would therefore be ambiguous here. Knowing so, what best characterizes his attitude towards her, and if it has evolved, how so?

Answering these questions is the onus on this characterization of Finn and Princess Bubblegum's relationship around the values of familiarity, investment and altruism, which I state to be fundamental tenets informing their interactions. However, before embarking on this characterization, I need to make a second assumption about them; in particular, about the underlying "desire" that compels Finn to pine for her. I assume, especially, that the "[unrequited] puppy love" Finn harbors for her is not one borne out of *eros*. In making this assumption, I consider the propensity for Finn's definition of "romance" to be as transient as that of a child undergoing adolescence in the time that he entertains such an idea might be, as well as the openness of the dictionary definitions of "puppy love" and "crush," both of which certainly involve infatuation, but make no qualification that said infatuation be sexual. Justifying this assumption in-universe requires me to frame the problem of clarifying his feelings towards her as an epistemological problem in the form of: "How do I surely know that it is one and not another?" I endeavor to resolve this through rationalizing his language and behavior relating to his love interests in the context provided by scenes on-screen.

I begin by establishing that the "want" Finn feels for Princess Bubblegum is of a different nature from the "want" he feels for another love interest of his, Flame Princess. This he states plainly to the latter in "Hot to the Touch":

> I'm not trying to [antagonize you]. I just like you. I think I… I think I *like-like* you. Listen, when I look at you, my brain goes all stupid. And I just wanna hug you, and sit on the couch and play BMO with you. I can't explain why, but, I never felt this way before and I think we should be together.[7]

Is Finn lying? Here we recall that this episode takes place immediately after "Incendium," the episode in which Princess Bubblegum rejects a "romantic" advance from him, and with it the possibility that he could be saying this to spite her. This possibility is not demonstrated in any obvious sense in the scene in which this dialogue occurs. Instead, I have in mind the tension pervading the scene and the tremor in Finn's voice, as he is placed at fireball-point to account for his intentions in following an irate Flame Princess, and infer that he would be in a state of intense fear, perhaps like anybody in his situation, that would overwhelm any alternative emotion or grudge which may motivate dishonesty in his response. Therefore, insofar as my judgment on his honesty is no more credible than that of the audience, the setting of the scene provides us with the context by which an implication that he is being dishonest could be conveyed to us. No such implication is apparent, and we thus have to conclude that he is being honest about his inclinations.

What are those inclinations? In particular, what is this feeling of "like-[liking]" someone that he has "never felt [before]"? Recalling that Finn honestly states that the type of "want" he feels for Flame Princess is not a "want" he has felt for anyone else, we can say that whatever he feels in that sense for Flame Princess would not be what he feels for Princess Bubblegum. In all this we note that lust, or *eros*, is not a sensation which can be eliminated, and we have no reason to conclude that any lust Finn might feel for Princess Bubblegum would disappear even if Finn were to change his mind about pursuing her romantically. We might thus expect this lust to be indexed in imagery associating him with her at any point in the series, in a clear measure which would be absent in imagery associating him with Flame Princess. In which case, we would expect to see depictions which index the lust he feels for Princess Bubblegum, and that any dreams he has of Flame Princess would lack such innuendo.

Further investigation requires us to compare explicit imagery associating him with Princess Bubblegum, with explicit imagery associating him with Flame Princess. For his perspective on Princess Bubblegum, we revisit the opening scene of "What Was Missing"; for the comparison, we revisit his hallucinations of Flame Princess in "Frost and Fire." In the former, we see Finn nuzzling a lock of hair Princess Bubblegum gave him. He presses the hair to his cheek and rubs it against his face with a contented smile, savoring the closeness of the contact. In the latter, we witness Flame Princess aiming a steady stream of fire directly at his groin. He sports a bizarre expression, seemingly caught between discomfort and ecstasy in the moment. He does not try to escape his predicament. Instead, he moves his arms and legs up and down, much like how someone might trace out cherubic shapes in soft snow. Just as one might relish in the texture of soft snow while playing in it, Finn appears to relish in a certain "fuzziness" he feels as his groin is set aflame. Knowing that these are the most explicit exhibits associating him with either character, we must acknowledge that the difference in intensity of depiction speaks to this difference in nature of his desire for either character; in particular, that the direct physical stimulation of Finn's genitals in the latter scene is markedly absent in the former, and does not feature again in any other dream he has about Princess Bubblegum. I note the precision in the Confucian proverb, "the beginning of wisdom is to call things by their right names," for its utter appropriacy in describing this distinction; that Flame Princess is, in the words of Rebecca Sugar, a "new love interest" not only in the sense of being a novel object of Finn's infatuation, but also in the form of infatuation she arouses within him.

Relating Finn's extraordinary visuals of her to his confessions of "like-liking" her and having never "felt this way before," we are now certain that this unique sensation he feels for Flame Princess corresponds to the distinctive features of his dreams with her and how he clearly feels while captivated by them; namely, his expression, his ecstasy and the clear vision of constant contact between his genitals and her flames. Effectively, in "Frost and Fire," we are witnessing Finn's sexual awakening! Conversely, the absence of such imagery in both the opening scene of "What Was Missing" and in the various premonitions Finn has had of Princess Bubblegum implies that this lust he clearly feels for Flame Princess is not something he feels for her.

More importantly, did Princess Bubblegum recognize what Finn felt for her? It would certainly explain the prolonged, profound confusion evident on her countenance following his tirade against her in "Burning Low." Cue Finn: "What am *I* talking about?! PB, I was ... geh ... eh.. I was in love with you! Okay?! And you didn't love me back! Now I'm ready to move on, and it's like ... rrmph!! You're gonna build me up all over again! Well, I'm done! I'm done."[8]

What about his tirade confuses her? Any confusion she could have over his nomenclature would center around a conflict between her understanding of the present context, namely, her "advising" Finn against dating Flame Princess, and his understanding of it. Further, as this examination centers solely on her understanding, it would be better determined separately from the issue of whether Finn understood her or not. What is unambiguous, however, is the clarity of Finn's message to her behind his stuttering: it seems to him that her being the one telling him not to date Flame Princess suggests an intentional backtracking on her part. We recall that Princess Bubblegum "[building] up" Finn from his perspective would entail her either luring him in by increasing his expectations that she cares about him, only to deceive him against the backdrop of those expectations, or simply reviving the painful memories of her treatment of him prior to his encounter with Flame Princess. Either way, he views her as a harbinger of misery, and no longer believes that she has good intentions. This is a message conveyed to her at face value, accounting clearly for how she has deeply hurt him, how this relates to his issues with Flame Princess and why he brings it up at all. Did she hear him? Evidently, an awareness, or lack thereof, of Finn's message does not enlighten her, as her subsequent dialogue with Jake reveals:

> JAKE: You heartless monster! Do you have any idea how much he's CRIED OVER YOU? Finn deserves to be happy, even if his blooping face gets burned off! You should be ashamed! You're SICK!
> PRINCESS BUBBLEGUM: What are you..? This isn't about some petty love triangle![9]

Her confusion has not abated; if anything, the stress lines under her eyes in this scene suggest that it has grown. However, in acknowledging that Finn and Jake have interpreted the situation as a "petty love triangle," she communicates an understanding of how she could be seen as the triggering harbinger that Finn charges her with earlier, and therefore her confusion is not one borne out of obliviousness to Finn's feelings, but an informed one in which her understanding of Finn's feelings towards her before conflicts with her understanding of his feelings now. Since she understands that the situation has been interpreted as a "petty love triangle" in which Finn's crush on her is on the same plane as his crush on Flame Princess, a featuring of genuine confusion alongside her denial reflects not a desire to overrule their feelings, but a prior understanding that Finn's feelings for Flame Princess is not in the same modality as his feelings for her.

What desire, then, drives his behavior towards her? That it is a "want" separate from lust does little to describe his interactions with her, let alone rationalize the language with which he describes said interactions. He owes his knowledge of "romance" substantially to Jake, who views Finn's relationship with Princess Bubblegum in the same vein as his with Flame Princess and who has been informed by the "half-baked" Cinnamon Bun, of all characters, of his inability to focus. No wonder Finn speaks of "[getting] dumped" at the end of "Too Young," or having "no expectations" in "Too Old," or "future farming" his interactions with females. However, do these phrases communicate precisely what he seeks in her? Disregarding his language, Finn's interest in "dating" Princess Bubblegum apparently lies not as much in the activities they engage in as in her company and her physical affection. The latter is something he craves insatiably; he blushes at her kisses and the thought of them, or when she leans on him, rubs her hand longingly across his face, headlocks (almost strangles) and elbows her, rubs his finger on hers after a high five much to her consternation ("Hey!"), sneaks or drapes his arms over her immediately after breaking into her bedroom and scares her in the wee hours of the morning, to give "a hundred percent of his being all for [her]." Does he pursue her "love" out of a desire fueled by mystery, or out of a "silly" emotional dependence on her affection from which she insists he "move on"? That he should be so comfortable behaving so "loosely" with her, and that she tolerates said behavior without protracted animosity reflects on inherent bases of trust and familiarity which undergird their interactions throughout the series. It is these bases that I hope to explore in the rest of this essay. After all, what is their dynamic premised on?

Characterization

I hereby embark on my description of Finn and Princess Bubblegum's relationship proper. Before doing so, however, I believe it useful to recall the two preliminary assumptions grounding it:

1. Situational logic followed by human beings about conscious activity applies to all episodes, scenes and interactions in *Adventure Time*, insofar as it supports plot progression.
2. While Finn pines for her out of a crush he considers romantic, it is not a crush motivated by *eros*, and hence not a crush in the same spirit as his on Flame Princess. Knowing that she is both conscious and confused otherwise without semblance of, and reason for ill-intent, Princess Bubblegum recognizes this.

The first assumption justifies the usage of logic as a schema to establish reason behind all insights proposed in this essay. The second guides my exploration into how the concepts of familiarity, investment and altruism characterize their interactions in the light of a parental denomination.

I speak first of familiarity; in particular, familiarity among two individuals involved in either a parental or pseudo-parental relationship, such as that shared by a child and a permanent caregiver. From the perspective of an involved parental figure, this familiarity would be utter and thorough, entailing an intimate knowledge of their child's personality, physicality and psychology. By virtue of the roles she plays in Finn's life, Princess Bubblegum is heavily invested in it. Observations made in the preamble of this essay about her interactions with him prove some of this familiarity with him implicitly. It is reflected in her placid reaction to his involuntary nudity in "Obsidian," and in her confidence to defy Jake's exhortations to her in "The Tower" to "give the kid a chance." That Jake exalts her to "give [Finn] a chance" reflects his acknowledgment of her involvement in Finn's well-being beyond an authoritative capacity. We note allusions to its longevity in her childlike utterances of "bong-bong" in that episode and "bub-bub-bub" in "The Pajama War," expressions referring to neither a situation nor a subject and are speech ticks unique to her dialogues with Finn. It is a familiarity that relaxes her conversation with him, and motivates her confident intervention in his life.

This familiarity underpins mutual trust, motivating altruism. Facing his imminent, indefinite departure in "The Invitation" into the great unknown, Princess Bubblegum jabs her finger at him and issues him an imploration so fervent, it reads like an order: "You have to promise me ... *promise* me ... that you'll come home safe." It is therefore interesting that her priority is for him to "come home safe," above all. Is she certain that Finn refers to wherever she refers to as "home"? Moreover, where does she refer to as "home"? More importantly, this seems irrelevant. As she does not impose her definition of "home" on him in what she knows could be her final words to him, she leaves it open to his definition. Nevertheless, she wants him to be "safe" throughout, while unable to verify so. Ergo, this is not her instruction, but her wish. Indeed, it is a wish from a woman who worries for him as much as he worries for himself, despite knowing him; arguably, better than she knows herself. Here, Bubblegum, despite having been betrayed by just about every single character she has let intimately into her life, sets one such character free for himself, not knowing if he will return with a heart imbued with gratitude, vengeance, or at all. Such is a display of a love so selfless and unconditional; such, is altruism.

We witness this again in the finale, before the war, as Finn screams at her to back down, "Please, listen to me! We've been friends for a long time!" Cue Princess Bubblegum experiencing a flashback; one that focuses on the robot arm attached to Finn and rewinds it back in time to the robot arm attached to Shoko, his past incarnate. Likewise, we are reeled back to our impressions of Shoko in "The Vault" who, after receiving the arm Princess Bubblegum made selflessly for her, went on with her ill-fated mission to steal her amulet. In that cycle of life, the soul in Shoko traded an act of betrayal for one of altruism. In this cycle, that soul resides in Finn, imploring her to let her guard down to Uncle Gumbald; the first character to betray her and who had betrayed her again just the night before using Finn himself, the embodiment of said soul. Placing her faith in Finn, she goes, "Okay, Finn. We'll give him one last chance." Doing so, in the hands of this soul she rests her heart once more, and in the throes of war, her kingdom. Only so, for the soul is embodied by her hero, and not by someone less open.

What drives this cycle of familiarity, altruism and trust for Princess Bubblegum? As the imagery of the arm sans the wearer connotes, it is neither the bodies housing the soul nor the soul, but more the investment of her time, resources and workmanship in maintaining them both. She loses a candy person, James, for Finn in "James." Her reasoning? "He's candy, but you're not. I can't clone another you." The reductive statement would be: "You are irreplaceable to me." Knowing that this takes place after the events of "The Vault," it would have been just as reasonable for her to say that even if Finn and Jake had perished in that toxic pit, reincarnations of them would always visit her eventually and by that logic, they would be equally dispensable. Clearly, she does not believe in this syllogism, and Finn is somehow singular.

To better understand what Finn might be to her, we may explore the implications posed by the psychic stalemate between two of her creations, Goliad and Stormo. Where Goliad is an impressionable sphinx borne out of her DNA, Stormo is one borne out of Finn's. Superficially, their conflict, one between tyranny and selflessness, may metaphorize a diametric opposition between Princess Bubblegum and Finn's personalities and thus their propensity to equilibrate. It is thus interesting that Goliad was not conditioned by Princess Bubblegum, but by Jake. More compelling still is the fact that Princess Bubblegum is unaware of this, and thus remains convinced that Finn and Jake trained Goliad together. Henceforth, when she creates Stormo to counter Goliad after learning of Goliad's corruption, she creates a counter not to her, but to an impression of her. How do we reconcile her actions with her impression that Finn and Jake were conditioning Goliad? She would be countering the damage caused by corruption which two individuals were responsible for, with a counterpart borne out of one of said individuals. Like the transcendental trust she places in Finn in "The Invitation" and in the finale, this would be taking a gambit on Finn which she would only have known to work against her.

She takes the gambit nonetheless, for the same reason that she presents Finn her newest experiments, creations and expeditions before anyone else, and lets Finn and Jake substitute as ambassadors for her. It is, after all, a reason informed by her complete and utter supervision of him from various positions of mentorship. As her charge, Finn is familiar; an open book which she has written in and read from various angles and perspectives. The clash between Goliad and Stormo, then, would represent the diametrically opposed aspects to their personalities as embodied by him. Finn has therefore become a vessel for the worst in her authority and the best in her intentions; a living piece of her legacy. In here her perspectives on investment, familiarity and altruism interact in perfect harmony; mutually informing, catalyzing and motivating. The epitome of said harmony is Finn's significance to her.

What then, is Princess Bubblegum to Finn? My second assumption simplifies this description. Free from erotic connotations, she is a beacon of chaste and potent significances. In "Breezy" and in "The Hall of Egress," she assumes the omniscient voice that leads him out of despair and darkness respectively. The moments they share in "The Pajama War" permeate the "happy place" that, in "Hero Heart," will him out of his insanity. They are moments pure and simple, forming an oasis in which he relives his company with her. Free from undertones, they are unassumingly fun; something he will never be too young for. They are moments that he cherishes beyond his wildest dreams, punctuated by a mortality he arguably fears in her just as she fears in herself. He witnesses her naked, liquefied dying form and is forced to kill her demonic possessed form in "Mortal Recoil." He questions the ethics behind her sacrifice in *James*, unsure as to why he will not be sacrificed next, whenever "next" comes. In much the opposite fashion to her familiarity with him, he has seen more to her than he understands. However, he wants to understand. This is meaningful, as it informs us that his loyalty to her is not blind. She might deserve it, as she gives his life structure and purpose; purpose which compels him to fulfil Shoko's unfinished burden. It is, ultimately, why he smiles.

By this same assumption, the appreciation he has for her affection is also justifiable and never depraved, for it is a limerent appreciation of her loving, radiant touch. This ostensibly attached him to her as a child and continues to hold him as a teenager beyond his developmental stages. He is, by then, too close for both his growth and her comfort. Her discomfort resolves her emphasis on "really gotta" in "You really gotta move on" and justifies the exasperation with which she says, "Oh, you." It thus compels her to push him away in "Incendium," which, beyond a rejection, is an act of intervention. Parallels can be drawn with her confiscation of Cinnamon Bun's night light in "Five More Short Graybles" here, suggesting that this intervention is practiced. To Cinnamon Bun, this is ruthlessness from an overbearing mother; to Finn, it is unexpected coldness from a "bro."

Was she always a "bro"? I conclude my exploration by discussing what is to be made of Finn's visage of her in "Don't Look." Specifically, I ask what is to be made of her appearance relative to Jake's. She is a "teen boy heartthrob" next to "varsity bro Jake." The two caricatures are similar, resembling older brothers who thrive in socially complex environments on a combination of their appearance and reputation. There are also the apparent uniformities in sex and age, despite Princess Bubblegum being female. Would it matter, had her visage been an older female? Its apparent age can either be tied to her biological age or taken to mean that Finn does not factor age into his appreciation of her. However, it being female would transform the scene into that of an adolescent boy meeting an adolescent girl. Would it have undermined a portrayal of fraternity? Prior assumptions leave this open.

Ad interim, a mother's love needs no advocate but her child. As Finn steps into the hollow housing the waiting Lich, the abomination of death sneers, "Aren't you *cold*?" The pink sweater put about him by Princess Bubblegum beams in defiance, exuding an aura reflective of its symbolic purpose; to augment his heroic will to shred the skull of death. If the cold is one associated with death, the sweater, as anathema, is to enshroud and overcome it with a warmth associated with life. Reductively, it is a power, and as it never destroys the princess who guides the hands from which it comes and never destroys again, it is a power inimitable and indomitable. Indeed, it is the power of "lo-liking someone a lot"; a power associate but never secondary to love, for it is one so unmistakably stable, pure and true.

Notes

1. In the sense of C.S. Lewis' definition of it in *The Four Loves*.
2. Lewis.

3. For examples, see: Julie C. Bowker and Rebecca G. Etkin, "Evaluating the Psychological Concomitants of Other-Sex Crush Experiences During Early Adolescence"; Canadian Paediatric Society, "Understanding Adoption"; Robbie Duschinsky and Sophie Reijman, "Filming Disorganized Attachment."
4. Andrew Tran, "The Annotated *Adventure Time*."
5. For a fuller discussion, see: Karl Popper, *Objective Knowledge*.
6. Matt Moen, "In Conversation."
7. "Hot to the Touch" (season 4, episode 1).
8. "Burning Low" (season 4, episode 16).
9. "Burning Low."

References

Bowker, Julie C., and Rebecca G. Etkin. "Evaluating the Psychological Concomitants of Other-Sex Crush Experiences During Early Adolescence." *Journal Of Youth and Adolescence* 45, no. 5 (2016): 846–857.

Canadian Paediatric Society. "Understanding Adoption: A Developmental Approach." *Paediatrics & Child Health* 6, no. 5 (2001): 281–283.

Duschinsky, Robbie, and Sophie Reijman. "Filming Disorganized Attachment." *Screen* 57, no. 4 (2016): 397–413.

Koertge, Noretta. "The Methodological Status of Popper's Rationality Principle." *Theory and Decision* 10, no. 1 (1979): 83–95.

Lewis, C. S. *The Four Loves*. New York: Harcourt Brace Jovanovich, 1960.

Moen, Matt. "In Conversation: Rebecca Sugar and Noelle Stevenson." PaperMag, 2020. https://www.papermag.com/rebecca-sugar-noelle-stevenson-2646446747.html.

Popper, Karl. *Objective Knowledge: An Evolutionary Approach*. Rev. ed. Oxford, UK: Oxford University Press, 1979.

Tran, Andrew. "The Annotated *Adventure Time*: Dis-Gendered Origin Myths and Birth Trauma in 'Bonnie and Neddy.'" Overmental, 2015. https://overmental.com/content/the-annotated-adventure-time-dis-gendered-origin-myths-and-birth-trauma-in-bonnie-and-neddy-42018.

Of Lacan and Lemons
A Psychoanalytic Reading of Season Six's "The Mountain"

PAUL A. THOMAS

Many fans and critics alike consider the sixth-season episode "The Mountain" (storyboarded by Sam Alden and Jesse Moynihan) to be one of the show's headiest installments, and for good reason. Over eleven minutes, viewers are privy to esoteric dialogue and kaleidoscopic set pieces as Lemongrab and Finn traverse the inside of the titular mountain to meet a mysterious being named Matthew. The episode is, to be blunt, a mind-screw. What then is one to make of it? To answer that question, this essay will consider the episode with regard to the theories put forth by Jacques Lacan. With the help of Lacan, I argue that "The Mountain" is best read as a psychoanalytic "self-analysis," in which Lemongrab attempts to attain full happiness by finding his "One True *objet petit a*." The episode—and Lemongrab's analysis—concludes when Lemongrab "traverses his fantasy," thereby recognizing the nature of his desire and why his goal is an impossibility.

My decision to use the writings of Lacan as my theoretical starting point may be controversial to some. Lacan has, after all, been long lambasted for his esotericism and his apparent inanity; in their book *Fashionable Nonsense* (1997), Alan Sokal and Jean Bricmont went so far as to call Lacan's writing "gibberish."[1] And while Lacanians will defend their founder by insisting that his style was a deliberate method to disrupt the Symbolic, this has not stopped many a scholar from chucking their copy of *Écrits* across the room in a fit of frustration. All of this is a shame, because Lacan's body of work—while at times maddeningly dense—is replete with valuable concepts that can help us better discuss that particular yearning in the heart of all human subjects for something more. If only Lacan were somehow more accessible....

This is where the current essay comes into play. Inspired by the approach of Slavoj Žižek (an idiosyncratic academic and fervent proponent of Lacan who has long used pop culture as a vehicle to express psychoanalytic ideas), I intend for this essay to serve not only as an explication of one of *Adventure Time*'s more confusing episodes, but also as a sort of "pop culture primer" that uses the antics of animated characters to explain the core tenets of Lacan's notoriously challenging body of work. Put most simply, this essay is my attempt to present both "The Mountain" and Lacan in a way that is—as Lemongrab might say—acceptable.

"The fruit of the ~~lemon~~ Lacan is impossible to ~~eat~~ read": From the Earl of Lemongrab to Jacques Lacan

At the start of "The Mountain," things are going rather well for Lemongrab and his earldom. His people have worthwhile jobs, plenty of lemon candies to eat, a meaningful schedule, and even what appears to be freedom of artistic expression. But despite how much the earldom has evolved since the despotic days of Lemongrab I, something is awry, and deep down, Lemongrab is unhappy. One night, while laying himself down to sleep, Lemongrab glances at a mural atop his canopy bed that depicts the legend of the Mountain of Matthew. According to this tale, Matthew is a great, imposing being who can offer peace unto those who have felt as if something is missing from their life. It is while examining the mural that Lemongrab notices a small crack in the fresco. It is tiny—hardly noticeable—but it causes Lemongrab extreme distress. What is it about this tiny, insignificant fissure that causes Lemongrab so much unease?

To explicate Lemongrab's psychological dilemma, let me first explore the theories of the somewhat controversial French psychiatrist Jacques Lacan (1901–81). Lacan is today remembered largely for single-handedly remixing the psychoanalytic canon by encouraging "a return to Freud" while also attacking the prevailing approaches to psychoanalysis that had developed in the 20th century. Using Freud's seminal work as a springboard, Lacan reinterpreted many psychoanalytic concepts, freeing them from sexual literalism and giving them a more socio-linguistic spin. While many of Lacan's texts have had a major impact in the academy, much of his work remains unknown to those outside the domains of psychoanalysis and critical theory. This is largely due to Lacan's notoriously dense prose, his numerous allusions to literature, his frequent use of puns that do not translate well into English, and his pseudo-mathematical equations. Another difficulty is that Lacan often discusses concepts that, by their very nature, defy coherent explanations, such as "non-meaning" and "lack." When taken together, these challenges can make reading Lacan feel like one is divining a religious text for hidden meaning. Despite this hurdle, this essay will attempt to synthesize Lacan in a way that can then help us understand what exactly is going on with Lemongrab.

Let me start by considering Lacan's articulation of how subjects understand, inform, and are informed by the world around them. Lacan postulated that there are fundamentally three orders (or "registers") to subjective existence: the Imaginary, the Symbolic, and the Real. The first register, that of the Imaginary, is—despite its name—not strictly the realm of imagination or the make-believe. Rather, it is, as the philosopher Adrian Johnston puts it, "the restricted spheres of consciousness and self-awareness. It is the register with the closest links to what people experience as non-psychoanalytic quotidian reality."[2] The Imaginary thus not only comprises the world that we literally see with our senses, but also how we mentally perceive other people—and ourselves—to be. For a clear *Adventure Time* example, think of Finn's dilemma in the eighth-season episode "Don't Look," in which a curse causes his mental perception of people to physically change the way they look, thereby eliding the difference between "seeing with the eye" and "seeing with the mind." This is the domain of the Imaginary.

It is at the Imaginary level that the human subject creates a workable fiction of our wholeness that "offers [us] a sense of self"[3]—this is the Ego, which Lacan calls the "seat of illusions."[4] Lacan refers to the Ego as such because no human is truly a singular, consistent entity. Instead, we are all "fragmented, chaotic bod[ies]"[5] flying through time and space, further decentered by the split between our conscious and unconscious minds. A solid, unified Ego is therefore a mirage, and because of this, the Imaginary register as a whole can best be understood as a register of (mis)recognition, illusion, narcissism, and ego-centric thinking.

The second register, the Symbolic, is the realm of signification, which gives us meaning and allows us to make sense of our lives by means of socio-cultural structures. According to Lacan, "language is [the] symbolic behavior *par excellence*,"[6] and as such, humans fully enter this register when, as babies, we begin to learn language. An important aspect of this pre-existing web of signification is that for the child, it immediately begins dividing up the world into discrete units. Prior to the entrance into language, newborns do not perceive categories like "swords," "lemons," or "bacon pancakes"; we only perceive existence as an "undifferentiated continuum" of sensorial information.[7] But once we begin to learn language, this totality is broken down and the constituent parts of reality are labelled as specific objects (e.g., "*This* is a sword. *That* is a lemon. *These* are bacon pancakes"). While this naming provides meaning, it also results in the Symbolic register being built upon a fundamental "lack," as the existence of discrete objects logically implies that those objects can become lost. And given that human subjects are christened in the Symbolic (that is, given a name, an identity, a social role, etc.), it can be said that we too are built upon this lack. The lack at the heart of the subject becomes a traumatic void over which the Symbolic, despite its best efforts, cannot perfectly plaster.

The Symbolic is also the realm of what Lacan called the "big Other," which can be effectively glossed as systems of laws, customs, and sociocultural protocols to which human subjects are expected to adhere if they want to "fit in" with society. It is important to note that while the big Other is not some singular, panoptic entity who is "out there"—like Orwell's Big Brother, or Princess Bubblegum with her massive surveillance state—it is nevertheless always there, always watching. This is because the big Other is equivalent to those structures that we use to make sense of reality even when we are alone, such as language, logic, morality, and cultural norms. While the big Other can operate in obvious ways (such as when a new law is passed or when someone is punished for a crime), it often functions on an unconscious level by suggesting what it is that subjects should strive for to be considered successful, thereby shaping the desires of subjects *and* convincing subjects that these desires are really their own. It is for this reason that Lacan famously argued that one's desire is really "the desire of the Other."[8]

Finally, the Real "resists symbolization absolutely"[9] and is beyond what we can possibly conceive. Some people take this to mean that the Real is "that which is 'really' [out] there, unprocessed, underneath or behind the symbolic patterning … that we call reality."[10] This is not quite right. Instead, Lacan's Real is more like the direct inverse of human subjectivity—a sort of pure, unknowable materiality encompassing everything that a human subject is not and cannot comprehend. Perhaps the Real can be best likened to a sort of psychic dark matter, in that it exerts itself on human subjects at all times but remains undetectable in its totality.

To make matters even more confusing, the Real is often articulated in two seemingly paradoxical ways: the pre–Symbolic Real and the post–Symbolic Real.[11] When it comes to the pre–Symbolic Real (also called $Real_1$ or the "Primordial Real"),[12] the Real is conceptualized as a mythical form of complete, perfect existence preceding the Imaginary and Symbolic orders, in which every possible need is immediately satisfied.[13] Given this form's highly acceptable nature, subjects yearn to reach and/or experience this Real in its "fullness" (or, rather, its "lack of lack")[14] by locating "*das Ding*" (literally: "the Thing"); this is the "impossible-real object of desire"[15] that subjects believe must lie far beyond the gates of symbolization and imagination, beating in the heart of the Real. Alas, because the Real resists signification and humans enter the world of signification during birth, it could be said that subjects are closest to *das Ding* and the plentitude of the Real only when they are newborns, ignorant of language and other symbolic devices that divide up the world into discrete units.[16]

Though the pre–Symbolic Real is forever out of a subject's grasp, many seek it out nonetheless. But in doing so, a subject runs the risk of sliding into the second modality of the Real: the Real-as-lack (sometimes called $Real_2$ or the "Leftover Real").[17] This avatar of the Real is perhaps most commonly experienced as a painful, negative force that disrupts the Imaginary-Symbolic matrix that we call reality by foregrounding the pure, meaningless "materiality of our existence."[18] This mode of the Real shatters our carefully-constructed understanding of the world and prevents us from making sense of what is happening around us (given that "sense" is a product of the Imaginary and Symbolic registers). For an example of such an eruption in *Adventure Time*, think of when Princess Bubblegum was possessed by the Lich in season two's "Mortal Folly"/"Mortal Recoil." This event shook Bubblegum, making her feel small, fragile, and so very mortal. What is more, because such an accident did not happen "for a reason" (i.e., it was a freak accident), it could not be integrated into Bubblegum's Symbolic order of signification. It was thus a modality of the Real which "resists symbolization,"[19] hence the use of the "post–Symbolic" modifier.

It is important to note that both the pre–Symbolic Real and the post–Symbolic Real are actually one in the same, and are different only in the positive or negative way we attempt the impossible task of trying to conceive of that which cannot be symbolized: It is either a heaven beyond all imagination, or a pure void of meaninglessness that swallows all.

With the three levels of existence defined, Lemongrab's unease at the crack in his mural can now be understood from a psychoanalytic angle. First, consider the mural itself. As a large painting replete with intricate designs and rich visual motifs, it can be understood as a representative of the larger Symbolic order, given that it is "a complex network of linguistic and cultural signs—a chain of signification that makes sense of the world and our position within it."[20] It is for this reason that Lemongrab looks to the mural for an answer as to why he is unhappy, as he believes it will provide him with a sense of understanding. But what about the hole? This crack, I argue, is representative of a traumatic rupture in the Symbolic order. In other words, it is lack, through which the pure unknowability of the Real—represented by the darkness of the crack and the low, eerie, howling emanating from within—is bleeding.

The reason this crack causes Lemongrab such distress is because it reminds him of a similar rupture that lies at the heart of his subjective being. As was discussed earlier, this lack is created when human subjects enter the Symbolic and are fully severed from the Real. For Lemongrab, however, this lack also has a literal component. In his first few episodes, Lemongrab was the sole Lemonperson in existence, which alienated him from others. To make things better, Bubblegum created a clone-brother, Lemongrab II, to keep the original company, and while the two ruled peacefully together for some time, everything came crashing down in the fifth-season episode "Too Old," in which Lemongrab I ate part of his clone-brother. This disaster was compounded in the subsequent episode "Lemonhope," wherein Lemongrab I exploded; after this accident, Bubblegum fused the remnants of Lemongrab I with those of his cannibalized brother, resulting in Lemongrab III—a Frankensteinian "remix" of his predecessors' "brains and bodies"[21] who is the star of "The Mountain." Given that Lemongrab III is essentially a coreless composite of spare parts (which, by their very nature as part-objects, can become lost), the lack within the heart of his being is even more pronounced. Who even *is* he anymore?

This fundamental lack leads Lemongrab to feel as if some integral piece must be missing from his soul. This missing piece is what Lacan calls the *objet petit a* (French for "little object o[ther]"). This peculiar object is something of a contradiction, as it is both the object-cause of desire *and* the object of desire. In the guise of the former, it is perceived as a hole in the symbolic order through which the Real-as-lack bleeds, but in its latter guise, it is also perceived as an actual "sublime object"[22]— "an object elevated to the dignity of" *das Ding*[23]—that, once located, will complete the subject like a puzzle piece, allowing them to reconnect to the Real-as-excess. Put most simply, if *das Ding* is the impossible and incomprehensible object that we seek, then the *objet petit a* is the symbolic-imaginary embodiment of *das Ding*. Like a religious mystic, we believe that capturing the *objet petit a* in our symbolic-imaginary lifeworld will give us direct access to the Real of *das Ding*.

But there is a problem here: neither the *objet petit a* nor *das Ding* exist! In actuality, both are *post facto* phantasms created when the subject enters the Symbolic-Imaginary world at birth—a passage that gives rise to a retroactive feeling of being severed from some lost plentitude. Birth, in other words, imbues us with lack—a lack which we believe indexes the existence of something "out there" that, once located, will make us whole again. Unfortunately, this lack is just part of the human condition; this means that no part-object—no "One True *objet petit a*"—exists in our lifeworld which will function as a symbolic-imaginary embodiment of the impossible *das Ding*, ameliorating our lack. But, as mentioned before, this impossibility does not mean that subjects will cease their search efforts, and indeed, subjects spend much of their lives hopping from part-object to part-object seeking out their missing piece, only to be disappointed when their efforts result in failure. To make it all worse, Lacan argues that if a subject does manage to get ahold of what they believe to be their One True *objet petit a*, they will be unsatisfied, since it is not the final part-object that they are so desperately seeking. This makes any pleasure the object confers limited at best and utterly upsetting at worst.

With the concept of the *objet petit a* in mind, let us return to the mural. Because it is representative of the Symbolic order writ large, the mural can also be understood as a manifestation of the "big Other"—that which, among other things, tells us what to do and what to desire. In this case, the mural tells Lemongrab that Matthew is his One True *objet petit a* that he must find to remedy the lack upon which he is constituted as a subject; only through Matthew, the fresco whispers, can Lemongrab locate *das Ding* and reconnect with the long-lost Real-as-excess. Staring at this Symbolic command night after night has caused Lemongrab to unconsciously internalize this desire for Matthew, coming to mistake that desire for his own rather than a demand thrust upon him by the big Other.

Lemongrab has usually been content to simply fantasize about Matthew as he falls asleep, but the appearance of the crack—a metaphorical "void in the centre of the symbolic order"[24]—reminds him of his deeper yearning for wholeness and the call of the One True *objet petit a* that he believes to be Matthew. The crack thus inaugurates the episode by encouraging Lemongrab to seize his fantasy object. And so the character sets out for the legendary Mountains of Matthew.

The Mirrors of Matthew: Finn, Lemongrab, and the Mirror Stage

In the bowels of the mountain, Lemongrab stumbles into a cavernous room holding three fantastic mirrors, each of which arguably show him a scenario reflective of one of the agents in Sigmund Freud's understanding of the human mind: In the first, Lemongrab sees his creator-mother, Princess Bubblegum, attempting to relate to his "lemon styles"; this vision expresses an oedipal want, and is thus a reflection of his Id. In the second, he sees Lemonhope usurping the lemon throne and promising to "undo all the order" imposed on the lemon people by Lemongrab; this represents Lemongrab's fixation with what is "correct" and is representative of his Superego. In the final mirror, he witnesses spectral images of Lemongrab I and II arguing over Lemonsweets, a lemon "child" and a scion of his compound Ego. After a mystical voice demands that he pick one mirror, Lemongrab chooses the third, and thanks to trippy magics, he is swallowed whole by Lemonsweets, tumbling into a black void containing nothing but cascading versions of himself. During this vision, Lemongrab is told to taste the grease on his lemony skin, leading him to question if he is nothing but "grease"—a disgusting bodily fluid.

As the Earl experiences this strange vision, Finn enters into the same mirror chamber. Earlier, he and Jake had spied Lemongrab journeying into the mountain, and, being suspicious of his motives, they followed him. At the base of the Mountain, a mystical guardian allowed Finn to pass, but barred Jake from entering. The reason is simple: Finn, much like Lemongrab and unlike Jake, feels as if there is a hole in his soul. This was caused largely by his break-up with Flame Princess in the fifth-season episode "Frost & Fire," as well as the loss of both his arm and father in the sixth-season episode "Escape from the Citadel" (the latter of which can be psychoanalytically understood as a symbolic castration courtesy of the father).

When Finn steps into the mirror room, he too sees three different scenarios that represent the tripartite model of the human psyche: In the first, Finn sees a hollowed-out Cinnamon Bun, who beseeches Finn to wear him like a suit so that he can spend time with his ex-girlfriend Flame Princess; this represents the sexual/romantic wishes of his Id. In the second, he sees Jake chiding BMO for attempting to eat a freshly baked Finncake, which represents his worry about cultural rules and prohibitions, ergo his Superego. In the third, he sees a butterfly, which (as evidenced in previous episodes) is his spiritual avatar and a manifestation of his Ego. Just like Lemongrab before him, Finn is ordered by a voice to select a mirror. Finn obliges by choosing the third and jumps onto the back of the butterfly. The insect quickly flies into a dark void in which he sees, like Lemongrab before him, an endless cascade of himself.

In addition to recalling aspects of Freud's famous Id/Superego/Ego distinction, the mirrors in "The Mountain" are also evocative of Lacan's theory of the "mirror stage." Lacan argued that roughly six months after our birth, we inevitably look at ourselves in a mirror (or we see ourselves "reflected" in the "mirror" of a person, like our mother). Being babies, we are uncoordinated, sensorially discombobulated, and not in total control of certain biological functions (e.g., eating, defecating, moving). But when we gaze into a mirror, we see a phantasmic view of a seemingly whole individual. Yearning for that sense of wholeness, we buy into the idea that we *are* that specular image, and in doing so, we give birth to our Ego. This "mirror stage" thus marks our full movement into the Imaginary register, and also presages in many ways our full embracing of the Symbolic register.[25]

But what exactly does the mirror stage and Freud's tripartite model of the psyche have to do with Lemongrab and Finn's journey? To crack this mystery, let us first consider the "incorrect" mirrors, which reflect the wants of the Id and the Superego. Because the Id is the "unconscious origin of speech"[26] and the Superego is "consonant with the ... idea of the law,"[27] both are manifestations of signification and thus belong to the Symbolic register.[28] Logically, this means that the Id- and Superego-coded mirrors belong to this register, too. Conversely, the "correct" mirror—which leads Lemongrab and Finn to an infinite regress of their spectral images—focuses solely on the Ego, which is situated in the domain of the Imaginary. Since Lemongrab and Finn start off in the world of the Symbolic, and endeavor to reach the Real, their passage through the ego-mirror can thus be read as a sort of reverse-mirror stage: by passing through, the two characters "unhook" themselves from the Symbolic order and regress into the unmediated Imaginary, closing in on the unified Real-as-excess, which is accessible via Matthew.[29] All of this suggest that were either character to have chosen one of the "incorrect" mirrors, they would have landed right back in the Symbolic where they started.

Now, in the Ego-space of the mirror, Lemongrab and Finn must figure out a way to "unhook" themselves from the Imaginary. Lemongrab does this by pouring out into the inky darkness his "pure essence," while Finn chooses to run headlong into the void. Both methods lead the two into the junction of the Imaginary and the Real, depicted as a sort of subterranean vestibule, wherein Matthew—the "impassive, imaginary objectification of the Real"[30]—resides.

"Infinite stairs are unacceptable!" The Impossibility of the Real and the Recognition of the Other's Fantasy

Matthew speaks to Lemongrab and Finn, telling them how many others have journeyed to the mountain and merged with his great being, "distill[ing] themselves to their original source materials and ... [now] exist[ing] in oneness." This language about returning to some sort of primordial unity recalls in many ways one of psychoanalysis's more controversial ideas: the death drive. This concept was proposed by Freud, who argued that in opposition to *Eros* (that is, our instinct to live), humans possess a self-destructive impulse, often referred to as *Thanatos*, that compels us to, in effect, kill ourselves and return to the pre-differentiated state of (non)being in which we existed prior to our birth. This death drive, Freud argued, is why humans engage in self-destructive behaviors that go far beyond the simple pursuit of pleasure.

While Lacan eagerly embraced the idea of the death drive, he argued that it is not a desire to die, but rather the opposite. Sean Sheehan, glossing Lacan, argues that the death drive should really be understood as that which:

> constantly [compels human subjects to seek] something more than [our] mere biological existence. It seeks to reach the Real by filling the gap in the Symbolic order, the gap that is itself the Real, but, caught up as it must be in the loop of the signifying chain, this becomes an impossible task, hence the unremitting, never-to-be-satisfied rotation of the death drive.[31]

The Lacanian death drive is thus that relentless yearning subjects have to connect with *das Ding* via their One True *objet petit a* and thereby attain permanent psychic peace in the totality of the Real-as-excess. It is this "nostalgia for wholeness"[32] that Matthew appeals to when he suggests that Lemongrab and Finn merge with his being.

This parallel between "The Mountain" and the Lacanian death drive is made clearer when Lemongrab notes that by joining the Real vis-à-vis Matthew, he may finally experience "the ecstasy of [his] ego death." Lemongrab's use of the word "ecstasy" here also echoes another Lacanian term: *jouissance*. Originally meaning "orgasm" in French, *jouissance* is—as with all Lacanian terms and phrases—a hard one to pin down, and as such is usually left untranslated. With that said, *jouissance* should not be understood simply as "pleasure." Rather, it is something beyond, usually expressed as pleasure so intense that it is painful. Sheehan writes that *jouissance* can be understood as the burning "to realize a primordial connection of complete oneness,"[33] and Lewis Kirschner similarly describes it as "a persistent yearning for *total satisfaction*.... The desire for *jouissance* ... is the retroactive effect of becoming a separate subject, which leaves a permanent ache of desire in its wake" [emphasis added].[34] *Jouissance* can consequently be understood as total fulfilment in the oneness of the Real, which a subject retroactively believes was lost when they entered into Imaginary-Symbolic reality at birth. Lemongrab's yearning for the "ecstasy of [his] ego death" is thus really a yearning for *jouissance*.

Lemongrab's dreamed-of satisfaction can be called the "*jouissance* expected": "an illusory, mythicized 'full satisfaction,' namely, the re-finding of *das Ding*, the decisive, final quelling of the incessant clamoring of the drives."[35] However, when Lemongrab is before Matthew, realization dawns. If he merges with Matthew, he ceases to be himself, and thereby he does not experience either the Real or *jouissance* as a subject—it would be "impossible enjoyment"[36] beyond the pleasure principle, resulting in subjective annihilation. Conversely, if he does *not* merge with Matthew, the pure *jouissance* of the Real will still remain out of grasp. It is a catch-22, for both options lead neither to the "*jouissance* expected," but rather to the painfully disappointing "*jouissance* obtained."[37]

It is in that moment that Lemongrab realizes he has been tricked. The mural above his bed was not providing him with a serendipitous answer to his own desire; instead, it, as an avatar of the big Other, was telling him both what his desire was *and* how he could impossibly sate it. Matthew was all along just a fantasy object sustained by the desire of the big Other, whose capture will bring Lemongrab no closer to the full psychic peace for which he yearns.

As soon as Lemongrab recognizes that Matthew is not his ticket to *das Ding*, pure *jouissance*, or the Real-as-excess, the sublimity of Matthew evaporates and the great being instantly transmutes into an impossible monstrosity. This leads Lemongrab to shriek at the being in abject horror: "If you are the head that blooms atop the ziggurat, then the stairs that lead to you must be infinite!" Infinite stairs, Lemongrab reasons quite passionately, are "unacceptable"—and so is reaching for an impossible goal.

Lemongrab then reaches into his pocket and pulls out a handful of lemon drop candies. These were last seen in the fifth-season episode "All Your Fault," and were the remains of Lemonjon, a massive lemon being who, after experiencing emotions for the first time, "dissolve[d] the bonds uniting" his body, thereby becoming "component to all."[38] As piece-objects of a former subject, these candies thus embody the very concept of lack. Lemongrab then equates himself to the candies and muses that they have the power to destroy Matthew. On one level, Lemongrab is seeing in the candies his spectral image, given that they are part-objects of his biological scion (making them part of the Imaginary register), but on another, more important level, he is recognizing the lack inherent in both the candies and himself (making them part of the Symbolic register). This is a major moment in Lemongrab's development, for in making this connection, he is admitting to himself that being constituted in the Imaginary-Symbolic registers as a subject precludes the chance of ever connecting with *das Ding* and finding unity in the Real-as-excess. Lemongrab subsequently tosses the candies into Matthew's mouth, and the lack inherent in the candies instantly "cuts into the smooth façade of the Real,"[39] causing Matthew to explode into the individuals of whom he was formerly composed; what once appeared to be whole is thus revealed to be lacking.

What is one to make of Matthew's destruction? Simply put, it artistically depicts the prescribed end of Lacanian psychoanalysis: the traversal of fantasy. According to Lacanian thought, this process requires the subject to recognize that fantasy is a construct foisted on us by the big Other, thus making it "a primordial lie, covering up the impossible Real."[40] This, in turn, leads the subject to realize that the target of desire—*das Ding*, which is believed to be "out there," embodying total *jouissance*—was really always an ontological void and that any object claiming to lead the subject to *das Ding* "is simply an attempt to fill in the empty place of this loss."[41] This means the big Other does not really have all the answers (or, perhaps, any of the answers), it cannot lead us to the plentitude of the Real, and it, like the subject, is built on a fundamental lack. The big Other and the Subject are thus both on the same playing field. If this all is the case, why then should one obsess about what the big Other has to say when one can instead follow their own "lemon styles"?[42]

Many assume that a subject who has traversed the fantasy is in some utopic position. This is not the case, for traversing the fantasy requires the individual to recognize that subjectivity will always cause us to yearn for an impossible completeness. Our drive for an impossible, imagined *jouissance* cannot be quelled. We simply must learn to live with it. But this somewhat grim revelation has a silver lining, as Adrian Johnston notes:

> [A subject who traverses the fantasy] must, therefore, obey the logic of the forced choice, of "cure or worse" (*guérison ou pire*): Either accept that one cannot peacefully coexist with one's drives after analysis [i.e., that you will always yearn for something beyond], or endure even worse pain in believing that one is singled out to suffer in a unique, singular fashion. ... After [traversing the fantasy], the [subject] at least might be able to secure a bit more satisfaction from the little pleasures of quotidian existence, once these pleasures are not completely overshadowed by unattainable standards of a nonexistent enjoyment.[43]

This means that while the subject is not totally free from unhappiness, they should finally be free to "enjoy their enjoyment"[44]—that is, live their life and relish the little scraps of happiness that they find along the way—without having to worry that some missing piece is out there, held by the big Other just waiting to be discovered.

Evidence that Lemongrab traverses his fantasy in "The Mountain" comes at the end of the episode, when, after fleeing from the Mountain of Matthew and returning to his castle, Lemongrab looks up at the hole in the mural—that feature which had earlier convinced him that Matthew was his One True "Thing." He then takes a Lemonjon, chews it up, and spits it into the mural's crack, covering up the hole. This act can be read as a highly poetic equation about Lemongrab's newfound mental state: He (a subject born into the Imaginary-Symbolic registers) is the candy (an Imaginary-Symbolic part-object epitomizing lack), and the mural (which has a hole) is the big Other (which, it turns out, is lacking all the answers); by spitting the candy into the hole, Lemongrab is recognizing that the lack in the big Other is the same as his own. He further emphasizes this equivalence by musing to himself, "Yo, yo, it's grease." Just as he had earlier directed a similar comment at himself, he now directs it at the mural;

"Mind Games"

Lemongrab thus recognizes that he and the Other are united by their lack. Given that "the subject [traverses his fantasy] when his lack coincides with the lack in the Other,"[45] the ending of "The Mountain" thus sees Lemongrab at the logical end of his self-analysis.

Notes

1. Alan Sokal and Jean Bricmont, *Fashionable Nonsense*, 23.
2. Adrian Johnston, "Jacques Lacan."
3. Seán Sheehan, *Žižek*, 12.
4. Jacques Lacan, *Freud's Papers*, 62.
5. Dino F. Felluga, *Critical Theory*, 180.
6. Jacques Lacan and Wladimir Granoff, "Fetishism," 272.
7. Karen Coats, *Looking Glasses and Neverlands*, 2.
8. Jacques Lacan, *Four Fundamental Concepts*, 38.
9. Lacan, *Freud's Papers*, 66.
10. Sheehan, *Žižek*, 25.
11. Joseph Carew, *Ontological Catastrophe*, 30–31; Felluga, *Critical Theory*, 264, 330.
12. Carew, 30; Aron Dunlap, *Lacan and Religion*, 63.
13. Felluga, *Critical Theory*, 330.
14. Lacan, *Four Fundamental Concepts*, ix.
15. Slavoj Žižek, *Sublime Object of Ideology*, 221.
16. Dunlap, *Lacan and Religion*, 63; Bruce Fink, *Lacanian Subject*, 24.
17. Carew, *Ontological Catastrophe*, 31; Dunlap, 63.
18. Felluga, *Critical Theory*, 264.
19. Lacan, *Freud's Papers*, 66.
20. Sheehan, *Žižek*, 13.
21. To quote Princess Bubblegum. "Lemonhope II" (Season 5, episode 51).
22. Žižek, *Sublime Object of Ideology*, passim. I will hereafter refer to this object, which a subject mistakenly believes is *das Ding*, as the "One True *objet petit a*."
23. Slavoj Žižek, *Enjoy Your Symptom!*, 8, paraphrasing Jacques Lacan, *The Ethics of Psychoanalysis*, 112.
24. Žižek, *Sublime Object of Ideology*, 209.
25. Jacques Lacan, "The Mirror Stage."
26. Dylan Evans, *Introductory Dictionary*, 81.
27. Lacan, *Freud's Papers*, 102, 3.
28. Evans, *Introductory Dictionary*, 81, 202.
29. Lacan argued it is impossible to "eject" one or more of these registers in everyday life, given that "each [register] is sustained only in its topological relation with the others." Jacques Lacan apud Evans, *Introductory Dictionary*, ix. As such, Finn and Lemongrab's journey into the Ego-mirror should not be understood as a rejection of the Symbolic register, but rather as an artistic depiction of "thinking beyond"—or perhaps, *before*—"the Symbolic."
30. Žižek, *Sublime Object of Ideology*, 209.
31. Sheehan, *Žižek*, 31.
32. Jacques Lacan, "La Famille."
33. Sheehan, *Žižek*, 33.
34. Lewis Kirshner, "Rethinking Desire," 85.
35. Adrian Johnston, *Time Driven*, 239, 83.
36. Žižek, *Enjoy Your Symptom!*, 75.
37. Johnston, *Time Driven*, 239; Adrian Johnston, "Forced Choice."
38. "All Your Fault" (Season 5, episode 9).
39. Fink, *Lacanian Subject*, 24.

40. Guanjun Wu, "In Place of a Conclusion," 318.
41. Slavoj Žižek, *Interrogating the Real*, 52.
42. "You Made Me" (Season 4, episode 20).
43. Johnston, *Time Driven*, 249, 338.
44. Bruce Fink, *Clinical Introduction*, 216.
45. Slavoj Žižek, *Less Than Nothing*, 129.

References

Carew, Joseph. *Ontological Catastrophe: Žižek and the Paradoxical Metaphysics of German Idealism*. New Metaphysics. Ann Arbor: Open Humanities Press, 2014.
Coats, Karen. *Looking Glasses and Neverlands: Lacan, Desire, and Subjectivity in Children's Literature*. Iowa City: University of Iowa Press, 2004.
Dunlap, Aron. *Lacan and Religion*. New York: Routledge, 2016.
Evans, Dylan. *An Introductory Dictionary of Lacanian Psychoanalysis*. New York: Routledge, 1996.
Felluga, Dino F. *Critical Theory: The Key Concepts*. Routledge Key Guides. New York: Routledge, 2015.
Fink, Bruce. *A Clinical Introduction to Lacanian Psychoanalysis: Theory and Technique*. Cambridge, MA: Harvard University Press, 1997.
_____. *The Lacanian Subject: Between Language and Jouissance*. Princeton, NJ: Princeton University Press, 1997.
Homer, Sean. *Jacques Lacan*. Routledge Critical Thinkers. London: Routledge, 2005.
Johnston, Adrian. "The Forced Choice of Enjoyment: *Jouissance* between Expectation and Actualization." *Lacanian Ink: The Symptom*, no. 2 (2002). https://www.lacan.com/forced.htm.
_____. "Jacques Lacan." In *Stanford Encyclopedia of Philosophy*, edited by Edward N. Zalta. Stanford, CA: Metaphysics Research Lab, 2018. https://plato.stanford.edu/entries/lacan/.
_____. *Time Driven: Metapsychology and the Splitting of the Drive*. Evanston, IL: Northwestern University Press, 2005.
Kirshner, Lewis. "Rethinking Desire: The *Objet Petit a* in Lacanian Theory." *Journal of the American Psychoanalytic Association* 53, no. 1 (2005): 83–102. https://doi.org/10.1177/00030651050530010901.
Lacan, Jacques. *Écrits: The First Complete Edition in English*. Translated by Bruce Fink. New York: W. W. Norton, 2006. 1966.
_____. *The Ethics of Psychoanalysis, 1959–1960*. Translated by Dennis Porter. The Seminars of Jacques Lacan. Edited by Jacques-Alain Miller. Vol. 7, New York: W. W. Norton & Company, 1997.
_____. *The Four Fundamental Concepts of Psycho-Analysis*. Translated by Alan Sheridan. The Seminars of Jacques Lacan. Edited by Jacques-Alain Miller. New York: W. W. Norton & Company, 1981.
_____. *Freud's Papers on Technique, 1953–1954*. Translated by John Forrester. The Seminars of Jacques Lacan 1. Edited by Jacques-Alain Miller. New York: W. W. Norton & Company, 1991.
_____. "La Famille." In *Encyclopédie Française*, edited by A. de Monzie, 40.3–42.8. Paris, France: Société de Gestion de l'Encyclopédie Française, 1938.
_____. "The Mirror Stage as Formative of the I Function as Revealed in Psychoanalytic Experience." Translated by Bruce Fink. In *Écrits*, 75–81. New York: W. W. Norton, 2006.
Lacan, Jacques, and Wladimir Granoff. "Fetishism: The Symbolic, the Real and the Imaginary." In *Perversions, Psychodynamics and Therapy*, edited by Sandor Lordan and Michael Balint, 265–78. New York: Gramercy Publishing Company, 1956.
Sheehan, Seán. *Žižek: A Guide for the Perplexed*. London: Continuum International Publishing Group, 2012.

Sokal, Alan, and Jean Bricmont. *Fashionable Nonsense: Postmodern Intellectuals' Abuse of Science*. New York: Picador, 1998.

Wu, Guanjun. "In Place of a Conclusion: Traversing the Fantasy." In *The Great Dragon Fantasy: A Lacanian Analysis of Contemporary Chinese Thought*, 313–53. Singapore: World Scientific Publishing, 2014.

Žižek, Slavoj. *Enjoy Your Symptom! Jacques Lacan in Hollywood and Out*. New York: Routledge, 1992.

———. *Interrogating the Real*. Edited by Rex Butler and Scott Stephans. London: Bloomsbury Academic, 2005.

———. *Less Than Nothing: Hegel and the Shadow of Dialetical Materialism*. London: Verso, 2012.

———. *The Sublime Object of Ideology*. 2nd ed. London: Verso, 2008.

Trauma and the Body in *Adventure Time*

Steven Kielich

Trauma plays a pivotal role in Pendleton Ward's seminal animated fantasy series *Adventure Time* (2010–2018). Its narrative is, after all, to borrow a phrase from Alexander Burry, "dominated by an apocalyptic, end-oriented sensibility,"[1] precisely because the series itself demonstrates striking similarities to post-apocalyptic narratives. To be sure, its wide cast of characters find themselves in the aftermath of a catastrophic event, the destruction of which shares obvious similarities with nuclear holocaust.[2] However, it is not an obvious choice to examine the effects of trauma because *Adventure Time* is, after all, an animated children's fantasy show starring a boy and his dog. We should not allow this fantasy space, however, nor the very categorization of the series as a "children's show," to prevent us from recognizing the darker, more challenging dimensions of *Adventure Time*. The series alerts us to the ways that, among other things, trauma inscribes itself on the body: the primary site on which trauma and its symptoms are written. In this way, by displaying trauma and its effects visually on the body, rather than through textual or oral means, *Adventure Time* accurately depicts the inherent challenge of traumatic fiction: the onerous if not impossible task of properly narrativizing a traumatic event into a relatively cohesive narrative structure.

Adventure Time is one of those unique examples of mass-market entertainment that appeals to all audiences while simultaneously expressing something personal and quite possibly challenging about the world that we live in today. Despite its distant, fantastical setting, the show confronts reality in very harrowing and striking ways. While it is rife with off-beat humor and juvenile antics, those who are old enough to see past the seemingly incoherent and unpredictable narrative, as well as its child-like innocence, find themselves subjected to a post-apocalyptic narrative that aggressively confronts disturbing adult themes such as abandonment, loneliness, addiction, cannibalism, and existential anxiety. In the episode "Memory of a Memory," for example, we see the vampire Marceline in conflict with her ex, Ash, who literally steals her memories of his abusive behavior to get her back. This episode is just one example of how *Adventure Time* explores the consequences of trauma and abuse, particularly how these two violent or psychological acts can warp our conception of time and affect our literal memory recall. To this end, although trauma is not the primary focus of *Adventure Time*, its subject matter nevertheless repeatedly deals with extremely distressing experiences.

In this essay—which is inspired and informed heavily by the argumentation of Electra Georgiades, Slavoj Žižek, and Dominick LaCapra, among others—I will look at *Adventure Time* vis-à-vis the topics mentioned in this introduction, thereby reevaluating the series through the theoretical lens of trauma aesthetics. This will allow viewers and scholars alike to receive and critically examine the series in new and exciting ways. In particular, closely reading how *Adventure Time* represents and addresses trauma will help produce insight into how the psychic devastation or suffering that many undergo because of a traumatic experience contributes extensively to the fragmentation of one's identity, their individuality, as well as their sense of community.[3]

Adventure Time as Trauma Fiction

Adventure Time is, I claim, an example of trauma fiction. The very setting of the show, for example, the Land of Ooo, is the very center of trauma on the most elementary dimension. When we watch *Adventure Time*, we see Ooo in the aftermath of what can be claimed as the most horrible event any person can experience or witness: nuclear holocaust. The Land of Ooo is a veritable post-apocalyptic wasteland, which is precisely why we see ruined pieces of modern technology scattered throughout Ooo, as well as great architectural feats diminished to radiated ruins. In this way, *Adventure Time* can be comfortably placed alongside other narratives that are deeply rooted in the aftermath of major historical catastrophe. Correlatively, *Adventure Time* revolves around "an overwhelming sense of absence and non-belonging which manifests in ellipsis and fragmentation, deprivation and lack, and a distinctive resort to repetition."[4] The very "deprivation and lack" that exists writ large in the very landscape of Ooo produces intense images that reinforce the notion that it is a landscape consisting of remnants from a previous existence affected by an unprecedented catastrophe. Similarly, characters like Whisper Dan (that silent and subservient iron golem, who, in the episode "The Silent King," appears to be nothing more than a servant) are entirely deprived of a personality and will. Characters like Whisper Dan, moreover, serve as salient examples of what happens when one's individual self is ostensibly deprived of their subjectivity: they are, as a result of this transformation, reduced to a helpless servant. Both content and form are unsettled thanks to the traumatic core of the show. *Adventure Time's* post-war environment is also highly evident in those grotesque and ghastly creatures known as Oozers—humans who have mutated over time from prolonged exposure to radiation, causing them to physically and mentally deteriorate at an alarming rate, turning them into mindless, aggressive creatures, who, unable to speak or reason, act on instinct. The Oozer creatures are just one example that we can look to in order to help center ourselves amid the interminable manifestations of trauma that permeate the series.

Reading *Adventure Time* through a post-war lens allows us to examine the series' themes and aesthetics with respect to trauma studies. *Post-war* is a decidedly singular historical period, one that is predicated upon the experience of a conflict with emotionally severe repercussions, consisting of unspeakable horrors and traumas that have injurious effects on the physical and psychological levels, generating crises of various dimensions in both communal and individual structures. Of course, community plays a very important role within *Adventure Time*. Suffice to recall *Adventure Time's* very simple, quirky theme song. What is it that these lyrics are telling us? Basically, they are telling us to grab our friends as we journey to distant and uncharted lands, and, moreover, with Jake and Finn, the fun will never end. The injunction to "grab your friends" is effectively suggesting that in order to be filled with joy, to have fun, during one's adventures, one needs to be with friends, with company, and so on. *Adventure Time* is predicated on social relationships; certain characters have, more or less, a companion-counterpart who joins, or at least follows, them as they journey throughout the Land of Ooo. The most obvious of this companion-counterpart relationship is the protagonist-duo Finn (the human) and Jake (the anthropomorphic dog—with whom the "fun never ends") who rarely, if ever, leave each other's side; they are inseparable. Finn, we must remember, because he is the last human alive in this post-war period, is ultimately denied the "fundamental source … of communality"[5] and thus his only option is to stick with Jake in an attempt to restore his "radically impaired sense of belonging"[6] in this post-apocalyptic world. The dynamic that exists between Finn and Jake—the dynamic of company—suggests that, after an apocalyptic event like a nuclear war, there is purpose and value in the "presence of another."[7] The purpose and value are compensatory, in that social relations help one cope with traumatic events. The idea of company, of community, is an undeniably major thematic concern with trauma narratives.

To further explain this point, let us quickly examine how the concept of company plays a central, thematic role in other works of popular culture. Post-apocalyptic narratives—premised on either nuclear holocaust or the ever-popular zombie apocalypse which are so often locatable in popular culture (i.e., films and video games)—frequently emphasize this very topic. It is as if these works propagandized the prodigious importance of interpersonal companionship as it relates to sheer survival and survivability. Suffice to recall Romero's *The Night of the Living Dead* (1968), or Sam Raimi's *The Evil Dead* (1981): two seminal horror cinema classics that ultimately remind us to, in the event that the dead rise from their shoddy graves, join forces with others in order to effectively capitalize on one's chances of survival. Similarly, the critically-acclaimed and commercially-successful video game franchise *Fallout* (1997–2015) from Bethesda Studios reminds us that to travel throughout the post-apocalyptic wastes alone is a dangerous thing; this is why the game recommends the player establish a companionship with another character to travel and combat enemies with. These popular culture examples bring to light "depiction of human company [and its] value ... in the aftermath of a period of profound atrocity."[8] This is precisely why company and trauma are inextricably related in these narratives; they ultimately suggest that there is a fundamental weakness inherent in remaining alone, while explicitly addressing and demonstrating that to remain in a group or to be a part of a community is of the utmost importance.[9]

This theme of company carries over into *Adventure Time*, only it is taken to its most obscene dimensions; there are many characters in the series who emphatically express obsession with being in the company of another character, but Ice King is perhaps the most revealing example of this extreme obsession. Ice King has the habit of kidnapping princesses with whom he has become infatuated, snatching them away from their homes, bringing them to his lair in his Ice Kingdom. The reason behind Ice King's kidnappings is that he is trying to fill the void that was left by his fiancé, Betty, who abandoned him. Before nuclear war waged throughout Ooo, she and Simon Petrikov (Ice King's real name) were in a committed relationship until Petrikov, under the arcane enchantments of a magical crown that he discovered, gradually began to alter his body and warp his mind. This abandonment—the literal severing of company—is the primary source of Ice King's trauma and the reason behind his constant kidnapping. This emphatic obsession over the prodigious desire to be in the company of another individual is undoubtedly suggestive of traumatic loss: Ice King, continuously bombarded with emotions of a past that intrudes and effectively overpowers the present, "is left to endure the consequences of a trauma, the persistence of which is suggested [to be] the result" of absence.[10]

Adventure Time, as a model of trauma fiction, is very much preoccupied with loss and lack. Suffice to recall Ice King's trauma, which is, after all, that of a perpetual presence of absence. It is absence, in the wake of a traumatic event, that shapes the very world of *Adventure Time*. Here, we can turn to Dominick LaCapra (whose psychoanalytic work in trauma and Holocaust studies is indispensable) and his essay "Trauma, Absence, Loss" (1999) which proposes radical notions about how time, space, and language are to be revived after key elements of symbolic life have collapsed under the traumatic events of the Holocaust:

> In an obvious and restricted sense losses may entail absences, but the converse need not be the case. Moreover, I would situate [...] absence [...] on a transhistorical level, while situating loss on a historical level. In this transhistorical sense absence is not an event and does not imply tenses (past, present, or future). By contrast, the historical past is the scene of losses that may be narrated as well as of specific possibilities that may conceivably be reactivated, reconfigured, and transformed in the present or future. The past is misperceived in terms of sheer absence or utter annihilation. Something of the past always remains, if only as a haunting presence or revenant.[11]

The last line, for me, is the most important because it brings forth this possibility that something from the past can be, if only as a spectral presence, ever-existing in the present. This idea of something returning from the past into the present, where it remains as a powerful and overwhelming force, is very much alive in *Adventure Time*. In *Adventure Time*, the residue of one's past trauma is repeatedly displayed as a confronting and haunting presence.

This image of something returning from the past, actively haunting and threatening one's present reality, is precisely what LaCapra calls revenant. In folklore, the revenant is an animated corpse that, believed to have been revived by some act of necromancy, and, driven by revenge, haunts the living.[12] This is a classic topic that has been explored in all sorts of art forms, but one of the best contemporary examples would be the aptly-titled 2015 film from Alejandro G. Iñárritu, *The Revenant*. This film tells the story of the explorer Hugh Glass who, after a debilitating grizzly bear attack, is buried alive and left behind to die by his expedition crew somewhere in the Dakota wilderness. His crew members, believing Glass to have died from his wounds, forget about Glass completely; he is, upon burial, removed, in their minds, from reality. Glass, however, survives this premature burial and, fueled by an inextinguishable desire, emerges from his grave and makes it his mission to hunt down and exact revenge on his crew. Glass effectively occupies the figurative position of the returning dead[13] whose drive fits perfectly into the answer proposed by Žižek in *Looking Awry* (1992) for why the dead return. Žižek writes:

> Apropos of this phenomenon, let us then ask a naive and elementary question: why do the dead return? The answer offered by Lacan is the same as that found in popular culture: because they were not properly buried, i.e., because something went wrong with their obsequies. The return of the dead is a sign of a disturbance in the symbolic rite, in the process of symbolization; the dead return as collectors of some unpaid symbolic debt.[14]

Glass' symbolic debt here is obvious: He wants to exact revenge and will go to the utmost extremes to ensure that his vengeance is fulfilled. However, it is, as Žižek points out for us, his improper burial that ultimately allows him to haunt his contemporaries. The crew's quick and dodgy burial of Glass is an effort to push Glass out of their symbolic reality. From the point of view of the expedition crew, Glass' return is not only deeply unwanted but also terribly traumatic, in the sense that Glass' return not only contaminates reality but also severs one's deliberate distancing from the past. One might say that Glass' "death" was traumatic because a collective ritual intended to overcome the anguish of loss was not carried out properly. The revenant's return, then, whether figurative or literal, is a symptom of a trauma that can only be cured through a symbolic coming to terms with death.

The consequences of trauma function almost exactly like a revenant insofar as it emerges as a radical disruption of reality whereby something from the past taints the present.[15] Just like the crew members who believed Glass to have left their reality, we often associate past events with the past, i.e., we assume they no longer exist in the present. However, when trauma from some past event does reemerge, we are overwhelmed then with a sense of something not being over. It is as if we are literally watching the dead emerge from their graves, disrupting our reality, and so on. This metaphor can easily be applied to trauma insofar as despite perceiving an event to have been concluded, there are nonetheless these excremental remainders that simply refuse to be properly buried.[16]

Adventure Time, the narrative of which takes place in the aftermath of a nuclear war, plays with this threshold very nicely. In nuclear war, the event happens, but there are, of course, material remains of a time that, like revenants, threaten and haunt the present. Littered throughout Ooo are visual reminders of a past that are suggestive of the land as *corpsed*: The Land of Ooo is a veritable graveyard of artefacts from a previous age, for the rubble that is scattered throughout the land comprises bombs, television sets, radios, junk floating on the rivers' surfaces, cars, crashed helicopters, and so on. Moreover, there are craters that certainly are not natural, but are instead the products of munitions and explosions.

The Land of Ooo, while once a beautiful and magical place, is now in the aftermath of a dreadful nuclear conflict known as The Mushroom War when "frightful bombs, poised to bathe the land in mutagenic horror"[17] were dropped on Ooo. While this landscape and all the objects scattered throughout it evoke a post-war atmosphere, they nonetheless also evoke the unprocessed trauma that cannot be tamed, domesticated, or rendered palpable. One might say here that the external landscape mirrors or expresses the devastated condition of the internal world, of a subjectivity overwhelmed by what has happened. Not only does this effectively suggest that a traumatic event has no beginning, middle, or end, it also suggests that however much we would like to escape it—to deny its existence—we are forever haunted in the present by a traumatic past.

The Body as Site of Trauma: Ice King and the Crown

Just as the very landscape of *Adventure Time* serves to mirror or express the devastated condition of its internal world, so too does the body serve as a site on which we can read the impact of trauma.[18] The bodies of characters in the series serve as sites on which we can locate, and therefore decode, a profound personification of trauma. No other character in *Adventure Time* is more plagued by the everlasting experience of trauma and its effects than Ice King, that lonely wizard who has the magical capabilities to wield and manipulate ice and snow. Initially introduced as a villain, Ice King slowly but positively becomes a rather kind-hearted but terribly misunderstood aging man with perverse senses of morality and social behavior, suffering from debilitating loneliness, loss of memory, and frequent confrontations with horrors from his past. On the most elementary level, Ooo and Ice King share the image of a "dysfunctional, deteriorating, and often disappearing body"[19] that is always reminding them (and us) about their past. Ice King, in particular, suffers from the traumatic experience of utter loss—he was abandoned by his fiancé—and his body reflects such loss. On an elementary level, Ice King is no longer a human being; he has lost his humanity and is instead an undead creature. Moreover, his skin, being a sickly blue and incredibly cold to the touch, is deprived of the color and warmth that we often identify with living things. His poor eyesight, his fragile bones, etc., all emphasize physical decline which, with Ice King, is utterly relentless. His progressive physical deterioration is his ultimate loss of the self and it matches his fiancée's perceived abandonment. His unsuccessful acceptance of a past loss is resurrected in its most obscene dimensions in the present, where it remains with extreme persistence.

Because he belongs to "the realm of the abject," we can turn to Ice King's physical body in order to decode, interpret, and transcribe his traumatic past into a coherent account.[20] Borrowing Georgiades' phrasing once again, "the depiction of corporeal decline," in *Adventure Time*, "serves to express vividly the trauma that cannot be fully addressed in personal history, captured in memory or coherently articulated in speech."[21] A consequence of trauma and a traumatic past is a display of reluctance, or more generally, inability, to successfully narrate one's personal accounts of a traumatic encounter—the memories of which are often repressed—in a clear, concise, and articulate manner. When a subject is no longer capable of articulating, in a coherent or relevant manner, the events surrounding their trauma, the body itself can function as a site from which the very essence of trauma can be extracted, conveying it in a visual way, which is especially relevant when the work of remembering faces the obstacle of trauma.

The interesting thing about Ice King's corporeal being, however, is that, although he is deteriorating (his body is literally becoming undone), there is a definite bodily persistence. He is very much in a situation shared with zombies, the creatures who, despite progressive decay (a limb lost here, a chunk of flesh torn off there, etc.) nonetheless shuffle forward with a limping gait. The classic example of how to successfully destroy a zombified individual is to remove the head or destroy the brain, for until those organs are destroyed, the zombie knows no end. Ice King, I claim, is in the same unfortunate condition. He knows that he is actively decaying; yet, despite this decay, he knows that there is no definitive end. Finding himself trapped in an undead state, where he is rapidly declining mentally and physically, Ice King fails to consider a limit simply because, for him, there is no limit.

Ice King's body is not naturally undead; it is under the control of the magic crown that he wears. His body, under the marred influence of the crown, "constrains his interaction with the world" around him[22]; it excessively poses as an authoritarian identity over his entire self. An extreme example of this is, of course, the Hollywood narrative concept of the invasion of the body snatchers: People are trapped in their own body, unable to break free from the control of alien forces; the aliens, of course, use the bodies of their victims as mere vessels for their momentary humanly existence.[23] Those possessed are arguably aware of what is happening, yet their actions and movements are entirely beyond their control, manipulated like puppets by a powerful, outside force. A similar concept is present in *Adventure Time* with Ice King particularly. Somewhere deep beneath the surface of Ice King exists Simon Petrikov—Ice King's former self before he underwent the traumatic transformation into the undead creature that he is now. The crown that he wears is what ultimately controls him; it is the powerful, outside force that, like the body-snatching aliens, controls Ice

King, using his body as nothing more than a mere passive vessel. Considering this, Ice King's body is totally independent of his inner self; in other words, his corporeal being fails to function analogously with his subjectivity. The bodily dissociation from the self, "like the inherent struggle between memory and language," suggests further "victimization symptomatic of trauma."[24] The possession by an authoritarian bodily entity is exemplified by Ice King.

Perhaps the most striking characteristic of this dissociated authoritarian body that can be located in Ice King is the very fact that he is undead. Ice King—his body assuming the qualities of a veritable prison—is unable to, indeed cannot, escape the clutches of immortality that his undead body perpetuates. In other words, Ice King cannot die; he simply lives on and on indefinitely. It is the crown that preserves Ice King indefinitely, bestowing an immortality onto its wearer that is both disgusting and terrifying: it allows its wearer the possibility of persisting endlessly beyond the limitations of natural, organic life.[25] Ice King is undead, then, not in the sense that he has achieved nirvana, this sublime immortal sense of spirit, but instead as a zombie is undead. This very distinction evokes what can be classified as an *obscene immortality*[26]: No matter the annihilation, the "living dead" rise once again, shuffling round unharmed and unaffected despite the effects of their previous violent encounter. Ice King is, we learn, some 1,000 years old, and, moreover, he is also the survivor of perhaps the most devastating and brutal examples of annihilation: a nuclear holocaust. The crown is the very object that kept him alive through that nuclear holocaust which turned Earth into the Land of Ooo. Ice King is, to cut it short, simply immortal. He exists in this obscene dimension of undeadness thanks to the crown that he wears.

The crown embodies what Slavoj Žižek, interpreting Freud, insists is an undead partial object. Žižek provides us with a beautiful example that perfectly illustrates precisely what an undead partial object is using Andersen's fairy-tale *The Red Shoes* (1845).

> In Andersen's fairy tale *The Red Shoes*, an impoverished young woman puts on a pair of magical shoes and almost dies when her feet won't stop dancing. She is only saved when an executioner cuts off her feet with his axe. Her still-shod feet dance on, whereas she is given wooden feet and finds peace in religion. These shoes stand for drive at its purest: an 'undead' partial object that functions as a kind of impersonal willing: 'it wants,' it persists in its repetitive movement (of dancing), it follows its path and exacts its satisfaction at any price, irrespective of the subject's well-being. This drive is that which is 'in the subject more than herself': although the subject cannot ever 'subjectivize' it, assume it as 'her own' by way of saying 'It is I who want to do this!' it nonetheless operates in her very kernel.[27]

The red shoes in Anderson's fairy tale are, in other words, the internalization of the dancer's[28] passion for dance taking over; the shoes, immortal in their undeadness, are literally the undead object. We can easily locate a similar obsceneness in the Ice King's crown, which serves in this case as the undead partial object.

The crown, like Anderson's red shoes, is more powerful than a simple object; it has a particular will of its own. Likewise, the crown, through the sympathetic magic that it promises, enslaves its wearer. Just as the red shoes, which promise the pleasure of dance, eventually force the young girl to amputate her legs in order to free herself from them, so too does the power of the crown reveal itself to be no more than a mere deception, destroying Ice King's mental and physical capacities, and effectively obliterating him. It can be surmised then that the crown is endowed with a malevolent sentience that enables it to manipulate its bearer to the point where the bearer ultimately loses themselves completely.

Although his body is deteriorating, he nonetheless remains alive. Ice King is distinctly neither human nor inhuman; he is instead marked by a terrifying excess which effectively negates his humanity, or at least what is left of it. It is this excess, in particular, that indicates trauma, because trauma is not simply an assault on the mind—it is also a powerful force that impacts individuals on a physical level. This is precisely the reason why Ice King often complains of his ill health and incessantly comments on his body-image (throughout the series, and it is quite obvious at times, Ice King goes through apparent cycles of binge eating and starvation; he fluctuates in weight because of either his over- or under-eating).[29] It is as if Ice King's body is effectively and continually turning against him.[30] The crown is very much to blame for this aggression on the bodily level; it is, like a drug, the very life force that dictates Ice King's every movement, as if he were nothing more than a simple puppet, "foreground[ing] a profound level of dehumanisation."[31]

Ice King's deeply traumatic past literally manifests itself on his body. We must remember that profound loss—his abandonment by his fiancée, Betty—is what informs Ice King's trauma. In remembering this, we can then read Ice King's body as his loss realized. His body is gradually decaying; it is a literal loss of the physical self—a figural embodiment of a psychic loss. What is more, his skin, as already mentioned, is an obscene blue, visually indicative of a dead body turned cold. The body is the very canvas on which the unassimilable qualities of trauma are effectively conveyed to us, the audience, without dissipating or obscuring the truth.

The truth here, of course, is that trauma not only exists "in his head"; it is very real and it impacts the body, too. *Adventure Time* reveals to us that trauma physically exists and that it is as palpable as the very skin of a person. By displaying trauma as a physical presence, *Adventure Time* reinforces the notion that upon confronting a traumatic memory one is often left completely powerless, unable to effectively distance oneself from the immediate dangers that traumatic memory often promises. In other words, because *Adventure Time* displays trauma physically, in an either geographic or bodily sense, it reinforces this sense that any resistance to it is futile and that there is no effective separation or escape from a traumatic memory or presence. More to the point, despite Ice King's ostensible distance from his traumatic past, as an aged and immortal sorcerer, he nevertheless cannot escape his traumatic past precisely because the trauma is always immediate—it is on his very body. There is no way, in other words, for Ice King to effectively distance himself from his trauma precisely because his traumatic wounds exist not only within his mind as memories but, in a much more immediate way, on his flesh.

Suffice to recall "trauma" in the original Greek literally signifies "wound." This wound, of course, refers to a physical injury of or on the body. With Ice King, the concept and imagery here is obvious: his wounded, ruptured body accurately symbolizes what lies beneath the exterior such as the emotions, the memories, the vulnerabilities, and so on. Furthermore, this wounding evokes the vulnerability of not only the psyche but of the flesh itself as far as trauma is concerned. Ice King's body, replete with scabs, blotches, dead skin, all colored by an obscene blue, is rendered harmed—the flesh, maimed. Ice King's wounded body displays a very real, immediate violence that forever subjects him to continuous sensations that are predicated upon a dark and disturbing past when terrible things happened.

In this sense, the body lies at the very core of *Adventure Time*'s exploration of trauma. By displaying trauma and its effects visually on the body rather than textually or orally (i.e., a direct telling or explaining of one's trauma), *Adventure Time* accurately depicts the difficulty of articulating one's traumatic experience into a succinct narrative form. When something is so traumatic, it often resists effective—and therapeutic—narrative reconstruction. Recognizing the impossibility of integrating the events of one's past into a coherent narrative, *Adventure Time* presents us with the alternate possibility of reading and interpreting trauma visually.

Conclusion

Despite the fantastical setting and seemingly childlike innocence of *Adventure Time*, we can comfortably situate the series in the ambit of trauma fiction. The Land of Ooo, after all, is presented to us in the aftermath of what can be claimed as the most horrible event any person can experience or witness: nuclear holocaust. It is precisely through a post-war lens that we are fully able to examine the series' thematic and stylistic preoccupations with respect to growing critical discourse in trauma studies. This allows us to further examine and interrogate the consequences of a conflict with emotionally severe repercussions, consisting of unspeakable horrors and traumas that have injurious effects on the physical and psychological levels, generating crises of various dimensions in both communal and individual structures.

Trauma, therefore, plays a pivotal role in the series. With its profound commentary on trauma, the series alerts us to the ways that trauma inscribes itself on the body. When the attempt to remember faces the obstacle of trauma, and communicability is consigned to an impossibility, the body and physicality in general can be used as physiological measurements of trauma. What we find is that the very Land of Ooo, consisting of remnants from a previous existence affected by an unprecedented catastrophe, evokes the consequences of unprocessed trauma that fails to meet the demands of verbal narrativization. The very landscape mirrors or expresses the devastated condition of the internal world—of a subjectivity overwhelmed by what has happened. Correlatively, we can locate, and therefore decode, trauma that is personified on the body of certain characters, namely Ice King. With Ice King, and the very geography of the Land of Ooo, we discover that the body is the very canvas on which the unassimilable qualities of trauma are effectively conveyed.

Adventure Time serves as an incredibly salient example of how the body can potentially offer answers to the enshrouding mysteries behind the traumatic encounter, and it functions therefore as a legitimate source of traumatic cognition. This is directly apropos of the inherent difficulty of what we might call the "narrative problem" of trauma fiction. More precisely, this "narrative problem" or dilemma of trauma fiction is that trauma, in general, is bound up in the question of ethics, politics, and the very epistemology of witnessing. In considering the (im)possibilities of the very narrativization of a traumatic event, we must confront the possibility of whether or not an event can be told at all. This is the inherent paradox of trauma studies, one that is especially prevalent in Holocaust studies.[32] Frequently, the very nature of trauma is such that those who would bear witness to an event are incapable of successfully recounting it properly. This occurs for one of two reasons: Either the individual did not survive the traumatic event; or, while there is a survivor, it is because of the event that they nonetheless might be stripped of all ability to speak about it. *Adventure Time*, then, is a cinematic experimentation of how, precisely because of the innate difficulty of performing a verbal narrative that does justice to the traumatic, cataclysmic event, the trauma itself can be rendered, represented, and interpreted, elsewhere—namely, the body.

Narratively, the series is best understood as a work predicated on traumatic experiences of the past, including a nuclear war that occurred one thousand years before the series main timeline; despite this war being ancient history, its "consequences ... are still endured in the present,"[33] revealing a fundamental need for secondary markers to be analyzed. These secondary sources, whether it is the human body or the various artifacts of a bygone time that wound the very geography of the Land of Ooo, are precisely those objects that represent and address trauma in original and profound ways. This effectively produces insight into how the psychic devastation or suffering that many undergo because trauma contributes extensively to the complete loss of subjectivity and one's sense of community. When we combine the two modes of trauma fiction and trauma aesthetics, we can create a more complete picture of how a series like *Adventure Time* channels the various motifs and tropes of trauma.

NOTES

1. Alexander Burry, "Execution, Trauma, and Recovery in Dostoevsky's *The Idiot*," 259.
2. Burry, 259.
3. Electra Georgiades, *Trauma, Company, and Witnessing in Samuel Beckett's Post-War Drama, 1952–61*, 213.
4. Georgiades, 213.
5. Georgiades, 36.
6. Georgiades.
7. Georgiades, 47.
8. Georgiades, *Trauma, Company, and Witnessing*, 9.
9. In Kai Erikson's "Notes on Trauma and Community," he writes that "trauma can create community" (185). The protagonists and characters of *The Night of the Living Dead*, *Evil Dead*, the *Fallout* franchise, and especially *Adventure Time*, are, "like trauma victims, 'not drawn together by feelings of affection'" (Georgiades, *Trauma, Company, and Witnessing*, 171), but, because they find themselves embedded in a tragic world.
10. Georgiades, *Trauma, Company, and Witnessing*, 38.
11. Dominick LaCapra, "Trauma, Absence, Loss," 700.
12. Lindahl, Carl, et al, *Medieval Folklore: A Guide to Myths, Legends, Tales, Beliefs, and Customs*, 424.
13. Although Glass' status as a revenant is purely figurative, since he himself was never truly "dead," this does not invalidate the analysis. The circumstances surrounding Glass' "death," his incomplete burial, as well as his eventual incessant haunting of his foes with the vengeful intention all perfectly align themselves—more than any ordinary zombie narrative would—with the ideas that both Žižek and LaCapra have on the subject.
14. Slavoj Žižek, *Looking Awry*, 23.
15. Georgiades, *Trauma, Company, and Witnessing*, 38.
16. What happens when waste, much to our horror, reemerges? Think, for a moment, of a toilet: Waste goes into a toilet, and that waste is then flushed away. It is, like a revenant, who is buried and then forgotten. When we flush any waste down the toilet, we recognize the waste as leaving our reality, entering another space which we phenomenologically identify as a kind of netherworld, or a place of non-existence. When the flushing does not function properly and the waste reemerges, we are horrified, overwhelmed then with a sense of something not being over. It is as if we are literally watching the dead emerge

from their graves, disrupting our reality, and so on. This metaphor can easily be applied to trauma insofar as despite perceiving an event to have been concluded, there are nonetheless these excremental remainders that simply refuse to be properly buried. These are symptoms that a trauma has occurred. There is perhaps a difference between flushing away something and working through it emotionally. The first is a kind of repressive gesture that may not solve the problem. The second is more therapeutically oriented and has a chance of overcoming the anguish related to the traumatic event.

17. "Finn the Human" (Season 5, Episode 1)
18. Georgiades, *Trauma, Company, and Witnessing*, 108.
19. Georgiades, 142.
20. Karen O'Donnell, *Ruptured Voices: Trauma and Recovery*, 76.
21. Georgiades, *Trauma, Company, and Witnessing*, 142.
22. Georgiades, 145.
23. Although the phrasing here might inspire one to recall Jack Finney's *The Body Snatchers* and its many cinematic adaptations, we must be very careful here. In the traditional *Body Snatcher* narratives, human possession is predicated not on an external force but an internal one. The crucial component of these narratives is that the "infected" bodies are taken over and controlled by something within them as opposed to something beyond them in an external sense. Nevertheless, the idea of "body snatching" as such from an external force is certainly present in similarly structured narratives such as John Carpenter's masterpiece *They Live* (1988). Carpenter's film adheres to the classic formula that there are aliens among us who are also invisible to our gaze, but subverts it slightly. By using subliminal messages, silently disseminated via televised broadcasts, the aliens effectively manipulate, control, and possess their victims. It is only when the broadcasting antenna is destroyed by the film's hero John Nada, effectively severing the aliens' only possible means of control, that their guises are revealed.
24. Georgiades, *Trauma, Company, and Witnessing*, 145.
25. Slavoj Žižek, noticing the inextricable connection that exists between the "disgustingly-terrifying" and "comical" representations of immortality in popular culture, provides a very beautiful and concise explanation of what is otherwise a very basic Lacanian reading of immortality. The most basic form of immortality, writes Žižek, "resides in what Lacan calls the Sadean fundamental fantasy: the fantasy of another, ethereal body of the victim, which can be tortured indefinitely and nonetheless magically retains its beauty (recall the Sadean figure of the young girl sustaining endless humiliations and mutilations from her depraved torturer and somehow mysteriously surviving it all intact, in the same way Tom and Jerry and other cartoon heroes survive all their ridiculous ordeals intact)" (Žižek, "The Obscene Immortality and Its Discontents," 2).
26. This phrase—"obscene immortality"—is borrowed from Slavoj Žižek who, addressing player subjectivity in video games, uses it to explain the "undead dreamspace of video games": "When I am immersed in a game, I dwell in a universe of undeadness where no annihilation is definitive since, after every destruction, I can return to the beginning and start the game again" (Žižek, "The Obscene Immortality and its Discontents," 1).
27. Slavoj Žižek, "Bruce Fink: *The Lacanian Subject*," 161.
28. In Michael Powell and Emeric Pressburger's beautiful *The Red Shoes* (1948), the heroine is a ballerina. Those who have seen the Powell and Pressburger film will know that, unlike Andersen's tale where the dancer must have her feet brutally cut off with an axe, the ballerina-protagonist throws herself in front of a moving train. While she is bleeding to death, and a crowd of on-lookers surround her, her red shoes are taken off and she finally dies. Whether she throws herself before a speeding locomotive because she is entirely subservient to the sentient power of the red shoes or because she simply wishes to commit suicide to free herself from ever having to dance again is left ambiguous.
29. Ice King's fickle fluctuations in his weight are suggestive of a loss of control. According to Susan J. Brison (2002, 73), losing control is "one of the most serious harms of trauma." We can argue then that this frequent and drastic fluctuation in weight defines a state of complete helplessness in the face of an overwhelming force. Indeed, as Herman

(1992, 33) notes, "traumatic events overwhelm the ordinary systems of care that give people a sense of control, connection, and meaning."

30. From a psychoanalytic perspective, his body is partially siding with the trauma's search for expression, and partially offering the disorders and illnesses as a compromise with the social reality he is in. To continue the toilet metaphor from earlier: Ice King's dehumanized condition is representative of the repressed in his body. Analytically speaking, the problem here, then, is not that the toilet is backed up; rather, it is that we flush things away. It is interesting that proper symbolic payment of debt is different from flushing the toilet.

31. Georgiades, *Trauma, Company, and Witnessing*, 146.

32. See Dominick LaCapra's *History and Memory after Auschwitz* (1998) for further reading on this particular subject. There, LaCapra attempts to distinguish between "primary and secondary memory" (20). He suggests that, because "memory almost invariably involves lapses relating to forms of denial, repression, suppression, and evasion" (20), the event must be "reconstructed from its effects and traces" (21). He then arrives at the conclusion that, because trauma produces "a gap or hole in experience," there is never an "immediate access to the experience itself even from the original witness, much less for the secondary witness and historian" (21).

33. Georgiades, *Trauma, Company, and Witnessing*, 10.

REFERENCES

Brison, Susan J. *Aftermath: Violence and the Remaking of a Self*. Princeton, NJ: Princeton University Press, 2011.

Burry, Alexander. "Execution, Trauma and Recovery in Dostoevsky's *The Idiot*." *Slavic and East European Journal*, vol. 54, no. 2, 2010, pp. 255–71.

Erikson, Kai, "Notes on Trauma and Community." *American Imago*, vol. 48, no. 4, The Johns Hopkins University Press, 1991, pp. 455–72.

Georgiades, Electra. *Trauma, Company and Witnessing in Samuel Beckett's Post-War Drama, 1952–61*. ProQuest Dissertations Publishing, 2015.

González Iñárritu, Alejandro, et al. *The Revenant* / Directed by Alejandro G. Iñárritu; Screenplay by Mark L. Smith & Alejandro G. Iñárritu; Produced by Arnon Milchan, Steve Golin, Alejandro G. Iñárritu, Mary Parent, Keith Redmon, James W. Skotchdopole; a Regency Enterprises Presentation in Association with Ratpac Entertainment; a New Regency/Anonymous Content/M Productions/Appian Way Production; an Alejandro G. Iñárritu Film. 20th Century Fox Home Entertainment, 2016.

Herman, Judith Lewis, *Trauma and Recovery*. New York: Basic. 1992.

LaCapra, Dominick. *History and Memory after Auschwitz*. Ithaca. NY: Cornell University Press, 1998.

_____. "Trauma, Absence, Loss," *Critical Inquiry*, Vol. 25, No. 4 (1999): 696–727.

Lindahl, Carl, et al. *Medieval Folklore: A Guide to Myths, Legends, Tales, Beliefs, and Customs*. Edited by Carl Lindahl et al., Oxford, UK: Oxford University Press, 2002.

O'Donnell, Karen. *Ruptured Voices: Trauma and Recovery*. Oxford, UK: Inter-Disciplinary Press, 2019.

Žižek, Slavoj, "Bruce Fink: *The Lacanian Subject*," *Journal for the Psychoanalysis of Culture and Society*, Vol. 1, No. 1, 1991: 161.

_____. *Looking Awry: An Introduction to Jacques Lacan through Popular Culture*. Cambridge, MA: MIT Press, 1992.

_____. "The Obscene Immortality and its Discontents," *The International Journal of Žižek Studies*, Vol. 11, No. 2 (2017): 1–14.

"Is that where creativity comes from?"
Adventure Time *and the Artistic Medium*

The Japanese Spirit and Aesthetic in Western Animation

The Influence of Anime on Adventure Time

KENDRA N. SHEEHAN

Nowadays, many Westerners are familiar with the terms "anime" and "manga"—the Japanese words for animation and comics, respectively. These terms are often associated with distinctly Japanese forms of entertainment that are trendy, colorful, and "fun." But while these art forms may have originated in Japan, they have both moved outside of Japan and can be found worldwide. This popularity is plainly evident in other countries'—and, in particular, the United States'—use of what might be referred to as the Japanese aesthetic: Today, anime and manga characters adorn numerous products produced for worldwide consumption, including video games, advertisements, and food packaging. Thanks to the globalization of Japanese pop products, the Japanese aesthetic has left an evident mark on Western popular culture.

While the United States is a hard power in terms of military and economic might, Japan is arguably one of the world's leading soft powers, whose pop culture products are influential through cultural or ideological means.[1] This is especially true when it comes to its animation, and by some estimates anime now makes up approximately sixty percent of the world's animation.[2] Notably, the emergence of Japan as a prominent soft power and the subsequent globalization of Japanese anime has influenced American animation significantly, not only in terms of art style, but also in terms of its increased interest in engaging storylines, more mature themes, and stylized music. This essay examines the many ways that the anime tradition has informed *Adventure Time*'s visual and narrative approach, with the *Stakes* miniseries serving as an example.

Globalization of Japanese Pop Culture and "Japanese Cool"

Japanese pop culture, as defined by William Tsutsui, is a commercial culture, i.e., a culture that is mass-produced for worldwide consumption and designed to appeal to mainstream tastes by encompassing a wide range of forms and media.[3] As such, many Japanese pop products are created with both Japan and the West in mind. Douglas McGray, in his article "Japan's Gross National Cool," uses Sanrio's popular *Hello Kitty* line as an example. Although globally recognized as a Japanese product created by a Japanese company, the main character, known as "Kitty White," was envisioned as British. McGray argues that this dual identity means that, on one hand, "Hello Kitty is Western, so she will sell in Japan," but on the other, "she is Japanese, so she will sell in the West."[4] The character has been specifically designed to straddle global consumer tastes, appearing foreign to both Eastern and Western consumers.[5]

Scholars like McGray have argued that one reason Japanese pop culture has become so popular outside Japan is because its "Japaneseness" connotes an exotic sort of "coolness" to the Western world. This is no accident, and as we just discussed, many of the products Japan exports have been carefully crafted to be just Japanese enough for non–Japanese consumers. In other words, they have been manufactured to appeal to Western sensibilities about an idealized Japan. The "cool" factor arises when these products are perceived in the minds of Western consumers as being both genuinely and uniquely Japanese, and thereby somehow "different" from other products (even though they often are not that different from the pop culture products of other countries). This "coolness" is furthered by a product's use of Japanese names, Japanese words, or stylized art (e.g., an anime or manga character), which visually reinforces the exotic "otherness" of the product. It has been through the production and exporting of "distinctly Japanese" video games, consumer electronics, architecture, fashion, food, and art that Japan has managed to attain great cultural influence.[6]

Japan's cultural influence is unique and unlike America's. For many, America's influence is seen as the result of pop culture giants like Hollywood, McDonald's, or the film enterprise of Disney. But as Shabao Xie argues, America's pop culture hegemony was never an inevitability; instead, it was the result of American imperialism and the nation's military and commercial power, which has exerted great cultural and economic influence on other cultures.[7] Japan, on the other hand, is a soft power[8] that holds sway over Asia and the rest of the globe, neither through military might nor economic hegemony, but instead through raw cultural appeal.[9] This appeal is the previously discussed "Japanese cool," which manifests as cute mascots and anime characters; media that embodies romanticized ideas of samurai culture and friendship; and a bevy of other products that are seen as distinctly Japanese. With a worldwide demand for its "cool" culture, Japan proves that it does not need a military to be influential.

Of Japan's many "cool" products, anime is one of the most popular, with the internet functioning as the primary platform that enables international fans to watch, download, share, and discuss anime series. In the United States, many high schools and college campuses now have anime clubs, and the spread of anime has even permeated the American film industry: For instance, Walt Disney Studios originally had a contract with Japan's famed Studio Ghibli to release films in the West (a contract now held by GKIDS), and in 2003, Studio Ghibli's *Spirited Away* won an Oscar for Best Animated Feature at the seventy-fifth Academy Awards, which helped anime gain international recognition while also setting a standard for other animated films that would follow. Today, anime can easily be found airing on American television during certain programming blocks (such as Cartoon Network's Toonami and Adult Swim), and an increasing number of anime films are being translated and released in theaters to American audiences.

The Origin of Anime and Its Popularity in the United States

Japanese anime has its origins in both Western and Japanese culture. On one hand, anime "builds on previous high cultural traditions" in Japan, including the art of *kabuki* (traditional dance) and the artistic technique of woodblock printing.[10] On the other, anime also embraces the "worldwide artistic traditions of twentieth century cinema and photography ... often in surprisingly complex ways" to explore "issues familiar to viewers of contemporary art cinema and even to the readers of contemporary literature."[11] Anime tends to use a variety of cinematic techniques—such as dramatic close-ups and panning shots of scenery—to aid in storytelling, heighten emotions, and help make social commentary about topics as serious as "homelessness, the patriarchal exploitation of women, the ever-expanding power of the media, and the politics of historical revisionism."[12]

When discussing the emergence and evolution of anime, it is important to start with the work of one man: Osamu Tezuka (1928–1989). Considered by many to be one of the most influential artists in the world, Tezuka's work left an impact on Japanese artists and animators that can still be seen today. Known as the "god of comics,"[13] Tezuka was initially inspired by Japanese adaptations of Western literature, films from the West, and the cartoons of Walt Disney—especially Mickey Mouse.[14] His love of Disney's films, in particular, influenced his early work as a manga artist, and he even created manga adaptions of several Disney films, most notably Disney's *Bambi*.[15] Drawing inspiration from Walt Disney Studio cartoons and films, as well as other Western animation, it was Tezuka who helped create the distinctive large eyes style that is so often found in anime and manga.[16]

Disney was a major influence on other Japanese animators as well, and many Japanese animation studios, such as Toei, quickly adopted the standard "Disney formula" for films, focusing their energy on "high-quality animated cartoon adventures based upon classic folktales, sprinkled with musical numbers and featuring human protagonists surrounded by cute animal companions."[17] Along with Disney cartoons, Max Fleischer productions (such as *Betty Boop* and *Popeye the Sailor* shorts) helped inform the exaggerated expressions, dramatic situations, and aforementioned wide eyes that became common to Japanese animation.[18]

In 1960, Keiko Osonoe's *Mittsu no hanashi* (*Three Tales*) became the first anime to be broadcast on Japanese televisions rather than debut in a movie theater.[19] Then, in 1963, Tezuka and his studio Mushi Productions created the first popular anime television series, *Tetsuwon Atomu*—a program that is often credited as signaling the "birth of a popular culture phenomenon in Japan."[20] The series was imported to the West in 1964 as *Astro Boy* and became a hit, thereby helping to lay the groundwork for other anime aimed at the *shōnen* (literally, "boy" or "youth") demographic. The works targeted toward this demographic (works now commonly referred to simply as "*shōnen* anime" or "*shōnen* manga") are characterized by their focus on adventure, action, martial arts, and comedy. Most *shōnen* protagonists also tend to work towards bettering themselves as well as strengthening their bonds with friends. As the genre name suggests, *shōnen* anime is mainly aimed at early to late teen boys, although there is a large cross-readership with early to late teen girls, too. As such, *shōnen* anime and manga are commonly translated and published in the West. Popular anime series that belong to the *shōnen* genre include *Dragon Ball Z, Gundam Wing, Bleach,* and *Naruto* among many others.

Other early anime series that were imported in the 1960s to the West include works like *Gigantor* and *Speed Racer*; however, anime did not gain a large fan base in the United States until the 1970s, after the success of *Star Wars*, which led to the anime programs *Space Cruiser Yamato* and *Gatchaman* being aired in California under the new names *Star Blazers* and *Battle of the Planets*, respectively.[21] In the 1980s, Streamline Pictures became the first U.S. company "to import, translate, and subtitle or over-dub anime for distribution in the U.S. theater and home-video markets."[22] In 1995–96, the anime programs *Sailor Moon* and *Dragon Ball Z* gained success with American audiences, thanks to the licensing, localization, and dubbing efforts of DIC Productions and Funimation Productions, respectively (both series would find even wider success on Cartoon Network's "Toonami" and "Adult Swim" programming blocks in the late 90s and early 2000s). Then, in 1997, the *Pokémon* anime (based on the video game series of the same name), became a hit in the United States, resulting in the robust marketing of *Pokémon*-themed video games, manga, and merchandise. Due to its massive popularity, *Pokémon* is often seen as a key program that proved anime could achieve mainstream success outside of Japan.[23]

Why did anime begin to gain popularity in the United States at this time? It is likely that this was in part due to anime's storytelling methods. In the 1970s, '80s and '90s, classic American cartoons—perhaps best exemplified by *Scooby-Doo*—often featured loose, episodic plots with little to no consistency between episodes. Japanese anime, on the other hand, offered "suspenseful drama," "more intense personal relationships," and "more complex plots," thanks largely to the "Japanese TV tradition of presenting these dramas as a continuing serial rather than as independent stories," similar in style to that of the American comic book.[24] Put differently, at a time when the American market was saturated with cartoons that lacked plot or character development, anime provided audiences with more complex stories and well-rounded characters.

In the late 1990s and early 2000s, anime had a cult American following, spurred on largely by internet message boards and websites that provided enthusiasts with a way to share fan translations and the like. Since then, anime has steadily occupied a more visible place in Western animation markets, and its distinct aesthetics have noticeably impacted the look of American animation. Consider, for instance, the many television series, such as the recent reboot of *Thundercats*, that feature protagonists with gravity-defying hair, large eyes, and plot-driven episodes. Many contemporary animators are not secretive about their fondness for anime, with some—such as *Adventure Time* creator Pendleton Ward,[25] *Steven Universe* creator Rebecca Sugar,[26] and *The Owl House* creator Dana Terrace[27]—having discussed in interviews how anime has directly inspired their work.

Stylistically, anime is often defined by the use of particular cinematic techniques such as close-up, tracking and panning shots, and even unique lighting. One particular shot common to anime is the "pillow shot," the name of which was coined by critic Noël Burch and alludes to the stylistic *makurakotoba* (English: "pillow words") used in classical Japanese poetry.[28] In this type of shot, the "camera cuts away from the main action to a static view of scenery, such as buildings, trees, or objects within a room."[29] These peaceful shots, while common in anime, are rarely seen in American cartoons, which tend to fill silences and transitions with constant movement, action, or noise instead.

Voice acting showcases another major difference between Japanese and American animation; anime voice actors tend to deliver dramatic performances rather than the exaggerated and cartoonish approach associated with American cartoons. Recently, however, this has changed and a number of American productions—including shows like *Avatar the Last Airbender*, *The Dragon Prince*, *The Legend of Korra*, and *Star Wars: The Clone Wars*—have started to place a greater focus on anime-like voice acting. Additionally, in Japan, voice actors for anime often gain a certain level of celebrity, and while there are American voice actors who are recognizable (such as Mel Blanc, Nancy Cartwright, or Jim Cummings), American voice actors for general animation have historically tended to not reach a similar level of popularity as their Japanese counterparts.

In addition to the abovementioned visual and technical influences in the development of anime, there are four popular themes that Japanese animation often touches upon: *kawaii*, *mecha*, *yōkai*, and the apocalypse. Each of these themes represents an aspect of Japanese culture and may influence the overall visual and/or narrative style of the anime in general. *Kawaii*, a Japanese term meaning "cute," focuses on "childishness, vulnerability, smallness, and sweetness."[30] The idea of *kawaii* can also refer to a nostalgia for childhood. *Mecha*, on the other hand, refers both to humanoid robots and to technology as a whole; *mecha* anime thus often "explor[es] the limits of the human" and "consider[s] the imaginative possibilities of the fusion of human beings and machines."[31]

The idea of *yōkai*—a term which can be translated into English simply as "monster" or "demon"—has its origins in Japanese folklore and often focuses on what constitutes being human and what makes something monstrous.[32] William Tsutsui argues that, in anime, *yōkai* "are ever present and everywhere, a ubiquitous imaginative feature of the Japanese landscape."[33] By this, he does not mean that literal *yōkai* are always the focus of the story, but instead that they are understood as lurking in either the background or the details of the plot (for instance, a legend about a *yōkai* may be mentioned, or a character may have a *yōkai* mascot sticker or keychain). The final anime theme to consider is that of the apocalypse. This topic pervades much of Japanese pop culture, and this obsession with destruction and the end of the world "is one distinguishing feature of the contemporary pop imagination in Japan."[34] Japan's history provides a reasonable explanation for this fascination, give that it is the only country in the world to have been devastated by atomic bombs, and to this day it is under constant threat of earthquakes, tsunamis, and other natural disasters.

Adventure Time, *Anime, and Japanese Influence*

Created by Pendleton Ward, *Adventure Time* is a show that has captured the imagination of millions, and Fred Seibert (the series' executive producer) has argued that the show represents "the future of how people ... tell stories in animation."[35] Since its first season in 2010, *Adventure Time* has inspired several pop culture products, including comics, Lego sets, and video games, and it has been the recipient of numerous awards, including Annie Awards, several Primetime Emmy Awards, and a Sundance Film Festival Award. Interestingly, despite airing on Cartoon Network (a network primarily targeted at children), *Adventure Time* has attracted adult viewers due to the show's darker themes, its philosophical ponderings, and its whimsy. But unlike other mainstream cartoons popular with adults, such as *Family Guy* and *Futurama*, *Adventure Time* managed to appeal to a diverse audience of children, teens, *and* adults. This child-friendly but irreverent approach was arguably inspired by Cartoon Network's earlier series, *The Marvelous Misadventures of Flapjack*, as well as the aesthetic of the various animators that worked on *Flapjack*, including Pendleton Ward himself.

As was mentioned in the previous section, Pendleton Ward has long acknowledged that anime played a role in shaping the series: In a 2010 interview with Animation World Network, for instance, series creator Pendleton Ward explicitly cited Hayao Miyazaki (the famed Japanese anime artist and director who co-founded Studio Ghibli) as a great influence on the series, and he expressed his wish to capture moments of beauty similar to that found in Miyazaki's film *My Neighbor Totoro* (1988).[36] In an interview with Wizards of the Coast the following year, Ward again cited Miyazaki as an inspiration, this time applauding Miyazaki's understanding of pacing: "We pull inspiration from.... Hayao Miyazaki and we try to take our time with the stories even though they're 11 minutes each. I try to pace [episodes] out, so the characters can have moments to breathe and appreciate the world that they're in."[37] Other *Adventure Time* artists who have cited anime as an influence on their work include Rebecca Sugar,[38] Ian Jones-Quartey,[39] Natasha Allegri,[40] Jesse Moynihan,[41] Bert Youn,[42] and Hanna K. Nyström.[43] In this section, we will explore how exactly the anime tradition influenced *Adventure Time* by looking at various thematic, visual, and tonal parallels.

When considering the relationship between *Adventure Time* and anime, perhaps it is best to start by considering the show's main character, Finn the Human. At the start of the series, Finn is a twelve-year-old boy who grows throughout the show's ten seasons. His development, both physically and emotionally, is shown in various ways: his voice deepens, he has birthdays, he experiences crushes and love, and he deals with existential crises. In many ways, Finn reflects the common elements befitting a *shōnen* anime protagonist: He is enthusiastic, he wants to be a great warrior and protect others, and he shows honorable intentions even towards his opponents. Finn is thus similar to protagonists like Naruto from the anime of the same name, who wants to be the best and highest ranked ninja, or Tanjiro Kamado of *Demon Slayer: Kimetsu no Yaiba*, who wants to protect people while also showing sympathy to his opponents.

When Finn trains to hone his skill, *Adventure Time* often features visuals that call to mind the *shōnen* anime tradition. Consider, for instance, season six's "Rattleballs," in which a former guard for the Candy Kingdom, the titular Rattleballs, teaches Finn swordsmanship. In one scene, Rattleballs leaps forward and, after one swing of his sword, everything behind him either falls to pieces or splits in half. The scene is reminiscent of one wherein a typical anime mentor displays his skill, a trope commonly seen in *shōnen* anime like in *Naruto* or *Rurōni Kenshin* when swordsmen slice through their opponents or objects. On top of these visual cues, it is worth noting that as a reclusive swordmaster who teaches Finn how to properly wield a sword, Rattleballs functions like a wandering *rōnin* (i.e., a masterless samurai)—an archetypal character found in many Japanese works, including various anime like Mugen in *Samurai Champloo*, Manji in *Blade of the Immortal*, or Gintoki in *Gintama*, to name a few. Rattleballs' *rōnin*-like appearance is furthered by his vaguely East Asian pattern of speaking, and by the Zen-inspired philosophies that he imparts to Finn.

In terms of art style, *Adventure Time* is visually indebted to a distinctly Japanese art aesthetic known as "Superflat." This term, coined by Japanese artist Takashi Murakami, refers to a postmodern form of art influenced by both anime and broader Japanese popular culture. The style is "highly influenced by digital technologies and Japanese animation, characterized by the interplay of mobile, flat surfaces."[44] In terms of visuals, Superflat art is "eclectic, bringing together … both the traditional Japanese early modern woodblock prints and postwar Japanese anime; pop and subculture with 'high' art."[45] We see something similar in *Adventure Time*: Finn and Jake are animated in a flat, two-dimensional style, and the world they navigate is a combination of clear black outlines (recalling the lines and colors found in traditional Japanese woodblock prints) and brightly colored designs that border on the eccentric (recalling the aesthetic of modern anime).

A solid example of *Adventure Time*'s Superflat-like aesthetic comes to us in the season five episode "The Vault," which features vibrant background designs, eclectic characters, and a bittersweet story. In one poignant scene, the character Shoko dies near a sapling that would later grow into Finn and Jake's treehouse. As the character collapses near the tree, she is dwarfed by a large red sun and mountains, reminiscent of the striking images of nature in woodblock prints like Hokusai's "Fine Wind, Clear Morning" or any of the prints from his *Thirty-Six Views of Mount Fuji*. Additionally, Shoko herself—having metamorphosed into a green, mutated monster—resembles the images of Japanese *yūrei* ("ghosts") with disheveled hair and uncanny features, commonly found in Japanese woodblock prints, or *ukiyo-e*. These decidedly traditional elements, however, contrast sharply with the episode's bright palate, flat coloring, eccentric character designs, and modern dialogue.

On the topic of design, it should be noted that *Adventure Time* owes much to *kawaii* elements commonly found in certain genres of anime. Finn, for instance, is drawn in a cute, simple manner, not unlike the style of Hello Kitty: He is a bit pudgy, and his signature fashion accessory is a white hat with rounded ears on top. The other characters in *Adventure Time* seem to similarly be inspired by this style of animation, as they are drawn with rounded edges that reflect their fun, quirky personalities. In contrast, many of the show's major villains—such as the Ice King or the Lich—are drawn with sharper lines and angles, visually differentiating them from the show's heroes. (This recalls the way many anime villains are depicted, with examples including Tomura Shigaraki from *My Hero Academia* or Hisoka Morow from *Hunter X Hunter*.) Of note, many of the show's lesser villains (a number of whom are not actually evil but rather misunderstood creatures doing what they think is right) are not particularly threatening, and as such, they are often depicted as *kawaii* in their comedic attempts to deal with Finn and Jake.

Technology and the *mecha* theme figure into the series as well. Throughout the show, we get glimpses of Finn's past lives or alternate reality versions of the character, and all of them have a robotic or artificial arm (two notable examples being the alternate reality "Farmworld Finn," introduced in season four's "The Lich," as well as Finn's previous incarnation, the aforementioned Shoko, introduced in "The Vault"). Additionally, in the sixth-season episode "Escape from the Citadel," during the main timeline of the series, Finn loses his arm, which is replaced a few episodes later in "Breezy"; his arm is lost again in the season-eight episode "Reboot," whereupon it is replaced with a robotic prosthetic. Another instance of technology and *mecha* playing a major role in the narrative is found in the episode "Hot to the Touch," wherein Finn creates a *mecha*-like suit that he pilots with the help of NEPTR (a robot companion who Finn created in the first season episode "What Is Life?"). This *mecha* allows Finn to track down and reason with Flame Princess, a love interest with whom he has had a misunderstanding.

The *yōkai* (monster or demon) theme is touched upon repeatedly in the show, with numerous characters fitting into this category, including Marceline the Vampire Queen, the Elementals (that is, the embodiments of slime, candy, ice, and fire), the Hyoomans, the Snow Golems, and the Fire Wolves. Indeed, Ooo is overflowing with a variety of unique monsters and creatures, and Finn spends many an episode meeting these creatures. Sometimes Finn is forced to fight these beings, but more often, he chooses to help them. This is important to take note of, for while most of the show's *yōkai*-like creatures are "monsters" in the technical sense, many are harmless, and some are even friendly. The decision to feature "good monsters" is in line with much of Japanese anime, in which *yōkai* are not always representative of evil. On top of this, Finn's decision to befriend these superficially monstrous characters mirrors plot elements found in *shōnen* anime—such as *Hunter X Hunter*, *Naruto*, or *My Hero Academia*—wherein a normal or weak protagonist grows stronger over the course of the series, thanks not only to training, but also to their friendship with more powerful beings.

Apocalyptic themes, too, loom ever-present in the background of Finn's adventures, and these ideas are occasionally made explicit through flashbacks. As discussed in the previous section, anime series often revolve around fears of an apocalyptic future, due to Japan being the only country in the world to have experienced the devastating effects of a nuclear bomb. Explorations of the anxiety surrounding war and destruction are a key element of anime series like *Gundam* or *Neon Genesis Evangelion*. While *Adventure Time* never quite reaches the levels of violence or darkness of these two series, several of Finn's adventures focus on him saving the Land of Ooo from total destruction courtesy of villains like the Lich or the godlike Golb.

Anime often explores what could be considered "adult" themes, like puberty or sexuality, and, while not as explicit as many Japanese programs, *Adventure Time* manages to address "mature" topics, too. The show often handles these topics in a serious yet subtle way. Perhaps the best example of this approach is the way in which the show depicts Finn going through puberty. This plot thread is introduced in the fifth-season episode "Frost & Fire," in which Finn essentially experiences a sexual awakening.[46] He has a dream about his girlfriend, Flame Princess, shooting flames at his groin, and he laughs, happily exclaiming, "My body is engulfed in flames!" and "Oh, so good!"[47] He then spends the rest of the episode trying to recreate the previous day's conditions in order to have the same dream, but it ultimately costs him his relationship with Flame Princess. *Adventure Time*'s willingness to explore a topic like budding sexuality is likely indebted to an element of anime that appeals to many: the exploration of the sexual and romantic relationships of characters, which provides a more mature examination of life in a way that is often absent in mainstream Western animation.

Adventure Time has also featured elements of the Japanese writing system, including kanji and kana. In the fifth-season episode "Simon & Marcy," a water bottle with the kanji for "water" (水) and "human life" (人生) is seen on the floor of a car. A few episodes later in "One Last Job," Jake pushes a button marked with the Japanese kana "キュウ・いそ.ぐ いそ.ぎ," which means "hurry," "emergency," and "sudden" in English.[48] Another fifth-season episode, "Candy Streets" features a sign with the Japanese katakana "ファーマシー," which means "pharmacy."

Finally, it is worth noting that the seventh episode of season six, "Food Chain," was directed, written, and storyboarded by famed experimental anime director Masaaki Yuasa, who is known for his use of vivid and bizarre colors as well as abstract figures. Some of the popular productions he has worked on include *Crayon Shin-chan*, *My Neighbors the Yamadas*, *Kemonozume*, and *Samurai Champloo*, among others. His animation studio, Science Saru, was also responsible for animating the openings for the three *Adventure Time* miniseries (i.e., *Stakes*, *Islands*, and *Elements*), as well as its finale "Come Along with Me." Arguably, Yuasa's participation in the production of the series makes *Adventure Time*'s connection to anime most clear.

Analyzing the Stakes *Miniseries*

Finn starts off as the focus of the show, and over the course of the series, his companions are fleshed out and given their own side plots. One such character is Marceline the Vampire Queen. During the first two seasons, Marceline is a chaotic prankster who hangs out with Finn, teases Jake, and has a strained relationship with Princess Bubblegum. With the airing of the season three episode "What Was Missing," however, it became clear that there was much more to this eternal teen vampire than what the surface suggested. Marceline's story is more fully explored in the seventh-season miniseries *Stakes* (2015), which fleshes her out and ties her into *Adventure Time*'s wider mythology. In particular, *Stakes* explores

Marceline's vampirism and other heavy topics, like her (im)mortality, her existential dread, her parental abandonment issues, and her relationship with Princess Bubblegum.

As has been discussed thus far, *Adventure Time* has taken many influences from anime, and the *Stakes* miniseries is no exception. The parallels are perhaps most obvious when you consider the nature of lead characters. For instance, just as *Stakes* stars Marceline the vampire, many Japanese anime and manga are also populated by numerous half-demons or half-vampires, such as Inuyasha from the anime of the same name, and Anzai from *Devil's Line*. Like both Inuyasha and Anzai, Marceline, too, was born to a demon father and a human mother. Marceline's relationship with Princess Bubblegum also lightly mirrors that of Inuyasha and his love interest Kagome, albeit with less bickering and stereotypical behavior. Princess Bubblegum tries to use science and technology much like Kagome uses products from her time period to help Inuyasha in the Sengoku period. Additionally, Marceline's battle with the Vampire King in "Vamps About" is reminiscent of the many fights Inuyasha has with the powerful demonic enemies he comes across.[49]

Stakes also seems indebted to the tropes and story beats common to *shōnen* anime. Like the protagonist of a *shōnen* anime, Marceline is introduced at the beginning of *Stakes* as a character needing to "grow up."[50] And so she sets off on an adventure to better herself, develop as a person, and strengthen the bonds with her friends along the way; after episodes' worth of self-sacrifice and hardship, Marceline returns a mature hero. But in addition to a similar structure, *Stakes* and *shōnen* anime are united in another, arguably more profound way: their fundamental philosophy. In *shōnen* anime, protagonists are often driven or inspired by the tenets of Zen Buddhism and Japan's native religion, Shinto, due to how deeply both are rooted in Japanese culture. *Stakes*, too, seems to pull from these same traditions, exploring several decidedly Shinto-Buddhist concepts: suffering is a part of life, there are spirits all around us, karma exists, having the right intentions matter, and moderation is important.[51]

The last two ideals—that intentions matter, and that moderation is important—are perhaps the most interesting for our present discussion. In anime, many protagonists (in both *shōnen* anime and other types of anime) learn the importance of these precepts through sacrifice, self-reflection, and hardship. This is not unlike what we find with Marceline's development in *Stakes*. Before she was a vampire, Marceline grew up in the aftermath of the Great Mushroom War, cared for by her father figure, Simon Petrikov. Unfortunately, due to the impact of his magical ice crown, Simon's memories and personality eventually faltered and Marceline was left alone. Marceline encountered a group of humans who were being terrorized by vampires, and so Marceline decided to protect these humans by hunting the vampires into extinction. Like most *shōnen* protagonists early in their journey, Marceline starts off with good intentions—her decision to protect the remaining humans was noble, given that the vampires were excessive in their consumption of the living—but because she does nothing in moderation and does not pause for self-reflection, her intentions begin to shift. Her desire to protect humans is soon replaced by a desire to zealously kill *all* vampires. It is this shift from protection to hatred, combined with her tendency to act before thinking, that tragically results in Marceline becoming a vampire herself.

Marceline's struggle with intentionality and moderation is also explored in her relationship with Princess Bubblegum—another character who does not do things in moderation. A major reason that their relationship fell apart was that Princess Bubblegum spent too much time trying to run her kingdom perfectly, whereas Marceline spent too much time mindlessly pranking, having fun, and playing her axe bass. Neither character initially took the time to self-reflect on their actions, and their excessive tendencies negatively impacted one another. Traditional Japanese culture requires that one be mindful of those around them and the results of their actions. Japanese Zen Buddhism stresses not only the idea of living in the moment, but also the importance of being mindful, and recognizing the ties that we share with others. Because Marceline and Bubblegum initially acted in a way that did not take the other into account, their relationship fell apart. In *Stakes*, however, Marceline and Bubblegum are more mindful of their behavior and their bond, and as a result, their relationship starts to repair itself.

Another interesting parallel between *Stakes* and anime comes to us by way of technology. In many anime and manga, there is often a blending of the supernatural, the magical, or the religious with modern technology. For instance, many of the films directed by Hayao Miyazaki combine technology with the magical or supernatural, such as *Nausicaä of the Valley of the Wind* (1984), *Princess Mononoke* (1997), *Spirited Away* (2001), and *Howl's Moving Castle* (2004). This is likely a result of Shinto and Buddhism fusing with modern elements of Japanese culture: For instance, the Kodaiji Temple in Kyoto hosts a Buddhist priest named Mindar—who also happens to be a telenoid robot.[52] Similarly in Chiyoda, Tokyo, near the famed Akihabara, the Shinto shrine Kanda-myōjin features *omamori* (charms) that resemble the motherboard of a computer.[53] *Stakes*, too, features a similar blending of the supernatural with the technological, specifically with regard to Princess Bubblegum's development. Throughout much of the miniseries, she relies entirely on technology to the point of excess, refusing to acknowledge supernatural or magical possibilities. She wishes to use her skills as a scientist and not the supernatural options presented to her in order to fight the vampires. In the end, Bubblegum moderates her stance, and a happy balance is struck, which is illustrated in the miniseries' penultimate episode, "Checkmate," in which Bubblegum uses technology to revert the Vampire King—a unquestionably supernatural creature—into a normal lion.

Marceline's experiences and characterization can be connected to another element of Japanese culture that is often found in anime: *mono no aware*. This particular concept comes from Buddhism and can be translated as "the pathos of things"; in essence, it is the gentle sadness we feel when recognizing that nothing is permanent, perfect, or complete. A deeper understanding of this concept can be gained by noting that Japanese culture, early and contemporary, contains an "acute appreciation for the ephemeral nature of man, his struggles in the face of great odds and the inevitability of his downfall and disappearance."[54] Japanese art and entertainment, especially pop culture media, portray death or loss in a way that actually impacts the characters and narrative, such as the deaths of major characters in *Naruto* and *Demon Slayer: Kimetsu no Yaiba*. Loss reminds the characters (and the reader or viewer) that life moves on, and *Mono no aware* reflects an appreciation for the transience of life.

While *mono no aware* runs throughout *Adventure Time* as a whole, Marceline's story arc in *Stakes* is heavily predicated on the concept, with the miniseries featuring its fair share of sad, quiet moments as Marceline wistfully contemplates the world around her. (These scenes often mirror those found in anime and manga, like in *Hunter X Hunter* when the protagonist Gon is not strong enough to fight Neferpitou and mourns the possible fate of Kite, or in *Neon Genesis Evangelion* when Misato listens to Kaji's message on her answering machine.) Arguably, the idea of *mono no aware* is most noticeable at the end of *Stakes*, when Marceline's sings "Everything Stays." This song, originally a lullaby sung to Marceline by her mother, explores the idea that while existence itself might seem static, everything within it is constantly changing. The song is melancholic—perhaps haunting even—but its placement at the conclusion of *Stakes* nevertheless feels triumphant, for it signals Marceline's embrace of life's transience. This allows her to reject a fatalist approach to her vampiric curse and instead recognize that the pain caused by her vampirism is temporary, like everything else.

But of all the parallels between *Stakes* and anime, perhaps the clearest is a visual from the *Stakes* finale, "The Dark Cloud." At the end of this episode, Marceline flies into the air and begins to brightly glow a light blue, then bright pink color. Silhouetted against a black background speckled with white dots that resemble stars, Marceline begins to consume the essence of the Vampire King, once again becoming a vampire. This particular scene is a direct nod towards the *henshin* ("transformation") sequence—a staple of Japanese shows like *Super Sentai*, but most commonly associated with the series *Sailor Moon*. In this series, whenever the clumsy fourteen-year-old protagonist Usagi Tsukino transforms, she becomes "more like a woman ... newly focused, powerful, and self-assured."[55] Likewise, following Marceline's transformation, she becomes a more permanent, mature figure with "fresh mortal memories" and "more empathy."[56] Of course, there are differences between the two (Sailor Moon ends up in a sailor suit at the end of her transformation, whereas Marceline's transformation results only in the return of the fang marks on her neck), but in both instances the *henshin* sequence is a visual indicator that the character—be it Usagi or Marceline—has changed on a deeper level.

Conclusion

Examining the influence of Japanese animation on a show like *Adventure Time* provides a better understanding of how the globalization of popular culture can inspire creative works. This understanding in turn leads to better ways of analyzing and recognizing how cultures interact with one another. As an element of the "mainstream," the popular cultures of other countries illuminate how cultural and historical events influence and affect the creation of art and literature, and even shape society at large. Anime is "a useful mirror on contemporary Japanese society, offering an array of insights into the significant issues, dreams and nightmares of the day," and arguably American animation is moving in this direction due to anime's influence.[57] The production and consumption of pop products like anime and manga offer insight into what resonates with the creators and consumers of pop culture.

Japan never developed the idea that animation is just for children, as many in the West still believe. More recently, however, American shows like *Adventure Time* have, by emulating aspects of Japanese animation, started to change people's opinions about the worth of children's animation. Though not an exact replica of the anime-inspired animation style found in other action cartoons on American television, *Adventure Time* certainly captures many of the elements and aesthetic details that first attracted fans to anime. As such, there is something cyclical about the influences and inspirations that have been exchanged between the U.S. and Japan. Disney animation influenced early Japanese animators and now that inspiration has come back to American animation. *Adventure*

"Is that where creativity comes from?"

Time is emblematic of this cyclical relationship between Japanese and American animation, and it clearly demonstrates the impact of Japanese culture, its aesthetics, and the stylings of one of its most popular contemporary art forms: anime.

Notes

1. Christine R. Yano, "Wink on Pink."
2. Tze-yue G. Hu, "Frameworks of Teaching and Researching Japanese Animation," 5.
3. William M. Tsutsui, *Japanese Popular Culture and Globalization*, 4.
4. Douglas McGray, "Japan's Gross National Cool," 50.
5. Douglas McGray, "Japan's Gross National Cool," 50.
6. McGray, "Japan's Gross National Cool," 47.
7. Shaobo Xie, "Is the World Decentered? A Postcolonialist Perspective on Globalization," 53–75.
8. McGray, 53.
9. Tsutsui, *Japanese Popular Culture and Globalization*.
10. Rudyard C. Pesimo, "'Asianizing' Animation in Asia," 139.
11. Pesimo, 139–140.
12. Steven T. Brown, "Screening Anime," 7–8.
13. Fred Patten, *Watching Anime, Reading Manga*, 198.
14. Raz Greenberg, *Hayao Miyazaki*, 2; Jasper Sharp, *Historical Dictionary of Japanese Cinema*, 249
15. Patten, *Watching Anime*, 146, 179, 234.
16. Northrop Davis, *Manga and Anime Go to Hollywood*, 369; Greenberg, *Hayao Miyazaki*, 2.
17. Patten, *Watching Anime*, 52–53.
18. Robin E. Brenner, *Understanding Manga and Anime*, 6–7.
19. Michael Daliot-Bul and Nissim Otmazgin, *The Anime Boom in the United States*, 15.
20. Andrew C. McKevitt, "'You Are Not Alone!,'" 897.
21. Jonathan Clements, *Anime*, 148.
22. McKevitt, "'You Are Not Alone!,'" 903.
23. Roland Kelts, *Japanamerica*, 101–102; Fred Ladd with Harvey Deneroff, *Astro Boy and Anime Come to the Americas*, 2, 120–121.
24. Patten, *Watching Anime, Reading Manga*, 56.
25. Pendleton Ward, "Time for Some Adventure with Pendleton Ward."
26. Susana Polo, "Crystal Gems, *Beavis and Butthead*, and the *Goofy Movie*."
27. Joe Amarante, "Hamden-Raised Animator Finds Home in LA, Creates *Owl House* at Disney."
28. Deborah Shamoon, "Films on Paper," 22.
29. Shamoon.
30. Tsutsui, *Japanese Popular Culture and Globalization*, 20.
31. Tsutsui, 21.
32. Kendra Sheehan, "Modernizing and Marketing Monsters in Japan," 4–5.
33. Tsutsui, *Japanese Popular Culture and Globalization*, 20.
34. Tsutsui, 18.
35. Ramin Zahed, "And Now for Something Entirely Brilliant!"
36. Rick DeMott, "Time for Some Adventure."
37. Bart Carol, "Spotlight Interview."
38. Rebecca Sugar in "The Chamber of Frozen Blades" commentary.
39. Ian Jones Quartey in "To Cut a Women's Hair" commentary.
40. ChannelFrederator, "Exclusive Interview w/ Natasha Allegri."
41. Jesse Moynihan, "Adventure Time Season 5."

42. Jesse Moynihan in "Princess Monster Wife" commentary.
43. Hanna K. Nyström, "What were your favorite cartoons…"
44. Yano, "Wink on Pink," 685.
45. Thomas Looser, "Superflat and the Layers of Image and History in 1990s Japan," 92.
46. Oliver Sava, "*Adventure Time*: 'Frost & Fire.'"
47. "Frost & Fire" (season 5, episode 30).
48. "One Last Job" (season 5, episode 23).
49. "The Empress Eyes" (season 7, episode 9).
50. "Marceline the Vampire Queen" (season 7, episode 6).
51. For more on these ideals, see: Randall L. Nadeau, *Asian Religions*.
52. Erica Baffelli, "The Android and the Fax," 249–263.
53. YABAI Writers, "Kanda Myojin."
54. Boye Lafayette De Mente, *The Japanese Have a Word for It*, 263.
55. Anne Allison, "Sailor Moon," 272.
56. "The Dark Cloud" (Season 7, episode 13).
57. Pesimo, "'Asianizing' Animation in Asia," 140.

REFERENCES

Allison, Anne. "Sailor Moon: Japanese Superheroes for Global Girls." In *Japan Pop!* Edited by Timothy J. Craig, 259–278. Armonk, NY: M.E. Sharpe, 2000.
Amarante, Joe. "Hamden-Raised Animator Finds Home in LA, Creates *Owl House* at Disney." *New Haven Register*, 2020. https://www.nhregister.com/news/article/Hamden-raised-animator-finds-home-in-LA-creates-14945817.php.
Anders, Charlie Jane. "The New *Adventure Time* Miniseries Was an Amazing Meditation on Change." *Gizmodo*, 2015. https://io9.gizmodo.com/the-new-adventure-time-miniseries-was-an-amazing-medita-1743802434.
Baffelli, Erica. "The Android and the Fax: Robots, AI and Buddhism in Japan." In *Itineraries of an Anthropologist: Studies in Honour of Massimo Raveri*. Edited by Giovanni Bulian and Silvia Rivadossi, 249–263. Venice, Italy: Edizioni Ca' Foscari, 2021.
Bocking, Brian. *A Popular Dictionary of Shinto*, Surrey: Curzon, 1996.
Brown, Steven T. "Screening Anime." In *Cinema Anime*. Edited by Steven T. Brown, 1–22. New York: Palgrave Macmillan, 2006.
Carroll, Bart. "Spotlight Interview." *Dungeons & Dragons*, 2011. https://dnd.wizards.com/articles/features/pendleton-ward-interview.
"The Chamber of Frozen Blades" commentary track. *Adventure Time: The Complete Second Season*. DVD. Los Angeles: Cartoon Network, 2013.
Daliot-Bul, Michael, and Nissim Otmazgin. *The Anime Boom in the United States: Lessons for Global Creative Industries*. Cambridge MA: Harvard University Asia Center, 2020.
Davis, Northrop. *Manga and Anime Go to Hollywood*. New York: Bloomsbury Publishing, 2015.
De Mente, Boye Lafayette. *The Japanese Have a Word for It: The Complete Guide to Japanese Thought and Culture*. Chicago: Passport Books, 1997.
DeMott, Rick. "Time for Some Adventure with Pendleton Ward." *Animation World Network*, 2010. https://www.awn.com/animationworld/time-some-adventure-pendleton-ward.
Franich, Darren. "Adventure Time Review." *Entertainment Weekly*, 2013. https://ew.com/article/2013/02/22/adventure-time-2/.
Greenberg, Raz. *Hayao Miyazaki: Exploring the Early Work of Japan's Greatest Animator*. New York: Bloomsbury Publishing, 2018.
Hu, Tze-yue G. "Frameworks of Teaching and Researching Japanese Animation." In *Japanese Animation: East Asian Perspectives*. Edited by Masao Yokota and Tze-yue G. Hu, 3–14. Jackson: University Press of Mississippi, 2013.
Kelts, Roland. *Japanamerica: How Japanese Pop Culture Has Invaded the U.S.* New York: St. Martin's Press, 2006.

Ladd, Fred, and Deneroff, Harvey. *Astro Boy and Anime Come to the Americas: An Insider's View of the Birth of a Pop Culture Phenomenon*. Jefferson, NC: McFarland, 2014.

Looser, Thomas. "Superflat and the Layers of Image and History in 1990s Japan." *Mechademia* 1 (2006): 92–106.

McCarthy, Helen "Art for the Masses—Manga on Television." In *Manga, Comic Strip Books from Japan*. Edited by Kyoichi Tsuzuki and Alfred Birnbaum, xiii–xiv. New York: Saunders & Williams, 1991.

McGray, Douglas. "Japan's Gross National Cool." *Foreign Policy* 130 (2002): 22–54.

McKevitt, Andrew C. "'You Are Not Alone!': Anime and the Globalizing of America." *Diplomatic History* 34.5 (2010): 893–921.

Nadeau, Randall L. *Asian Religions: A Cultural Perspective*. Oxford, UK: Wiley-Blackwell, 2014.

Newitz, Annalee. "Magical Girls and Atomic Bomb Sperm: Japanese Animation in America." *Film Quarterly* 49.1 (1995): 2–15.

Nyström, Hanna K. "What were your favorite cartoons growing up as a child?" Tumblr, 2016. https://hannakdraws.tumblr.com/post/139323248857/what-were-your-favorite-cartoons-growing-up-as-a.

Patten, Fred. *Watching Anime, Reading Manga: 25 Years of Essays and Reviews*. Berkeley: Stone Bridge Press, 2004.

Pesimo, Rudyard C. "'Asianizing' Animation in Asia: Digital Content Identity Construction within the Animation Landscapes of Japan and Thailand." *Reflections on the Human Condition: Change, Conflict and Modernity*. Edited by Anna Liza Magno, 124–160. Bangkok: The Nippon Foundation, 2007.

Polo, Susana. "Crystal Gems, *Beavis and Butthead*, and the *Goofy Movie*: An Hour with Rebecca Sugar." *Polygon*, 2019. https://www.polygon.com/2019/8/30/20837281/steven-universe-movie-rebecca-sugar-cartoon-network.

"Princess Monster Wife" commentary track. *Adventure Time: The Complete Fourth Season*. DVD. Los Angeles: Cartoon Network, 2014.

Sava, Oliver. "*Adventure Time:* 'Frost & Fire.'" *AV Club*, 2013. https://tv.avclub.com/adventure-time-frost-fire-1798177575.

Shamoon, Deborah. "Films on Paper: Cinematic Narrative in Gekiga." In *Mangatopia: Essays on Manga and Anime in the Modern World*. Edited by Timothy Perper and Martha Cornog, 21–36. Santa Barbara: ABC-CLIO, 2011.

Sharp, Jasper. *Historical Dictionary of Japanese Cinema*. Lanham, MD: Scarecrow Press, 2011.

Sheehan, Kendra. "Modernizing and Marketing Monsters in Japan: Shapeshifting *Yōkai* and the Reflection of Culture." In *Exploring the Macabre, Malevolent, and Mysterious: Multidisciplinary Perspectives*. Edited by Matthew Hodge and Elizabeth Kusko, 2–20. Newcastle upon Tyne, UK: Cambridge Scholars Publishing, 2020.

"To Cut a Woman's Hair" commentary track. *Adventure Time: The Complete Second Season*. DVD. Los Angeles: Cartoon Network, 2013.

Tsutsui, William. *Japanese Popular Culture and Globalization*. Ann Arbor, MI: Association for Asian Studies, Inc., 2010.

YABAI Writers, "Kanda Myojin—An Ancient Shrine with A Techie Twist." YABAI, 2018. http://www.yabai.com/p/3812?fbclid=IwAR2MygG829hbVnc_p3BlYwIKck-C7rnnbvMJIKr-oRlsaL1A8CKhipx01Pg.

Yano, Christine R. "Wink on Pink: Interpreting Japanese Cute as It Grabs the Global Headlines." *The Journal of Asian Studies* 68.3 (2009): 681–688.

Zahed, Ramin. "And Now for Something Entirely Brilliant!" *Animation Magazine* (2010): https://www.animationmagazine.net/tv/and-now-for-something-entirely-brilliant/.

"Bad Jubies"
Giving Value to the Intangible in Artistic Professions

CATALINA MILLÁN SCHEIDING

Spending some time in a lush green meadow under a dazzling sun, Jake, Finn and Lumpy Space Princess are interrupted by an announcement through BMO: a terrible storm is about to arrive. Finn jumps into action! It's time to build a bunker and they all pitch in ... all except Jake, who's working on something. Something that is making Lumpy Space Princess increasingly nervous, because there is nothing to be seen—while the work on the bunker progresses. But when the storm rages, and the bunker doesn't live up to expectations, who will save the crew?

About two years after "Bad Jubies" had been aired, I attended a faculty training workshop led by Robert Lagueux, the Associate Vice President of Academic Affairs at Berklee. The main focus of the session was the generational change of the students that would make up the larger population of the cohort during the coming years at the College. He incorporated clips from the HBO series *Girls* and most of the "Bad Jubies" episode. At the time, I had been teaching the "Professional Development Seminar" for about five years and the experience was quite enlightening—if the department head could engage the faculty body with this example, why not implement a similar idea in the classroom? The way "Bad Jubies" presents the creative process and highlights how it is judged from the outside offers a way to meet members of the music industry through storytelling, and it shares, through characters' actions, awareness of music cognition issues.

The Background: Adventure Time *and Music*

Although scholarship on *Adventure Time*, as noted in this book's introduction, has delved mostly into gender studies[1] and the philosophy of the series,² as a series with over 200 episodes that explore a diversity of topics, including death, reincarnation and the soul, political and power structures and even the tribulations of maturity and acquiring responsibilities, the potential for *Adventure Time* to stimulate spaces to explore different perspectives is rich, for both the academic world as well as for the viewer. Additionally, the multimodality of *Adventure Time* (a series that has been adapted for videogames, comic books, story books, cookbooks, and even cosplay) exemplifies the dialogic and multifaceted nature of contemporary entertainment, opening the conversation between viewers, creators and creation.

The key elements that this chapter intends to highlight in relation to *Adventure Time*, however, are the references to creativity and music, specifically in the episode "Bad Jubies." While these references cannot technically be considered metareferential, as the characters do not display awareness of being in a story, the references *Adventure Time* incorporates in relation to creativity³ and the openness to including diverse animation and illustration techniques, even changing episode lengths, could be considered self-referential in relation to the creative process in general. "Bad Jubies" would incorporate this function as an example of the creative openness in *Adventure Time*'s production, being guest-written and directed by Kirsten Lepore and produced entirely in stop motion animation.

While the series thematically relies heavily on both technology and magic, art and, specifically, music play a key role in *Adventure Time*. Whether it is as a background score or a song that one of the characters breaks into, numerous genres and styles are incorporated into the series, from lullabies to folk to electronic music to rap. Many times, these musical moments are part of the general conversation characters are having, or they are activities that organically occur when "hanging with pals." Other times, they are meant to share the angst or backstory of a character and are sung by one character to another, or they serve as an accompaniment while characters complete an activity. In an indirect way, *Adventure Time* represents throughout its ten seasons many of the fields that music cognition focuses on and intends to address through case studies.

On the one hand, *Adventure Time* illustrates the link between music and autobiographical memories. Considering that "music activates the entire limbic system, which is involved in processing of emotions and in controlling memory,"⁴ studies which have intended to compile data on how this process work indicate that musical pieces that are considered attractive make it easier for non-musicians to remember them while also considering how musical memories are directly related to specific situations and, subsequently, the construction of self.⁵ Recent studies have linked the emotional content of music to the creation of long-term memories by analyzing involuntary musical imagery, known in general as "earworms."[6]

On the other, the link between emotion and music as a tool to "elicit emotions—rather than merely expressing an emotion that the listener recognizes"[7] is one of the reasons why music causes pleasure. It is used to enhance emotions, whether these are positive or negative and, therefore, can be recognized as an incorporeal companion to the listener's feelings.[8] *Adventure Time* embodies this idea of "music as a friend" superbly.

The Work: Bad Jubies, Art, and Creativity

Following the premise of storytelling as a tool for empathy building, the episode "Bad Jubies" was selected for several reasons. While "Bad Jubies" is not the only episode in *Adventure Time* to focus on the creative process, it addresses the completion of an artistic piece and its impact on the storyline. For example, the fifth-season episode "James Baxter the Horse," centers on the creative process with a specific aim (making people happy) and inspiration (James Baxter), and incorporates ideas of documenting the creative process, perfecting the result including the use of both theory and technology, and adding personality. In contrast, two seasons later, "Bad Jubies" follows a creative process to completion without the involvement of the viewer. In fact, in "Bad Jubies," the viewer is invited to observe the creative process from the outside and follow the perceptions of other characters in an episode starring only Jake, Finn, BMO, Lumpy Space Princess and the storm—accompanied by several animals. Jake uses his time before the critical storm to generate an artistic response and the other characters gradually turn on him as they do not understand the tangible outcome of his work.

The defense of creative work is stated throughout the seasons, specifically in reference to music and its many contemporary styles. In the aforementioned "James Baxter the Horse," Jake makes an interesting consideration about rock music and originality: "No, it's like, he's shredding on a guitar and learning how to shred isn't just copying the exact notes as someone else's solo. You need to learn how to do your own solo." Another episode, "The Music Hole" is used as an example of how music can give answers in rough times while it can also be used as a competitive marketing tool in a battle of the bands. Even *Adventure Time*'s finale "Come Along with Me" not only closes the storyline with a song, but opens the episode with a not-so-subtle conversation about beatboxing that illustrates common misconstructions about the genre:

BETH: [*blows raspberry*] Shermy, this is silly as heck. Beatboxing is for babies.
SHERMY: [*robotic voice*] No, it's not. I am a man.[9]

"Bad Jubies," which received a Primetime Emmy Award, Outstanding Individual Achievement in Animation, proves to be a perfect display of many of the points that most music students pertaining to the Professional Development Seminar mentioned when considering their current status in the professional world and their worries about the future. The episode focuses on three main points that were addressed in class: how they engage in the creative process, how productivity is measured, and what type of support system they need to build and foster.

The Creative Process

"Bad Jubies" depicts the creative process as a solitary practice that requires time, concentration, and a reconnection to nature. Although there is no clear aim to the process in this episode, it appears as a reaction to the critical news of the storm coming and could be considered a coping mechanism. Much like Björk's comments about her creative process in relation to nature,[10] the way Jake generates the "Good vibes" composition is by actively listening to the surroundings and engaging with nature. The Icelandic artists mentions that "I started writing melodies as a kid, walking to school and back, and it just always was my way of coping or dealing with the world."[11] This type of work appears in "Bad Jubies" to connect an emotional need with spiritual fulfillment, with Jake's encounter with Lumpy Space Princess taking place at the edge of a mountain cliff, connecting with the surrounding animals, and watching a sunset. Nonetheless, the predominant feature of this idea of the creative process in "Bad Jubies" appears to be the ability of connecting in a different way and developing a unique type of perception—a specific way of viewing or listening. This appears in stark contrast with the practical work fulfilled by the other characters in the episode.

Evaluation of Productivity

"Bad Jubies" addresses one of the issues consistently found in psychological studies with musicians in relation to their work: its value. From children musicians[12] to electronic music producers,[13] the judgement that a certain culture lays on an artistic object marks the creator. Nonetheless, this value is clouded in the synchronic situation of its creation: politics, economics, social structures, specific communities, and the reception of the piece.[14] In the musical field, this need to measure value has been linked to the marketability of the piece, regardless of discussions of "functionality" or "aesthetical value"—that is to say, if an artist sells, they are recognized by the music industry and their selling numbers and awards become a tangible measure of their success.[15]

The music industry, however, is not formed only of big artists, but of a myriad of small and mid-size artists. For these, music is a profession with which they make a living, and they are able to measure their success through performance and gauging the emotional connection between audience and the musical creation. In an interview with the *Southwest Review*, Spencer Krug of the bands Wolf Parade and Sunset Rubdown (among several other projects) espoused this attitude when he said:

> It's really built into the career that you're gonna go out and share your work over and over again. You have a chance to hone that part of what you do, the performance of it, and you get to share it with people that are guaranteed to at least be curious. They bought a ticket to be there. You have this already biased audience in front of you. You're totally spoiled. Then you get to perform the songs that you already know they are interested in hearing. It really does boost one's ego.[16]

Therefore, while some musicians measure the validity of their music in terms of tangible metrics (e.g., ticket and record sales, accolades, marketing and licensing revenue), many others believe, like Krug, that the value of music lies in its intangible characteristics (e.g., emotional expression, personal connection), with live performances in particular being especially prized, given that they are ephemeral, connective events that can never be repeated exactly the same way twice.

"Bad Jubies" illustrates this very complex idea that encompasses the artistic world throughout the episode. The idea of tangible results as the way the characters are contributing to the final result (the construction of the bunker) falls in line with the general way *Adventure Time* illustrates the corporate world and its measure of success, starting with the introduction of Business Men in season one. In this case, Lumpy Space Princess is the character who most obviously points out the issue and comments on it to the other characters throughout, making them all doubt the usefulness of Jake's activity, as it cannot be measured by the productivity parameters of the episode. She pushes other characters to also question his position, for example asking BMO to check on Jake and requiring an explanation of the value of a work in progress:

> JAKE: Well, thing is, I've been working in this thing, & ah.... I've been collecting, like, lots of stuff! Uh.... I just can't really show anyone yet. But trust me, man! It'll be great! I promise!
> BMO: But.... But Jake I don't see anything here.[17]

While work is shared by the other characters, they all focus on the immediate necessities: shelter, water, food, which ultimately are not up to par. Jake's investment in his creativity generates another type of "food" for the soul, and proves to be crucial for the critical moment the characters are in.

The episode ends with two main ideas in relation to intangible productions and how to value them. On the one hand, Jake requires the other characters to join and (re)create the composition he's been working on throughout the episode. BMO, Lumpy Space Princess and Finn have heard Jake's work and have connected with it, and they must collaborate in its construction when the storm crashes into the bunker:

> FINN: Jake, you got to help us get back to our happy place. The only way to fight bad jubies is with good jubies!
> JAKE: Aah! Finn, I can't keep this up solo! [...] No time to be self-conscious, man! Get on this beat![18]

On the other, it illustrates the idea that has become a commonly shared meme in the virtual world, attributed to Michel Serres, of the artistic creation and the act of teaching as something that enriches the audience through sharing, and does not follow the common rules of the market exchange.

Both ideas are illustrated when the storm crashes into the bunker, is "confronted" with Jake's work and leaves with the only tangible item of the creation itself, Jake's notebook. Jake points out how the storm is in a state of depression and lashes out in anger because of its inability to slow down and focus on experiencing, following the ideas of Eisner on art education, who once noted that "if there is any lesson that the arts teach, it is the importance of paying close attention to what is at hand, of slowing down perception so that efficiency is put on a back burner and the quest for experience is made dominant. [...] The arts are about savoring."[19] When Jake brings this idea to the forefront, Finn aligns with his purpose:

> FINN: Yeah. You get to hear life happening. Makes you feel good.
> TORNADO MAN: Ahhhh. You're right! I've been a freaky storm for so long that I forgot it's okay to be a breeze sometimes. If you'll excuse me, I'm going to explore the rest of this beautiful day.[20]

Support System

The last issue illustrated in the episode of "Bad Jubies" has to do with the support system for creators and the trust required to foster intangible creations, without the need to follow the rules of productivity. In the case of this episode, both ideas are linked together. BMO and Finn initially trust Jake and give him time to work on what he requires. Finn visits Jake when he is taking time to create and, although he is unable to understand the relevance of Jake's activity and asks him to join the general work distribution, he trusts Jake enough to give him time.

However, Lumpy Space Princess worries about Jake's activities and criticizes him several times throughout the episode to his friends, slowly eroding the trust they have in him. The general disapproval is based upon comparison. Lumpy Space Princess states her anger which stems from the idea of shared responsibility: if they are to share a space of survival, they should all pitch in equally (from her perspective) and the only measure of work is a tangible result:

> LUMPY SPACE PRINCESS: THAT'S IT!! IS JAKE STAYING IN THIS BUNKER OR WHAT?!
> FINN: I mean, of course. It's for everyone.
> LUMPY SPACE PRINCESS: BUT HE HASN'T LUMPING DONE ANYTHING![21]

After pressuring both BMO and Finn to try to convince Jake to join their bunker project, Lumpy Space Princess confronts Jake herself, deriding him for "working on nothing."[22] This perception becomes the norm in the group, with Finn echoing the idea once things get complicated in the bunker: At one point, he shouts: "Well, maybe…. I could've built [a better shelter] if I had some help from, oh, I don't know, my best friend!"[23]

The Framework: Storytelling for Empathy Building

The inclusion of these topics in "Bad Jubies" offered several interesting opportunities. It primarily displays a completed creative process, while it additionally illustrates the surrounding environment: how do others perceive and judge this process? How is art or, in this case, music, regarded and why?

Furthermore, "Bad Jubies" places the need for creativity at a critical moment: a storm is approaching and none of the protagonists are sure if they will be able to survive. Therefore, "Bad Jubies" reveals not only a way of coping with a crisis through creativity, but a way of responding to it. In a moment where Covid-19 has had a severe impact in the response to music creation by the cancelation of most live events, thereby decimating the creative economy in the western world,[24] finding an answer about the relevance and position of creativity and music is paramount, especially for creators.

The issues to be examined are whether the opportunities for discussion about creativity that "Bad Jubies" offers can be measured and whether they work cross-culturally. The premise on why The Land of Ooo could offer a "middle ground" to revisit and reassess personal concepts is based on a theory probably as old as humanity itself: storytelling as an empathy building tool.

The field of children's literature has mentioned this idea often when considering storytelling in books, picture books and audiovisual material.[25] Petit considers children's books as "a vehicle to discover oneself or build oneself, to elaborate a subjectivity"[26] or, said in simpler words: a window to a fantasy world. Storytelling becomes a place to create a personal and intimate space, but it also provides something to imitate, a model of a different world, which does not necessarily have to represent part of the cultural reality of the child reader. Petit gives examples of reading *The Jungle Book* or *Tarzan*[27] and how this act builds a bridge between the reader, their culture, the references found in the text. She contends that reading can empathetically reflect the views of a character or a writer, even if they are from another time and place: the texts become "a sudden awareness, light shed over a piece of personal space that had previously been dark and troubling"[28] that can also provide ideas, models and options that do not belong to the reader's immediate culture but which are nonetheless valid.[29]

The clinical use of storytelling has also seen a surge lately, especially in the field of caring professions such as nursing, social work or even teaching[30] while it has also been included in the discussion on how to connect humanity in an increasingly digital world[31] with the added possibilities of virtual and immersive storytelling. Heinemeyer highlights the link and feedback between the individual and the communal that storytelling generates in both subjectivity and in social change.[32] In her analyses, she considers how storytelling is not only used to build relationships, generating a space for connectivity, but also how it offers the possibility to create a new "vernacular": "an alternative, situated language and established practices for free-ranging, creative, narrative dialogue"[33] based on a community's level of comfort, knowledge of each other and ability to answer the group's regenerative needs. Artistic practices, including storytelling, are considered to suspend the regular norms, "unite a disparate group around an intense experience, and bring individuals' and groups' perceptions to the attention of a culture, which succeed in generating moments of creative confluence between different perspectives."[34] This "vernacular" language of creativity can be harvested by the external impact: a storyteller in the case of Heinemeyer, an episode of *Adventure Time*, in the case study presented.

Heinemeyer establishes an additional need for storytelling, which is linked to mental health in the current socioeconomic scenario. She underlines how "a growing body of thought drawing on critical psychology and youth studies links the rise in mental distress to neoliberalism itself, particularly the impact of austerity, precarious employment, competitive education systems, and the individualization of responsibility for survival and success."[35] The results of this distress reflect on the younger generations,[36] with Francis and Horn mentioning that "today's college students experience unprecedented levels of mental health concerns, mainly anxiety and depression."[37] The Covid-19 pandemic is expected to increase this trend.

The response in the field of professional development counselling has had to adapt to these requirements. Currently, the rhetoric of "do what you love" has been highly questioned—mostly, because it generally stems from a privileged position, while first-generation college students or students from mid-to-low-income families are under more pressure to become self-sufficient and to fulfil the expectations of their support groups (families, communities, etc.),[38] but additionally because many people might not have a clear zeal towards a single professional path.[39] In the search for a healthier and more realistic career development path, the language of passion is slowly being replaced by the language of purpose, linked manly to the idea that "possessing a strong purpose when engaging in work-related decisions can lead to more satisfying and meaningful lives for college students."[40] But considering the limited knowledge of the type of work and the variety of positions in a certain field, this needs to be explored and adjusted to the needs, obligations and requirements of students.[41] Lastly, one of the key elements that the language of purpose focuses on is the fluidity of "passions," following the theories of interest.[42] This idea of change and transformation through the acquisition of new experience and knowledge is also applied in conversations in the classroom, especially as data from the current market indicates that a person entering the professional world in this decade in North America will likely not only be changing job positions but also shifting careers entirely throughout their working life.[43]

Connecting the possibilities of storytelling as an empathy building tool and searching for a space to open the discussion on music focusing on the three elements "Bad Jubies" offers (the creative process, the evaluation of productivity and the support system), a qualitative study took place during the semester of Fall 2020 to survey the impact *Adventure Time* had on fostering a space for regenerative conversation and on offering the convergence of different perspectives and multicultural backgrounds.

The Case Study: Professional Development for Musicians

The case study took place in a course required for graduation offered by Berklee College of Music, called "Professional Development Seminar," with the current code number LHUM 400. This course is mandatory and is recommended to be taken after the fourth semester has been completed. The main learning outcomes of LHUM 400 are split into two different sections. The first focuses on career exploration and preparation: what is out there? What is the typical entry point into different types of careers? What materials should the student prepare? This type of research is proposed from a practical perspective, with the creation of specific documents and materials that can be assessed, from resumes to Electronic Press Kits (EPKs) or networking notebooks. The second section of the course intends to offer a space to foster conversations about the position of the student in the professional world: do they have a specific mission, or have they thought about business ethics? How do they want to engage with coworkers? What is their definition of success? These conversations do not offer a single answer, as each student brings their own background to the table and is set on different goals. In these conversations, the job of the faculty member is mostly as a facilitator, and having an updated knowledge of the trends in career development is key.

"Bad Jubies" was screened as part of this second objective, with a group of 25 students in a section of the course offered remotely due to Covid-19 restrictions. The age of students ranged between 19 and 28, with the largest percentage being 20 (32%) and the second largest group being 22 (20%). The cohort included students from the USA (8), China (6), South Korea (3), India (2), Israel (2), England (1), Lithuania (1), Spain (1), and Australia (1). Of the total, 36 percent of students had two semesters left to graduate, 32 percent had three semesters left, 12 percent had four semesters left, 12 percent had one semester left, and for two students (8%) this was their last semester.

The activity followed the subsequent structure: (1) warm up: introduction of one of the conversational topics—total of 5 minutes; (2) viewing of the complete episode of "Bad Jubies"—total of 12 minutes; (3) discussion about the three key elements of the episode: the creative process, evaluation of productivity and the support system in an open class forum—total of 20 minutes, and (4) completing an anonymous survey on the activity to create immediate feedback—total of 5 minutes.

The survey was divided into purely quantitative yes-or-no questions and additional open-ended questions to assess the impact of the open forum discussion through the summaries of the main ideas the students had reflected upon. The answers to the quantitative questions were mainly positive, with "Did you enjoy the activity (watching 'Bad Jubies')?" and "Do you think the episode connects musicality and spirituality (or emotion)?" both receiving an 84 percent yes, 12 percent unsure and 4 percent no, and the question "Do you think it illustrates a common issue that artists/creators are confronted with?" receiving 88 percent yes and 12 percent unsure.

In relation to their support system, many students linked the emotional support to economic sustenance, as they were still in a position of investing in their career. Fifty-two percent of students considered that their close family was supportive of their decision to pursue a musical career. Thirty-two percent added to their close family their extended family, amounting to a total of 84 percent of students that considered they were backed both in their vocation as well as in their economic situation. Eight percent (2 students) acknowledged that their economic efforts to study music were a combination of their own income and family support, while one student (4%) mentioned no support, either economically or emotionally.

The open-ended questions presented were two. One was related to the episode and their current scenario as creators during the Covid-19 pandemic ("How do you think art responds/helps respond to a crisis [like in the episode]?"). Most responses pointed towards the connection between music and emotion, using terms such as 'coping mechanism,' 'remedy,' "support" and "escape." The second question focused on the episode's portrayal of art and its echo in the larger student's environment ("Would you like to add any thoughts about the episode? Or about artistry and its perception in general?"). In relation to the evaluation of productivity, several students highlighted the intangible rewards of creativity, linking it to mental health ("Artistry should be perceived as a tool for healthy development of society") and spirituality ("I've always believed that everything we carry inside spiritually in our lives, has the highest value and no matter what anyone says, music is one of the artistic 'lenses' I can filter my emotions and values and communicate them to other people. No matter who you are, everyone is searching for inner peace and stability."). Additionally, the consideration of the value of art was linked to its potential as a documentation tool ("Art can record history, convey emotion and bring people spiritual comfort") and a way to analyze the synchronic character of a group. ("During times of crisis, emotions are high, and art is a direct reflection of prevalent emotions during a given time period.") The link between art and creative problem-solving also appeared, pointing to its potential. ("It definitely portrays the situation that people are facing with—and potentially suggests [a] solution to overcome [them].")

When considering the creative process, participants considered mainly the illustrated scenario "Bad Jubies" offers of music as an answer to a crisis. Most comments highlighted the connection that the episode created between music and emotions, through comments such as "Art can evoke repressed emotion, such as happiness and comfort, and be a much-needed relief in a tense or uncomfortable situation," and "Art [has] the power of forming and shaping one's emotions. In crisis, art could help people simply feel better."

During the session, the participants commented on the fact that, although they had different backgrounds and career paths, their concerns were similar, and they were able to empathize and find new perspectives from the conversation generated by the Land of Ooo.

Discussion

Adventure Time's ten seasons touch upon innumerable topics that concern all different ages. This chapter focuses specifically on the relevance of music in *Adventure Time*, a common thread that brings characters together and illustrates nuances in their identities throughout the series. The way *Adventure Time* integrates music into its plot via key storytelling techniques exemplifies current trends in music cognition research, demonstrating the connection between music and emotion, as well as the elusive concept of "music as a friend."

"Bad Jubies" specifically addresses the creative process as seen from the outside, and illustrates its development and its link to societal ideas on productivity and the impact a support system has on artistic work. By following the perception of the characters that are not creating the piece, the artistic work appears subject to judgement. The episode focuses on three main ideas: (1) the creative process, with creation as a solitary experience that requires reflection and contributes to the creator's ability to connect in a different way; (2) the evaluation of productivity, with art as an intangible result that does not represent the rules of the market but which nonetheless is constantly subjected to the values of others, affecting the creative production itself; (3) the support system, which ought to trust in the emotional relevance of works that are not tangible and explore value outside traditional understandings of productivity.

For these reasons, musicians can use "Bad Jubies" as an example of how storytelling can build empathy. Considering the generation of constructive conversation has the potential to open new perspectives and enhance communal communication, "Bad Jubies" could be a common ground to generate a 'vernacular,' that is a distinctive group language built from a common story. This potential was explored in the college classroom, specifically with musicians, as a response to a critical moment in the music industry, the students' position in the ever-changing musical scene and increased mental health awareness. The case study sample intends to incorporate the perspective of the musician by analyzing the responses of future workers in the music industry, and questions whether the use of storytelling in empathy building and the vernacular that it creates is cross-cultural. The responses display how music students use the story posed by "Bad Jubies" to engage in conversation about their future, and how it generated mostly positive feedback.

Adventure Time's weaving of topics and growth of characters offers us the unique potential to use its storytelling to reevaluate and evolve opinions. While "Bad Jubies" offers this option specifically to artistic creators, the opportunity for empathy building through storytelling could be explored further by single episode viewers and the series' followers.

Notes

1. As seen, for example, in the articles presented by Emma Jane, "Gunter's a Woman," and Carolyn Leslie, "Adventure Time and Gender Stereotypes."
2. Nicolas Michaud, *Adventure Time and Philosophy*.
3. Erin Fuller, "How My Son's Favorite Cartoon Made Be a Better Creative."
4. Lutz Jäncke, "Music, Memory and Emotion."
5. Steven Eschrich, Thomas Münte and Eckart Altenmüller, "Unforgettable Film Music."
6. Benjamin, M. Kubit and Petr Janata, "Spontaneous Mental Replay."
7. Geoffrey Miller, "The Biology of Music."
8. Robert J. Zatorre and Valorie N. Salimpoor, "From Perception to Pleasure," 10430–10437.
9. "Come Along with Me" (season 10, episode 13–16).
10. Panos Panay and R. Michael Hendrix. "How Björk Helped Iceland Weather the Global Financial Crisis."
11. Panay.
12. Michael J.A. Howe and John Sloboda, "Problems Experienced by Talented Young Musicians," 16–18.
13. Anna Jordanous, Daniel Allington, and Byron Dueck. "Measuring Cultural Value Using Social Network Analysis," 100–117.
14. Simon Frith. *Performing Rites*, 13–14.
15. Frith, 15
16. Zach Linge, "An Interview with Spencer Krug."
17. "Bad Jubies" (season 7, episode 20).
18. "Bad Jubies."
19. Elliot W. Eisner, "The Arts and the Creation of Mind," 207.
20. "Bad Jubies."
21. "Bad Jubies."
22. "Bad Jubies."
23. "Bad Jubies."
24. GESAC and Ernst & Young Consulting, "Rebuilding Europe."
25. As commented in Margaret Meek, "Introduction. Definitions," 1–12; Tony Watkins, "History and Culture," 76–98; and Michèle Petit, "Pero ¿y Qué Buscan Nuestros Niños en sus Libros?" Note, translations of quotes provided by the author of this article.
26. Petit, 14.
27. Petit, 18.
28. Petit, 29–30.
29. This paragraph is based on content from the author's thesis, *The Translation of Nursery Rhymes into Spanish: A Methodological Framework*.

30. Gavin J. Fairbairn, "Ethics, Empathy and Storytelling," 22–32.
31. Patricia J. Maney, "Empathy in the Time of Technology," 51–61.
32. Catherine Heinemeyer, *Storytelling in Participatory Arts*, 211–250.
33. Heinemeyer, 213.
34. Heinemeyer.
35. Heinemeyer, 212.
36. American Psychological Association, "College Students' Mental Health," 44–6.
37. Perry C. Francis and Aaron S. Horn, "Mental Health Issues," 263–277.
38. Michael J. Stebleton, "Moving Beyond Passion," 163–171.
39. Michal Bohanes, "Following your Passion is Dead."
40. Stebleton, "Moving Beyond Passion," 164.
41. Stebleton, 165.
42. Paul A. O'Keefe, Carol S. Dweck, and Gregory M. Walton, "Implicit Theories of Interest," 1653–1664.
43. Eddy S.W. Ng, Linda Schweitzer, and Sean T. Lyons, "New Generation, Great Expectations," 281–292.

References

American Psychological Association. "College Students' Mental Health Is a Growing Concern, Survey Finds." *Monitor on Psychology Monitor on Psychology* 44, no. 6 (2013): 13. http://www.apa.org/monitor/2013/06/college-students.

Bohanes, Michal. "'Following your Passion is Dead'—Here's What to Replace it With." *Forbes*, 2018. https://www.forbes.com/sites/michalbohanes/2018/07/05/following-your-passion-is-dead-heres-what-to-replace-it-with/#5b3a3aa7f832.

Eschrich, Steven, Thomas Münte, and Eckart Altenmüller, "Unforgettable Film Music: The Role of Emotion in Episodic Long-Term Memory for Music." *BMC Neuroscience* 9, no. 48 (2008): 1–7.

Fairbairn, Gavin J. "Ethics, Empathy and Storytelling in Professional Development." *Learning in Health and Social Care* 1, no. 1 (2002): 22–32.

Francis, Perry C., and Aaron S. Horn. "Mental Health Issues and Counseling Services in US Higher Education: An Overview of Recent Research and Recommended Practices." *Higher Education Policy* 30, no. 2 (2017): 263–277.

Frith, Simon. *Performing Rites: On the Value of Popular Music*. Cambridge, MA: Harvard University Press, 1996.

Fuller, Erin. "How My Son's Favorite Cartoon Made Be a Better Creative" Muse, 2018. https://musebycl.io/worklife/how-my-sons-favorite-cartoon-made-me-better-creative.

GESAC and Ernst & Young Consulting. "Rebuilding Europe: the Cultural and Creative Economy before and after the COVID-19 Crisis." rebuilding-europe.eu, 2021. https://www.rebuilding-europe.eu.

Heinemeyer, Catherine. *Storytelling in Participatory Arts with Young People. The Gaps in the Story*. Cham, Switzerland: Palgrave Macmillan, 2020.

Howe, Michael J.A., and John A. Sloboda. "Problems Experienced by Talented Young Musicians as a Result of the Failure of Other Children to Value Musical Accomplishments." *Gifted Education International* 8, no. 1 (1992): 16–18.

Jäncke, Lutz. "Music, Memory and Emotion." *Journal of Biology* 7, no. 6 (2008): 1–5.

Jane, Emma A. "'Gunter's a Woman?!'—Doing and Undoing Gender in Cartoon Network's Adventure Time." *Journal of Children and Media* 9, no. 2 (2015): 231–247.

Jordanous, Anna, Daniel Allington, and Byron Dueck. "Measuring Cultural Value Using Social Network Analysis: A Case Study On Valuing Electronic Musicians." In *Proceedings of the Sixth International Conference on Computational Creativity*, edited by Hannu Toivonen, Simon Colton, Michael Cook, and Dan Ventura, 100–117. International Association for Computational Creativity, 2015.

Kubit, Benjamin M., and Petr Janata. "Spontaneous Mental Replay of Music Improves

Memory for Incidentally Associated Event Knowledge." *Journal of Experimental Psychology: General.* Advance online publication (2021).

Lent, R. W. "Future of Work in The Digital World: Preparing for Instability and Opportunity." *The Career Development Quarterly* 66, no. 3 (2018): 205–219.

Leslie, Carolyn. "*Adventure Time* and Gender Stereotypes" *Screen* 78 (2015): 44–47.

Linge, Zach. "An Interview with Spencer Krug." *Southeast Review*, 2021. https://www.southeastreview.org/single-post/an-interview-with-spencer-krug.

Maney, Patricia J. "Empathy in the Time of Technology: How Storytelling Is the Key to Empathy." *Journal of Evolution & Technology* 19, no. 1 (2008): 51–61.

Meek, Margaret. "Introduction. Definitions, Themes, Changes, Attitudes." In *International Companion Encyclopedia of Children's Literature*, edited by Peter Hunt, 1–12. 2nd ed., vol. 1. New York: Routledge, 2004.

Michaud, Nicolas, ed. *Adventure Time and Philosophy: The Handbook for Heroes.* Chicago: Open Court Publishing Company, 2015.

Miller, Geoffrey. "The Biology of Music." *The Economist*, 2000, https://www.economist.com/science-and-technology/2000/02/10/the-biology-of-music.

Ng, Eddy S.W., Linda Schweitzer, and Sean T. Lyons. "New Generation, Great Expectations: A Field Study of the Millennial Generation." *Journal of Business and Psychology* 25 (2010): 281–292.

O'Keefe, Paul A., Carol S. Dweck, and Gregory M. Walton. "Implicit Theories of Interest: Finding Your Passion or Developing It?" *Psychological Science* 29, no. 10 (2018): 1653–1664.

Orellana, Natalia. "Extending the Scope: Career Guidance in Higher Education." Global University Network for Education, 2018. http://www.guninetwork.org/articles/extending-scope-career-guidance-higher-education.

Panay, Panos, and R. Michael Hendrix. "How Björk Helped Iceland Weather the Global Financial Crisis." *Literary Hub*, 2021, https://lithub.com/how-bjork-helped-iceland-weather-the-global-financial-crisis.

Petit, Michèle. "Pero ¿y Qué Buscan Nuestros Niños en sus Libros?" *Lecturas sobre Lecturas.* Mexico DF: Consejo Nacional para la Cultura y las Artes, 2002.

Stebleton, Michael J. "Moving Beyond Passion: Why 'Do What You Love' Advice for College Students Needs Reexamination." *Journal of College and Character* 20, no. 2 (2019): 163–171.

Sutton, Gene, and Rhonda Gifford. "Career Counseling Centers and the College Level" In *Career Development in Higher Education*, edited by Jeff Samide, Grafton T. Bliason, and John Patrick 119–135. Charlotte, NC: Information Age Publishing, 2011.

Watkins, Tony. "History and Culture." In *International Companion Encyclopedia of Children's Literature*, edited by Peter Hunt, 76–98. 2nd ed., vol. 1, New York: Routledge, 2004.

Zatorre, Robert J., and Valorie N. Salimpoor. "From Perception to Pleasure: Music and its Neural Substrates." *Proceedings of the National Academy of Sciences* 110, Supplement 2 (2013): 10430–10437.

About the Contributors

Bridget M. **Blodgett** is an associate professor in the Division of Science, Information Arts, and Technology at the University of Baltimore. Her research analyzes Internet culture and the social impacts thereof on offline life. Her research takes a critical eye to online game communities regarding gender, inclusiveness, and identity. *Toxic Geek Masculinity in Media* (2017, with Anastasia Salter) is the summation of this work to date.

Camille **Chane** is a doctoral student in the Laboratoire d'Études et de Recherche sur le Monde Anglophone (LERMA) research center at Aix-Marseille University in Marseille, France. He is working on a dissertation about linguistic stereotyping and the representation of East Asians in American cartoons of the studio era.

Zhi Hwee **Goh** earned a bachelor of engineering degree in electronic and electrical engineering (with a minor in intelligent systems) from University College London in 2021. His research interests include mathematics, philosophy, as well as the portrayal of the main character relationships in *Adventure Time*.

Mage **Hadley** is a writer and filmmaker from England who crafts essays and online reviews that focus predominantly on bisexuality, mythology, and the analysis of queer media and online spaces. Her videos can be found on her YouTube channel, "black and white thinking."

Steven **Holmes** is a lecturer in the English department at the University of Hawai'i at Mānoa. He teaches classes on argumentative writing, science fiction, fantasy literature, digital art, and even Shakespeare. His work has been published in *Studies in the Fantastic*, *The Written Dead: The Zombie as a Literary Phenomenon*, *War Gothic in Literature and Culture*, and *Gender and Sexuality in Contemporary Popular Fantasy*.

Birdy Wei-Ting **Hung** is an MFA candidate at the School of Cinema, San Francisco State University. She is interested in documentaries and experimental aesthetics and has screened at the University of California Berkeley Art Museum Pacific Film Archive, the San Francisco Independent Film Festival, and the Golden Melody Awards. She has published in the online journal *cinemedia* and is a contributor to Aaron Kerner's book, *Abject Pleasures in the Cinematic*.

Aaron **Kerner** is the director of the School of Cinema at San Francisco State University where he has taught since 2003. His publications include *Extreme Cinema*

(2017, with Jonathan Knapp), *Theorizing Stupid Media* (2019, with Julian Hoxter), and *Abject Pleasures in the Cinematic* (2023).

Steven **Kielich** is a visiting scholar and researcher at the State University of New York at Buffalo. His areas of academic research and interest are primarily Lacanian psychoanalysis and psychoanalytic theory, continental philosophy, film theory, twentieth-century American and British literature, and popular culture. He teaches in Buffalo, New York.

Jenine **Oosthuizen** is working on her master of arts degree. Her research focuses on the intersection of postmodernism, film/TV, and literary theory, including the examination of meta-fiction in popular TV series. She is also a creative writer, and her short story "Quick or Ink?" was published in *MacQueen's Quinterly*.

Anastasia **Salter** is an associate professor of English at the University of Central Florida, and author of *Twining: Critical and Creative Approaches to Hypertext Narratives* (2021, with Stuart Moulthrop), *Portrait of the Auteur as Fanboy* (2020, with Mel Stanfill), and *Adventure Games: Playing the Outsider* (2020, with Aaron Reed and John Murray).

Catalina Millán **Scheiding** is an associate professor in the Liberal Arts Department at Berklee College of Music Valencia Campus and a member of the Grupo de Investigación TALIS of the University of València. Her areas of research include children's poetry, multimodality and translation, as well as narratology in fantasy and fiction.

Kendra N. **Sheehan** is a senior lecturer in the Department of Classical & Modern Languages at the University of Louisville, and an adjunct instructor for Indiana University Southeast and for Kentucky Community and Technical Colleges. Her research interests include popular culture, religion, Japanese culture and film, and the humanities.

Sequoia **Stone** received her bachelor of arts degree in English from SUNY New Paltz, and her master of arts degree in English with a specialization in children's literature from San Diego State University. Her research interests include queer literature, media and theory, young adult literature, Gothic literature, and fan studies.

Paul A. **Thomas** is a library specialist at the University of Kansas and holds a Ph.D. in library and information management from Emporia State University. He is the author of *Exploring the Land of Ooo* (rev. ed., forthcoming), *Inside Wikipedia* (2022), and *I Wanna Wrock!* (McFarland 2018).

Al **Valentín** is a Ph.D. candidate in women's, gender and sexuality studies at Rutgers University, writing their dissertation on how videogames shape our conceptions of (in)humanity. A queer, nonbinary, writer, educator and artist, their work exists at the intersection of affect theory, black feminist thought, woman of color feminisms and media and technology studies. They are also a poet and visual artist.

Olivia M. **Vogt** is a graduate of North Dakota State University. They are particularly interested in the interactions between media, identity, and culture, with a current focus on how queerness and media combine to impact cultural norms. Their research has been presented at the National Communication Association and International Communication Association conferences.

Index

Adult Swim 227, 229
Alden, Sam 192
allegory 4, 6, 22, 23, 24, 25, 181
Allegri, Natasha 47, 231
Andersen, Hans Christian 215
anime 13, 18, 96, 225–240
apocalyptic narratives and themes 55–68, 208–210, 230
Archie Comics 57, 64
artistic value 243–255
Avatar the Last Airbender 230

Bakhtin, Mikhail 7, 10, 105–118
Battle of the Planets 228
Behar, Katherine 165
Bethesda Studios 210
Betty Boop 228
Birds of Prey 65
Blade of the Immortal 232
Bleach 228
BMO 6, 9–10, 43, 110, 133, 140–141, 158, 166–172, 183, 199, 243, 245, 247–249; and accent 84–100; and gender 29–39
"Bubbline" 6, 9, 43–52, 55, 58–59, 63, 67–68
Buffy the Vampire Slayer 17, 20
Butler, Octavia 61

Cake the Cat 116–118, 145–150, 153; see also Fionna the Human
CalArts 1
Camus, Albert 11, 123, 134
carnivalesque 7, 10, 105, 108, 114–119
Cartoon Network 1, 5–8, 21, 34, 43, 45–49, 52, 56–59, 66, 68, 72, 96, 105, 110, 114, 159, 227, 231
ChalkZone 1
Children of Men 64
Cho, Margaret 89
Covid 249, 251–253
Crayon Shin-chan 235
Crenshaw, Kimberlé 164
Cuber 11, 138, 144, 148–150, 153

Dawn of the Dead 60
Demon Slayer 232, 238

Devil's Line 236
DiMaggio, John 2, 87, 117
das Ding 195–198, 201–203; see also Lacan, Jacques
Disney 65, 75, 226–228, 239
Distant Lands 1, 9, 11, 36, 43, 68, 113, 158–159, 166, 168, 171–172
Dragon Ball Z 228–229
Dragon Prince 230
Dungeons and Dragons 1

Elements (miniseries) 139–141, 235
existentialism 11, 123–134, 208, 236

The Fairly OddParents 1
Fallout 210
Family Guy 231
Finn 1–4, 9, 12, 18–23, 30, 34–39, 44, 46, 49–50, 56–57, 71–81, 84, 87, 89–98, 106–119, 122, 131–134, 139–140, 142–146, 151, 153, 170, 172, 192, 194, 198–201, 209, 232–235, 243, 245, 248–249; and his relationship to Princess Bubblegum 179–190
Fionna the Human 116, 145–150, 153; see also Cake the Cat
Fleischer, Max 228
Freud, Sigmund 193, 198–200, 215
Futurama 2, 231

Gatchaman 228
gender and *Adventure Time* 29–68
Gigantor 228
Gintama 232
Graybles *see* Cuber
grotesque realism 10, 105–107, 114, 117–118
Gundam franchise 228, 234

Harley Quinn 9, 55, 64–66, 68
Harman, Graham 159–163, 166, 168
HBO Max 43, 52, 65, 68, 113, 159
Hello Kitty 226, 233
henshin sequence 239
Herpich, Tom 23, 24
heteroglossia 10, 111–119
heteronormativity 33, 36, 57–58, 62, 64, 79

261

262 Index

Howl's Moving Castle 237
Hunter X Hunter 233–234, 238

Ice King 3–4, 11–12, 21, 50, 58, 71–73, 79–80, 94, 114–117, 125, 127, 138, 144–153, 210–218, 233; see also trauma and *Adventure Time*
Islands (miniseries) 19, 139–141, 235

Jack London 61
Jackson, Zakiyyah Iman 164–165
Jake 1–4, 9–10, 18, 20–23, 30–31, 35–39, 44, 49, 56–57, 87, 89–99, 106–116, 122, 128, 132–134, 139–146, 153, 170, 172, 181, 185–190, 199, 209, 232–233, 235; black-coding of 117–118; as a creative 243–255; and masculinity 71–82
Japan 13, 57, 85, 88–89, 95–97, 116, 225–240
Jesus 24, 60
Jones-Quartey, Ian 231
jouissance 12, 201–202; see also Lacan, Jacques
The Jungle Book 250

kawaii theme 230, 233
Kellner, Douglas 8, 17–19, 23–24
Kemonozume 235
Kenny, Tom 3
Kipo and the Age of Wonderbeasts 60

Lacan, Jacques 12, 192–204, 212
Lady Rainicorn 10, 33, 62, 77, 79, 81, 84–89, 92–97, 116, 145
Legend of Korra 52, 67, 230
Lemongrab, Earl of 12, 59, 192–204
The Lich 4, 21, 72, 170, 190, 196, 233–234
"little-narratives" 138, 141
Lumpy Space Princess 48, 86, 145–148, 243, 245–249

Mad Max 56, 61–62, 64
manga 225–229, 236–239
Marceline 3, 6, 9, 19, 21, 31, 35, 43–52, 55–59, 63, 68, 72–73, 98–99, 110, 113–114, 122, 124–134, 139–141, 145–148, 168–169, 172, 182, 208, 234–239; see also "Bubbline"
The Marvelous Misadventures of Flapjack 1, 231
Mathematical! (series) 9, 45–47, 51
McHale, Patrick 20, 91
mecha theme 230, 233–234
Men's Right Activism 71, 80
meta-fiction 11, 138, 144–148, 151, 153–154
miniseries 139–142; see also *Elements* (miniseries); *Islands* (miniseries); *Stakes* (miniseries)
Mr. Belvedere 126
Mittsu no hanashi 228
Miyazaki, Hayao 231, 237
Morton, Timothy 160–161, 163, 167, 169, 172–173

Moynihan, Jesse 19, 23–24, 48, 51, 192, 231
multilingualism 10, 84, 92, 97
Mushroom War 4, 12, 21–22, 56, 59, 63, 68, 124–125, 213, 236
Muto, Adam 2, 45–47, 49, 51, 98
My Hero Academia 233–234
My Neighbor Totoro 231
My Neighbors the Yamadas 235
mythology 7, 19–22, 123, 235

Naruto 228, 232, 234, 238
Nausicaä of the Valley of the Wind 237
Neon Genesis Evangelion 234, 238
Netflix 29, 65–66
Nickelodeon 1, 4, 52
Nyström, Hanna K. 51, 231

object-oriented ontology 11, 158–173
objet petit a 12, 192, 197–198, 201
Olson, Olivia 3, 48
The 100 62
Ortega, José 161–162
Osborne, Kent 23
Osonoe, Keiko 228
The Owl House 45, 229
Ozu, Yasujirō 111

Peabody Awards 2
Perlman, Ron 4
Petrikov, Simon 4, 125, 210, 214, 236
Pokémon 229
Popeye the Sailor 228
Popper, Karl 12
post-apocalypse see apocalyptic narratives and themes
Postman 61, 64
postmodernism 11, 124, 137–1154, 232
Princess Bubblegum 3, 6, 9, 12, 19, 31, 43–52, 55–59, 63, 68, 73, 95, 98, 110, 112–114, 122, 125–127, 132, 139, 145, 168–169, 172, 195–198, 235–238; and relationship to Finn 179–190; see also "Bubbline"
Princess Mononoke 237
Prismo 24, 79–81
psychoanalysis 12, 192–194, 196, 200, 202, 211; see also Freud, Sigmund; Lacan, Jacques

queer discourse analysis 32
queer theory and *Adventure Time* 29–82
queerbaiting 6, 50–51

realist narratives 18–19, 139, 142; see also grotesque realism
The Revenant 211
Rickmers, Dan 46–47
The Road 61, 64
Robbie, Margot 65
Rurōni Kenshin 232

Sailor Moon 57, 229, 239
Samurai Champloo 232, 235
Scooby-Doo 229
Seibert, Fred 46–47, 231
Shada, Jeremy 2
She-Ra and the Princesses of Power 9, 45, 52, 55, 63–68
Shermy and Beth 110, 133–134, 142, 246
shinto 236–237
shōnen anime 228, 232, 234, 236–237
Sinophone world 115–116
Sisyphus 11, 123, 126, 131, 134
"slice of life" narratives 18–19
Snyder, Zack 60–61
Song of Ice and Fire series 62
Space Cruiser Yamato 228
Speed Racer 228
Spirited Away 227, 237
SpongeBob Squarepants 4
Stakes (miniseries) 6, 13, 49–50, 122, 125–133, 139–140, 225, 235–238
Star Blazers 228
Star Wars 228, 230
Steven Universe 6, 30, 45, 49, 55, 57, 59, 64–68, 153, 229
straight time 36–37
Studio Ghibli 227, 231
Sugar, Rebecca 30, 44–49, 57–58, 68, 182–184, 229, 231
Suicide Squad 65
"superflat" aesthetic 232–233

Tarzan 250
Teen Titans 3
Terrace, Dana 229
Tetsuwon Atomu 228
Tezuka, Osamu 227–228
Thundercats 229
Toonami 227, 229
trauma and *Adventure Time* 207–219

UPN 17

Walch, Hynden 3, 50, 181
The Walking Dead 60, 62
Wall-E 64
Ward, Pendleton 1, 20, 46, 48, 51, 71–72, 86, 91, 95–96, 207, 229, 231
Warmhammer 62
The WB 17
Wynter, Sylvia 164

The X-Files 20

Yang, Niki 10, 33, 84–87, 90–92, 95, 97
"yellow English" 88–90
"yellow voice" 87
yōkai theme 230, 234
Youn, Bert 95, 231

Zen 232, 236–237
Žižek, Slavoj 193, 208, 212, 215

www.ingramcontent.com/pod-product-compliance
Lightning Source LLC
Chambersburg PA
CBHW021852230426

43671CB00006B/364